This is an impressive volume, spanning some of the most fascinating areas of legal and criminological psychology. Top contributors and superb editors. I recommend this book!

Pär Anders Granhag, *Professor of Psychology, University of Gothenberg, Sweden; Director of CLIP; and former President of the European Association of Psychology & Law (EAPL)*

Written by experts in their respective fields, this collection will prove to be a valuable resource for both researchers and students.

Clive Hollin, *Emeritus Professor, University of Leicester, UK*

Kapardis and Farrington's *The Psychology of Crime, Policing and Courts* is a superb collection of empirical papers by twenty-two experts, who bring state of the art information to practitioners, researchers, students and policy makers. An indispensable read for all who are interested in the welfare of young offenders and reducing their contact with the police and the courts.

Rolf Loeber, *Ph.D., Distinguished Emeritus Professor of Psychiatry, University of Pittsburgh, PA, USA*

A stimulating journey through some of the most critical topics of legal and criminal psychology. This book, which includes contributions from several prestigious scholars, provides academics, students and professionals with an excellent text and guide for their work and research.

Santiago Redondo, *Professor of Criminology, University of Barcelona, Spain*

The Psychology of Crime, Policing and Courts

This book brings together an international group of experts to present cutting-edge psychological research on crime, policing and courts. With contributors from the UK, Germany, Italy, Norway, Cyprus, Israel, Canada and the USA, this volume explores some of the most interesting and contemporary areas of criminological and legal psychology.

The Psychology of Crime, Policing and Courts is divided into three parts. Part I explores crime and anti-social behaviour, including the concentration of offending within families, juvenile delinquency, adolescent bullying, cyber-bullying, violence risk assessment and psychopathy. Part II examines policing and the detection of deception, with chapters on interrogational practices, police interviews of children and modern detection methods. Part III focuses on courts and sentencing, with chapters exploring wrongful convictions, the role of juries, extra-legal factors in sentencing decisions and an examination of sentencing itself.

Representing the forefront of research in developmental criminology and criminological and legal psychology, this book is a comprehensive resource for undergraduate and postgraduate students studying psychology and criminology, with particular value for those studying forensic psychology. This book is also a valuable resource for psychologists, lawyers, social scientists and law enforcement personnel.

Andreas Kapardis is Professor of Psychology and Law in the Department of Law, University of Cyprus.

David P. Farrington, OBE, is Emeritus Professor of Psychological Criminology at the Institute of Criminology, Cambridge University.

Routledge Studies in Criminal Behaviour

1 **Criminal Behaviour from School to the Workplace**
Untangling the Complex Relations Between Employment, Education and Crime
Edited by Frank Weerman and Catrien Bijleveld

2 **Pathways to Sexual Aggression**
Edited by Jean Proulx, Eric Beauregard, Patrick Lussier, and Benoit Leclerc

3 **The Psychology of Crime, Policing and Courts**
Edited by Andreas Kapardis and David P. Farrington

The Psychology of Crime, Policing and Courts

Edited by Andreas Kapardis and
David P. Farrington

LONDON AND NEW YORK

First published 2016
by Routledge
2 Park Square, Milton Park, Abingdon, Oxon OX14 4RN

and by Routledge
711 Third Avenue, New York, NY 10017

Routledge is an imprint of the Taylor & Francis Group, an informa business

© 2016 Andreas Kapardis and David P. Farrington

The right of the editors to be identified as the authors of the editorial matter, and of the authors for their individual chapters, has been asserted in accordance with sections 77 and 78 of the Copyright, Designs and Patents Act 1988.

All rights reserved. No part of this book may be reprinted or reproduced or utilised in any form or by any electronic, mechanical, or other means, now known or hereafter invented, including photocopying and recording, or in any information storage or retrieval system, without permission in writing from the publishers.

Trademark notice: Product or corporate names may be trademarks or registered trademarks, and are used only for identification and explanation without intent to infringe.

British Library Cataloguing-in-Publication Data
A catalogue record for this book is available from the British Library

Library of Congress Cataloging in Publication Data
Names: Kapardis, Andreas, editor. | Farrington, David P., editor.
Title: The psychology of crime, policing and courts / edited by Andreas Kapardis and David Farrington.
Description: First Edition. | New York, NY : Routledge, 2016. |
Series: Routledge studies in criminal behaviour ; 3 | Includes bibliographical references and index.
Identifiers: LCCN 2015045847| ISBN 9781138931213 (hardback) |
ISBN 9781315679860 (ebook)
Subjects: LCSH: Criminal psychology. | Criminal behavior. | Forensic psychology. | Correctional psychology.
Classification: LCC HV6080 .P837 2016 | DDC 364.01/9–dc23
LC record available at http://lccn.loc.gov/2015045847

ISBN: 978-1-138-93121-3 (hbk)
ISBN: 978-1-315-67986-0 (ebk)

Typeset in Times New Roman
by Wearset Ltd, Boldon, Tyne and Wear

Contents

List of figures	ix
List of tables	x
List of contributors	xii
Foreword	xiv
PROFESSOR RAY BULL	

Introduction: psychology, crime, policing and courts   1

ANDREAS KAPARDIS AND DAVID P. FARRINGTON

PART I

Crime and antisocial behaviour   5

1 **The concentration of convictions in two generations of families**   7

DAVID P. FARRINGTON AND REBECCA V. CRAGO

2 **Self-reported juvenile delinquency in three surveys over 38 years: a German study on the crime drop**   24

FRIEDRICH LÖSEL, DORIS BENDER, ZARA SÜNKEL AND MARK STEMMLER

3 **What factors protect adolescent bullies from developing into criminal and violent offenders?**   44

MARIA M. TTOFI AND DAVID P. FARRINGTON

4 **Cyberbullying: does parental online supervision and youngsters' willingness to report to an adult reduce the risk?**   57

ANNA C. BALDRY, ANNA SORRENTINO AND DAVID P. FARRINGTON

viii *Contents*

5 **Violence risk: the actuarial illusion** 75
DAVID J. COOKE

6 **The psychopath: continuity or change? Stability of
psychopathic traits and predictors of stability** 94
HENRIETTE BERGSTRØM, ADELLE E. FORTH AND
DAVID P. FARRINGTON

PART II
Policing and detecting deception 117

7 **Questioning the interrogational practices of US law-enforcement
officers: legal and psychological perspectives** 119
DAVID WALSH, SEAN O'CALLAGHAN, AND
REBECCA MILNE

8 **Police interviews of sexually abused children: the state of
the art in differentiating truthful and false accounts** 136
MARILENA KYRIAKIDOU

9 **Psychophysiological detection of deception: a review of
detection methods, recent research and potential forensic
applications** 155
GERSHON BEN-SHAKHAR

PART III
Courts and sentencing 173

10 **Wrongful convictions: psychological and criminal justice
system contributors** 175
C. RONALD HUFF

11 **The English jury: issues, concerns and future directions** 188
NICOLA PADFIELD

12 **Extra-legal factors that impact on sentencing decisions** 201
ANDREAS KAPARDIS

13 **Reflections on sentencing in England and Wales** 231
NICOLA PADFIELD

Index 259

Figures

2.1	Mean scores in self-reported delinquency at different survey times	30
4.1	Prevalence of school and cyberbullying and victimization	66
5.1	Natural frequency diagram of reoffending by RM2000S risk category data from Barnett et al. (2010)	82

Tables

1.1	Prevalence of convictions up to age 32 among all family members (G1–G2)	15
1.2	The concentration of convictions up to age 32 in families (G1–G2)	15
1.3	Percentage of G2 males convicted up to age 32, given convicted or unconvicted relatives up to age 32 (G1–G2)	16
1.4	Percentage of families with a G2 brother or G2 sister convicted up to age 32, given a convicted or unconvicted G1 parent up to age 32 (G1–G2)	17
1.5	Prevalence of convictions up to age 32 among all relatives (G2–G3)	18
1.6	The concentration of convictions up to age 32 in families (G2–G3)	18
1.7	Percentage of G3 sons convicted up to age 32, given convicted or unconvicted relatives up to age 32 (G2–G3)	19
1.8	Percentage of G3 daughters convicted up to age 32, given convicted or unconvicted relatives up to age 32 (G2–G3)	19
2.1	Hypotheses on the explanation of the international crime drop	25
2.2	Percentages of boys who reported various forms of delinquent behaviour in the three surveys	31
2.3	Percentages of boys who reported at least six offences that indicate relatively serious delinquency when carried out frequently	32
3.1	Bullying versus convictions and violence	50
3.2	Protective effects against violence convictions	50
3.3	Protective effects against criminal convictions	51
3.4	Interactive protective effects	52
4.1	Summary of key findings on the role of parents and cyberbullying	59
4.2	Summary statistics of the study's variables	66
4.3	Gender differences between school bullying and cyberbullying	67
4.4	Correlations between cyberbullying and cybervictimization and different parental supervision activities, willingness to report, gender and hours online	69

Tables xi

4.5	Hierarchical regression for cyberbullying	70
4.6	Hierarchical regression for cybervictimization	71
5.1	Univariate associations between risk and aggravating factors and proven sexual reoffending in a two-year follow-up period for the RM2000S	80
5.2	Final two-stage logistic regression model of risk and aggravating factors and proven sexual reoffending in a two-year follow-up period for the RM2000S	81
6.1	Overview of longitudinal studies investigating rank-order stability of psychopathic traits	96
6.2	Overview of longitudinal studies investigating mean-level stability of psychopathic traits	98
6.3	Overview of potential predictors/moderators and time of measurement	102
6.4	Correlations corrected for attenuation	104
6.5	Mean level stability of psychopathic traits	105
6.6	Partial correlations between predictors and psychopathic traits while controlling for time 1 psychopathic traits	106
6.7	Partial correlations between predictors and psychopathic traits while controlling for time 2 psychopathic traits	106

Contributors

Anna C. Baldry is Associate Professor in the Department of Psychology, Second University of Naples, Caserta, Italy.

Doris Bender is Senior University Lecturer in the Institute of Psychology, University of Erlangen-Nuremberg, Germany.

Gershon Ben-Shakhar is President, Open University of Israel, and Emeritus Professor of Psychology, Hebrew University of Jerusalem, Israel.

Henriette Bergstrøm is Lecturer in the Psychology of Criminal Investigation, Department of Law, Criminology and Social sciences, University of Derby, England.

Ray Bull is Emeritus Professor of Forensic Psychology in the Department of Neuroscience, Psychology and Behaviour, University of Leicester, England, and Professor of Criminal Investigation in the Department of Law, Criminology and Social sciences, University of Derby, England.

David J. Cooke is Professor of Forensic Clinical Psychology, Glasgow Caledonian University, Glasgow, Scotland, and Visiting Professor, Faculty of Psychology, University of Bergen, Norway.

Rebecca V. Crago is a Ph.D. student in the Department of Psychology, University of East Anglia, Norwich, England.

David P. Farrington is Emeritus Professor of Psychological Criminology at the Institute of Criminology, Cambridge University, England.

Adelle E. Forth is Associate Professor, Department of Psychology, Carleton University, Ottawa, Canada.

C. Ronald Huff is Emeritus Professor, Department of Criminology, Law and Society, University of California, Irvine, USA.

Andreas Kapardis is Professor of Legal Psychology and Chair of the Law Department, University of Cyprus, Nicosia, Cyprus.

Marilena Kyriakidou is Research Fellow, Violence and Interpersonal Aggression Research Team, Coventry University, England.

Contributors xiii

Friedrich Lösel is Emeritus Director of the Institute of Criminology, Cambridge University, England, and Emeritus Professor, Institute of Psychology, University of Erlangen-Nuremberg, Germany.

Rebecca Milne is Professor of Forensic Psychology, Institute of Criminal Justice Studies, University of Portsmouth, England.

Sean O'Callaghan is a Ph.D. student at the University of Portsmouth, England.

Nicola Padfield is Master of Fitzwilliam College, Cambridge University, and Reader in Criminal and Penal Justice, Faculty of Law, Cambridge University, England.

Anna Sorrentino is a Ph.D. student in the Department of Humanities, Federico II University of Naples, Italy.

Mark Stemmler is Professor of Psychological Assessment, Methodology and Legal Psychology in the Institute of Psychology, University of Erlangen-Nuremberg, Germany.

Zara Sünkel carries out research in the Regional Psychiatric Hospital, Ansbach, Germany.

Maria M. Ttofi is University Lecturer in Psychological Criminology at the Institute of Criminology, Cambridge University, England.

David Walsh is University Reader in Criminal Investigation, International Policing and Justice Institute, University of Derby, England.

Foreword

Professor Ray Bull

In 2016 the importance of further improving our understanding of crime, of how best to police and of judicial procedures has continued to increase. Indeed, in 2015 many horrendous crimes were committed around the world; and in response substantial further funds were devoted to detecting and reducing crimes, especially the most serious types. However, quality research continues to be needed on how to do this effectively. 'Political' decision-making will be less valid if it is not in line with what past and ongoing research has discovered.

In this book the editors have purposely attracted chapter authors from a large variety of countries who are at various stages of their careers. In particular, some of the authors are from countries in which the psychological study of crime, policing and the courts is at a relatively early stage (compared to other countries such as the USA and England). Therefore, much of what this book contains will be new to the reader and it describes exciting innovations. The established, major topics of crime and antisocial behaviour rightly receive considerable attention but from several new perspectives. The fast growing topic of how investigators and police do and should interview suspects and witnesses is overviewed in two of the 13 chapters. The related topic of detecting truth and lies rightly deserves a chapter. The crucial topics of courts and sentencing are covered in four other chapters.

Thus, this book makes a meaningful contribution to the reduction of crime, to successful policing and to effective judicial procedures, things of great importance in all continents. The two editors and the many authors and co-authors are to be commended for their efforts on behalf of society.

Introduction

Psychology, crime, policing and courts

Andreas Kapardis and David P. Farrington

The main aim of this book is to present new psychological research on crime and antisocial behaviour, policing and detecting deception, and courts and sentencing. Most of the chapters are revised and updated versions of papers given at a European Association of Psychology and Law (EAPL) conference in Nicosia, Cyprus. The EAPL is now 25 years old. At a conference in Nuremberg, Germany, in 1990, it was resolved to found the EAPL, and the 25th anniversary conference was held in Nuremberg in 2015.

The first six chapters report research on crime and antisocial behaviour. It has often been discovered that offending tends to be concentrated in families. In Chapter 1, David P. Farrington and Rebecca V. Crago show that this was true of two generations of families in the longitudinal Cambridge Study in Delinquent Development. In the first generation, 6 per cent of families accounted for half of all convictions of all family members (fathers, mothers, sons and daughters). In the second generation, 8 per cent of families accounted for half of all convictions of all family members. Farrington and Crago go on to document significant intergenerational transmission of convictions from parents to children for both generations. Interestingly, the strength of intergenerational transmission was greater for children who had not been separated from their parents, suggesting that environmental influences on offending were important.

In many Western industrialized countries, aggregate crime rates increased from the 1970s to a peak in about 1995, and then decreased. In Chapter 2, Friedrich Lösel, Doris Bender, Zara Sünkel and Mark Stemmler investigate this phenomenon by analysing self-reported delinquency surveys completed by 14–15 year old boys in one Bavarian city in 1973, 1995 and 2011. Interestingly, they find that delinquency increased slightly from 1973 to 1995, but then decreased substantially from 1995 to 2011. They study numerous possible explanations of the crime drop, and suggest that the implementation of developmental prevention programmes and improved parental child-rearing behaviour may have been contributory factors.

The next two chapters focus on bullying, which is a type of antisocial behaviour that is significantly related to offending. In Chapter 3, Maria M. Ttofi and David P. Farrington investigate factors that interrupt the continuity from bullying at age 14 to offending at ages 15–50. They find that the main protective

2   A. Kapardis and D.P. Farrington

factors against criminal convictions tended to be environmental (e.g. high family income, good child-rearing, attending a low delinquency rate school), whereas the main protective factors against violence convictions tended to be individual (e.g. low daring, high intelligence, low extraversion). They conclude that protective factors should be taken into account in the design of bullying prevention programmes.

In Chapter 4, Anna C. Baldry, Anna Sorrentino and David P. Farrington investigate the involvement of Italian students (average age 15) in cyberbullying and cybervictimization. They find that 30 per cent of boys and 19 per cent of girls admitted cyberbullying in the previous six months, whereas 25 per cent of boys and 27 per cent of girls reported that they had been cybervictims. Interestingly, parental supervision of online activities was negatively related to cyberbullying (as expected) but positively related to cybervictimization, suggesting that cybervictimization may have caused increased parental online supervision. They conclude that more parental awareness, supervision and control of children's online activities are needed in order to reduce these modern-day problems.

The next two chapters focus on violence risk assessment and psychopathy. In Chapter 5, David J. Cooke questions the usefulness of actuarial risk assessment instruments, especially when they are used to make predictions about individuals rather than about groups. He further argues that the Area under the ROC Curve (AUC) is useful in diagnostic testing but is not useful for prognosis, when outcomes are not known. He also points out that information about differences between individuals is not necessarily relevant for conclusions about causal relationships within individuals. Overall, he recommends structured professional judgement in dealing with offenders, rather than the mechanical application of actuarial instruments.

Psychopathy is a very important personality dimension that is correlated with offending and antisocial behaviour. In Chapter 6, Henriette Bergstrøm, Adelle E. Forth and David P. Farrington investigate the relative stability of psychopathic traits from age 8–10 to age 48. The stability over time was remarkable; for example, psychopathy scores at age 8–10 correlated 0.40 with psychopathy scores at age 48, and psychopathy scores at age 16–18 correlated 0.66 with psychopathy scores at age 48. The most consistent predictors of later psychopathy scores were an antisocial family and antisocial peers.

The next three chapters focus on policing and detecting deception. The interrogation of suspects of crime is a central feature of criminal investigations and plays a crucial role in the process of obtaining justice. However, as David Walsh, Sean O'Callaghan and Rebecca Milne point out in Chapter 7, we do not know enough about how police officers in different countries approach the task in practice. The authors discuss the development of approaches to police questioning of suspects in the United States, demonstrate how certain beliefs have underpinned particular unethical questioning tactics, and focus on and critique the widespread and influential Reid model. The legal framework within which police question suspects is also considered, including both legislation and case law governing arrest, and "Miranda" rights, defining coercion and cruel and unusual

Introduction   3

punishment, in order to show what tactics and techniques are permitted. Differences between states in the recording of police interviews and interviewing of juvenile suspects are also reviewed, increasing concern about the risk of false confessions.

Differentiating true and false accounts is of great interest to the public and especially to criminal investigators and judicial officers. False sexual allegations have devastating effects on people's lives, send innocent people to prison, and cause unnecessary inconvenience to a lot of individuals, communities and legal personnel as well as to economic systems. In Chapter 8, Marilena Kyriakidou describes the phenomenon of false sexual allegations, focusing in particular on how best to differentiate between truthful and false accounts by children. It is perhaps comforting to know that the state of the art in identifying false accounts lies in unifying fabrication characteristics into testing instruments and, importantly, by conducting carefully structured police interviews with children, as detailed in Chapter 8.

While the debate about the accuracy of the lie-detector or polygraph continues unabated, two well-known psychophysiological detection methods used by polygraph examiners are the Comparison Questions Test (CQT), designed to detect deception, and the Concealed Information Test (CIT), designed to detect concealed knowledge. Gershon Ben-Shakhar in Chapter 9 shows that only the CIT meets basic scientific standards, although its external validity has been questioned. Furthermore, he suggests useful recommendations for enhancing the use of the CIT as an aid to criminal investigations.

A great deal of psycholegal research over the years been concerned with courts and sentencing. Miscarriages of justice are a worldwide concern. DNA profiling has made it possible to document wrongful convictions, that is the convictions of individuals who are factually innocent of the crimes for which they were convicted and even executed. In Chapter 10, C. Ronald Huff throws much-needed light on the causes of wrongful convictions by addressing important factors that contribute to miscarriages of justice at the investigation stage (eyewitness misidentification, false confessions, the use of informants/"snitches", bad lawyering, false accusations), and the prosecution stage (prosecutorial misconduct). He also highlights the significance of "tunnel vision" in the form of confirmation bias and belief perseverance, and provides suggestions about how wrongful convictions can be reduced.

The last three chapters concern judicial and juridic decision making. One of the arguments against the jury is that jurors are influenced by non-legal factors. A great deal of the empirical evidence on this for criminal trials is based on numerous mock-juror experiments of questionable external validity. In Chapter 11, Nicola Padfield addresses both the fairness and effectiveness of the jury process and poses a number of questions which psychologists are better suited to answer than lawyers by conducting "real world" research, such as: Should juries be given pre-trial summaries of the issues? Should the judge's summing up be oral or in writing? When does the jury need the help of an expert? And: Has the time come to allow the judge to retire with the jury?

4 *A. Kapardis and D.P. Farrington*

Unjustifiable inconsistencies in sentencing have been a cause for concern for over a century now. In Chapter 12, Andreas Kapardis evaluates the empirical evidence that such extra-legal factors as a defendant's race and physical attractiveness, and characteristics of magistrates and judges, influence the severity of the sentence imposed. The evidence is discussed and policy implications considered against the backdrop of the contemporary legal framework for sentencing in western English-speaking common law countries, including constraints on judicial discretion, the concepts of "sentence" and "disparity" and the nature of the sentence decision-making process.

For most people, the "sentence" means the penalty imposed by a criminal court on a defendant who has pleaded guilty or has been found guilty. Such a view of the sentence ignores the fact that, in reality, as Nicola Padfield shows in Chapter 13, a sentence should be considered a process that encompasses decisions made at the point of the initial sentence, on what happens throughout that sentence, and at the end of that sentence. By recasting the concept of "sentence", Chapter 13 provides both a fresh perspective on the purposes of sentencing and contributes significantly to a greater understanding of the real meaning of the "sentence" as well as to a more credible, orderly and efficient system, thus leading to increased fairness and justice.

This book is extremely wide-ranging in its coverage of important topics in psychology, crime and the law. It is also extremely international, as contributors are drawn from nine countries (England, Scotland, Germany, Italy, Norway, Cyprus, Israel, Canada and the United States). We believe that this book advances knowledge greatly about some of the most interesting areas of contemporary criminological and legal psychology.

Part I

Crime and antisocial behaviour

1 The concentration of convictions in two generations of families

David P. Farrington and Rebecca V. Crago

Introduction

The main aim of this chapter is to investigate the concentration of offending in two successive generations of families in the Cambridge Study in Delinquent Development (CSDD). It has been known for many years that offending tends to be concentrated in certain individuals in a birth cohort. For example, Wolfgang, Figlio and Sellin (1972) found that 6% of a cohort of Philadelphia males accounted for 52% of all their offences up to age 18, and called these 6% the "chronic" offenders. Similar results have been obtained in several later studies (e.g. Blumstein, Farrington, & Moitra, 1985; Farrington & West, 1993; Piquero, Farrington, & Blumstein, 2007).

There has been much less research, however, on the concentration of offending in families. The first extensive analyses of this topic were completed by Farrington, Gundry, and West (1975) and West and Farrington (1977). These analyses were carried out in the CSDD, which is a prospective longitudinal study of 411 London males, mostly born in 1953 and followed up from age 8; this project is described in more detail later. These analyses were based on convictions of the Study males, their biological parents and their biological siblings up to December 31, 1973, when the Study males were aged 20 on average. Brothers and sisters who had not reached age 17 by this date (the minimum age for adult court at that time) were not included in the analyses.

Out of 1763 persons searched in 394 families, 397 (22.5%) had been convicted; 28.2% of Study males, 26.7% of fathers, 13.4% of mothers, 37.4% of brothers and 7.6% of sisters. This was an average of one convicted person out of 4.5 persons per family. There were a total of 1217 convictions, or an average of 3.1 per family. Importantly, only 18 families (4.6%) accounted for nearly half (47.7%) of all the convictions, and 45 families (11.4%) accounted for nearly half (47.1%) of all the convicted persons.

These analyses were repeated by Farrington, Barnes and Lambert (1996) for convictions up to December 31, 1993, when the Study males were aged 40 on average. Out of 2203 persons searched in 397 families, 601 (27.3%) had been convicted; 39.0% of Study males, 27.9% of fathers, 13.6% of mothers, 44.2% of brothers and 12.1% of sisters. This was an average of 1.5 convicted persons out

8   *D.P. Farrington and R.V. Crago*

of 5.5 persons per family. There were 2442 convictions, or an average of 6.2 per family. Importantly, only 20 families (5.0%) accounted for nearly half (46.4%) of all convictions, and 48 families (12.1%) accounted for nearly half (44.3%) of all convicted persons.

The main aim of the present chapter is to repeat these analyses for two generations of CSDD families. In the interests of clarity, the original 411 males are termed generation 2 (G2), their biological parents are termed generation 1 (G1) and their biological children are termed generation 3 (G3). We aim to investigate to what extent the previous results, obtained by comparing G1 parents with G2 children, are replicated when G2 parents are compared with G3 children.

Method

The CSDD is a prospective longitudinal survey of 411 London males (G2 males) from age eight to age 56. The results of the Study have been described in six books (Farrington, Piquero, & Jennings, 2013; Piquero et al., 2007; West, 1969, 1982; West & Farrington, 1973, 1977), and in five summary articles (Farrington, 1995, 2003; Farrington, Coid, & West, 2009; Farrington & West, 1981, 1990). The original sample of G2 males is described next. Since the analyses are based on criminal record searches of all three generations, these are also described. As the record searches were based on identifying particulars obtained in interviews, these interviews are described as well.

The sample of G2 males

At the time they were first contacted in 1961–62, the G2 males were all living in a working-class area of South London. The vast majority of the sample was chosen by taking all the boys who were then aged 8–9 and on the registers of six state primary schools within a one mile radius of a research office which had been established. In addition to 399 boys from these six schools, 12 boys from a local school for educationally subnormal children were included in the sample, in an attempt to make it more representative of the population of boys living in the area. Therefore, the boys were not a probability sample drawn from a population, but rather a complete population of boys of that age in that area at that time.

Most of the G2 boys (357, or 87%) were Caucasian in appearance and of British origin, in the sense that they were being brought up by parents who had themselves been brought up in England, Scotland or Wales. Of the remaining 54 boys, 12 were Afro-Caribbean, having at least one parent of West Indian (usually) or African origin. Of the remaining 42 boys of non-British origin, 14 had at least one parent from the North or South of Ireland, 12 had parents from Cyprus, and the other 16 boys were Caucasian and had at least one parent from another Western industrialized country.

On the basis of their fathers' occupations when they were aged eight, 94% of the G2 boys could be described as working-class (categories III, IV or V on the

Registrar General's scale, describing skilled, semi-skilled or unskilled manual workers), in comparison with the national figure of 78% at that time. The majority of the boys were living in conventional two-parent families with both a father and a mother figure; at age 8–9, only 6% of the boys had no operative father and only 1% had no operative mother. This was, therefore, overwhelmingly a traditional Caucasian, urban, working-class sample of British origin.

Interviews with the G2 males

The G2 males have been interviewed nine times, at ages eight, ten, 14, 16, 18, 21, 25, 32 and 48. At ages eight, ten and 14, they were assessed in their schools. The tests in schools measured individual characteristics such as intelligence, attainment, personality and psychomotor impulsivity. At all ages except 21 and 25, the aim was to interview all the G2 males who were still alive, and it was always possible to interview a high proportion: 405 (99%) at age 14, 399 (97%) at age 16, 389 (95%) at age 18, 378 (94%) at age 32 and 365 (93%) at age 48. The survey received ethical approval from the Ethics Committee of the Institute of Psychiatry, Kings College London. At age 48, 17 males had died, five could not be traced and 24 refused, which meant that 365 out of 394 who were still alive were interviewed. Because of inadequate funding, only about half of the males were interviewed at age 21, and about a quarter at age 25.

In addition, the boys' teachers completed questionnaires when the G2 males were aged about 8, 10, 12 and 14. These furnished data about their troublesome and aggressive school behaviour, their restlessness or poor concentration, their school attainments and their truancy. Ratings were also obtained from the boys' peers when they were in the primary schools at ages eight and ten, about such topics as their daring, dishonesty, troublesomeness and popularity.

Interviews with the G1 parents

Interviews with the G1 parents were carried out by female social workers who visited their homes. These took place about once a year from when the G2 boy was about eight until when he was aged 14–15 and was in his last year of compulsory education. The primary informant was the mother, although many fathers were also seen. The G1 parents provided details about such matters as family income, family size, their employment histories, their child-rearing practices (including attitudes, discipline and parental disharmony), their degree of supervision of the boy, and his temporary or permanent separations from them.

Interviews with the G2 wives and female partners

Information about the wives and female partners (cohabitees) of the G2 males was sought during all interviews from age 18 onwards. For convenience, the G2 wives and female partners will simply be referred to as the G2 wives. They filled in a child-rearing questionnaire when the G2 male was aged 32, and 234 G2

10 *D.P. Farrington and R.V. Crago*

wives (77.2% of 303) were interviewed when the G2 male was aged 48. This interview included information about child-rearing, health and family violence (see Theobald & Farrington, 2012).

Interviews with the G3 children

Only biological G3 children aged at least 18 (born up to 1995) were targeted. We knew about and had identifying information for 691 G3 children. In order to meet the ethical standards of the South-East Region Medical Ethics Committee, we were required to contact the G2 male and/or his female partner in trying to interview the G3 children. Therefore, 20 G3 children whose G2 fathers refused at age 48, and seven children who father was dead at age 48 (and where no female partner was available) were not eligible to be interviewed. An additional six G3 males who had died and three who were disabled (one Down's syndrome, one mental health problems, one severe attention deficit-hyperactivity disorder), together with two who did not know that the G2 male was their father, were considered to be not eligible.

Of the 653 eligible G3 children, 551 were interviewed (84.4%) at an average age of 25; 291 of the 343 G3 males (84.8%) and 260 of the 310 G3 females (83.9%). Of the remainder, 39 children refused, 33 parents refused, 13 children could not be traced, 14 were elusive (agreeing or not refusing but never being available to interview) and three were aggressive or problematic. Of the 29 eligible children living abroad since birth, 17 were interviewed, usually by telephone. (For more information, see Farrington, Ttofi, Crago, & Coid, 2015.) Big efforts were made to establish which G2 wife was the mother of which G3 child.

Criminal record searches of the G2 males

Up to 1994, searches were carried out in the central Criminal Record Office or National Identification Service (CRO/NIS) at Scotland Yard in London to try to locate findings of guilt of the G2 males and their biological relatives. The minimum age of criminal responsibility in England is ten. The Criminal Record Office contained records of all relatively serious offences committed in Great Britain or Ireland, and also acted as a repository for records of minor juvenile offences committed in London. In the case of 18 males who had emigrated outside Great Britain and Ireland by age 32, applications were made to search their criminal records in the eight countries where they had settled, and searches were actually carried out in five countries. Two males were counted as not at risk of conviction, because they emigrated permanently before age 10, were not convicted and were not searched abroad.

Between 1964 and 1979, paper records were consulted in the CRO/NIS at Scotland Yard. In 1979, the records were transferred on to microfiche, and microfiche records were then consulted in the CRO/NIS at Scotland Yard until 1994. However, from 1995, the microfiche collection was discontinued and all convictions were recorded on the Police National Computer (PNC). There was

Convictions in two generations of families 11

only limited copying of old records to the PNC, generally when a person received a new conviction.

The last search of conviction records in the CRO/NIS took place towards the end of 1994, when most of the G2 males were aged 41. Convictions were counted for offences committed up to the end of 1993, when most of the males were aged 40 (Farrington et al., 1996; Farrington, Lambert, & West, 1998). The recorded age of offending is defined here as the age at which an offence was committed, not the age on conviction. There can be delays of several months or even more than a year between offences and convictions, making conviction ages different from offending ages. In investigating criminal careers, it is vital to study when offences were committed.

Further searches of criminal records of the G2 males took place in July 2002 and December 2004 in the PNC, at which time most of the males were aged 51. Many records of old convictions were not found in the PNC, and several convictions before 2002 were not found until the 2004 search, which covered NIS as well as PNC. The earliest date listed in the PNC was counted as the date on which an offence was committed. A Home Office report (Farrington et al., 2006) and many previous analyses were based on the criminal records up to age 50 derived from these searches. A further search of the PNC was completed in March 2011, when most males were aged 57. The criminal records of the G2 males are therefore now known up to age 56 (Farrington et al., 2013).

For comparability with the G3 children, it was decided to count officially recorded cautions as well as convictions in the PNC, since cautions were routinely recorded on a national basis from 1995. In total, 177 G2 males were convicted up to age 56 (43.8% of 404 at risk) for a total of 909 offences, including 51 cautions. In this chapter, "convictions" include officially recorded cautions. Convictions were only counted if they were for "standard list" (more serious) offences, thereby excluding minor crimes such as minor traffic infractions and simple drunkenness. The most common offences included were thefts, burglaries and unauthorized takings of vehicles, although there were also quite a few offences of violence, vandalism, fraud and drug abuse. The definition of what is a "standard list" offence changed over time. In particular, common assault became a standard list offence in July 1995, drunk driving was added to the standard list from January 1996, and being drunk and disorderly was added in April 1997. All of these types of offences were counted (see Farrington, Ttofi, Crago, & Coid, 2014).

Offences are defined as acts leading to convictions, and only offences committed on different days were counted. Where two or more offences were committed on the same day, only the most serious one was counted. This rule was adopted so that each separate incident could only yield one offence; if all offences had been counted, the number of offences would have been greater than the number of criminal incidents, and therefore the number of criminal incidents would have been overestimated. The most serious offence was defined as the one which received the most severe sentence or – where sentences were equal – the one with the longest maximum sentence. Most court appearances arose from

12   D.P. Farrington and R.V. Crago

only one offending day; the 909 recorded offences up to age 56 corresponded to 826 separate occasions of conviction. Offences "taken into consideration" were not counted.

The paper and microfiche records were extremely detailed (e.g. in their descriptions of the circumstances of offences) but the computerized PNC records (actually the Home Office/Ministry of Justice extract from the PNC) are not. There were major problems in deciding whether a G2 male found in a search was really our man, particularly in the case of people with common names and no middle names, and when there were slight differences in names or dates of birth between PNC and our own records. Fortunately, it was possible to establish whether each G2 male in the PNC data was our man unambiguously in all cases, using our prior searches, interview information and knowledge about the man's age and address (compared with his places of arrest and conviction, which were listed in the PNC file). In many cases, the G2 male and/or the G2 wife provided information about convictions in interviews. It would have been difficult to establish with certainty who was or was not our person in the PNC data in the absence of the interview data.

Criminal record searches of the G2 wives

We knew about and had identifying information for 413 wives of the G2 males. Theobald and Farrington (2010) studied the effect of getting married on convictions of the G2 wives. They were searched in the CRO/NIS in 1994, and in the PNC in 2004 and 2011. Of these 413 wives, 55 were convicted (13.3%), with a total of 129 offences. The counting rules were similar for all relatives (e.g. only convictions on different days were counted) except that cautions up to 1994 were only counted for G2 males.

Criminal record searches of the G2 brothers and G2 sisters

The full biological brothers and sisters of the G2 males were also searched from 1964 to 2011. Farrington and Painter (2004) reported on their convictions and compared G2 brothers, G2 sisters and G2 males; Besemer (2012) investigated intergenerational transmission from G1 parents to all G2 sons and G2 daughters.

The sample of 411 G2 males contained 14 pairs of brothers. In the interests of studying the 397 families, one G2 male from each pair (each younger brother and one randomly selected member of each of the five twin pairs) was counted as a G2 brother instead of a G2 male. Only family members who survived at least to age ten, and who had sufficient identifying particulars (name and date of birth), were searched. Because of our extensive contacts with the families over many years, very few family members had insufficient identifying particulars.

Up to 2011, when the average G2 brother was aged 56, 214 out of 489 G2 brothers (43.8%) were convicted, with a total of 1078 offences. Similarly, up to 2011, when the average G2 sister was aged 56, 68 out of 525 G2 sisters (13.0%) were convicted, with a total of 190 offences.

Criminal record searches of the G1 fathers and G1 mothers

The G1 fathers and G1 mothers were repeatedly searched in the CRO/NIS between 1964 and 1994, when the average G1 father (neglecting deaths) would have been 72 and the average G1 mother would have been 69. Up to this time, 110 G1 fathers (27.9% out of 394 known) were convicted, with a total of 318 offences, and 54 G1 mothers (13.6% out of 397) were convicted, with a total of 258 offences.

Criminal record searches of the G3 children

As mentioned, there were 691 children whose name and date of birth were known. Their median year of birth was 1981, and more than half were born between 1977 and 1985. They were first searched in the microfiche records in 1994, and they were then searched in the PNC in 2003, 2006 and 2011–12. The 31 G3 children who had been abroad since birth could not be searched, but 656 of the remaining 660 were searched. These included 343 G3 males and 313 G3 females. The mean age at which they were last searched was 29, and more than half were last searched between ages 25 and 33. Of the 343 G3 males, 95 (27.7%) were convicted, with a total of 537 offences, and 27 of the 313 G3 females (8.6%) were convicted, with a total of 53 offences. In the present analyses, only G3 children who had been searched after age 21 were included; their mean age searched was 30. In the interests of having comparable conviction data on all relatives, only convictions up to 32 are counted in this chapter. This age was chosen because 93.8% of the G2 males were interviewed at age 32, and it was close to the mean age of searching of the G3 males.

Statistical methods

The main measure of strength of relationship that is used in this chapter is the Odds Ratio (OR). This statistic has the advantage that it is not dependent on the overall sample size (unlike chi-squared for example) or on the row and column totals (Fleiss, 1981). Conventionally, its confidence interval (CI) is given, and it is statistically significant on a two-tailed test when the lower CI is 1.00 or greater. One-tailed tests would be justifiable in light of the directional predictions. Again conventionally, an OR of 2.00 or greater is considered to indicate a strong relationship (Cohen, 1996).

Because the G3 children are not all independent, it is necessary to adjust the variance of the OR in G3 analyses to take account of the clustering of G3 children in G2 families. It is easiest to do this by referring to the standardized mean difference d. Clustering has no material effect on the value of d but it increases the variance of d (see e.g. Hedges & Hedberg, 2007). The variance is multiplied by $[1 + (n-1) \times ICC]$, where n is the number of individuals in a cluster and ICC is the intraclass correlation. This correction has been known for many years and has been called the design effect (e.g. Kish, 1965) or the variance inflation factor (e.g. Donner, Birkett, & Buck, 1981).

14   D.P. Farrington and R.V. Crago

It is well known (see e.g. Lipsey & Wilson, 2001, p. 202) that

$$\ln (OR) = pi \times d/sqrt(3)$$

$$\text{or } \ln(OR) = 1.81 \times d$$

$$\text{Therefore, SE } [\ln(OR)] = 1.81 \times SE(d)$$

Since SE [ln(OR)] increases in direct proportion to SE(d), it follows that the variance of Ln(OR), like the variance of d, needs to be multiplied by $[1+(n-1) \times ICC]$ to take account of clustering.

For the dichotomized measure of convictions of G3 males, the ICC was 0.31, indicating a considerable degree of clustering of convictions in families. Since there were 275 G3 males in 186 families, the average number of G3 males in a family was 1.48. Therefore, the variance of ln(OR) was multiplied by $[1+0.48 \times 0.31]$, or increased by 15%, to take account of the clustering of convictions. This is equivalent to increasing the standard error of ln(OR) by 7.2% for G3 males. For G3 females, the ICC was only 0.027, corresponding to an increase in the variance of ln(OR) of only 1.3%. Because this was very small, the standard error of ln(OR) was not increased for G3 females.

It is not necessary to adjust the OR in analyses of G2 males because there is only one G2 male per family.

Results

G1–G2 families

There were 397 families in the CSDD. However, three G1 fathers were not searched because of insufficient identifying particulars, and two G2 males moved abroad before the age of criminal responsibility of ten and so were not at risk of being convicted in England and Wales. This left 392 families with a G1 father, a G1 mother and a G2 male who were all searched and at risk of conviction. There were 485 G2 brothers and 525 G2 sisters in these families who were searched and at risk of conviction, after excluding those who died or emigrated before age ten.

Table 1.1 shows the prevalence of convictions up to age 32 for all G1–G2 family members; 38.5% of G2 males were convicted, compared with 19.6% of G1 fathers, 7.1% of G1 mothers, 41.2% of G2 brothers and 11.8% of G2 sisters. The fact that the percentage of G2 brothers who were convicted is similar to the percentage of G2 males who were convicted suggests that the repeated personal contacts with the G2 males had very little effect on their likelihood of being convicted. In total, 518 out of 2186 birth family members (G1 fathers, G1 mothers, G2 males, G2 brothers and G2 sisters), or 23.7%, were convicted, and they accumulated 1934 convictions, an average of nearly one each. In addition, Table 1.1 shows that 8.7% of G2 wives (including female partners) were convicted up to

Convictions in two generations of families 15

Table 1.1 Prevalence of convictions up to age 32 among all family members (G1–G2)

Relative	Number searched	Number convicted	% convicted	Number convictions	Convictions per offender
G2 Male	392	151	38.5	696	4.6
G1 Father	392	77	19.6	183	2.4
G1 Mother	392	28	7.1	49	1.8
G1 Parent	784	105	13.4	232	2.2
G2 Older brother	227	104	45.8	443	4.3
G2 Younger brother	258	96	37.2	397	4.1
G2 Brother	485	200	41.2	840	4.2
G2 Older sister	243	29	11.9	92	3.2
G2 Younger sister	282	33	11.7	74	2.2
G2 Sister	525	62	11.8	166	2.7
G1–G2 Family member	2186	518	23.7	1934	3.7
G2 Wife	391	34	8.7	72	2.1

age 32. The number of convictions per offender was 4.6 for G2 males, 4.2 for G2 brothers, 2.4 for G1 fathers, 1.8 for G1 mothers, 2.7 for G2 sisters and 2.1 for G2 wives.

Table 1.2 shows the concentration of convictions in G1–G2 families. For example, eight families (2.0% of all families), containing 80 persons (G1 fathers, G1 mothers, G2 males, G2 brothers and G2 sisters), or 3.6% of all persons, accounted for 489 convictions (about a quarter of all convictions). Twenty-five families (6.4% of all families), containing 233 persons (10.7% of all persons),

Table 1.2 The concentration of convictions up to age 32 in families (G1–G2)

Families		Persons		Convictions	
No.	%	No.	%	No.	%
4	1.0	38	1.7	307	15.9
8	2.0	80	3.6	489	25.3
12	3.1	115	5.3	625	32.3
16	4.1	147	6.7	738	38.2
20	5.1	186	8.5	840	43.4
25	6.4	233	10.7	954	49.3
30	7.6	261	11.9	1054	54.5
35	8.9	292	13.4	1137	58.8
40	10.2	332	15.2	1207	62.4
50	12.8	401	18.3	1321	68.3
60	15.3	462	21.1	1417	73.3
70	17.9	546	25.0	1494	77.2
100	25.5	756	34.6	1674	86.6
150	38.3	1025	46.9	1832	94.7
200	51.0	1294	59.2	1903	98.4
300	76.5	1833	83.9	1934	100.0
392	100.0	2186	100.0	1934	100.0

16   D.P. Farrington and R.V. Crago

accounted for 954 convictions (about half of all convictions). Only 161 families (41.1%) contained no convicted persons.

Table 1.3 shows the percentage of G2 males who were convicted up to age 32, given convicted or unconvicted relatives up to age 32. For example, 68.8% of G2 males with a convicted G1 father were themselves convicted, compared with 31.1% of G2 males with an unconvicted G1 father. Similarly, 64.3% of G2 males with a convicted G1 mother were themselves convicted, compared with 36.5% of G2 males with an unconvicted G1 mother. The figures in Table 1.3 are based on G2 males, whereas those in Table 1.1 are based on relatives. For example, 122 G2 males had at least one convicted G2 brother in Table 1.3, whereas 200 G2 brothers were convicted in Table 1.1; and 120 G2 males had only unconvicted G2 brothers in Table 1.3, whereas 285 G2 brothers were unconvicted in Table 1.1.

The strongest relationship in Table 1.3 was between G2 males and G2 wives; 78.8% of G2 males with a convicted wife were themselves convicted, compared with 35.1% of G2 males with an unconvicted wife. The relationship between convictions of husbands and wives was even stronger in G1; 71.4% of G1 fathers with a convicted G1 mother were themselves convicted, compared with 15.7% of G1 fathers with an unconvicted G1 mother (OR = 13.47, CI = 5.66–32.05).

Following Thornberry, Freeman-Gallant and Lovegrove (2009), it might be expected that the relationship between a convicted parent and a convicted child would be less strong if the child was separated (permanently or temporarily) from the parent, and this was indeed found. Of the 392 G2 males, 254 (64.8%) were not separated from their G1 father up to age ten, 64 (16.3%) were separated because of death or hospitalization, and 74 (18.9%) were separated because of other reasons, usually connected with parental conflict.

Of G2 males who were not separated, 66.7% of 33 with a convicted G1 father were themselves convicted, compared with 27.6% of 221 with an unconvicted G1 father (OR = 5.25, CI = 2.40–11.46). Of G2 males who were separated because of death or hospitalization, 66.7% of 12 with a convicted G1 father were themselves

Table 1.3 Percentage of G2 males convicted up to age 32, given convicted or unconvicted relatives up to age 32 (G1–G2)

Relative	Convicted relative (N)	Unconvicted relative (N)	Odds ratio	CI
G1 Father	68.8 (77)	31.1 (315)	4.89	(2.86–8.37)
G1 Mother	64.3 (28)	36.5 (364)	3.13	(1.40–6.97)
G1 Parent	65.9 (85)	30.9 (307)	4.31	(2.59–7.17)
G2 Older brother	65.8 (79)	29.2 (72)	4.68	(2.35–9.31)
G2 Younger brother	57.1 (70)	27.1 (85)	3.59	(1.83–7.05)
G2 Brother	57.4 (122)	27.5 (120)	3.55	(2.07–6.08)
G2 Older sister	71.4 (21)	39.6 (149)	3.81	(1.40–10.39)
G2 Younger sister	61.5 (26)	43.0 (151)	2.12	(0.90–4.97)
G2 Sister	62.8 (43)	37.7 (239)	2.79	(1.43–5.47)
G2 Wife/Partner	78.8 (33)	35.1 (285)	6.87	(2.88–16.39)

Convictions in two generations of families 17

convicted, compared with 32.7% of 52 with an unconvicted G1 father (OR=4.12, CI=1.09–15.61). Of G2 males who were separated for other reasons, 71.9% of 32 with a convicted G1 father were themselves convicted, compared with 47.6% of 42 with an unconvicted G1 father (OR=2.81, CI=1.06–7.49).

Table 1.4 shows the relationship between convicted G1 parents and convicted G2 brothers and G2 sisters. For example, 71.9% of families with a convicted G1 father also had a convicted G2 brother, compared with 43.8% of families with an unconvicted G1 father; and 39.1% of families with a convicted G1 mother also had a convicted G2 sister, compared with 13.1% of families with an unconvicted G1 mother. It is noteworthy that the relationship between G1 fathers and G2 brothers was stronger than between G1 fathers and G2 sisters; and that the relationship between G1 mothers and G2 sisters was stronger than between G1 mothers and G2 brothers.

G2–G3 families

There were 254 G2–G3 families with a G2 male, a G2 wife and at least one G3 child searched and at risk of conviction. Nine G2 males had two G2 wives and therefore were included in two G2–G3 families. As a consequence, the 254 G2–G3 families included 245 different G2 males.

Table 1.5 shows the prevalence of convictions up to age 32 of all G2–G3 family members; 41.2% of the different G2 males were convicted, compared with 10.2% of G2 wives, 31.3% of G3 sons and 8.7% of G3 daughters. In total, 235 out of 1028 different birth family members (22.9%) were convicted, and they accumulated 1054 convictions, or about one each. The number of convictions per offender was 4.7 for G2 males, 1.9 for G2 wives, 5.6 for G3 sons and 2.0 for G3 daughters.

Table 1.5 also shows the convictions of the G1 grandfathers and G1 grandmothers of the G3 children; there were some duplicates, but 23.7% of different G1 grandfathers and 8.9% of different G1 grandmothers of these families were convicted.

Table 1.4 Percentage of families with a G2 brother or G2 sister convicted up to age 32, given a convicted or unconvicted G1 parent up to age 32 (G1–G2)

	Convicted G1 father	*Unconvicted G1 father*	*Odds ratio*	*CI*
% with G2 Brother convicted (N)	71.9 (57)	43.8 (185)	3.29	(1.72–6.28)
% with G2 Sister convicted (N)	25.8 (62)	12.3 (220)	2.49	(1.24–4.99)
	Convicted G1 mother	*Unconvicted G1 mother*	*Odds ratio*	*CI*
% with G2 Brother convicted (N)	76.5 (17)	48.4 (225)	3.46	(1.09–10.93)
% with G2 Sister convicted (N)	39.1 (23)	13.1 (259)	4.25	(1.71–10.59)

18   *D.P. Farrington and R.V. Crago*

Table 1.5 Prevalence of convictions up to age 32 among all relatives (G2–G3)

Relative	Number searched	Number convicted	% convicted	Number convictions	Convictions per offender
G2 Male	254 (*245)	105 (*101)	41.3 (*41.2)	498 (*477)	4.7 (*4.7)
G2 Wife	254	26	10.2	50	1.9
G2 Parent	508 (*499)	131 (*127)	25.8 (*25.5)	548 (*527)	4.2 (*4.1)
G3 Sons	275	86	31.3	483	5.6
G3 Daughters	254	22	8.7	44	2.0
G3 Children	529	108	20.4	527	4.9
G2–G3 Family member	1037 (*1028)	239 (*235)	23.0 (*22.9)	1075 (*1054)	4.5 (*4.5)
G1 Grandfather	252 (*245)	60 (*58)	23.8 (*23.7)	146 (*143)	2.4 (*2.5)
G1 Grandmother	254 (*247)	23 (*22)	9.1 (*8.9)	45 (*42)	2.0 (*1.9)

Notes
* excluding nine G2 male duplicates (4 convicted, with 21 convictions), *excluding seven G1 grandfather and G1 grandmother duplicates (2 grandfathers convicted, with 3 convictions, 1 grandmother convicted, with 3 convictions).

Table 1.6 shows the concentration of convictions in the G2–G3 families. For example, six families (2.4% of all families), containing 32 persons (G2 male, G2 wife, G3 sons, G3 daughters), or 3.1% of all persons, accounted for 244 convictions (almost a quarter of all convictions). Twenty families (7.9% of all families), containing 91 persons (8.8% of all persons), accounted for 532 convictions (about half of all convictions). Only 112 families (44.1%) contained no convicted persons.

Table 1.6 The concentration of convictions up to age 32 in families (G2–G3)

Families		Persons		Convictions	
No.	%	No.	%	No.	%
3	1.2	14	1.4	155	14.4
6	2.4	32	3.1	244	22.7
9	3.5	48	4.6	313	29.1
12	4.7	59	5.7	378	35.2
15	5.9	69	6.7	441	41.0
20	7.9	91	8.8	532	49.5
25	9.8	109	10.5	611	56.8
30	11.8	128	12.3	677	63.0
35	13.8	148	14.3	735	68.4
40	15.7	168	16.2	781	72.7
50	19.7	210	20.3	855	79.5
60	23.6	250	24.1	911	84.7
70	27.6	292	28.2	953	88.7
100	39.4	414	39.9	1032	96.0
150	59.1	631	60.8	1075	100.0
254	100.0	1037	100.0	1075	100.0

Convictions in two generations of families 19

Table 1.7 shows the percentage of G3 sons who were convicted up to age 32, given convicted or unconvicted relatives up to age 32. For example, 39.7% of G3 sons with a convicted G1 grandfather were themselves convicted, compared with 29.2% of G3 sons with an unconvicted G1 grandfather. However, convictions of G1 grandfathers and G1 grandmothers did not significantly predict convictions of G3 sons. Convictions of G2 males, G2 wives, G3 brothers and G3 sisters did significantly predict convictions of G3 sons. The comparison between G3 sons and their G3 siblings was based on families; for example, 59 G3 sons had at least one convicted brother, 107 G3 sons had only unconvicted brothers, and the remaining 109 G3 sons had no brothers. Therefore, it was not necessary to adjust these analyses for non-independence.

Table 1.8 shows the percentage of G3 daughters who were convicted up to age 32, given convicted or unconvicted relatives up to age 32. For example, 17.2% of G3 daughters with a convicted G1 grandfather were themselves convicted, compared with 5.9% of G3 daughters with an unconvicted G1 grandfather. Convictions of G1 grandfathers, G2 wives and G3 brothers significantly predicted convictions of G3 daughters, but convictions of G1 grandmothers, G2 males and G3 sisters were not significantly predictive.

Table 1.7 Percentage of G3 sons convicted up to age 32, given convicted or unconvicted relatives up to age 32 (G2–G3)

Relative	Convicted relative (N)	Unconvicted relative (N)	Odds ratio	CI
G1 Grandfather	39.7 (58)	29.2 (216)	1.60	(0.84–3.05)
G1 Grandmother	40.0 (25)	30.4 (250)	1.53	(0.62–3.78)
G2 Male	47.7 (109)	20.5 (166)	3.54	(2.00–6.26)
G2 Wife	67.9 (28)	27.1 (247)	5.67	(2.30–13.97)
G3 Brother	52.5 (59)	19.6 (107)	4.53	(2.25–9.12)
G3 Sister	66.7 (15)	27.1 (129)	5.37	(1.72–16.82)

Note
The CI for G1 grandfather, G1 grandmother, G2 male and G2 wife was increased to take account of the non-independence of G3 sons (see text).

Table 1.8 Percentage of G3 daughters convicted up to age 32, given convicted or unconvicted relatives up to age 32 (G2–G3)

Relative	Convicted relative (N)	Unconvicted relative (N)	Odds ratio	CI
G1 Grandfather	17.2 (64)	5.9 (187)	3.32	(1.36–8.09)
G1 Grandmother	17.4 (23)	7.8 (231)	2.49	(0.77–8.11)
G2 Male	10.9 (110)	6.9 (144)	1.64	(0.68–3.95)
G2 Wife	19.4 (36)	6.9 (218)	3.27	(1.23–8.69)
G3 Brother	16.4 (55)	3.1 (97)	6.13	(1.58–23.73)
G3 Sister	10.0 (20)	9.2 (131)	1.10	(0.23–5.33)

20   D.P. Farrington and R.V. Crago

We again investigated whether the relationship between a convicted parent and a convicted child was less strong if the child was separated (permanently or temporarily) from the parent, and indeed this was true for G3 sons. Of the 275 G3 sons, 46 were not interviewed; of the remainder, 176 (76.9%) were not separated from their father before age 16, but 53 (23.1%) were. Of G3 sons who were not separated, 41.4% of 58 with a convicted G2 father were themselves convicted, compared with 16.9% of 118 with an unconvicted G2 father (OR=3.46, CI=1.70–7.04). Of G3 sons who were separated, 55.6% of 27 with a convicted G2 father were themselves convicted, compared with 30.8% of 26 with an unconvicted G2 father (OR=2.81, CI=0.91–8.68).

As mentioned, convictions of G2 fathers did not significantly predict convictions of G3 daughters, and this relationship was not stronger for G3 daughters who had not been separated; OR=0.89 (CI=0.22–3.59) for unseparated G3 daughters, and OR=1.18 (CI=0.26–5.47) for separated G3 daughters.

Conclusions

Compared with the previous article by Farrington et al. (1996), in this chapter convictions are studied up to the same age (32) for all relatives. However, one limitation of the present analysis is that the criminal records of the G3 children up to age 32 are not complete. Quite a few of the G3 children were last searched before age 32: 67.3% of G3 sons and 64.2% of G3 daughters. Nevertheless, the majority (65.1% of G3 sons and 70.1% of G3 daughters) were aged at least 28 when they were last searched, and so they were well past the peak age for first convictions. Another difference from the previous article is that the present chapter includes G2 wives and female partners, whereas in the previous article only G2 wives were included. The previous article showed that very little of the concentration of offending in families was attributable to co-offending.

Our main conclusions are that offending is strongly concentrated in families as well as in individuals and that it is transmitted from one generation to the next. However, the concentration of offending was somewhat less in the G2–G3 analysis than in the G1–G2 analysis. While 6% of G1–G2 families accounted for half of all their convictions, 8% of G2–G3 families accounted for half of all their convictions. This was mainly because the average family size decreased from G2 (5.6 persons per family) to G3 (4.1 persons per family), and because variations in family size were less for G3. In G2, the 25 most criminal families (6.4% of families) contained 233 persons (an average of 9.3 each; 10.7% of all persons); in G3, the 20 most criminal families (7.9% of families) contained 91 persons (an average of 4.6 each; 8.8% of all persons).

While the concentration of offending was clearly less in the G2–G3 analysis, the strength of intergenerational transmission was not clearly lower. The OR was 4.89 for G1 fathers versus G2 males, 3.29 for G1 fathers versus G2 brothers, and 3.54 for G2 males versus G3 sons. The OR was 3.13 for G1 mothers versus G2 males, 3.46 for G1 mothers versus G2 brothers and 5.67 for G2 wives versus G3

Convictions in two generations of families 21

sons. Perhaps surprisingly, there was only one significant relationship between G1 grandparents and G3 children: convicted G1 grandfathers predicted convicted G3 daughters.

In the G1–G2 analysis, same-sex intergenerational relationships were generally stronger than opposite-sex relationships. The G1 father–G2 male relationship was stronger than the G1 mother–G2 male relationship; the G1 father–G2 brother relationship was stronger than the G1 father–G2 sister relationship; and the G1 mother–G2 sister relationship was stronger than the G1 mother–G2 brother relationship. Rowe and Farrington (1997) also found in the CSDD that intergenerational and intragenerational same-sex relationships were stronger than the corresponding opposite-sex relationships.

The greater strength of same-sex intergenerational relationships was less clear in the G2–G3 analysis. While the G2 wife–G3 daughter relationship was stronger than the G2 male–G3 daughter relationship, the G2 wife–G3 son relationship was stronger than the G2 male–G3 son relationship. Also, as already noted, the only significant relationship between G1 and G3 was between G1 grandfathers and G3 daughters.

It is not possible to study the importance of genetic influences in the CSDD because no genetic material (e.g. DNA) has been collected. However, it is possible to study the importance of environmental influences by comparing children who have been separated from their parents with children who have not. To the extent that genetics is important, separated and unseparated children should be similar. However, in the G1–G2 analysis, the relationship between convicted G1 fathers and convicted G2 males was clearly stronger for G2 males who had not been separated from their G1 fathers. Furthermore, this result was replicated in the G2–G3 analysis in comparing G2 males with their G3 sons. Therefore, environmental influences are important.

The main implications of this chapter for policy and practice are that interventions should be targeted on criminal families rather than on individuals and should particularly aim to interrupt the intergenerational transmission of offending. Successful interventions would have greater and longer-lasting benefits by reducing the offending not only of one generation but also of succeeding generations.

Acknowledgements

For funding the Cambridge Study in Delinquent Development, we are very grateful to the Home Office, the Department of Health, the Department for Education, the Rayne Foundation, the Barrow Cadbury Trust and the Smith-Richardson Foundation.

References

Besemer, S. (2012). *Intergenerational transmission of criminal and violent behaviour.* Leiden, Netherlands: Sidestone Press.

22   D.P. Farrington and R.V. Crago

Blumstein, A., Farrington, D. P., & Moitra, S. (1985). Delinquency careers: Innocents, desisters and persisters. In M. Tonry & N. Morris (eds), *Crime and justice*, vol. 6 (pp. 187–219). Chicago: University of Chicago Press.

Cohen, P. (1996). Childhood risks for young adult symptoms of personality disorder: Method and substance. *Multivariate Behavioral Research, 31*, 121–148.

Donner, A., Birkett, N., & Buck, C. (1981). Randomization by cluster. *American Journal of Epidemiology, 114*, 906–914.

Farrington, D. P. (1995). The development of offending and antisocial behaviour from childhood: Key findings from the Cambridge Study in Delinquent Development. *Journal of Child Psychology and Psychiatry, 36*, 929–964.

Farrington, D. P. (2003). Key results from the first 40 years of the Cambridge Study in Delinquent Development. In T. P. Thornberry & M. D. Krohn (eds), *Taking stock of delinquency: An overview of findings from contemporary longitudinal studies* (pp. 137–183). New York: Kluwer/Plenum.

Farrington, D. P., Barnes, G., & Lambert, S. (1996). The concentration of offending in families. *Legal and Criminological Psychology, 1*, 47–63.

Farrington, D. P., Coid, J. W., Harnett, L., Jolliffe, D., Soteriou, N., Turner, R., & West, D. J. (2006). *Criminal careers up to age 50 and life success up to age 48: New findings from the Cambridge Study in Delinquent Development*. London: Home Office (Research Study No. 299).

Farrington, D. P., Coid, J. W., & West, D. J. (2009). The development of offending from age 8 to age 50: Recent results from the Cambridge Study in Delinquent Development. *Monatsschrift fur Kriminologie und Strafrechtsreform (Journal of Criminology and Penal Reform), 92*, 160–173.

Farrington, D. P., Gundry, G., & West, D. J. (1975). The familial transmission of criminality. *Medicine, Science and the Law, 15*, 177–186.

Farrington, D. P., Lambert, S., & West, D. J. (1998). Criminal careers of two generations of family members in the Cambridge Study in Delinquent Development. *Studies on Crime and Crime Prevention, 7*, 85–106.

Farrington, D. P., & Painter, K. A. (2004). *Gender differences in offending: Implications for risk-focussed prevention*. London: Home Office (Online Report 09/04).

Farrington, D. P., Piquero, A. R., & Jennings, W. G. (2013) *Offending from childhood to late middle age: Recent results from the Cambridge Study in Delinquent Development*. New York: Springer.

Farrington, D. P., Ttofi, M. M., Crago, R. V., & Coid, J. W. (2014). Prevalence, frequency, onset, desistance and criminal career duration in self-reports compared with official records. *Criminal Behaviour and Mental Health, 24*, 241–253.

Farrington, D. P., Ttofi, M. M., Crago, R. V., & Coid, J. W. (2015). Intergenerational similarities in risk factors for offending. *Journal of Developmental and Life-Course Criminology, 1*, 48–62.

Farrington, D. P., & West, D. J. (1981). The Cambridge Study in Delinquent Development (United Kingdom). In S. A. Mednick & A. E. Baert (eds), *Prospective longitudinal research* (pp. 137–145). Oxford: Oxford University Press.

Farrington, D. P., & West, D. J. (1990). The Cambridge Study in Delinquent Development: A long-term follow-up of 411 London males. In H.-J. Kerner & G. Kaiser (eds), *Kriminalitat: Personlichkeit, lebensgeschichte und verhalten (Criminality: Personality, behavior and life history)* (pp. 115–138). Berlin, Germany: Springer-Verlag.

Farrington, D. P., & West, D. J. (1993). Criminal, penal and life histories of chronic

Convictions in two generations of families   23

offenders: Risk and protective factors and early identification. *Criminal Behaviour and Mental Health, 3,* 492–523.

Fleiss, J. L. (1981). *Statistical methods for rates and proportions* (2nd edn) New York: Wiley.

Hedges, L. V., & Hedberg, E. C. (2007). Intraclass correlations for planning group randomized experiments in rural education. *Journal of Research in Rural Education, 22,* 1–15.

Kish, L. (1965). *Survey sampling.* New York: Wiley.

Lipsey, M. W., & Wilson, D. B. (2001). *Practical meta-analysis.* Thousand Oaks, CA: Sage.

Piquero, A. R., Farrington, D. P., & Blumstein, A. (2007). *Key issues in criminal career research: New analyses of the Cambridge Study in Delinquent Development.* Cambridge: Cambridge University Press.

Rowe, D. C., & Farrington, D. P. (1997). The familial transmission of criminal convictions. *Criminology, 35,* 177–201.

Theobald, D., & Farrington, D. P. (2010). Should policy implications be drawn from research on the effects of getting married on offending? *European Journal of Criminology, 7,* 239–247.

Theobald, D., & Farrington, D. P. (2012). Child and adolescent predictors of male intimate partner violence. *Journal of Child Psychology and Psychiatry, 53,* 1242–1249.

Thornberry, T. P., Freeman-Gallant, A., & Lovegrove, P. J. (2009). Intergenerational linkages in antisocial behaviour. *Criminal Behaviour and Mental Health, 19,* 80–93.

West, D. J. (1969). *Present conduct and future delinquency.* London: Heinemann.

West, D. J. (1982). *Delinquency: Its roots, careers and prospects.* London: Heinemann.

West, D. J., & Farrington, D. P. (1973). *Who becomes delinquent?* London: Heinemann.

West, D. J., & Farrington, D. P. (1977). *The delinquent way of life.* London: Heinemann.

Wolfgang, M. E., Figlio, R. M., & Sellin, T. (1972). *Delinquency in a birth cohort.* Chicago: University of Chicago Press.

2 Self-reported juvenile delinquency in three surveys over 38 years

A German study on the crime drop

Friedrich Lösel, Doris Bender, Zara Sünkel and Mark Stemmler

Introduction

Although criminology is a multidisciplinary field, sociological and legal approaches have dominated over many years. However, in the last decades psychology became more influential. This is visible in developmental and life-course criminology (e.g. Farrington, 2005), early prevention of delinquency (e.g. Farrington & Welsh, 2007), offender treatment and rehabilitation (e.g. Lösel, 2012a) and – most recently – in neuropsychological contributions to criminology (e.g. Raine, 2013). However, psychology seems to be less involved in discussions on macro-social issues of criminology, although these may be related to mediating processes on the individual and micro-social level (motivation, family stress, parenting, group dynamics, etc.). Such an example is the discussion on the 'crime drop' in which mainly authors with a background in sociology, economy or political science are taking part. Therefore, we found it worthwhile to contribute a study on this topic to a book on psychology and law.

Data from the United States, Canada, Australia and some European countries have shown decreasing crime rates since the early 1990s (e.g. Blumstein & Wallman, 2006; Farrell, 2013; Farrell, Tilley, Tseloni, & Mailley, 2010; Tilley, Tseloni, & Farrell, 2011; Tonry & Farrington, 2005; van Dijk, 2008; van Dijk, Tseloni, & Farrell, 2012). This trend has not only been reported for official police statistics, but also for regular victim surveys that are carried out in some countries. The literature on the crime drop refers to crime in general, violent crime and sometimes to specific other offences such as burglary or car theft. In the US National Crime Victimization Survey, for example, violent victimization decreased from 79.8 per 1,000 persons at age 12 or older in 1993 to a rate of 20.1 in 2014 (Truman & Langton, 2015). This is a drop of approximately 75%. The decrease in property victimization (per 1,000 households) was approximately two-thirds, i.e. from 351.8 in 1993 to 118.1 in 2014. For both types of crimes the curve of decrease flattened since the early twenty-first century. With regard to violent crime one may relate the crime drop to a long-term historical trend of decreasing violence (Eisner, 2003; Pinker, 2011). However, such an interpretation is perhaps too far-reaching, particularly when recent wars and civil wars are taken into account. One should also bear in mind that substantial crime drops (and later increases) already took place before the recent decline in the 1990s (Knepper, 2015).

Due to the complexity of the topic it is not surprising that many 'theories' or hypotheses have been proposed to explain the crime drop. In thorough reviews Levitt (2004) analysed ten of these explanations, Blumstein and Rosenfeld (2008) 12, Farrell (2013) 15 and Farrell et al. (2010) 21. Table 2.1 shows the 15 hypotheses from the brief review of Farrell (2013).

He applied five 'tests' to these explanations: 1. reasonable empirical evidence; 2. cross-national applicability; 3. compatibility with prior increases of crime; 4. compatibility with increases of specific crimes such as phone theft or e-crime; and 5. compatibility with variations in the timing of crime falls between countries and crime types. Whereas Blumstein and Rosenfeld (2008) found empirical support for 'increased prison population', 'consumer confidence' and 'waning crack market' as explanations of the crime drop in the United States, only 'improved security' passed the more international tests of Farrell (2013).

From a perspective of psychology and law in Europe it is noteworthy that most of the hypotheses in Table 2.1 are US-focused and mainly derived from rational choice, routine activity and strain theories. Some hypotheses are irrelevant for Europe (e.g. death penalty), some seem to be in conflict with each other (e.g. the two hypotheses on guns), and others contradict the experience in most European countries (e.g. crime *reduction* due to immigration). From a psychological perspective one may ask why explanations such as a decrease of corporal

Table 2.1 Hypotheses on the explanation of the international crime drop

Hypothesis	Potential mechanism
1 Strong economy	People with resources commit less crime
2 Concealed weapon laws	More defensive guns, less crime
3 Capital punishment	More death penalty deterred crime
4 Gun control laws	Less guns, less crime
5 Rising prison populations	Incapacitation and deterrence reduce crime
6 Policing strategies	Policing focused on crime prevention
7 More police	Increased police forces detect and deter more crime
8 Legalization of abortion	More abortion (since 1973) less later offending
9 Immigration	Immigrants commit less crime, so crime fell as immigration rose
10 Consumer confidence	Wealthy buy less from stolen good markets
11 Waning crack markets	2nd generation youth deterred by violence and prison for elders
12 Childhood lead	Less lead poisoning in childhood reduced youth crime
13 Changing demographics	Ageing population means fewer young offenders
14 Civilizing process	Social institutions more legitimate (1960–80s = age of protest)
15 Improved security	Improved security, reduced crime opportunities

Note
Based on Farrell, 2013; slightly modified.

26   *F. Lösel et al.*

punishment in families are rarely mentioned in the crime drop discussion, although social learning theory and empirical research have shown its relevance for delinquency (e.g. Straus, 2010). One may also ask why the crime drop is often explained by single factors. In developmental criminology there is clear evidence that only the accumulation of several risk factors and a lack of protective factors lead to a strong increase of criminal and violent behavior (Farrington, 1996; Lösel & Farrington, 2012). On the macro level, consideration of multiple factors may lead to puzzling results. For example, Ignatans and Pease (2015) found in an analysis of data from the Crime Survey of England and Wales that crime against the multiply defined most victimized families dropped, but the proportion of crime experienced by these households increased.

The problem of complex outcomes versus single explanatory variables can be seen in the hypothesis on the impact of incarceration rates. Blumstein and Rosenfeld (2008) convincingly reported that the rise in incarceration rates in the United States contributed to the crime drop. However, there was also a similar crime drop in Canada where incarceration did not increase in the 1990s (Zimring, 2006). Blumstein and Rosenfeld (2008) also emphasized local differences and showed, for example, big differences in the change of crime rates of major US cities. The more recent development in US incarceration underlines this complexity. The US, as world leader of imprisonment, has recently experienced a decrease in incarceration rates, but there is no simple relation to crime rates. Across some US states reduced incarceration rates correlated with decreasing crime rates, however, there were also lower crime rates in states where incarceration remained stable or even increased. An increased transfer from state to local prisons (with less rehabilitative efforts) makes the picture even more difficult (Petersilia & Cullen, 2015). As already Blumstein and Beck (1999) have shown, there is only a minor correlation between crime rates and incarceration rates, but more complex political processes need to be taken into account. In addition, Hofer and Lappi-Seppälä (2014) analysed justice data in Finland and Sweden over more than 250 years and found no lasting impacts of law and policy reforms on crime.

Such examples suggest that the thinking about the crime drop is sometimes too US-focused and too broad. For example, one may doubt whether it is meaningful to expect that hypotheses apply to such heterogeneous offences such as professional burglary, sexual child abuse and juvenile shoplifting. Exceptions from the crime drop such as cybercrime also need to be taken into account (Farrell et al., 2010). Although some authors seem to view the crime drop as a relatively general development in Western countries (e.g. Knepper, 2012; Tseloni, Malley, Farrell, & Tilley, 2010), others emphasize international differences (e.g. Aebi & Linde, 2010, 2012a; Killias & Lafranconi, 2012). For example, Aebi and Linde (2010) combined police statistics and crime victim surveys in Western Europe from 1988 to 2007. They found a decrease for property crime, but an increase for violent and drug offences. In another study, Aebi and Linde (2012b) analysed conviction studies from the European Sourcebook of Crime and Criminal Justice Statistics. The data showed different trends in

Self-reported delinquency in Germany 27

Central and Eastern Europe and also between various offences. Accordingly, the authors concluded that there is no general crime drop in Europe.

A more specific example is Germany. This country was influenced by the fall of the iron curtain in 1990 and did not experience a strong crime drop during the 1990s. According to the official crime statistics of the Federal Police Office there was a slight, but not continuous, decrease in overall crime figures per 100,000 of the population after 1993 (when the first valid crime statistics of the unified country were available). However, the rates for identified suspects per 100,000 showed a slight continuous increase until 2004. In contrast to the overall moderate changes, the figures for some offences strongly declined in the 1990s. For example, probably due to the electronic key and to preventive police and insurance programs, car theft decreased from *c.*215,000 cases in 1993 to *c.*37,000 in 2008 (Lösel, 2004a). However, more recent police data show again an increase that may be attributed to more sophisticated techniques of (often foreign) organized criminals (Bundeskriminalamt, 2015). A German 'deviance' from the international crime drop is particularly obvious in the crime rates of young people that strongly increased in the 1990s until 2001. We will refer to this in the discussion section. Since the police crime statistics show a more recent decrease, there is perhaps a 'delayed crime drop' in Germany.

However, all discussions of official crime data have to take their well-known problems into account: they only contain offences that were registered by the police and therefore depend on the action of victims, witnesses and the police. With regard to the crimes of juveniles (age 14<18 in the German crime statistics) or other age groups the data only refer to cleared offences for which a suspect has been detected. The overall clearance rates for registered offences in Germany are around 55% and vary substantially for different offences. The police-recorded offence category and suspect may not be confirmed in the later justice process, counting criteria changed repeatedly (e.g. for multiple offenders), the size and composition of the population (i.e. foreign offenders) also vary over longer time periods.

As a consequence of these and other problems a regular victim survey in Germany would be welcome. However, in spite of repeated proposals from researchers, the Government has not yet introduced such a measure to cross-validate official statistics. As shown above, analyses of a crime drop should cover relatively long time periods, data before a drop, and also more specific types of crime or age groups. Otherwise there is a risk of over-interpreting more or less normal statistical fluctuation and regressions to the mean.

Since there are no regular and comparable surveys in Germany, the following study aims to make a small contribution to the crime drop discussion that is not based on official statistics. We present data on self-reported delinquency in three cohorts of juveniles (1973, 1995 and 2011) from low-income neighbourhoods of a southern German city. Although the three samples are not representative, the study is insofar unique as it contains identical delinquency self-reports of boys who attended the same (or similar) schools before, during and after the

28   *F. Lösel* et al.

internationally postulated crime drop. We are not aware of a comparably long-term comparison of cohort data on self-reported juvenile delinquency in Germany or other European countries.

Method

Samples of the three surveys

The first survey took place in *1973* at Nuremberg (Bavaria) within the context of a larger project on juvenile delinquency funded by the German Research Foundation (e.g. Lösel & Wüstendörfer, 1976). In the present study on self-control and delinquency $n=161$ male students answered a delinquency self-report scale (Lösel, 1975). For details of the scale see the section on instruments below. Nuremberg is an industrial city in Middle Franconia with a population of $c.500,000$ ($c.$ one million in the wider region). The study was carried out in two state secondary modern schools ('Hauptschulen'). This school type is mostly for students who do not qualify for superior secondary schools/high schools ('Real-schule', 'Gymnasium'). The two schools had been selected because they were located in areas of Nuremberg with many families from lower class and migrant backgrounds. Because German cities at this time did not have as much heterogeneity between neighbourhoods as many US cities, one may not call these areas 'deprived', but they were clearly at the low end with regard to income, housing conditions and prestige in Nuremberg. The sample contained nearly all male 8th grade students of the two schools. The mean age of the boys was $M=14.30$ ($SD=0.64$). Like all other instruments the delinquency self-report was answered anonymously.

The assessment in *1995* was part of an intensive survey and experimental investigation of school bullying and delinquency. It was funded by the German Federal Police Office (Lösel & Bliesener, 2003). In this study we applied the same delinquency self-report as in 1973. Since the whole study contained 1,163 male and female students from all school types in Nuremberg and near-by Erlangen, we selected 66 boys from the total sample for a comparison with the 1973 data (Lösel, Bliesener, & Averbeck, 1998). These boys attended the 8th grade of the same schools in low-income neighbourhoods of Nuremberg as the 1973 sample. More than 90% of the eligible boys participated. The mean age of the boys was $M=14.62$ ($SD=0.78$). The delinquency data were again gathered anonymously.

The third survey that is included in the present study was carried out in *2011*. It was part of a larger project on chances and risks in the life course, funded by the German Research Foundation (e.g. Reinecke et al., 2013). The assessments in this project took place in Nuremberg and the North Rhine-Westphalian city of Dortmund (Wallner & Stemmler, 2014). The Nuremberg survey applied the same instrument on self-reported delinquency as we used in 1973 and 1995. Only two items had a slightly different wording to be comparable with the Dortmund part of the project. Due to now more restrictive data protection regulations in Germany and a further increased proportion of students from migrant backgrounds, the participation rates were lower than in 1973 and 1995 (in some classes less than 50%). In addition, the classes were smaller and the overall survey involved both sexes and different grades. Therefore, we could not limit our sample to the two schools of the previous studies, but included data from other state secondary schools in under-privileged neighbourhoods of Nuremberg. We selected four similar schools that had high rates of students from families with a low socioeconomic status (SES) and migration background. Although in 2010 the former 'Hauptschulen' were labelled 'Mittelschulen' in Bavaria, the selected schools were basically the same type of state schools as in the two previous surveys. The 2011 sample contained $n=96$ boys at 9th grade with a mean age of $M=15.52$ years $(SD=0.85)$.

Instruments

In all three assessments we applied a scale on self-reported delinquency that has been developed by Lösel (1975). Various studies have shown that the scale has sound psychometric quality and criterion validity (e.g. Bender & Lösel, 2011; Lösel & Bliesener, 2003; Lösel, Stemmler, & Bender, 2013). The scale contains 27 items that cover a broad range of delinquent behaviour and non-criminal violations ('status offences'). As in other self-reports on juvenile delinquency, items on extremely serious offences (e.g. murder, rape) are not included because they are unlikely and not accepted by schools and parents. The item format of the scale asks at first whether the youngster has carried out the respective offence and then how often he did it in the last year. To reduce skewness, the item frequencies are coded into the following categories: never$=0$, once$=1$, 2–5 times$=2$, 6–10 times$=3$ and more than 10 times$=4$. In addition to the *Total Delinquency* score there are subscales on *Property Offences* (12 items, e.g. shoplifting, theft from schoolmates, vehicle theft), *Aggressive/Violent Offences* (seven items, e.g. robbery, assault, weapon use) and *Status Offences* (non-criminal norm violations; five items, e.g. truancy, substance misuse, staying out overnight without parental permission).

Results

Figure 2.1 contains a visualization of the main findings, i.e. the average mean scores in the various delinquency scales at the three times of assessment. The means and standard deviations of the Total Delinquency scale were: $M=15.02$ $(SD=11.33)$ in 1973, $M=17.78$ $(SD=15.31)$ in 1995 and $M=6.31$ $(SD=7.50)$ in 2011. An ANOVA showed that the mean differences between the three assessments were highly significant: $F(2,279)=15.68, p<0.001$. The respective statistics for the subscale on Property Offences were $M=6.73$ $(SD=5.39)$ in 1973, $M=8.18$ $(SD=7.34)$ in 1995 and $M=3.34$ $(SD=3.42)$ in 2011. The test of the differences was again clearly significant; $F(2, 288)=13.35, p<0.001$. The mean scores for Aggressive/Violent Offences were $M=3.68$ $(SD=3.80)$ in 1973,

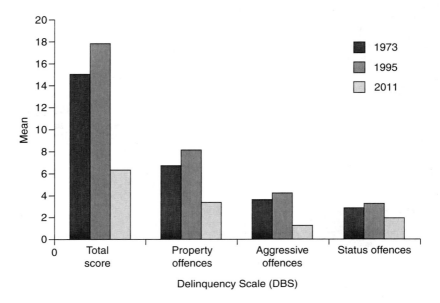

Figure 2.1 Mean scores in self-reported delinquency at different survey times.

$M=4.23$ ($SD=4.51$) in 1995 and $M=1.26$ ($SD=1.78$) in 2011, and the differences were highly significant; F (2, 315)=16.31, $p<0.001$. The scale on Status Offences (non-criminal norm violations) showed the following mean scores: $M=2.85$ ($SD=3.04$) in 1973, $M=3.22$ ($SD=3.48$) in 1995 and $M=1.96$ ($SD=3.14$) in 2011; F (2, 315)=3.55, $p<0.05$.

Overall, Figure 2.1 shows somewhat more self-reported delinquency in 1995 than in 1973. In contrast, there was a substantial decrease in the 2011 assessment. The pattern over time is similar for the three subscales and the total score.

For a more differentiated description of the data we compared the prevalence rates for individual items (see Table 2.2).

Overall, the item prevalence rates confirm the patterns of Figure 2.1. With the exception of one item, the percentages were lowest in the 2011 assessment. For many items the decrease in comparison to 1995 is substantial. Most differences across the three measurements were statistically significant. The items with no significant change over time are some property offences (fare dodging, theft from a classmate) and non-criminal norm violations/status offences such as truancy or staying out overnight without permission of the parents. However, there were also more serious offences that showed no significant change, i.e. fire setting or threat of others with a weapon. In these cases one has to take into account that the p values were between 0.05 and 0.10 and that the items had rather low base rates which reduced the possibility of a significant change ('floor effect').

As our analysis has only descriptive purposes we did not apply a Bonferroni correction for multiple significance testing. To avoid a further inflation of

Self-reported delinquency in Germany   31

Table 2.2 Percentages of boys who reported various forms of delinquent behaviour in the three surveys

Type of behaviour[a]	1973	1995	2011	Difference, χ^2
Fare dodging	73	85	78	3.55 *ns*
Cheating at a vending machine	60	55	12	60.12***
Shoplifting; theft in a department store/shop	55	53	7	64.24***
Theft from a classmate	15	14	7	3.54 *ns*
Robbery; violence to get goods from someone	22	15	6	11.25**
Bicycle theft	29	32	9	16.52***
Motor vehicle theft; car, motor bike, moped	9	20	1	16.99**
Breaking and entering	28	32	4	25.72***
Handling stolen goods	26	55	4	50.69***
Damage of property	27	42	5	32.72***
Arson, fire setting	14	14	5	5.51 *ns*
Driving without licence	50	58	19	31.59***
Assault, brawl with wounding somebody	50	59	12	48.35***
Possession of illegal weapons	24	32	15	6.29*
Harassment of others in public	32	42	7	30.02***
Use of illegal drugs	10	15	8	2.15 *ns*
Truancy, at least one day	40	49	30	6.17*
Stayed out overnight without parental permission	16	29	18	4.88 *ns*
Threatening of others with a weapon	5	11	3	4.49 *ns*
Heavy drunkenness	67	57	33	29.41***

Note

a The prevalence rates refer to at least one act during the last 12 months before the assessment. The items contained concrete descriptions of the behaviour, but were shortened in the table.
* $p<0.05$;
** $p<0.01$;
*** $p<0.001$;
ns = non-significant.

multiple tests we did not carry out tests for the contrasts between two measurement points. A closer inspection of the results in Table 2.2 shows both similarity and some deviance from the findings in Figure 2.1, particularly for the comparison between 1973 and 1995. Although two thirds of the items showed a higher prevalence in 1995, some of these differences were rather small. For other offences the rates were even lower in 1995 than in 1973, e.g. for robbery or cheating at a vending machine. However, these differences were also small, so that the analysis of single items is mainly in accordance with the general trend of an increase of self-reported delinquency between 1973 and 1995 and a decrease in the 2011 data. The latter change is clearly stronger than the first one. This is particularly the case for motor vehicle theft, shoplifting, assault, breaking and entering, property damage and driving without licence. With some exceptions the most substantial decrease took place in more serious and violent offences.

The latter finding leads to the question whether not only the prevalence of more serious delinquency had decreased in the 2011 survey, but also the number of boys who were particularly 'active' in such offences. Therefore, we selected some criminal acts and compared the proportions of boys who admitted more

32   *F. Lösel* et al.

than five of the respective offences in the last year. The results are shown in Table 2.3.

A majority of the differences in prevalence rates (Table 2.2) were not significant in Table 2.3 on frequent offending. This was the case for theft from a classmate, motor vehicle theft, robbery, assault, driving without licence, arson, use of illegal drugs and threatening others with a weapon. Of course this is partially due to the much lower frequencies (particularly in 2011), that led to a 'floor effect'. However, various items also showed that the frequent offending in 2011 happened similarly or even slightly more often than in 1973 and 1995. This was the case for theft from a classmate, robbery, use of illegal drugs and threatening others with a weapon. Perhaps, this pattern may be due to a few intensive offenders, however, in other items the proportion of frequent offenders dropped substantially (e.g. in shoplifting, motor vehicle theft, assault and handling stolen goods). Therefore, a cautious view on Table 2.2 only suggests that the crime drop in 2011 was less obvious and consistent when we analysed the frequent execution of criminal acts.

Discussion

Main findings

The present study contains a very rare data set on longitudinal comparisons of self-reported juvenile delinquency at three surveys over a period of 38 years.

Table 2.3 Percentages of boys who reported at least six offences that indicate relatively serious delinquency when carried out frequently

Type of behaviour[a]	1973	1995	2011	Difference $\chi^{2\,b}$
Shoplifting; theft in a department store/shop	9	20	1	14.74***
Theft from a classmate	1	0	4	2.12 *ns*
Robbery; violence to get goods from someone	5	2	3	0.80 *ns*
Bicycle theft	3	11	1	6.08*
Motor vehicle theft; car, motor bike, moped	3	5	0	2.11 *ns*
Breaking and entering	4	11	0	8.99*
Handling stolen goods	3	16	0	18.61***
Arson, fire setting	2	0	0	0.90 *ns*
Driving without licence	10	17	6	4.82 *ns*
Assault, brawl with wounding somebody	8	8	2	2.97 *ns*
Use of illegal drugs	4	8	7	2.02 *ns*
Threatening of others with a weapon	0	0	1	0.57 *ns*

Notes

a The percentages refer to committed offences during the last year before the assessment. The items contained concrete descriptions of the behaviour, but were shortened in the table.

b In cases of expected cell frequencies of less than $n=5$ we applied a Yates correction for the calculation.

* $p<0.05$;

** $p<0.01$;

*** $p<0.001$;

ns = non-significant.

Self-reported delinquency in Germany 33

Insofar, the study provides valuable information from a country that does not carry out regular victim surveys as a necessary supplement to the police crime statistics with its well-known distortions. It is also a strength that the assessments were carried out with the same self-report instrument, in the same city, at a similar age of the students, and mostly in the same schools from lower class neighbourhoods.

The main findings of our study are the following: Overall delinquency as well as the subscales on property, aggressive and status offences show a moderate *increase* between 1973 and 1995. In contrast, the data for 2011 reveal a *decrease* in all scales that was much greater than the previous increase. Although our study investigated only self-reported delinquency in relatively small samples, the drops from 1995 to 2011 in the scale means are in a similar range (e.g. 60%) as Truman and Langton (2015) reported for the 1993 vs 2014 comparisons of the large US victim survey that included very serious offences (see introduction). The decrease is also apparent in most of our single delinquency items. The difference in prevalence rates between 1995 and 2011 is rather strong for a majority of property and aggressive offences such as shoplifting, cheating at a vending machine, handling stolen goods, breaking and entering, motor vehicle theft, bicycle theft, property damage, assault and robbery. Some less serious forms of norm breaking or status offences show no significant or smaller differences, e.g. fare dodging, truancy and staying out overnight without parental permission. There were also mainly non-significant differences across time when we analysed the rates of frequent criminal acts, i.e. more than five respective offences during the last 12 months. Here only handling stolen goods, shoplifting and bicycle theft show significant differences over time. These findings may indicate that the crime drop phenomenon is more visible in occasional offending, but less relevant for a very small group of frequent offenders. However, one must also take into account that the overall low rates of frequent offending may have led to a 'floor effect' that made the detection of a significant change difficult.

Overall our findings clearly confirm a recent decrease in self-reported juvenile delinquency that is in accordance with the broader discussion of the crime drop. However, our findings from a German city diverge from the international literature insofar as we did not observe a decrease in 1995, but later. Our findings also suggest that the general discussion of a crime drop may be too broad and requires more attention to the development of specific types of delinquency (see also Aebi & Linde, 2010; Farrell et al., 2010).

Limitations

To avoid too far-reaching conclusions from our results it is necessary to emphasize some limitations. First, the sample sizes were not large and with their focus on lower-ranking state secondary schools neither representative for Nuremberg nor Germany. Second, although there were similar social and economic characteristics in the neighbourhoods of the selected schools, there may have been changes over the long time period covered in this study. Although

34   *F. Lösel* et al.

neighbourhood changes in Germany are less frequent and dynamic than in the United States, there is an increase in the proportion of students from families with a migration background (i.e. families from Turkey, Russia and the Balkans). As German surveys on self-reported juvenile delinquency show, these migrant groups exhibit somewhat more juvenile delinquency and violence than genuinely German youngsters (e.g. Baier, Pfeiffer, Simonson, & Rabold, 2009; Wallner & Stemmler, 2014). Insofar, a strong impact of this factor would have reduced the crime drop in our sample. A third limitation is the lower participation rate in 2011 as compared to the two previous surveys. As mentioned in the method section, this may have been due to various reasons. It is also not specific for our study because other recent German surveys on self-reported juvenile delinquency (e.g. Boers & Reinecke, 2007; Reinecke et al., 2013) reported lower participation rates than we had in our nearly complete recruitments in 1973 and 1995. If this selection bias had an influence on our 2011 data, it may have worked against the crime drop. This can be assumed because our field workers reported that in comparison to other students fewer boys from low SES migrant families provided the obligatory written consent of their parents. A fourth limitation is the slightly older mean age of the 2011 sample (15.52 vs 14.63 and 14.30 in the previous cohorts). This issue would again reduce a crime drop effect because both official crime statistics and many self-report studies show that delinquency is increasing during adolescence.

For all these reasons the observed crime drop between 1995 and 2011 cannot only be attributed to the above-mentioned methodological limitations. However, as in every self-report on norm-related behaviour, we cannot exclude the possibility of a partial impact of social desirability. An increased sensitivity to crime and violence issues in the mass media and public discussion may have led to less open and more social desirable answers by the boys.

Comparison with other German data

With this caution in mind, our results are supported by rather low prevalence rates in other recent German surveys on juvenile delinquency that had larger samples. For example, Boers and Reinecke (2007) carried out a study of 9th grade students in North-West Germany and reported, for example, rates of 3% for vehicle theft, 6% for robbery, 10% for bicycle theft, 8% for handling, 12% for assault, 13% for damage of property and 20% for shoplifting. Similar to our 2011 prevalence rates, these data are substantially lower than what we found in 1973 and 1995. A survey of 9th grade students in Munich, the Bavarian capital, also revealed much lower prevalence rates than we found nearly 20 or 40 years ago: Baier et al. (2006) reported 2% for threat with a weapon, 4% for motor vehicle theft, 5% for breaking and entering, 13% for property damage, 16% for assault and 20% for driving without licence. As in our study, very minor or status offences had much higher prevalence rates; e.g. fare dodging 84% and truancy 50%.

Another question refers to the concordance between our self-report results and the German crime statistics of the Federal Police Office. In spite of the

Self-reported delinquency in Germany 35

problems of official crime data (see the introduction), it is necessary to compare our findings with them. In general, the pattern in our self-report study is roughly supported by the police crime statistics. For details of the official statistics see the annual yearbooks of the German Federal Police Office (Bundeskriminalamt, BKA) and two security reports of the German Government (BMI & BMJ, 2001, 2009). The absolute numbers for German *male* juvenile suspects were 118,895 in 1973, 195,260 in 1995 and 149,092 in 2011. Although the country's unification in 1990 led to a population increase of *c.*25%, this does not sufficiently explain the juvenile crime rise of *c.*64% between 1973 (in the former German Federal Republic) and 1995 (unified Germany). Migrant populations, the proportion of young people and international mobility after the fall of the iron curtain played a role. Such issues are also involved in the decrease of *c.*24% from 1995 to 2011. More meaningful are figures per 100,000 of the population in the respective age and gender group. Such population-relativized rates for German male juvenile suspects are not available for 1973, but the rate was 8,362 in 1993 and 8,114 in 2011. This difference is clearly smaller than what we observed in our self-report data, however, it does not contradict a recent crime drop in principle. One must be aware that the official data are limited to German suspects because there are no reliable population data for foreign nationalities to compare with. Contrary to the international discussion of the crime drop in the 1990s the population-relativized crime rates for juvenile suspects in Germany increased from 1993 (when the first valid data for unified Germany were available) to the late 1990s and up to 2001. In these later years the rates per 100,000 for male German juvenile suspects were around 10,000. After 2001 they decreased more or less continuously (in 2014: 6,698) and even became lower than those for young adults (Lösel, 2012b).

The more specific regional data for Bavaria show a similar decrease in the rate for male juvenile suspects from 10,193 in 2001 to 7,559 in 2011 and 7,167 in 2014 (Bayerisches Landeskriminalamt, 2015). For Nuremberg we do not have such differentiated data, but the recent security report of the city shows a decrease in absolute numbers of juvenile suspects from 2,241 in 2010 to 1,666 in 2014 (Stadt Nürnberg, 2015). This substantial change in four years cannot simply be explained by a smaller proportion of young people.

Taking all these official data into account we can state the following. First, our observed decrease in self-reported juvenile delinquency is basically concordant with the development in official crime figures. Second, the assessment at 1995 took place at a time when official juvenile crime was still on the rise. Third, the differences between 1995 and 2011 in our self-reported data are larger than those in official crime figures for male German juveniles. Fourth, the comparison with the German official data should be interpreted with caution because regional, age and migration factors are not controlled.

36   *F. Lösel* et al.

Application of international hypotheses on the crime drop

As other recent German self-reports and official crime figures suggest that our long-term findings are not an artefact, the question of an explanation of the crime drop in our data remains. Therefore we briefly evaluate the plausibility of potential hypotheses. For this we first refer to the international hypotheses that Farrell (2013) has reviewed (see Table 2.1).

Several mainly US-focused hypotheses are obviously irrelevant for our data on self-reported delinquency of German school boys at age 14–15; i.e. numbers 2, 3, 4, 5 and 11. Hypothesis no. 1 on the country's economic condition is partly related to no. 10 (consumer confidence) and has some, but not much plausibility. The economic situation (e.g. the increase of the GDP) was rather good in the mid-1990s, later it deteriorated and in the first years of the twenty-first century Germany was the 'ill man' in Europe before it recovered in the last decade. The better economic situation in 2011 may have led to financial resources in most families and, as a consequence, less family stress and perhaps less need for property offending of the youngsters. However, this would not explain the high prevalence of fare dodging and, in particular, why the delinquency rates in 1995 were larger than in 1973, although the German economic condition was similar at both times.

Hypothesis no. 7 (more police) is not plausible because the number of police officers in Bavaria increased only slightly after 1995 and then slightly decreased from 2006 to 2011. More relevant is the hypothesis on the impact of more preventive policing strategies (no. 6). Partly due to the increase in (juvenile) crime during the 1990s Germany established numerous 'prevention councils' on the state and community level. These aim for a close cooperation between the police, local authorities, schools, social services and other relevant institutions. Whereas previously schools wanted to keep police out, they became more open to police prevention and investigation of serious violence at schools. Within this context, the Bavarian Police introduced in the late 1990s a special programme to prevent truancy and related delinquency. Police officers searched in the city centre, department stores and other popular places at times when youngsters should have been at school. In cooperation with the schools the students were brought back to the school and the parents were informed. The programme was piloted at Nuremberg in a cooperation network of the local police, schools and social services. Unfortunately, there was no control group evaluation, but truancy rates decreased and the rate became clearly lower than in other cities. Our above data show a significant decrease of truancy rates from 1995 to 2011 (see Table 2.2) and the absence of more than one day was only half of what had been reported in 1995. Although we do not have experimental evidence on the effects of such programmes, one should bear in mind that a reduction of truancy may have side effects on property and violent offences because the youngsters have less time to hang around.

The hypothesis on effects of the legalization of abortion (no. 8) does not seem to be relevant for our results. A more liberal German regulation on abortion

Self-reported delinquency in Germany 37

(with mandatory counselling) was introduced in 1995. This may have led to a lower birth rate of children from high risk families/mothers and thus fewer high-risk boys in 2011. However, the sample sizes in our study are too small to assume that such a rare factor may have played a role for the substantial crime drop in 2011.

The hypothesis on reduced crime due to immigration (no. 9) is not relevant for our study. In contrast to the United States and other countries with a selective immigration policy Germany even has a somewhat higher crime rate of various groups of immigrants. As mentioned above, this may have played a role for the increase of the delinquency in our study from 1973 to 1995, but would be counter-acting the observed decrease in 2011.

The hypothesis on less lead poisoning in childhood (no. 12) got much attention in the Anglo-American mass media. Exposure to lead during pregnancy can reduce the head circumference (and brain development) of infants and lead exposure in childhood correlates with lower IQ, violence and other behavioural problems (e.g. Nevin, 2000; WHO, 2010). Although there is no doubt about the negative influence of very high lead exposure on human health, the impact of this factor on our data is questionable. For example, the correlation between head circumference in infancy and later behaviour problems is very small (Koglin & Lösel, 2014). Parallel curves between the amount of violent crime and gasoline lead tonnes intake 23 years before (Nevin, 2000) look impressive, but they are no causal proof. Lead free petrol was introduced in Germany in 1983 and therefore one could have expected already a crime drop in our 1995 cohort (that did not happen). There is some promise of a broader hypothesis on a nutrition impact (Gesch, 2005), i.e. with regard to omega-3 fatty acids (Raine et al., 2015). However, we do not assume that nutrition had a major impact on the 2011 drop in our study because nutrition awareness in Germany's families is rather heterogeneous: there are many families which have become increasingly aware of a healthy nutrition and lifestyle, but there is another large group that prefers junk food and has high rates of obesity.

Changing demographics (no. 13) is a reasonable explanation of a crime drop because ageing societies like Germany have a lower proportion of particularly crime prone young people. For our results this hypothesis is not relevant because we did not analyse population data, but cohorts of juveniles. The hypothesis on the civilization process (no. 14) is also not relevant for our findings because the time of the young generation's protest was long over when we investigated the crime drop.

The last hypothesis of Farrell (2013) refers to improved security measures (no. 15). This is a plausible assumption with regard to the decrease we observed in various offences. For example, cheating at vending machines became more difficult in 2011 than before because electronic technologies improved. Theft from department stores and other larger shops were better prevented by electronic good labelling, metal detectors, video surveillance and so forth. The decline in property damage and breaking and entering may partly be due to more private security measures and solid materials in public areas to prevent

38   *F. Lösel* et al.

vandalism. As mentioned in the introduction, the decrease in motor vehicle theft can be attributed to electronic security measures and police prevention programmes.

Additional psychological hypotheses

Although the above interpretations are mainly based on plausibility, our data seem to be in line with some of the international hypotheses. However, most of the international explanations were not plausible or even irrelevant for our data. Therefore, we also suggest a few more psychological explanations. For example, since the late 1990s there have been numerous preventive activities in German kindergartens and schools. Such programmes undertake concrete steps to improve social skills, reduce school bullying and contribute to a more civilized interaction among youngsters. A substantial number of programmes have shown significant effects in well controlled studies (e.g. Farrington & Ttofi, 2008; Farrington, Ttofi, & Lösel, 2016; Farrington & Welsh, 2007; Lösel & Bender, 2012) and their widespread dissemination may have contributed to reductions in juvenile delinquency.

Related issues that are rarely addressed in the discussion of the crime drop are family interaction and parenting. Similar to school-based prevention programmes there are now many international evaluations of family-oriented approaches to improve child rearing and parenting (Farrington et al., 2016; Farrington & Welsh, 2007). In a nationwide and representative survey of family-oriented prevention programmes Lösel, Schmucker, Plankensteiner, and Weiss (2006) found that more than 200,000 programmes have been offered per annum and reached *c.* two million families. Although the vast majority of these approaches are not well evaluated, a recent meta-analysis showed that evaluated German programmes have a significant effect on both parenting and child behaviour (Weiss, Schmucker, & Lösel, 2015). Together with school and community based programmes these interventions may have contributed to the drop in juvenile delinquency between 1995 and 2011.

One should also be aware of changes that have an indirect impact on juvenile delinquency. For example, our study confirms a decrease in the prevalence of heavy drunkenness. This is in accordance with national data on decreasing alcohol consumption in the young generation (e.g. Lambert, Kuntz, & KiGGS Study Group, 2014). Since alcohol is particularly related to violence, reduced alcohol consumption may have had an impact on the drop of violent offences in our study.

An increased sensitivity to alcohol misuse, violence in the family and other contexts seem to be part of a broader culture of 'civilization' and 'correctness' that developed in Germany as in other countries. Although already the Anti-Violence Commission of the German Government recommended a legal ban of corporal punishment of children (Schwind et al., 1990), it took a long time until a respective civil law regulation went into effect. There are some data that indicate a signal effect with regard to this issue (Bussmann, 2004). Beyond legal

Self-reported delinquency in Germany 39

regulations, there is a long-term decrease of physical punishment by German parents (Schneewind & Ruppert, 1995). Although the impact of occasional slapping in otherwise intact parent-child relations is discussed controversially (e.g. Gershoff, 2010; Larzelere & Baumrind, 2010; Straus, 2010), there is no doubt that severe physical and psychological abuse has a negative impact on child development (Bender & Lösel, 2015). Therefore, more positive parenting and less aggression in child rearing may be another promising path of explaining the juvenile crime drop we observed.

One should also take group dynamics into account. When there are many aggressive youngsters in a school class there are more opportunities for model learning and mutual reinforcement of antisocial behaviour (Kellam, Ling, Mersica, Brown, & Jalongo, 1998). In contrast, more prosocial classmates can function as a protective factor against the onset or aggravation of delinquency (Lösel & Farrington, 2012). Insofar one may assume group dynamics that – like self-fulfilling prophecies – promote non-deviant behaviour when delinquency in a school is dropping. As a consequence of this hypothesis we emphasize the very low number of frequent offending in 2011 (see Table 2.3). However, since there were only few significant differences to the respective rates in 1995 one should also be aware that there is still a small number of particularly delinquent youngsters who have not yet been sufficiently reached by preventive measures.

In conclusion, we need to emphasize the rather speculative character of our 'explanations' of the crime drop. However, this is similar to what is often seen in the literature on this topic. As mentioned in the introduction we do not assume that one or the other single factor is a sufficient explanation, but according to multi-level concepts of prevention (e.g. Lösel, 2004b) they may have a substantial combined effect. Researchers in the field of criminology and law are encouraged to address the highly interesting macro-social issue of a crime drop with stronger methods and data that we could use in the present study. There will also be new challenging questions, for example, how the crime drop will be influenced by the actual mass immigration of mostly young men to Europe. Scholars of psychology and law should not only address such issues in post-hoc analyses (as they are prevailing in the crime drop research), but contribute to the development and sound evaluation of prevention programmes.

References

Aebi, M. F., & Linde, A. (2010). Is there a crime drop in Western Europe? *European Journal on Criminal Policy and Research, 16,* 251–277.

Aebi, M. F., & Linde, A. (2012a). Crime trends in Western Europe according to official statistics from 1990 to 2007. In J. .J. M. van Dijk, A. Tseloni & G. Farrell (eds), *The international crime drop: New directions in research* (pp. 37–75). Basingstoke, UK: Palgrave Macmillan.

Aebi, M.F., & Linde, A. (2012b). Conviction statistics as an indicator of crime trends in Europe from 1990 to 2006. *European Journal on Criminal Policy and Research, 18,* 103–144.

40   *F. Lösel* et al.

Baier, D., Pfeiffer, C., Simonson, J., & Rabold, S. (2009). *Jugendliche in Deutschland als Opfer und Täter von Gewalt* [Juveniles in Germany as victims and perpetrators of violence]. Hannover: Kriminologisches Forschungsinstitut Niedersachsen.

Baier, D., Pfeiffer, C., Windzio, M., & Rabold, S. (2006). *Schülerbefragung 2005: Gewalterfahrungen, Schulabsentismus und Medienkonsum von Kindern und Jugendlichen* [School students survey 2005: Experiences of violence, truancy and media consumption of children and youths]. Hannover: Kriminologisches Forschungsinstitut Niedersachsen.

Bayerisches Landeskriminalamt (ed.). (2015). *Junge Menschen als Tatverdächtige und Opfer von Straftaten* [Young people as suspects and victims of crimes]. München: Bayerisches Landeskriminalamt.

Bender, D., & Lösel, F. (2011). Bullying at school as predictor of delinquency, violence and other antisocial behaviour in adulthood. *Criminal Behaviour and Mental Health, 22*, 99–106.

Bender, D., & Lösel, F. (2015). Risikofaktoren, Schutzfaktoren und Resilienz bei Misshandlung und Vernachlässigung [Risk factors, protective factors, and resilience in child abuse and neglect]. In U. T. Egle, P. Joraschky, A. Lampe, I. Seiffge-Krenke & M. Cierpka (eds), *Sexueller Missbrauch, Misshandlung, Vernachlässigung* (4th ed., pp. 77–103). Stuttgart: Schattauer.

Blumstein, A., & Beck, A. J. (1999). Population growth in U.S. prisons 1980–1996. In M. Tonry & J. Petersilia (eds), *Crime and justice* (Vol. 26, pp. 17–61). Chicago, IL: University of Chicago Press.

Blumstein, A., & Rosenfeld, R. (2008). Factors contributing to U.S. crime trends. In R. Rosenfeld & A. Goldberger (eds), *Understanding crime trends workshop report* (pp. 13–43). Washington, DC: The National Academies Press.

Blumstein, A., & Wallman, J. (eds). (2006). *The crime drop in America* (2nd ed.). New York: Cambridge University Press.

BMI, & BMJ (eds). (2001). *Erster Periodischer Sicherheitsbericht* [First periodic security report]. Berlin: Bundesministerium des Innern & Bundesministerium der Justiz.

BMI, & BMJ (eds). (2009). *Zweiter Periodischer Sicherheitsbericht* [Second periodic security report]. Berlin: Bundesministerium des Innern & Bundesministerium der Justiz.

Boers, K., & Reinecke, J. (eds). (2007). *Delinquenz im Jugendalter: Erkenntnisse einer Münsteraner Längsschnittstudie.* [Juvenile Delinquency: Findings of a longitudinal study from Münster]. Münster: Waxmann.

Bundeskriminalamt (ed.). (2015). *Polizeiliche Kriminalstatistik 2014* [Police crime statistics 2014]. Wiesbaden: BKA. [The annual statistics for previous years are not cited here.]

Bussmann, K. D. (2004). Evaluating the subtle impact of a ban on corporal punishment of children in Germany. *Child Abuse Review, 13*, 292–311.

Eisner, M. (2003). Long-term historical trends in violent crime. In M. Tonry (ed.), *Crime and justice: A review of research* (vol. 30, pp. 83–142). Chicago, IL: University of Chicago Press.

Farrell. G. (2013). Five tests of a theory of the crime drop. *Crime Science, 2*(5), 1–8.

Farrell, G., Tilley, N., Tseloni, A., & Mailley, J. (2010). Explaining and sustaining the crime drop: Clarifying the role of opportunity-related theories. *Crime Prevention and Community Safety, 12*, 24–41.

Farrington, D. P. (1996). Individual, family and peer factors in the development of delinquency. In C. R. Hollin & K. Howells (eds), *Clinical approaches to working with young offenders* (pp. 21–56). Chichester, UK: Wiley.

Self-reported delinquency in Germany 41

Farrington, D. P. (1997). Early prediction of violent and non-violent youthful offending. *European Journal of Criminal Policy and Research, 5*(2), 51–66.

Farrington, D. P. (ed.). (2005). *Integrated developmental and life-course theories of offending.* New Brunswick, NJ: Transaction.

Farrington, D. P., & Ttofi, M. M. (2008). School-based programs to reduce bullying and victimization. *Campbell Collaboration Reviews 2009*, 6.

Farrington, D. P., Ttofi, M. M., & Lösel, F. A. (2016). Developmental and social prevention. In D. Weisburd, D. P. Farrington, & C. Gill (eds), *What works in crime prevention and rehabilitation: Lessons from systematic reviews.* New York: Springer, in press.

Farrington, D. P., & Welsh, B. C. (2007). *Saving children from a life of crime: Early risk factors and effective interventions.* New York: Oxford University Press.

Gershoff, E. T. (2010). More harm than good: A summary of scientific research on the intended and unintended effects of corporal punishment. *Law and Contemporary Problems, 73*, 31–56.

Gesch, B. (2005). The potential of nutrition to promote physical and behavioural well-being. In F. A. Huppert, N. Baylis, & B. Keverne (eds), *The science of well-being* (pp. 171–214). Oxford, UK: Oxford University Press.

Hofer, H. von, & Lappi-Seppälä, T. (2014). The development of crime in light of Finnish and Swedish criminal justice statistics, circa 1750–2010. *European Journal of Criminology, 11*, 169–194.

Ignatans, D., & Pease, K. (2015). Distributive justice and the crime drop. In M. A. Andresen & G. Farrell (eds), *The criminal act: The role and influence of routine activity theory* (pp. 77–87). London: Palgrave Macmillan.

Kellam, S. G., Ling, X., Mersica, R., Brown, C. H., & Jalongo, N. (1998). The effect of the level of aggression in the first grade classroom on the course of malleability of aggressive behavior into middle school. *Development and Psychopathology, 10*, 165–185.

Killias, M., & Lafranconi, B. (2012). The crime drop discourse – or the illusion of uniform continental trends: Switzerland as a contrasting case. In In J. J. M. van Dijk, A. Tseloni & G. Farrell (eds), *The international crime drop: New directions in research* (pp. 268–278). Basingstoke, UK: Palgrave Macmillan.

Knepper, P. (2012). An international crime decline: Lessons for social welfare crime policy? *Social Policy and Administration, 46*, 359–376.

Knepper, P. (2015). Falling crime rates: What happened last time. *Theoretical Criminology, 19*, 59–76.

Koglin, U., & Lösel, F. (2014). Pregnancy and birth complications and externalizing behavioral problems in preschoolers. *Monatsschrift für Kriminologie und Strafrechtsreform/Journal of Criminology and Penal Reform, 97*, 451–461.

Lampert, T., Kuntz, B., & KiGGS Study Group (2014). Tabak- und Alkoholkonsum bei 11- bis 17-jährigen Jugendlichen [Tobacco and alcohol consumption among juveniles at age 11 to 17 years]. *Bundesgesundheitsblatt, 57*, 830–839.

Larzelere, R. E., & Baumrind, D. (2010). Are spanking injunctions scientifically supported? *Law and Contemporary Problems, 73*, 57–87.

Levitt, S. D. (2004). Understanding why crime fell in the 1990s: Four factors that explain the decline and six that do not. *The Journal of Economic Perspectives, 18*, 163–190.

Lösel, F. (1975). *Handlungskontrolle und Jugenddelinquenz: Persönlichkeitspsychologische Erklärungsansätze delinquenten Verhaltens: Theoretische Integration und empirische Prüfung* [Self-control and juvenile delinquency: Integration of personality theories on delinquency and an empirical test]. Stuttgart: Enke Verlag.

42   F. Lösel et al.

Lösel, F. (2004a). Entwicklungsbezogene und technische Kriminalprävention: Konzeptuelle Grundlagen und Ergebnisse [Developmental and technical crime prevention: Basic concepts and results]. In H. Schöch & J.-M. Jehle (eds), *Angewandte Kriminologie zwischen Freiheit und Sicherheit* (pp. 175–203). Mönchengladbach: Forum Verlag Godesberg.

Lösel, F. (2004b). Multimodale Gewaltprävention bei Kindern und Jugendlichen: Familie, Kindergarten und Schule [Multimodal prevention of violence: Family, preschool and school]. In W. Melzer & H.-D. Schwind (eds), *Gewaltprävention in der Schule* (pp. 326–348). Baden-Baden: Nomos.

Lösel, F. (2012a). Offender treatment and rehabilitation: What works? In M. Maguire, R. Morgan, & R. Reiner (eds), *The Oxford handbook of criminology* (5th ed., pp. 986–1016). Oxford, UK: Oxford University Press.

Lösel, F. (2012b). What works in correctional treatment and rehabilitation for young adults? In F. Lösel, A. E. Bottoms, & D. P. Farrington (eds), *Young adult offenders: Lost in transition?* (pp. 74–112). Milton Park, UK: Routledge.

Lösel, F., & Bender, D. (2012). Child social skills training in the prevention of antisocial development and crime. In D. P. Farrington & B. C. Welsh (eds), *Handbook of crime prevention* (pp. 102–129). Oxford, UK: Oxford University Press.

Lösel, F., & Bliesener, T. (2003). *Aggression und Delinquenz unter Jugendlichen: Untersuchungen von kognitiven und sozialen Bedingungen* [Aggression and delinquency in adolescence: Studies on cognitive and social origins]. Neuwied: Luchterhand.

Lösel, F., Bliesener, T., & Averbeck, M. (1998). Hat die Delinquenz von Schülern zugenommen? Ein Vergleich im Dunkelfeld nach 22 Jahren [Has delinquency at schools increased? A comparison of self-reports after 22 years]. *DVJJ Journal, 9*, 115–128.

Lösel, F., & Farrington, D. P. (2012). Direct protective and buffering protective factors in the development of youth violence. *American Journal of Preventive Medicine, 43*(2S1), 8–23.

Lösel, F., Schmucker, M., Plankensteiner, B., & Weiss, M. (2006). *Bestandsaufnahme und Evaluation der Elternbildung* [Survey and evaluation of parent education in Germany]. Berlin: Bundesministerium für Familie, Senioren, Frauen und Jugend.

Lösel, F., Stemmler, M., & Bender, D. (2013). Long-term evaluation of a bimodal universal prevention program: Effects from kindergarten to adolescence. *Journal of Experimental Criminology, 9*, 429–449.

Lösel, F., & Wüstendörfer, W. (1976). Persönlichkeitskorrelate delinquenten Verhaltens oder offizieller Delinquenz? [Personality correlates of delinquent behavior or of official delinquency?]. *Zeitschrift für Sozialpsychologie, 7*, 177–191.

Nevin, R. (2000). How lead exposure relates to temporal changes in IQ, violent crime and unwed pregnancy. *Environmental Research, Section A 89*, 1–22.

Petersilia, J., & Cullen, F. T. (2015). Liberal not stupid: Meeting the promise of downsizing prisons. *Stanford Journal of Criminal Law and Policy, 2*(1), 1–43.

Pinker, S. (2011). *The better angels of our nature: Why violence has declined.* New York: Viking.

Raine, A. (2013). *The anatomy of violence: The biological roots of crime.* New York: Pantheon Books.

Raine, A., Portnoy, J., Liu, J., Mahoomed, T., & Hibbeln, J. (2015). Reduction in behavior problems with omega-3 supplementation in children aged 8–16 years: a randomized, double-blind, placebo-controlled, stratified, parallel-group trial. *Journal of Child Psychology and Psychiatry, 56*, 509–520.

Self-reported delinquency in Germany 43

Reinecke, J., Stemmler, M., Arnis, M., El-Kayed, N., Meinert, J., Pöge, A., Schepers, D., Sünkel, Z., Kucur-Uysal, B., Wallner, S., Weiss, M., & Wittenberg, J. (2013). Entstehung und Entwicklung von Kinder- und Jugenddelinquenz: Erste Ergebnisse einer Längsschnittstudie [Origins and development of juvenile delinquency: First results of a longitudinal study]. *Neue Kriminalpolitik, 25*, 207–228.

Schneewind, A., & Ruppert, S. (1995). *Familien gestern und heute* [Families yesterday and today]. München: Quintessenz.

Schwind, H.-D., Baumann, J., Lösel, F., Remschmidt, Eckert, R., Kerner, H. J. et al. (eds), (1990). *Ursachen, Prävention und Kontrolle von Gewalt: Analysen und Vorschläge der unabhängigen Regierungskommission zur Verhinderung und Bekämpfung von Gewalt* [Origins, prevention and control of violence: Analyses and recommendations of the German Federal Government's Independent Commission for the Prevention and Control of Violence]. Berlin: Duncker & Humblot.

Stadt Nürnberg (ed.) (2015). *Sicherheitsbericht Stadt Nürnberg 2014* [Security report for Nuremberg 2014]. Nürnberg: Stadt Nürnberg.

Straus, M. A. (2010). Criminogenic effects of corporal punishment by parents. In M. Herzog-Evans & I. Dran-Rivette (eds), *Transnational criminology manual* (pp. 373–390). Amsterdam, NL: Wolf Legal Publishing.

Tilley, N., Tseloni, A., & Farrell, G. (2011). Income disparities of burglary risk: Security availability and the crime drop. *British Journal of Criminology, 51*, 296–313.

Tonry, M., & Farrington, D. P. (eds), (2005). Crime and punishment in Western societies 1980–1999. *Crime and justice: A review of research* (vol. 33). Chicago, IL: University of Chicago Press.

Truman, J. L., & Langton, L. (2015). *Criminal victimization, 2014*. Washington, DC: US Department of Justice.

Tseloni, A., Farrell, G., Tilley, N., Grove, L., Thompson, R., & Garius, L. (2012). Towards a comprehensive research agenda on opportunity theory and the crime falls. In J. J. M. van Dijk, A. Tseloni, & G. Farrell (eds), *The international crime drop: New directions in research* (pp. 286–299). Basingstoke, UK: Palgrave Macmillan.

Tseloni, A., Mailley, J., Farrell, G., & Tilley, N. (2010). Exploring the international decline in crime rates. *European Journal of Criminology, 7*, 375–394.

Van Dijk, J. J. M. (2008). *The world of crime*. London: Sage.

Van Dijk, J. J. M., Tseloni, A., & Farrell, G. (eds), (2012). *The international crime drop: New directions in research*. Basingstoke, UK: Palgrave Macmillan.

Wallner, S., & Stemmler, M. (2014). Jugendliche Gewaltdelinquenz, psychosoziale Merkmale und Migrationsstatus [Juvenile violent delinquency, psychosocial characteristics and migration status]. *Forensische Psychiatrie, Psychologie und Kriminologie, 8*, 84–95.

Weiss, M., Schmucker, M., & Lösel, F. (2015). Meta-Analyse zur Wirkung familienbezogener Präventionsmaßnahmen in Deutschland [Meta-analysis on the effects of family-oriented prevention programs in Germany]. *Zeitschrift für Klinische Psychologie und Psychotherapie, 44*, 27–44.

WHO (ed.), (2010). *Childhood lead poisoning*. Geneva, CH: World Health Organization.

Zimring, F. E. (2006). The value and necessity of transnational comparative study: Some preaching from a recent convert. *Criminology and Public Policy, 5*(4), 615–622.

3 What factors protect adolescent bullies from developing into criminal and violent offenders?

Maria M. Ttofi and David P. Farrington

Introduction

Bullying is a common problem throughout the world (e.g. Due et al., 2005; Smith et al., 1999). Existing surveys indicate that children's involvement in bullying, either as bullies, victims or bully-victims, tends to be significantly stable not only from one school term to the next (Boulton & Smith, 1994) but also for longer periods, such as four years (Kumpulainen, Rasanen, & Henttonen, 1999), eight years (Sourander, Helstela, Helenious, & Piha, 2000), and even from elementary school through to the college years (Chapell, Hasselman, Kitchin, & Lomon, 2006). In a longitudinal study of children between ages 12 and 18 in Toronto, Pepler, Jiang, Craig, and Connolly (2008) identified four different bullying trajectories: consistently high, consistently moderate, early moderate and no bullying. The longest follow-up study of bullying was carried out in the Cambridge Study in Delinquent Development (CSDD), which is analysed in this chapter. Farrington (1993) found that bullies at age 14 tended to still be bullies at age 32, and tended to have children who were bullies.

Any suggestion regarding the concurrent undesirable impact of bullying on children's lives seems reasonable even to the lay mind. Establishing, on the other hand, the long-term effects of school bullying, and demonstrating that children who perpetrate bullying are more likely to follow a criminal path (compared with non-involved students), is more challenging. Nevertheless, this research question is very important because of its practical implications. If school bullying is a significant risk factor for later offending, then bullying prevention programmes could be seen as a form of early crime prevention (Ttofi, Farrington, & Lösel, 2012).

A strong association between school bullying and later offending could either reflect the persistence of an underlying aggressive or antisocial tendency or a facilitating effect of school bullying on later offending, or both. In either case, school bullies would be more likely to follow a criminal path later in life compared with non-involved students. Therefore research should aim to examine protective factors that interrupt this continuity based on longitudinal research (Ttofi, Bowes, Farrington, & Lösel, 2014). This topic is investigated in this chapter, based on analyses of the Cambridge Study in Delinquent Development (CSDD).

School bullying and criminal offending later in life

Within the framework of our British Academy funded project on 'Health and Criminal Outcomes of School Bullying', we published a systematic review and meta-analysis of prospective longitudinal studies on the efficacy of school bullying in predicting offending later in life (Ttofi, Farrington, Lösel, & Loeber, 2011). We edited a special issue of *Criminal Behaviour and Mental Health* on this topic that presented results from major longitudinal studies (Farrington, Ttofi, & Lösel, 2011). Studies were included in the meta-analysis based on 'level analyses'. Levels of bullying perpetration were compared with later levels of offending. The results of the meta-analysis suggested that there might be significant long-term detrimental effects of school bullying on later offending. This was even the case when confounded variables that were risk factors for bullying as well as for offending were controlled for.

Since then, we have published a review of bullying as a predictor of later violence (Ttofi et al., 2012), and we have updated our review of bullying as a predictor of offending by adding further studies. A detailed report presenting updated results was published by the Swedish National Council for Crime Prevention (Farrington, Lösel, Ttofi, & Theodorakis, 2012). The studies included in the meta-analysis are described in this governmental report. All 15 longitudinal studies found that bullying predicted later offending. Also, a later analysis of the CSDD showed that bullying at age 14 predicted conviction trajectories up to age 56 (Piquero, Connell, Piquero, Farrington, & Jennings, 2013).

In our meta-analysis, after controlling for covariates, the adjusted summary effect size was OR = 1.89 (95% CI: 1.60–2.23; $z = 7.49$) This OR indicates quite a strong relationship between bullying perpetration and later offending. For example, if a quarter of children were bullies and a quarter were offenders, this value of the OR would correspond to 34.5% of bullies becoming offenders, compared with 21.8% of non-bullies. Thus, being a bully increases the risk of being an offender (even after controlling for other childhood risk factors) by more than half.

School bullying and resilience

Previous research has investigated individual (e.g. Farrington & Baldry, 2010; Woods & Wolke, 2004) and environmental (e.g. Rigby, 1994; Wolke, Woods, Stanford, & Schulz, 2001) risk factors for bullying; results are consistent with a systematic review on this topic that was recently published (Cook, Williams, Guerra, Kim, & Sadek, 2010). This research is very useful as we are now able to 'sketch' a fairly accurate profile of school bullies and victims. However, this focus on deficit-oriented models within the framework of school bullying has some disadvantages. At the practical level, the reduction of specific types of risks from children's lives is quite often impossible. For example, although family socioeconomic status and ethnicity are associated with school bullying (e.g. Kim, Koh, & Leventhal, 2004; Wolke et al., 2001), any suggestion for the

46 *M.M. Ttofi and D.P. Farrington*

'removal' of such risks from children's lives is rather difficult and impractical. At the theoretical level, reducing the polarization between deficit-oriented and strength-oriented models (i.e. the integration of both perspectives) is a more holistic approach and it has the potential to lead to a better understanding of human behaviour problems (Lösel & Bender, 2003).

Within the field of criminology, the question of why individuals do not set out on a deviant pathway, or why they leave it, gradually led to the discussion of promotive and protective factors, which, in turn, resulted in a paradigm shift from a focus on deficits to a focus on strengths (Snyder & Lopez, 2005). Although risk-focused prevention has been very popular, based on the idea that offending can be reduced by targeting and alleviating risk factors (e.g. Farrington, 2000; Farrington & Welsh, 2007), criminological research is now gradually paying more attention to the notion of resilience within new intervention initiatives (Farrington & Ttofi, 2011b). The need for a similar paradigm shift within the framework of bullying prevention has already been suggested (Ttofi & Farrington, 2012).

Risk and protective factors

In this chapter, the following terminology is used: A *Risk Factor* is defined as a variable that predicts a high probability of offending. A *Risk-Based Protective Factor* is defined as a variable that predicts a low probability of offending among a group at risk (in our case: school bullies). An *Interactive Protective Factor* is defined as a variable that interacts with a risk factor to buffer its effects. For example, if poor parental supervision predicts delinquency in low-income families but not in high-income families, then high income may protect against the effects of the risk factor of poor parental supervision.

Farrington and Ttofi (2011b) investigated protective factors in the CSDD. When the risk group was defined as being a troublesome boy at age 8–10, the most important risk-based protective factors that predicted a low prevalence of convictions up to age 50 were low daring, good parental supervision, small family size and high non-verbal intelligence (see later for descriptions of these variables). When the risk group was defined as living in poor housing at age 8–10, the most important risk-based protective factors were good child-rearing, small family size, low dishonesty and low troublesomeness.

Good child-rearing in poor housing was the clearest example of an interactive protective factor. Among boys who lived in poor housing at age 8–10, 33% of those who received good child-rearing at age 8–10 were convicted, compared with 66% of those who received less good child-rearing, which was a significant difference. Among boys who lived in good housing at age 8–10, 32% of those who received good child-rearing were convicted, compared with 30% of those who received less good child-rearing, which was a negligible difference. Therefore, good child-rearing in poor housing reduced the probability of offending to the same value as in good housing, and this was a significant interaction effect. More recently, Farrington, Ttofi, and Piquero (2016) have completed an

Protecting bullies from becoming offenders 47

extensive analysis of risk-based protective factors and interactive protective factors in the CSDD in predicting convictions between ages ten and 18.

Protective factors among bullies

The current study aims to investigate factors that protect adolescent bullies from developing into criminal and violent offenders. In the CSDD, definite and probable bullies were identified based on self-reports at age 14. The following research questions are addressed:

- What risk-based protective factors predict a low probability of convictions among definite bullies?
- What risk-based protective factors predict a low probability of violence convictions among probable and definite bullies?
- Are risk-based protective factors the same or different for criminal and violence convictions?
- What are the main interactive protective factors against criminal and violence convictions?

The first analyses of factors that protect bullies from developing into offenders were published in a special issue of the *Journal of School Violence* that we edited (Ttofi, Farrington, & Lösel, 2014). Five major longitudinal studies addressed this topic. In New Zealand, Fergusson, Boden, and Horwood (2014) measured risk factors at age 7–12, protective factors at age 14–16 and self-reported delinquency at age 16–30. In Australia, Hemphill, Tollit, and Herrenkohl (2014) measured risk and protective factors at age 16–17 and self-reported antisocial behaviour at age 18–19. In Germany, Lösel and Bender (2014) measured risk factors at age nine, protective factors at age 10 and self-reported violence at age 13. In Scotland, McVie (2014) measured risk factors at age 13–16, protective factors at age 15–16 and self-reported violence at age 17. In a second Australian study, Vassallo, Edwards, Renda, and Olsson (2014) measured risk and protective factors at age 13–14 and self-reported delinquency at age 19–20. Ttofi et al. (2014) carried out a systematic review of protective factors that interrupt the continuity from bullying perpetration and victimization to internalizing (e.g. anxiety/depression) and externalizing (e.g. antisocial) problems later in life. They concluded that the most important of these were good school achievement, good social skills, coming from an unbroken family, high attachment to parents and prosocial friends.

In most cases, for a protective factor to be effective, it should be implemented either before or at the same time as the risk factor. For example, if the risk factor is having sexual intercourse and the protective factor is wearing a condom, it would not be effective to put on the condom after the sexual intercourse. Only Hemphill et al. (2014) and Vassallo et al. (2014) measured the protective factor at the same time as the risk factor. None of the five longitudinal studies investigated protective factors that interrupted the continuity from bullying to criminal

48   *M.M. Ttofi and D.P. Farrington*

convictions. In the present chapter, the protective factors were measured at age 8–10, before the risk factor of bullying at age 14, and the outcome variable was conviction between ages 15 and 50. Therefore, this is the first study of protective factors against bullying that measures the protective factors before the bullying and investigates the prevention of later criminal convictions.

Method

The present analyses are based on the Cambridge Study in Delinquent Development (CSDD), which is a prospective longitudinal survey of 411 South London males (see Farrington, Coid, & West, 2009; Farrington et al., 2006; Farrington, Piquero, & Jennings, 2013). These males were first assessed at age eight in 1961–62, and they have been followed up to age 48 in nine repeated face-to-face interviews and up to age 56 in criminal records. Information was also collected in annual interviews with parents conducted by Study social workers when the boys were aged between eight and 14, from peer ratings at ages eight and ten and from teacher ratings at ages eight, ten, 12 and 14. The attrition rate has been very low; at age 48, 93% of the males who were still alive were interviewed (365 out of 394). Criminal record searches showed that 41% of the males were convicted up to age 50 (167 out of 404 searched, excluding seven males who emigrated before age 21 and were not searched in criminal records).

Measures

Self-reported bullying perpetration was measured at age 14 and was divided into four categories: 'definitely no', 'probably no', 'probably yes' and 'definitely yes'. Criminal and violent convictions (from official data) were measured after bullying, between ages 15 and 50 inclusive. Almost one-fifth of the males (71 out of 404, or 17.6%) were convicted for a violent offence (assault, robbery, threatening behaviour or carrying an offensive weapon; see Farrington, 2012; Farrington & Ttofi, 2011a) and two-fifths of males were convicted for a criminal offence (158 out of 404, or 39.1%).

Twenty major childhood factors measured at age 8–10 were included in the analyses investigating protective effects. These variables are described in detail elsewhere (e.g. Farrington & Ttofi, 2011b; Farrington et al., 2006, 2009, 2016). Non-verbal intelligence was measured using Raven's Progressive Matrices test, while verbal intelligence was based on verbal comprehension and vocabulary tests. School attainment was derived from school records of English, arithmetic and verbal reasoning tests. Daring was based on peer and parent ratings of taking many risks in traffic, climbing, exploring and so on. Poor concentration and restlessness in class (hyperactivity) were rated by the boy's teachers, and impulsiveness (psychomotor clumsiness) was measured using the Porteus Maze, Spiral Maze and Tapping tests. Extraversion and neuroticism were measured using the New Junior Maudsley Inventory. Sample items were "I like to tell my friends all about things that happen to me" (true-extraversion) and "It takes a lot to make

Protecting bullies from becoming offenders 49

me lose my temper" (false-neuroticism). Nervousness was based on parent ratings of nervous-withdrawn boys, and popularity was measured using peer ratings.

Family income was derived from information given by parents to social workers. Similarly, the social workers enquired about the number of children in the family (including full biological siblings of the boy) and about the job of the family breadwinner (usually the father). The socioeconomic status (SES) of this job was rated on the Registrar General's scale, ranging from professional and managerial to unskilled manual jobs. Delinquency rates of the schools were obtained from the local education authority. The age of the mother referred to her age at the time of her first birth, which was ascertained by the social workers. The nervousness of the mother was based on social worker ratings and also on records of her psychiatric treatment. Parental interest in the boy's education was rated by the social workers (based on their interviews with the parents).

The rating of child-rearing was based on maternal and paternal discipline, which reflected warm or cold parental attitudes as well as harsh or erratic discipline, and parental harmony, which identified parents who were in conflict. Parental supervision measured whether the parents knew where the boy was when he was out, and parental separation identified boys who had been separated from a parent (usually the father) for at least three months for reasons other than death or hospitalization. All these variables were rated by the Study social workers and based on interviews with the parents (usually the mother).

The 'best' and 'worst' categories are usually obvious. However, for nervousness of the boy, the 'best' category was being nervous-withdrawn, because of prior research suggesting that this variable was negatively related to offending (West & Farrington, 1973, p. 115). In contrast, for neuroticism, the 'worst' category was high neuroticism, because the neuroticism items referred to irritability and getting angry as well as nervousness. Neuroticism measured emotional instability versus stability (calm, even-tempered children). For the age of the mother at the time of her first birth, being a teenager was the 'worst' category. For the job of the mother, having a full-time job was the 'best' category, having a part-time job was the middle category and having no job was the 'worst' category.

In previous analyses focusing on risk factors for offending, these variables were often dichotomized into the 'worst' quarter versus the remainder. In order to investigate protective effects in the present chapter, all age 8–10 variables were divided into the 'best' quarter (the protective end) versus the remainder. The direction of each variable is positive. Therefore, 'hyperactivity' as a protective factor would refer to the quartile that scored the lowest on hyperactivity, and the same was true of other variables such as 'neuroticism' and 'nervous mother'. On the other hand, 'verbal intelligence' as a protective factor refers to the quartile that scored the highest, and the same was true of other variables such as 'school attainment' and 'popularity according to peers'.

Results

In the CSDD, there were 71 definite bullies (17.5% of 406 boys assessed at age 14) and 129 probable bullies (31.8%). This chapter investigates definite bullies as predictors of all convictions. Because of the relatively small number of violence convictions, probable and definite bullies are grouped together in predicting violence. As shown in Table 3.1, definite bullies were significantly more likely to be convicted for criminal offending (OR = 1.7; 95% CI: 1.0–2.8) and probable bullies were significantly more likely to be convicted for violent offending (OR = 1.8; 95% CI: 1.0–3.0) compared with the remainder.

Next, protective effects against violent convictions were investigated (see Table 3.2). The aim was to examine which protective factors predicted a low probability of violence among the bullies. For example, of 36 bullies with low daring (rated by peers and parents), only one was convicted for violence (3%), compared with 42 out of 161 bullies with medium or high daring (26%); OR = 12.4, 95% CI: 1.6–93.0. Daring was a protective factor because the percentage of low-daring bullies who were convicted of violence was much less than the percentage of all bullies who were convicted of violence (22%).

Table 3.2 shows the eight most important protective factors against violence. Six of them (all except attending a low delinquency-rate school and small family

Table 3.1 Bullying versus convictions and violence

	No convictions	Convictions	% convictions
Definite bullies versus convictions			
No bullies	210	121	37
Bullies	36	35	49
Probable bullies versus violence			
No Bullies	177	28	14
Bullies	154	43	22

Note
Probable bullies include definite bullies.

Table 3.2 Protective effects against violence convictions

Variable	% violent in protective category	% violent in non-protective category	Odds ratio	95% confidence interval
Low daring	3	26	12.4	1.6–93.0
High non-verbal IQ	5	26	6	1.4–26.2
High verbal IQ	6	25	5.3	1.2–23.3
Low extraversion	11	24	2.5	0.8–7.5
Low delinquency school	14	26	2.2	1.0–5.0
Small family size	13	25	2.2	0.9–5.3
High school attainment	13	24	2.1	0.8–5.4
Low impulsivity	14	24	2	0.8–5.2

size) were individual factors. The four strongest predictors were all individual factors. Because of small numbers in the dichotomies, only four of the ORs were statistically significant on a two-tailed test; one-tailed tests are justifiable in light of the clear directional predictions. All eight ORs indicated relatively strong effects according to Cohen's (1996) criterion of OR = 2.0 or greater (a doubling of the odds in the non-protective category compared with the protective category).

Similar analyses were conducted to investigate factors with a protective effect against criminal convictions and the results are shown in Table 3.3. Of the six strongest predictors, four were socio-economic or family factors, namely good child-rearing, high family income, a low delinquency rate school and small family size. So far, we have studied *risk-based protective factors*.

As a final step, tests of interaction effects were carried out to establish *interactive protective factors*. An interactive protective factor significantly interacts with bullying in predicting offending. As shown on Table 3.4, bullying did not predict offending within high-income families (32% of non-bullies versus 22% of bullies). If anything, the bullies were less likely to be convicted, suggesting perhaps that aggression in favourable circumstances might be advantageous (although this finding should not be overemphasized because it was not statistically significant). In contrast, bullying significantly predicted convictions in less favourable circumstances, namely lower-income families (38% of non-bullies versus 58% of bullies). The Analysis of Variance showed a significant interaction term in predicting convictions ($F = 4.16$, $p = 0.42$). The results were similar for the interaction effects involving child-rearing and daring.

Discussion

School bullying is a significant predictor of later offending. Protective factors that interrupt the continuity from school bullying to a later anti-social path could be very useful in designing future intervention initiatives. Previous research has

Table 3.3 Protective effects against criminal convictions

Variable	% convicted in protective category	% convicted in non-protective category	Odds ratio	95% confidence interval
High family income	22	58	4.9	1.4–17.0
Good child-rearing	24	56	4.1	1.2–14.3
High school attainment	23	55	4	1.0–16.3
Low delinquency school	28	59	3.8	1.2–12.2
Low hyperactivity	31	60	3.4	1.2–9.4
Small family size	28	57	3.4	1.1–10.9
Low daring	25	52	3.3	0.6–17.6
Low impulsivity	31	53	2.6	0.7–9.3
Low extraversion	33	52	2.2	0.6–7.1
High non-verbal IQ	33	52	2.1	0.5–9.3

52   M.M. Ttofi and D.P. Farrington

Table 3.4 Interactive protective effects

High income	Lower income	Interaction
NB (N) B (N) 32% (104) 22% (18) (OR=0.6; 95% CI: 0.2–2.0)	NB (N) B (N) 39% (227) 58% (53) (OR=2.2; 95% CI: 1.2–4.1)	$F=4.16, p=0.042$

Good child-rearing	Worse child-rearing	Interaction
31% (108) 24% (17) (OR=0.7; 95% CI: 0.2–2.3)	NB (N) B (N) 38% (210) 56% (52) (OR=2.0 95% CI: 1.1–3.8)	$F=2.87, p=0.091$

Low daring/risk taking	Higher daring/risk taking	Interaction
NB (N) B (N) 11% (75) 3% (36) (OR=0.2; 95% CI: 0.0–2.0)	NB (N) B (N) 15% (127) 26% (161) (OR=1.9; 95% CI: 1.0–3.4	$F=4.25, p=0.040$

Notes
Table 3.4 shows: (a) per cent convicted within high/lower income and within good/worse child-rearing and (b) per cent violent within low/higher daring; CI=Confidence Interval; NB=Non-Bully; B=Bully; N=Sample Size.

investigated the effectiveness of bullying prevention programmes and the content of these programmes (Farrington & Ttofi, 2009; Ttofi & Farrington, 2011) and has highlighted the failure to take account of information about protective factors in devising existing interventions (Ttofi & Farrington, 2012). To the best of our knowledge, this is the first time that longitudinal researchers have attempted to examine factors that protect bullies from becoming violent or criminal offenders (according to convictions) later in life.

It is interesting that most factors with protective effects against violent offending tended to be individual while most factors against criminal offending tended to be family and social. One possible implication is that family and social interventions, such as parent training, might interrupt the continuity from teenage bullying to criminal offending but not violence. It is possible that different types of interventions, such as child social skills training, may be more efficacious in interrupting the continuity from bullying to violence later in life. Of course, in future, further analyses from other major prospective longitudinal studies should be carried out to see to what extent these results might be replicable.

School bullies are children with a high likelihood of following an antisocial path later in life. Focusing on protective factors and on building the resilience of children at risk is a more positive approach, and more attractive to communities, than reducing risk factors, which emphasizes deficits and problems (Pollard, Hawkins, & Arthur, 1999). Resilience has mostly been studied within psychology. Within criminology, the evidence regarding protective factors and resilience is at a very early stage compared with research on risk factors (Werner, 2000). Protective factors, however, have started to receive increased attention

Protecting bullies from becoming offenders 53

and are considered a key challenge for the next generation of risk assessment research (Farrington, 2007).

It is necessary to develop an assessment instrument that can provide data on empirically identified risk and protective factors for school bullying based on findings from prospective longitudinal research and following guidelines from relevant research in other fields (Rennie & Dolan, 2010). Possible differences in measurement reliability and validity of such an instrument across gender, age and racial/ethnic groups should also be examined. Such an instrument would have important applications in needs assessment and strategic prevention planning. The time is ripe to mount a new programme of international collaborative research on risk and protective factors against school bullying and its long-term consequences based on prospective longitudinal studies from across the world.

Our research suggests that it would be valuable to target specific individual, family and social resilience factors in trying to prevent the escalation from bullying to violent and criminal offending. Effective programmes include cognitive-behavioural skills training and pre-school intellectual enrichment programmes (Farrington & Welsh, 2007). The time is ripe to devise, implement and evaluate anti-bullying programmes based on the results of longitudinal studies on risk and protective factors.

Acknowledgements

This research was supported by the Jacobs Foundation and the Swedish National Council for Crime Prevention. For funding the Cambridge Study in Delinquent Development, we are very grateful to the Home Office, the Department of Health, the Department for Education, the Rayne Foundation, the Barrow Cadbury Trust and the Smith-Richardson Foundation.

References

Boulton, M. J., & Smith, P. K. (1994). Bully/victim problems in middle school children: Stability, self-perceived competence, peer perceptions and peer acceptance. *British Journal of Developmental Psychology, 12*, 315–330.

Chapell, M. S., Hasselman, S. L., Kitchin, T., & Lomon, S. N. (2006). Bullying in elementary school, high school, and college. *Adolescence, 41*, 633–648.

Cohen, P. (1996). Childhood risks for young adult symptoms of personality disorder: Method and substance. *Multivariate Behavioral Research, 31*, 121–148.

Cook, C. R., Williams, K. R., Guerra, N. G., Kim, T. E., & Sadek, S. (2010). Predictors of bullying and victimization in childhood and adolescence: A meta-analytic investigation. *School Psychology Quarterly, 25*, 65–83.

Due, P., Holstein, B. E., Lynch, J., Diderichsen, F., Gabhain, S. N., Scheidt, P., & Currie, C. (2005). Bullying and symptoms among school-aged children: International comparative cross sectional study in 28 countries. *European Journal of Public Health, 15*, 128–132.

Farrington, D. P. (1993). Understanding and preventing bullying. In M. Tonry (ed.), *Crime and justice*, vol. 17 (pp. 381–458). Chicago: University of Chicago Press.

54 M.M. Ttofi and D.P. Farrington

Farrington, D. P. (2000). Explaining and preventing crime: The globalization of knowledge – the American Society of Criminology 1999 Presidential Address. *Criminology, 38*, 1–24.

Farrington, D. P. (2007). Advancing knowledge about desistance. *Journal of Contemporary Criminal Justice, 23*, 125–134.

Farrington, D. P. (2012). Predictors of violent young offenders. In B. C. Feld & D. M. Bishop (eds), *The Oxford handbook of juvenile crime and juvenile justice* (pp. 146–171). Oxford: Oxford University Press.

Farrington, D., & Baldry, A. (2010). Individual risk factors for school bullying. *Journal of Aggression, Conflict and Peace Research, 2*, 4–16.

Farrington, D. P., Coid, J. W., Harnett, L., Jolliffe, D., Soteriou, N., Turner, R., & West, D. J. (2006). *Criminal careers up to age 50 and life success up to age 48: New findings From the Cambridge Study in Delinquent Development*. London: Home Office (Research Study No. 299).

Farrington, D. P., Coid, J. W., & West, D. J. (2009). The development of offending from age 8 to age 50: Recent results from the Cambridge Study in Delinquent Development. *Monatsschrift fur Kriminologie und Strafrechsreform (Journal of Criminology and Penal Reform), 92*, 160–173.

Farrington, D. P., Losel, F., Ttofi, M. M., & Theodorakis, N. (2012). *Bullying perpetration and victimization versus later depression and offending: An updated systematic review of longitudinal studies*. Stockholm: Swedish National Council for Crime Prevention.

Farrington, D. P., Piquero, A. R., & Jennings, W. G. (2013). *Offending from childhood to late middle age: Recent results from the Cambridge Study in Delinquent Development*. New York: Springer.

Farrington, D. P., & Ttofi, M. M. (2009). School-based programs to reduce bullying and victimization. *Campbell Systematic Reviews 2009*, 6.

Farrington, D. P., & Ttofi, M. M. (2011a). Bullying as a predictor of offending, violence and later life outcomes. *Criminal Behaviour and Mental Health, 21*, 90–98.

Farrington, D. P., & Ttofi, M. M. (2011b). Protective and promotive factors in the development of offending. In T. Bliesener, A. Beelman & M. Stemmler (eds), *Antisocial behaviour and crime: Contributions of theory and evaluation research to prevention and intervention* (pp. 71–88). Cambridge, MA: Hogrefe Publishing.

Farrington, D. P., Ttofi, M. M., & Losel, F. (2011). Editorial: School bullying and later offending. *Criminal Behaviour and Mental Health, 21*, 77–79.

Farrington, D. P., Ttofi, M. M., & Piquero, A. R. (2016), Risk, promotive and protective factors in youth offending: Results from the Cambridge Study in Delinquent Development. *Journal of Criminal Justice*, in press.

Farrington, D. P. & Welsh, B. C. (2007). *Saving children from a life of crime: Early risk factors and effective interventions*. Oxford: Oxford University Press.

Fergusson, D. M., Boden, J. M., & Horwood, L. J. (2014). Bullying in childhood, externalizing behaviors, and adult offending: Evidence from a 30-year study. *Journal of School Violence, 13*, 146–164.

Hemphill, S. A., Tollit, M., & Herrenkohl, T. I. (2014). Protective factors against the impact of school bullying perpetration and victimization on young adult externalizing and internalizing problems. *Journal of School Violence, 13*, 125–145.

Kim, Y. S., Koh, Y. J., & Leventhal, B. L. (2004). Prevalence of school bullying in Korean middle school students. *Archives of Pediatrics and Adolescent Medicine, 158*, 737–741.

Protecting bullies from becoming offenders 55

Kumpulainen, K., Räsänen, E., & Henttonen, I. (1999). Children involved in bullying: psychological disturbance and the persistence of the involvement. *Child Abuse and Neglect, 23*, 1253–1262.

Losel, F., & Bender, D. (2003). Protective factors and resilience. In D. P. Farrington & J. W. Coid (eds), *Early prevention of adult antisocial behaviour* (pp. 130–204). Cambridge: Cambridge University Press.

Lösel, F., & Bender, D. (2014). Aggressive, delinquent, and violent outcomes of school bullying: Do family and individual factors have a protective function? *Journal of School Violence, 13*, 59–79.

McVie, S. (2014). The impact of bullying perpetration and victimization on later violence and psychological distress: A study of resilience among a Scottish youth cohort. *Journal of School Violence, 13*, 39–58.

Pepler, D., Jiang, D., Craig, W., & Connolly, J. (2008). Developmental trajectories of bullying and associated factors. *Child Development, 79*, 325–338.

Piquero, A. R., Connell, N., Piquero, N. L., Farrington, D. P., & Jennings, W. G. (2013). Does adolescent bullying distinguish between male offending trajectories in late middle age? *Journal of Youth and Adolescence, 42*, 444–453.

Pollard, J. A., Hawkins, J. D., & Arthur, M. W. (1999). Risk and protection: Are both necessary to understand diverse behavioral outcomes in adolescence? *Social Work Research, 23*, 145–158.

Rennie, C. E., & Dolan, M. C. (2010). The significance of protective factors in the assessment of risk. *Criminal Behaviour and Mental Health, 20*, 8–22.

Rigby, K. (1994). Psychosocial functioning in families of Australian adolescent schoolchildren involved in bully/victim problems. *Journal of Family Therapy, 16*, 173–187.

Smith, P. K., Morita, Y., Junger-Tas, J., Olweus, D., Catalano, R., & Slee, P. (1999). *The nature of school bullying: A cross-national perspective.* London: Routledge.

Snyder, C. R., & Lopez, J. (2005). *Handbook of positive psychology.* New York: Oxford University Press.

Sourander, A., Helstelä, L., Helenius, H., & Piha, J. (2000). Persistence of bullying from childhood to adolescence: A longitudinal 8-year follow-up study. *Child Abuse and Neglect, 24*, 873–881.

Ttofi, M. M., Bowes, L., Farrington, D. P., & Lösel, F. (2014). Protective factors interrupting the continuity from school bullying to later internalizing and externalizing problems: A systematic review of prospective longitudinal studies. *Journal of School Violence, 13*, 5–38.

Ttofi, M. M., & Farrington, D. P. (2011). Effectiveness of school-based programs to reduce bullying: A systematic and meta-analytic review. *Journal of Experimental Criminology, 7*, 27–56.

Ttofi, M. M., & Farrington, D. P. (2012). Risk and protective factors, longitudinal research, and bullying prevention. *New Directions for Youth Development, 133*, 85–98.

Ttofi, M. M., Farrington, D. P., & Lösel, F. (2012). School bullying as a predictor of violence later in life: A systematic review and meta-analysis of prospective longitudinal studies. *Aggression and Violent Behavior, 17*, 405–418.

Ttofi, M. M., Farrington, D. P., & Lösel, F. (2014). Interrupting the continuity from school bullying to later internalizing and externalizing problems: Findings from cross-national comparative studies. *Journal of School Violence, 13*, 1–4.

Ttofi, M. M., Farrington, D. P., Lösel, F., & Loeber, R. (2011). The predictive efficiency of school bullying versus later offending: A systematic/meta-analytic review of longitudinal studies. *Criminal Behaviour and Mental Health, 21*, 80–89.

56   M.M. Ttofi and D.P. Farrington

Vassallo, S., Edwards, B., Renda, J., & Olsson, C. A. (2014). Bullying in early adolescence and antisocial behavior and depression six years later: What are the protective factors? *Journal of School Violence, 13*, 100–124.

Werner, E. E. (2000). Protective factors and individual resilience. In J. P. Shonkoff & S. P. Meisels (eds), *Handbook of early childhood prevention* (pp. 115–132). New York: Cambridge University Press.

West, D. J., & Farrington, D. P. (1973). *Who Becomes Delinquent?* London: Heinemann.

Wolke, D., Woods, S., Stanford, K., & Schulz, H. (2001). Bullying and victimization of primary school children in England and Germany: Prevalence and school factors. *British Journal of Psychology, 92*, 673–696.

Woods, S., & Wolke, D. (2004). Direct and relational bullying among primary school children and academic achievement. *Journal of School Psychology, 42*, 135–155.

4 Cyberbullying

Does parental online supervision and youngsters' willingness to report to an adult reduce the risk?

Anna C. Baldry, Anna Sorrentino and David P. Farrington

Introduction

Cyberbullying affects boys and girls of different ages all around the world, since communication among peers has changed, and so have the risks of online communication. Cyberbullying has been defined as 'an aggressive act or behavior that is carried out using electronic means by a group or an individual repeatedly and over time against a victim who cannot easily defend him or herself' (Smith et al., 2008, p. 376). Even if most researchers agree that cyberbullying can be considered as a new type of aggression, made possible by the increasing spread of the Internet and the new information and communication technologies (ICTs) among young people (Slonje, Smith, & Frisén, 2013), assessing the prevalence and nature of cyberbullying is complex, since there is still a lack of consensus regarding how cyberbullying should be defined and measured (Kowalski, Giumetti, Schroeder, & Lattanner, 2014; Olweus, 2013; Smith, del Barrio and Tokunaga, 2013; Tokunaga, 2010; Ybarra, Boyd, Korchmaros, & Oppenheim, 2012). The same applies when we look at possible causes of cyberbullying, better identified as 'risk and protective factors'.

By adopting the *ecological system theory*, based on Bronfenbrenner's ecological framework (Bronfenbrenner, 1979, 1986, 1994), it is possible to divide risk factors associated with bullying and cyberbullying according to one of four levels: individual, interpersonal, social, or community and cultural. The underlying reasoning is that there is no one single cause of cyberbullying; risk factors can have a role and influence and this varies from individual to individual, and from context to context (Baldry, Farrington, & Sorrentino, 2015). Risk factors for cyberbullying therefore can be related to the individual level including age, gender, youngsters' internet activities, empathy, self-esteem, and to the interpersonal level including the relationship with the parents and parental roles in monitoring, moderating and mediating of internet communication of their children (Mesch, 2009).

The aim of the study presented in this chapter is to investigate the relationship between parental online supervision and cyberbullying, controlling for other personal variables such as gender, amount of time using the Internet and willingness to report cyberbullying to an adult.

58   *A.C. Baldry* et al.

The studies reviewed use different definitional criteria, different measures of parental support, and so in Table 4.1 we provide a summary of findings, which overall are mixed also because different constructs were used.

Ybarra and Mitchell (2004) measured the caregiver-child relationship (emotional closeness, general monitoring and discipline) and parents' restriction of their children's internet use. With regard to the caregiver-child relationship, they found that cyberbullies and cyberbully/victims, compared to students not involved in cyberbullying, reported having poorer emotional bonds with their parents and lower levels of parental general monitoring. The authors also found that about 30% of parents of students involved as cyberbullies and cyberbully/victims restricted their children's internet use by blocking software on their home computer, compared to 22.1% of parents of students not involved.

Dehue et al. (2008) administered two questionnaires (one for students and one for parents) to 1,211 Dutch students and their parents measuring students' involvement in cyberbullying and cybervictimization. Parents were asked about the presence of house rules about the Internet, and the prevalence and communication about their children's experience of being cyberbullies or cybervictimized. The results showed that about 60% of parents reporting having set clear rules about the frequency with which their children could use the Internet and 80% of them had also established rules about what activities were allowed on the Internet. With regard to students' communication with their parents about their experience of being a cyberbully or a cybervictim, there was a discrepancy between the prevalence rates of cyberbullying and cybervictimization reported by parents and students. Only 4.8% of parents reported that their children were involved as cyberbullies, but 17.3% of students reported being a cyberbully, indicating little knowledge by parents about what is going on.

Juvonen and Gross (2008) surveyed online 1,254 US students aged 12–17 years about their experiences of cybervictimization and their willingness to report these incidents to adults. The results showed that 90% of youth did not report any cybervictimization incidents to adults. In particular, according to students, the reasons for not reporting were tied to the need to deal with cybervictimization by themselves (50%) and to the fear of parents' reactions, that is parents might restrict or not allow them to use the Internet (31%). Slonje and Smith (2008) administered to 360 Swedish students aged 12–20 years a questionnaire about students' experience of school bullying and victimization and of cyberbullying and cybervictimization and students' propensity to report cyberbullying and cybervictimization. The results highlighted that 50% of cybervictims did not report to anyone; none of the cybervictims reported their experience to teachers, 35.7% reported being a cybervictim to a friend, 8.9% to parents and 5.4% to someone else. The study also highlighted that, according to participants, the different cybervictimization types had different probabilities of being reported to adults; it seems that only picture/video clip cybervictimization was likely to come to the notice of adults.

Smith et al. (2008) surveyed 533 UK students aged 7–11 years about their willingness to tell anyone about school bullying and victimization and

Table 4.1 Summary of key findings on the role of parents and cyberbullying

Study	Sample		Method/parental measures	Main results of parental role		
	N	Age				
Ybarra & Mitchell (2004) USA	1,501	10–17 years	Telephone survey At least once in the past 12 months Parent-child relationship Parents' internet control	Compared to subjects not involved, cyberbullies and cyberbully/victims have poor emotional bonds with their parents	Compared to subjects not involved, cyberbullies and cyberbully/victims reported low levels of parental monitoring	Only about 30% of parents of students involved as cyberbullies and cyberbully/victims used blocking software, compared to 22.1% of parents of students not involved
Dehue, Bolman, & Völlink (2008) NL	1,211	M=12.7 (sd=0.73)	Self-reported questionnaire At least once in last semester House rules about the Internet and text messaging Communication on bullying and being bullied	60% of parents reported having set rules about the frequency with which children were allowed to use the Internet, 80% of them also reported having set clear rules about allowed activities on the Internet	With respect to communication on cyberbullying and cybervictimization, only 4.8% of parents reported their child was a cyberbully, while 17.3% of students reported being involved as cyberbullies	11.8% of parents reported their child was a cybervictim, while 22.9% of students reported they have experienced cybervictimization
Juvonen & Gross (2008) USA	1,454	12–17 years	Online survey Reporting cyberbullying to adults	90% of students reported not telling adults about cybervictimization	The most common reason for not telling an adult was that participants believe they "need to learn to deal with it" themselves (50%)	Almost one third of the sample (31%) reported that the reason they do not tell is because they are concerned that their parents might find out and restrict their internet access

continued

Table 4.1 Continued

Study	Sample		Method/parental measures	Main results of parental role	
	N	*Age*			
Slonje & Smith (2008) Sweden	360	12–20 years	Self-reported questionnaire At least once or twice in the past couple of months Reporting cyberbullying and cybervictimization to adults	50% of cybervictims reported not telling anyone, 35.7% told a friend, 8.9% told a parent/guardian and 5.4% someone else. No cybervictim reported his/her experience of cybervictimization to teachers.	The different types of cybervictimization have different chances of being reported to adults. In particular, according to most participants only picture/video clip cybervictimization was as likely to be noticed by adults as school victimization.
Smith et al. (2008) UK	533	7–11 years	Self-reported questionnaire At least once in the past year Reporting cyberbullying and cybervictimization to anyone	Participants indicated the best ways to stop cybervictimization: blocking messages/identities (74.9%), telling a parent and or a teacher) (63.3%), changing email address/phone number (56.7%), keeping a record of offensive emails/texts (46.5%), ignoring it (41.3%), reporting to police (38.5%), contact service provider (31.1%), asking them to stop (21.4%), fighting back (19.6%)	70.2% of school victims told someone about his/her victimization experience, while only 58.6% of cybervictims reported cybervictimization incidents to someone

Mesch (2009) USA	935	12–17 years	Self-reported survey Parental restrictive and evaluative mediation	Parental monitoring Web sites visited by their children (restrictive mediation), decrease youth's risk of being involved in cyberbullying as cybervictims	The presence of rules on sites that the children are allowed to visit (evaluative mediation) decreases youth's risk of been involved in cyberbullying as cybervictims	Parental monitoring and rules on internet allowed activities decrease youngsters' risk of being involved in cyberbullying
Wang, Iannotti, & Nansel (2009) USA	7,182	6–10 grades	Self-reported questionnaire Only once or twice in the previous two months Parental support (higher or lower)	Higher levels of parental support were negatively associated with involvement in cyberbullying as cyberbullies, cybervictims and cyberbully/victims	There is an inverse relationship between levels of parental support and involvement in cyberbullying as a cyberbully	
Huang & Chou (2010) Taiwan	545	Junior high school	Anonymous survey (online and printed) Reasons for not reporting cyberbullying and cybervictimization to adults	Among bystanders of cyberbullying, only 11.2% told parents and 3.7% told teachers. According to bystanders of cyberbullying reasons for not reporting were: being afraid of getting into trouble; feeling a sense of uselessness in looking to adults for assistance.	Cybervictims were less likely to turn to adults, including parents (11.6%) and teachers (5.9%)	Many more cybervictims than bystanders of cyberbullying reported cyberbullying incidents 33.4% of cybervictims reported their experience to peers

continued

Table 4.1 Continued

Study	Sample		Method/parental measures	Main results of parental role		
	N	*Age*				
Holfeld & Grabe (2012) USA	665	7–8 grades	Self-reported survey At least once or twice in the past 30 days Reporting cybervictimization	64% of cybervictims told their experience of online victimization to their peers, 50% to parents and 8% to teachers In 37% of cases, participants told more than one person their experience of cybervictimization	The chance of end of cybervictimization was 59% when told adults, 54% when told peers and 46% when adults/ peers were told	Regardless of to whom they report, in 53% of cases cybervictimization ended when victims reported the incident
Floros, Siomos, Fisoun, Dafouli, & Geroukalis (2013) Greece	2,017	12–19 years	Cross-sectional study At least once during the last school year Parental bonding Internet use, experience and safety procedures	Secure online practice at home is a protective factor. There is a statistically significant difference on the parental security measures when comparing those adolescents who were cybervictimized to those who were not cybervictimized.	Parental supervision apparently did not prevent youngsters' involvement as cyberbullies	Lower levels of perceived care, higher levels of perceived overprotection and higher levels of pathological internet use were linked both to being involved as cyberbully and cybervictim

Cyberbullying 63

cyberbullying and cybervictimization. The results showed a statistically significant difference in students' reporting of school victimization and cybervictimization. In particular, school victims (70.2%) were more likely than cybervictims (58.6%) to tell someone about their victimization experiences.

Mesch (2009) surveyed 935 US students 12–17 years and their parents in order to assess students' likelihood of cybervictimization and parental mediation strategies (restrictive or evaluative). With regard to parents' mediation strategies, the results showed that only parental monitoring of the Web sites visited by their children (restrictive parental mediation) was a protective factor, that is parental monitoring decreased a youth's risk of cybervictimization. Also, the evaluative mediation strategy of setting clear rules on children's allowed online activities decreased students' experience of cybervictimization.

Wang et al. (2009) administered to 7,182 US 6–10 grade students a questionnaire about students' experience of school bullying and victimization and cyberbullying and cybervictimization and students' perceived parental support. The results showed that high levels of parental control were associated with low cyberbullying and low cybervictimization.

In another survey conducted by Huang and Chou (2010) with 545 Taiwan junior high school students about cyberbullying and cybervictimization and reasons for not reporting cyberbullying and cybervictimization to adults, it emerged that cybervictims reported their experience to peers/classmates in 33.4% of cases, to siblings in 16.1% of cases, while only 11.6% and 5.9% of students reported cybervictimization respectively to parents and teachers.

Holfeld and Grabe (2012) administered to 665 7–8 grade US students a questionnaire about their experience of cyberbullying and cybervictimization, investigating also students' willingness to report cybervictimization. About 60% of students reported cybervictimization. In particular, of these, 64% reported their experience of cybervictimization to peers, 50% to parents, 20% to siblings, 8% to teachers, 5% to cousins and 1% to grandparents. The most important result from this research underlines the importance of reporting cybervictimization, because, when cybervictims decided to report their experience, in 53% of cases the cybervictimization stopped.

Floros et al. (2013) conducted a cross-sectional study involving the entire high school population ($N=2,017$) of the island of Kos and all of their parents. The study aimed to investigate the relationship between cyberbullying and cybervictimization and parental bonding and parental monitoring of their children's internet use and online security rules. With regard to secure online practices at home, the results showed a significant difference between cybervictimized and not cybervictimized adolescents, that is the presence of secure online practices was a protective factor. The same was not found with regard to cyberbullying, so parental rules and monitoring seem to not prevent students' involvement as cyberbullies.

In our study we looked specifically at the role of parents in online monitoring (informing the child about online risk, monitoring the child's online activities, accessing the child's social network accounts) in relation to cyberbullying and

64   *A.C. Baldry* et al.

cybervictimization. We hypothesized that greater parental involvement and awareness would be associated with lower cyberbullying and lower cybervictimization, controlling for individual level variables (gender, numbers of hours spent online and willingness to talk to an adult about their cyber experience).

Method

Participants

The total sample taking part in the study consisted of 2,419 Italian students recruited from different schools in different locations in the northern part of Italy. Of all participants 45.7% were males and 54.3% were females. The average age of the students who filled in the questionnaires was 15.4 years ($SD=2.06$) and most of them (95.2%) were Italian. Almost all students (99%) taking part in the study reported using the Internet at home, and 82.9% of them reported having at least one profile on a social network.

Measures

Participants were handed a questionnaire packet that included the Italian version of the original Olweus Bully/Victim Questionnaire (Baldry & Farrington, 1999; Menesini et al., 1997; Olweus, 1993) and the translation of the Students' Needs Assessment Survey (Willard, 2007). The questionnaire also included socio-demographic measures, such as gender, age, country of birth, internet availability at home, and a set of questions on parental monitoring of the online activities.

At the beginning of the questionnaire, the school bullying and cyberbullying definitions were provided. For the purpose of the present study only measures of types and frequency of bullying were taken into consideration. Students' involvement in school bullying as a bully and/or a victim was measured on five-point scales ranging from: 'never', 'only once or twice', 'two or three times a month', 'once a week', to 'several times a week', in the previous six months.

To measure cyberbullying we used the translated version of the Students' Needs Assessment Survey (Willard, 2007). For the purposes of the present study only measures of types and frequency of cyberbullying were taken into consideration. Students' involvement in cyberbullying was measured using a set of questions about perpetrating different online actions (five items) or being victimized (five items). Students were asked whether they had experienced (as a bully and/or as a victim) in the previous six months the following cyberbullying types: flaming,[1] denigration, impersonation, outing and exclusion. Each cyberbullying type was measured on a 3-point scale: 'no' (scored 0), 'yes, 1 to 4 times' (1) and 'yes, 5 or more times' (scored 2).

To measure students' willingness to report cyberbullying and cybervictimization incidents to parents or other significant adults (teachers), we created a scale by adding together five (5) items measured on four-point scales: 'very unlikely' (scored 0), 'somewhat unlikely' (scored 1), 'somewhat likely' (scored 2), 'very likely' (scored 3). The score, ranging from 0 to 15, was reliable with a Cronbach's alpha=0.83. Example items are: 'I would report online bullying to an adult if it happened to me', and 'I would tell your parents or a school staff member that a student is cybervictimized'.

Parental online supervision was measured with three different items that were used separately. Parents' education about internet use was assessed using a dichotomous variable ('no'=0) ('yes'=1), while for parental control of children's online activities and parental social network supervision respondents could answer on a three-point scale ranging from 'never' (scored 0) to 'frequently' (scored 2).

Procedure

Questionnaires were administered in the school during lessons by the first two authors after a custodial adult's consent was ascertained by the school principal. Participants were handed the paper and pencil questionnaire in their classroom. Before completion, the meaning of the terms school bullying and cyberbullying were explained to students. Students were assured about the anonymity of the study and that their answers were collected and analysed at an aggregate level so their identity was protected and they could provide their answers freely according to what was actually going on in their lives.

Data analysis

To measure overall involvement in bullying and cyberbullying, descriptive statistics were calculated to measure the prevalence of bullying and cyberbullying and gender differences (see Table 4.2). To establish the relative impact on cyberbullying and cybervictimization of parents' role in monitoring and educating youngsters in safe internet use and parents' role in supervising youngsters' social network profile(s) and students' willingness to report cyberbullying and cybervictimization to adults, two hierarchical regression analyses were conducted controlling for students' age and gender.

Results

Overall frequency data

To gain a basic understanding of prevalence of bullying and cyberbullying overall frequencies were calculated. Analyses showed that 59% of the students experienced at least one school victimization episode in the previous six months, while 26.2% reported being cybervictims. About 61% of the students were school bullies and almost 24% had bullied others in cyberspace through the new technologies (see Figure 4.1).

The most common form of school victimization was verbal bullying (45.6%), followed by indirect bullying (33.4%) and physical bullying (23.3%). Likewise

Table 4.2 Summary statistics of the study's variables

Measures and items	
Gender	45.7% males
Age (12–20)	Mean=15.4, sd=2.06
Nationality	95.2% Italian
Internet users	99% yes
Number of hours a day	57.6% at least 2–4 hrs
Social network profile	82.9% yes
Parental supervision of internet use	39.5% never
Parental supervision of children's social network profile	57.6% never
Parental education on safe internet use	42.9% no
School bullying (score 0–28)	Mean=2.50, sd=3.76
School victimization (score 0–28)	Mean=2.43, sd=3.53
Cyberbullying (score 0–5)	Mean=0.38, sd=0.83
Cybervictimization (score 0–5)	Mean=0.39, sd=0.76
Willingness to report cyberbullying/cybervictimization to adult (score 0–15)	Mean=8.77, sd=3.95

Note
Internet hours were assessed in four categories: 0–1 hr/day=1, 2–4 hrs/day=2, 5–8 hrs/day=3, more than 9 hrs=4, N=2,419.

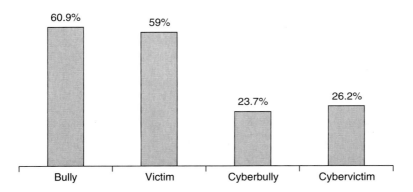

Figure 4.1 Prevalence of school and cyberbullying and victimization.

the most common type of school bullying was verbal bullying (48.4%), followed by indirect bullying (40.7%) and physical bullying (17.4%). With respect to students' involvement in cyberbullying, almost 13% of all respondents reported having sent nasty, cruel or mean messages to someone once or twice during the past six months, while the most common types of cybervictimization were denigration (11%), followed by outing (9.6%) taking place at least once or twice.

Although school bullying and victimization appear to be more prevalent than cyberbullying and cybervictimization, we believe it could be interesting to highlight that a significant number of the students participating in the study reported online web materials that denigrate and/or humiliate a school staff member

Cyberbullying 67

(33.7%), that threaten or suggest violence (26.5%) or suicide (6.1%), and harmful materials posted by homophobic and/or racist minorities (35%) or by gangs online (13.4%).

Parents' role in cyberbullying

More than half of students' parents had educated their children on how to behave correctly online, but about 40% of parents had never looked at or monitored their children's online activities and only 42.4% of parents had access and control of students' social network profile(s).

The data seem to suggest that students are not inclined to share their online experiences with their parents. In fact 23.8% of them would not turn to parents in order to report their cybervictimization experiences, and only 33.6% would tell them about another student's experience of cybervictimization.

Gender differences and involvement in school and cyberbullying

Gender differences in involvement in school and cyberbullying were investigated with a 2×2 cross-sectional cross tabulation (Table 4.3). The results showed that 67.8% and 61.2% of male students reported being involved in school bullying as bullies or victims respectively. The comparison using the chi-square test highlighted the existence of significant gender differences in students' involvement in school bullying; males were more likely than females to be involved in school bullying as bullies ($\chi^2_{(1)} = 39.001$, $p < 0.001$). Also for school victimization males were more involved than their female counterparts ($\chi^2_{(1)} = 4.024$ $p < 0.05$).

With regard to cyberbullying and cybervictimization, 29.8% of males and 18.7% of females admitted that they were cyberbullies, while 25% of males and 27.3% of females stated that they had been cybervictimized. The comparison using the chi-square test highlighted the existence of significant gender differences in students' involvement in cyberbullying; males were more likely to be involved as cyberbullies than females ($\chi^2_{(1)} = 40.242$, $p < 0.001$), but no significant gender differences were found with regard to cybervictimization.

Table 4.3 Gender differences between school bullying and cyberbullying

	Odds ratio	Male (%)	Female (%)
School bully	1.72***	67.8	55.1
School victim	1.18*	61.2	57.1
Cyberbully	1.84***	29.8	18.7
Cybervictim	0.89	25.0	27.3

Note
* $p < 0.05$;
** $p < 0.01$;
*** $p < 0.001$.

68   *A.C. Baldry et al.*

Hierarchical regression

To establish the relative impact of parents' role in monitoring and educating youngsters in safe internet use, and students' willingness to report cyberbullying and cybervictimization in incidence to parents or other significant adults (over and above individual variables such as gender and hours spent online) on involvement in cyberbullying and cybervictimization, two hierarchical regression analyses were conducted.

First, simple correlations between different risk factors and cyberbullying and cybervictimization were calculated to analyse the relationships between variables (see Table 4.4). Interestingly, parental education on internet use, parental control of online activities and parental social network supervision were negatively related to cyberbullying (as expected) but positively related to cybervictimization. Cyberbullying and cybervictimization were quite highly correlated ($r=0.403$), as were school bullying and school victimization ($r=0.558$). School bullying and cyberbullying were quite highly correlated ($r=0.466$) but school victimization and cybervictimization were somewhat less strongly correlated ($r=0.297$).

All predictive factors that were significantly correlated with cyberbullying and cybervictimization were entered into the regressions. The same predictors were used for cyberbullying and cybervictimization. The models are based on the theoretical model adopted which refers to the ecological approach to the explanation of the occurrence and nature of cyberbullying and cybervictimization. This means taking into account a set of risk factors related to individual, to interpersonal and to social levels. In this study, as mentioned, we focused only on the individual and interpersonal, or, familial, level.

In the first step of the analysis, gender and number of hours spent online a day were entered in the model first, and were statistically significant: gender (being a boy), and hours spent online a day (meaning more hours). In the second step, parental education on internet use, parental control of their children's online activities and parental supervision of their children's social network profile(s) were entered. Only parental education on safe internet use was negatively associated with cyberbullying ($\beta=-0.05$, $t=1.97$, $p<0.05$), meaning that the less parents educate their children on safe internet use, the more they are involved as cyberbullies. In the third step of the model, willingness to report cyberbullying/cybervictimization incidents was entered indicating that cyberbullying is negatively associated with willingness to report cyberbullying/cybervictimization incidents (see Table 4.5).

With regard to the prediction of cybervictimization, gender and number of hours spent online a day were entered in the model first and were statistically significant: gender (meaning being a girl), and hours spent online a day (meaning spending more hours on the Internet). In the second step, parental education on internet use, parental control of their children's online activities and parental supervision of their children's social network profile(s) were entered, significantly increasing the variance explained, though each risk factor reached only

Table 4.4 Correlations between cyberbullying and cybervictimization and different parental supervision activities, willingness to report, gender and hours online

	1	2	3	4	5	6	7	8	9	10
1 Willingness to report CB/CV	–									
2 Gender (female)	0.245**	–								
3 Numbers of hours on internet	−0.104**	−0.072**	–							
4 Parental education on internet use	0.242**	0.197**	−0.061**	–						
5 Parental control of online activities	0.242**	0.096**	−0.059**	0.301**	–					
6 Parental social network supervision	0.189**	0.076**	0.018	0.237**	0.466**	–				
7 Cybervictimization	−0.051*	0.036	0.109**	0.013	0.062**	0.070**	–			
8 Cyberbullying	−0.215**	−0.133**	0.139**	−0.090**	−0.072**	−0.052*	0.403**	–		
9 School victimization	−0.103**	−0.083**	0.102**	−0.046*	−0.009	0.003	0.297**	0.293**	–	
10 School bullying	−0.264**	−0.208**	0.158**	−0.121**	−0.119**	−0.071**	0.226**	0.466**	0.558**	–

Note

All variables are standardized;

* $p<0.05$;

** $p<0.01$;

*** $p<0.001$.

70   *A.C. Baldry* et al.

Table 4.5 Hierarchical regression for cyberbullying

	B	$SE\ B$	β
Step 1			
Gender	−0.25	(0.04)	−0.12***
Number of hours on internet	0.13	(0.02)	0.13***
Step 2			
Gender	−0.22	(0.04)	−0.11***
Number of hours on internet	0.13	(0.02)	0.13***
Parental education on internet use	−0.09	(0.05)	−0.05*
Parental control of online activities	−0.03	(0.02)	−0.03
Parental social network supervision	−0.02	(0.02)	−0.02
Step 3			
Gender	−0.15	(0.04)	−0.08***
Number of hours on internet	0.11	(0.02)	0.11***
Parental education on internet use	−0.04	(0.05)	−0.02
Parental control of online activities	−0.01	(0.02)	−0.005
Parental social network supervision	−0.01	(0.02)	−0.008
Willingness to report cyberbullying/cybervictimization	−0.18	(0.02)	−0.18***

Note
Total $R^2 = 0.242$; for step 1; $\Delta R^2 = 0.005$ for step 2 ($p < 0.05$); $\Delta R^2 = 0.027$ for step 3 ($p < 0.001$). All variables were standardized.

marginal significance ($p < 0.10$). In the third step of the model, willingness to report cyberbullying/cybervictimization incidents was entered, indicating that willingness to report cyberbullying/cybervictimization incidents was negatively associated with cybervictimization. Parental control of online activities and parental social network supervision were positively related to cybervictimization (see Table 4.6).

Discussion

Cyberbullying and cybervictimization are complex problems affecting a significant proportion of children and young people from the time they start using electronic ways to communicate. While school bullying affects children in school or around the school, making teachers and principals among the first ones to take responsibility to address the problem and develop and implement efficient programmes (Ttofi & Farrington, 2011; Ttofi, Farrington, & Baldry, 2008), cyberbullying occurs beyond the school borders (Ybarra & Mitchell, 2004). Therefore parents or any adult in charge of a child or youngster have specific responsibility to protect them from being victimized online as well as to prevent them from committing any cyberbullying online.

Youngsters are digital natives, meaning that they grew up with this form of communication technology and have expertise about electronic devices. Being online and communicating with their peers and unknown people, being popular, sharing photos, videos, thoughts and aspects of life, are things that parents are

Cyberbullying 71

Table 4.6 Hierarchical regression for cybervictimization

	B	$SE\ B$	β
Step 1			
Gender	0.09	(0.04)	0.04*
Number of hours on internet	0.11	(0.02)	0.11***
Step 2			
Gender	0.08	(0.04)	0.04
Number of hours on internet	0.11	(0.02)	0.11***
Parental education on internet use	−0.03	(0.05)	−0.01
Parental control of online activities	0.05	(0.03)	0.05
Parental social network supervision	0.05	(0.02)	0.05
Step 3			
Gender	0.11	(0.05)	0.05*
Number of hours on internet	0.11	(0.02)	0.11***
Parental education on internet use	−0.005	(0.05)	−0.003
Parental control of online activities	0.06	(0.03)	0.06*
Parental social network supervision	0.05	(0.02)	0.05*
Willingness to report cyberbullying/cybervictimization	−0.08	(0.02)	−0.08***

Note
Total $R^2=0.187$; $\Delta R^2=0.006$ for step 2 $(p<0.01)$; $\Delta R^2=0.005$ for step 3 $(p<0.001)$. All variables were standardized.

not used to. Parents or custodial adults could underestimate the dangers hidden online. The risk online is not only with regard to the risk of grooming or online sexual abuse by an adult, but it is related to cyberbullying, which can be done in several ways, via text messages, via social networks, video, email or chat rooms. These devices are not used in the same way by most adults and they may not even know that they exist.

In this chapter we investigated the role of some parental supervision and protection strategies (Mesch, 2009) in relation to involvement in cyberbullying and cybervictimization among a sample of over 2,400 Italian students. Parental relationships and supervision can be or should be considered as protective factors. However, students, according to the review of the literature presented in this chapter, often say that they did not talk to a parent about online harassment or would not do so because of fear of the consequences such as shutting down the use of mobile devices or of the computer in their bedroom (Juvonen & Gross, 2008). Therefore, even if parental supervision is a potential protective factor, it may not be one in practice. In fact, from our study, looking at the correlation between parental supervision and cyberbullying and cybervictimization, mixed results emerged.

Cyberbullying was negatively associated with parental education on internet use, whereas cybervictimization was positively associated, and the same was true of parental control of online activities and parental supervision of the activities that the child does in social networks. It could be that poor parental supervision and monitoring is a risk factor for cyberbullying, so that the less

72 *A.C. Baldry* et al.

parents are aware, and the less they inform their children or control their activities, the more it is likely that their child will cyberbully. Alternatively, the more caring parents may have less antisocial children without there being any causal effect of parenting on child behaviour. Surprisingly, cybervictims report higher levels of supervision, control and monitoring. This could be due to the fact that, if a child is victimized, the parents will supervise their child more, inform him or her more in order to prevent re-victimization and protect him or her more. To test these hypotheses, longitudinal studies would be required.

The overall model presented takes into account two different possible levels of risk factors of online bullying, according to the ecological theoretical framework (Bronfenbrenner, 1979, 1986, 1994): the individual and the interpersonal level. At the individual level, gender also explained part of the variance because being a boy is a risk factor for cyberbullying. Hours spent online (the more you are connected, the more you are exposed to actions committed and suffered) and willingness to talk to someone when in trouble were also related. As several studies have shown (Slonje & Smith, 2008), more than half of all students would not talk to an adult about what they have seen or what is going on.

This study has the limitation of being a correlational study, making it difficult to identify any causal relationships between the variables under investigation. However, it has investigated the strength of relationships between individual and interpersonal risk factors and cyberbullying and cybervictimization, underlining once more that the prevention and reduction of cyber activities has to be global and address different levels of risk and needs of youngsters (Baldry et al., 2015). In light of the cyberbullying results, we conclude that cyberbullying may be reduced by increased parental education of children on internet use, parental control of online activities and parental supervision of social networks.

Note

1 A 'flame' is a deliberately hostile and provocative message sent from one user to the community or an individual. Flaming is done by sending violent and vulgar electronic messages, in order to arouse verbal conflicts within the network between two or more users.

References

Baldry, A. C., & Farrington, D. P. (1999). Types of bullying among Italian school children. *Journal of Adolescence, 22*(3), 423–426.

Baldry, A. C., Farrington, D. P., & Sorrentino, A. (2015). Am I at risk of cyberbullying? A narrative review and conceptual framework for research on risk of cyberbullying and cybervictimization: The risk and needs assessment approach. *Aggression and Violent Behavior, 23*, 36–51.

Bronfenbrenner, U. (1979). *Ecology of human development: Experiments by nature and design*. Cambridge, MA: Harvard University Press.

Bronfenbrenner, U. (1986). Ecology of the family as a context for human development: Research perspectives. *Developmental Psychology, 22*(6), 723–742.

Bronfenbrenner, U. (1994). Ecological models of human development. In T. Husen & T. N. Postlethwaite (eds), *International encyclopedia of education* (2nd edn, pp. 1643–1647). New York: Elsevier Sciences.

Dehue, F., Bolman, C., & Völlink, T. (2008). Cyberbullying: Youngsters' experiences and parental perception. *CyberPsychology and Behavior, 11*(2), 217–223.

Floros, G. D., Siomos, K. E., Fisoun, V., Dafouli, E., & Geroukalis, D. (2013). Adolescent online cyberbullying in Greece: The impact of parental online security practices, bonding, and online impulsiveness. *Journal of School Health, 83*(6), 445–453.

Holfeld, B., & Grabe, M. (2012). Middle school students' perceptions of and responses to cyber bullying. *Journal of Educational Computing Research, 46*(4), 395–413.

Huang, Y. Y., & Chou, C. (2010). An analysis of multiple factors of cyberbullying among junior high school students in Taiwan. *Computers in Human Behavior, 26*(6), 1581–1590.

Juvonen, J., & Gross, E. F. (2008). Extending the school grounds? Bullying experiences in cyberspace. *Journal of School Health, 78*(9), 496–505.

Kowalski, R. M., Giumetti, G. W., Schroeder, A. N., & Lattanner, M. R. (2014). Bullying in the digital age: A critical review and meta-analysis of cyberbullying research among youth. *Psychological Bulletin, 140*(4), 1073–1137.

Menesini, E., Eslea, M., Smith, P. K., Genta, M. L., Giannetti, E., Fonzi, A., & Costabile, A. (1997). Cross-national comparison of children's attitudes toward bully/victim problems in school. *Aggressive Behavior, 23*(4), 245–258.

Mesch, G. S. (2009). Parental mediation, online activities, and cyberbullying. *Cyber-Psychology and Behavior, 12*(4), 387–393.

Olweus, D. (1993). *Bullying at school: What we know and what we can do.* Oxford, UK: Blackwell.

Olweus, D. (2013). School bullying: Development and some important challenges. *Annual Review of Clinical Psychology, 9*, 751–780.

Slonje, R., & Smith, P. K. (2008). Cyberbullying: Another main type of bullying?. *Scandinavian Journal of Psychology, 49*(2), 147–154.

Slonje, R., Smith, P. K., & Frisén, A. (2013). The nature of cyberbullying, and strategies for prevention. *Computers in Human Behavior, 29*(1), 26–32.

Smith, P. K., del Barrio, C., & Tokunaga, R. S. (2013). Definitions of bullying and cyberbullying: How useful are the terms? In S. Bauman, D. Cross & J. Walker (Eds). *Principles of cyberbullying research: Definitions, measures and methodology* (pp. 26–45). New York: Routledge.

Smith, P. K., Mahdavi, J., Carvalho, M., Fisher, S., Russell, S., & Tippett, N. (2008). Cyberbullying: Its nature and impact in secondary school pupils. *Journal of Child Psychology and Psychiatry, 49*(4), 376–385.

Tokunaga, R. S. (2010). Following you home from school: A critical review and synthesis of research on cyberbullying victimization. *Computers in Human Behavior, 26*(3), 277–287.

Ttofi, M. M., & Farrington, D. P. (2011). Effectiveness of school-based programs to reduce bullying: A systematic and meta-analytic review. *Journal of Experimental Criminology, 7*, 27–56.

Ttofi, M. M., Farrington, D., & Baldry, A. C. (2008). *Effectiveness of programs to reduce school bullying A systematic review.* Stockholm: Swedish National Council for Crime Prevention.

Wang, J., Iannotti, R. J., & Nansel, T. R. (2009). School bullying among adolescents in the United States: Physical, verbal, relational, and cyber. *Journal of Adolescent Health, 45*(4), 368–375.

74   *A.C. Baldry* et al.

Willard, N. E. (2007). *Cyberbullying and cyberthreats: Responding to the challenge of online social aggression, threats, and distress.* Champaign, IL: Research Press.

Ybarra, M. L., Boyd, D., Korchmaros, J. D., & Oppenheim, J. K. (2012). Defining and measuring cyberbullying within the larger context of bullying victimization. *Journal of Adolescent Health, 51*(1), 53–58.

Ybarra, M. L., & Mitchell, K. J. (2004). Online aggressor/target, aggressors and targets: A comparison of associated youth characteristics. *Journal of Child Psychology and Psychiatry, 45*(7), 1308–1316.

5 Violence risk

The actuarial illusion

David J. Cooke

In our infatuation with science and technology we overestimated our ability to manipulate and control the world around us. We forgot the power of the mind's irrational impulses. We were proud in our intellectual achievements, too confident in our abilities, too convinced that humans would stride across the world like gods.

(Peat, 2002, p. xiv)

Violence risk: the actuarial illusion

Describing the hubristic state of the natural sciences at the beginning of the twentieth century, Peat (2002) relates how Lord Kelvin – the then President of the Royal Society – indicated that everything in the physical world could be measured and understood in terms of the theories of Isaac Newton and James Clerk Maxwell. Peat (2002) described how quickly this scientific edifice dissolved from certainty to uncertainty: whether we embrace quantum theory, chaos theory or complexity theory, we know that our descriptions of physical systems, and our predictions, are inherently uncertain. Ironically, in its attempt to achieve respectability, psychology adopted Humean principles of causation and reductionism around the same period that the physical sciences were abandoning these approaches and adopting different conceptual approaches and different models (Richters, 1997). This is concerning. There can be little doubt that psychological systems are more complex, and less well understood, than the physical world: humans are active, reactive, interactive and adaptive organisms unlike the focus of the objects of Kelvin's physical world. No less an authority than Sir Isaac Newton made the position clear: "I can calculate the motions of the heavenly bodies, but not the madness of people."

While it would appear that the physical sciences have moved from a belief in certainty to embracing uncertainty – and the appreciation of the fundamental limits to knowing, predicting and managing the world around us – the science of violence risk assessment has sleep-walked towards a belief in certainty. This has led to somewhat hubristic statements about certain approaches; particularly those that have been termed actuarial risk assessment. Two examples will suffice; one applying to the actuarial approach, in general, the other to a specific test. "What

76 D.J. Cooke

we are advising is not the addition of actuarial methods to existing practice, but rather the complete replacement of existing practice with actuarial methods" (Quinsey, Harris, Rice, & Cormier, 1998, p. 171).

More recently, The State of California State Authorized Risk Assessment Tool for Sex Offenders Review Committee (2015) described the in-state study of the validity of one particular actuarial test – the STATIC-99R – as the "Crowning achievement of the SARARSO Committee in 2014" (p. 1). They informed parole and other decision makers that: "The Static-99 was found to be *very accurate* in predicting who would reoffend in California, predicting who would commit a new sex offense in about 82% of cases" (emphases added; www.saratso.org/index.cfm?pid=467).

Forensic practitioners providing expert testimony have a duty and responsibility to lay out the basis of their opinions and, in particular, explain the limitations of these opinions (*Brian Wilson and Iain Murray* v. *HMA*; [2009] Appeal No: HCJAC 58). Hubristic statements have no place in such evidence. This chapter explores some of the problems underpinning the application of actuarial risk assessment procedure in providing evidence about whether an individual will engage in violence in the future.

The task of risk assessment

Over the last two decades the task of violence risk assessment has taken centre stage in forensic practice (Cooke & Michie, 2010b, 2012; Otto & Douglas, 2010). Within clinical and correctional settings there has been the evolution of methods. Initially, the practice of unstructured professional judgement predominated. In essence, the assessor provided an unstructured personal view. Typically, it was unclear how the opinion was formed, what evidence was used, whether that evidence was consistent with empirical or clinical knowledge. Opinions were impressionistic, non-transparent, and thus they were not open to proper scrutiny and evaluation. In reaction to these practices psychologists developed simple statistical models – so called actuarial scales – that they believed could inform decision makers (Meehl, 1954).

These actuarial approaches have proved popular amongst practitioners and bureaucrats alike. Craig and Beech (2009) reported that: "in North America and the United Kingdom, actuarial risk assessment has permeated the entire criminal-justice system" (p. 197). One actuarial tool, the Risk Matrix 2000 (RM2000), is the most commonly used assessment procedure for sexual offenders in the English medium secure forensic units (Khiroya, Weaver, & Maden, 2009). The STATIC-99 (and its variants) is another widely used procedure: it is used routinely to inform decisions in civil Violent Sexual Predator hearings in the United States, and as was seen above, has many advocates. Those subject to this type of hearing can suffer long-term civil detention at the termination of their criminal detention. Clearly, actuarial risk assessment instruments (ARAIs) can influence serious decisions.

Despite their widespread application by a range of criminal-justice agencies (Craig & Beech, 2009), the use of ARAIs to make predictions about individuals has been subject to a large number of criticisms – logical, statistical and empirical. These criticisms include the problem of generalising from groups to individuals (i.e. the fallacy of division; Cooke & Michie, 2010a), the high degree of uncertainty associated with any probability estimates concerning individuals (Altman & Royston, 2000; Cooke & Michie, 2010b; Hart & Cooke, 2013; Hart, Michie, & Cooke, 2007a), the problem of field-reliability (Murrie et al., 2009) and the reference class problem, including, but not limited to, the selection of appropriate comparison samples (Hajek, 2007; Sreenivasan, Wienberger, Frances, & Cusworth-Walker, 2010). Further limitations, as noted by Barnett, Wakeling, and Howard (2010), are that actuarial tools can neither be used to capture individually relevant risk factors nor can they be used to individualise treatment plans. Despite these problems these approaches continue to be supported, authorised and, indeed, mandated by government agencies across the world.

A third approach has evolved in response to the fundamental limitations of the actuarial approach; this has been described as the structured professional judgement (SPJ) approach. SPJ approaches require the assessor to consider a number of risk factors known to be associated with violence risk from empirical research and systematic clinical practice (Douglas, Hart, Webster, & Belfrage, 2013; Otto & Douglas, 2010). Information about risk factors has to be gathered through interview, document review and formal testing. If risk factors are found to be present, the assessor has to determine whether they are relevant to future violent offending; relevant either because they are in some sense causally linked to future violence in this particular case, or because they may adversely affect any risk management strategy that might be put in place (Cooke, 2010b; Hart et al., 2003). The assessor is required to formulate an account of why the individual may be at risk of violence, consider what form that violence might take, and finally, the assessor should describe strategies for countering the perceived hazard. The process of formulating an opinion, therefore, is not a matter of merely adding up the number of risk factors present, it is a complex process. This approach is best exemplified by procedures such as the Risk for Sexual Violence Protocol (RSVP; Hart et al., 2003) and the HCR-20 (Douglas et al., 2013).

In this chapter I will consider the additional problems inherent in the use of ARAI approaches to risk assessment. I will start by considering the nature of the challenge confronting the risk assessor; I will then provide new empirical evidence that highlights the frailty of the approach. Finally, I will then consider the conceptual assumptions underpinning actuarial models.

The challenge of violence risk assessment

The area of risk assessment has become complex, the literature has the appearance of conceptual and statistical sophistication; arcane statistics and arcane discussion about probability theory abound. However, going back to basics, what is the risk assessor actually trying to achieve? In essence, the role of the assessor is to inform decision makers, in a court, parole hearing or other tribunal, about

78   *D.J. Cooke*

whether the person who is the focus of the report poses a risk of violence to another. The risk assessor should provide useful, valid, ethically sound information that is probative, and not prejudicial, in order that the decision maker can make principled and informed decisions (Cooke, 2010a). More nuanced approaches to risk assessment would require the assessor to characterise the nature of the risk posed – its likelihood, its form, its likely severity, imminence, frequency, whether it is enactable – and critically, what steps that could be taken to obviate any risk.

Clearly such an enterprise is not straightforward; this has long been appreciated. In his seminal paper Scott (1977) characterised the challenge faced by the risk assessor:

> Prediction of dangerousness is particularly difficult because: dangerousness is the resultant of a number of processes which occasionally may be synergistic amounting to more than the sum of their parts, some within the individual and some in society; it is not static; key factors are the individual's adaptiveness, resistance to change, and his intentions (which Emile Durkheim said in 1897 is "too intimate a thing to be interpreted by another person"): a common mistake is to confuse recidivism with dangerousness, they are not necessarily the same and may be combined in various patterns.
>
> (p. 128)

Let us consider the actuarial paradigm and whether it can serve to meet the challenge so eloquently expressed by Scott. The actuarial paradigm is *apparently* straightforward; procedures are developed to predict the future. A group of offenders, usually prisoners, is assessed, often in terms of features that are easy to assess or which are readily available in institutional files (e.g. age, marital status, criminal history variables, type of victims). These features may be selected empirically (i.e. on their association with the likelihood of reoffending) or rationally (i.e. on the basis of experience or theory). The items are combined using some algorithm (usually the sum of scores) and this algorithm is used to make a prediction about a new case. The score achieved by the new case is compared with a sample of offenders – the normative group – and the inference is made that the likelihood of reoffending for the new case will be the same as that for the normative group with which he is compared. By a process of analogue it is argued that this man resembles offenders in the high-risk group, therefore he *is* likely to reoffend at a level similar to the comparison group (Hart, 2009).

As in many walks of life the most dangerous assumptions are the unrecognised ones. Before considering these assumptions in some detail, I will first examine the empirical basis of one ARAI – the RM2000. I will demonstrate that it is important that independent researchers evaluate the data used to support the utility of these tests. This has been recognised by courts; for example, the use of the STATIC-99 in a Sexual Violent Predator hearing was ruled inadmissible due to the developers' refusal to share their underlying data with defence experts (*State of Wisconsin* v. *Homer L. Perren Jr.*, La Crosse County 2010-CI000003).

The empirical basis or violence: the case of the Risk Matrix 2000

The Risk Matrix 2000 (RM2000) is an ARAI that is widely used within criminal-justice settings in the United Kingdom; it is used to underpin expert advice to courts and other tribunals about whether an offender will reoffend or not; the focus is on sexual violence although there is a version of the RM2000 that considers non-sexual violence (Craig & Beech, 2009; Grubin, 2011). Barnett et al. (2010) published a study based on a very large and representative sample of offenders in England and Wales. They argued that their analysis demonstrated the robustness of the RM2000 for making predictions about offenders.

Barnett et al. (2010) argued for the empirical validity of actuarial tools such as the RM2000 because they "code factors that research has *reliably* linked to risk of reoffending to produce a score that indicates the probability of reconviction for a certain type of offense over a specified time period" (p. 444; emphases added). Other proponents of ARAIs, for example, Craig and Beech (2009), make similar claims stating that risk factors are selected because they have been "found to be *correlated highly* with sexual recidivism" (p. 194, emphases added). These are clearly strong claims; do the data support the claims? I sought and gained access to these data in order to evaluate the claims.

As noted above the RM2000 comes in two forms; here, I will focus on the most commonly used version, that which considers sexual reconvictions (RM2000S). The total RM2000S score is estimated in two steps. On the first step three risk factors are considered: *age of offender on release, number of sentencing occasions for a sexual offence* and *number of sentencing occasions for any criminal offence*. On the basis of this step offenders are allocated to one of four preliminary risk levels; namely, *Low, Medium, High* or *Very High*. On the second step four *aggravating* factors are considered; namely, *any male victim of sexual crime, any stranger victim of sexual crime, single (i.e. never in a stable live-in relationship for two years or more)* and *non-contact sex offence*. The preliminary risk level is modified on the basis of the presence of aggravating factors. The presence of two or three aggravating factors results in a risk level one higher than that previously given (e.g. *Medium* becomes *High*); the presence of all four aggravating factors results in a risk level two higher than previously given (e.g. *Medium* becomes *Very High*). A *Very High Risk* level, for example, may be reported as predicting that the offender has a 59% likelihood of reoffending in the next 15 years.

Is this empirically justifiable and defensible; are the results for the RM2000 robust? Barnett et al. (2010) based their conclusion on total RM2000 scores and reoffending rates; unfortunately, they failed to test the underlying statistical model underpinning the RM2000, that is, they failed to test whether the risk factors were in fact associated, either "reliably" or "highly", with outcome.

We (Cooke & Michie, 2014) were interested in two broad questions, first, whether each risk factor was associated with recorded recidivism either individually, or in combination, and second, whether the total score could provide any

80   D.J. Cooke

useful information about the key question the RM2000S claims to answer: will this particular offender reoffend sexually in the next 15 years?

RM2000 risk factors and recidivism

The Barnett et al. (2010) sample was large ($N=4,946$). As a consequence of the inherent statistical power any differences – even tiny differences – between recidivists and non-recidivists should have been readily detectable. We started by carrying out simple univariate analyses to determine whether each of the risk factors was independently associated with recidivism. Neither *age* nor having a *male victim of any sexual offence* demonstrated a statistically significant association with the outcome of sexual reoffending in the two-year follow-up period (see Table 5.1). So in this very large sample, in which it would be expected that even small effects should be detectable, only five of the seven risk factors were associated with the outcome, and indeed, having never been in a marital type relationship was just significant at the 5% level, and had a weak effect (odds ratio = 1.56). Of course, unsurprisingly, many of the RM2000S risk factors are correlated with each other, and therefore, simple univariate analyses overestimate the amount of information available; variance is shared. To model the relationships amongst the risk factors we carried out logistic regression analysis designed to mimic the two-step scoring process that is at the core of the RM2000S. First, we entered the three risk factors as a block; second we entered the four aggravating factors as a block. Only four of the seven factors fitted the final model (i.e. *age, number of sexual appearances, stranger victim* and *non-contact sex offence*) (see Table 5.2). Good model fit was achieved but the variance explained by the model was very low (Pseudo R^2 estimated between 0.013 and 0.068). Comparison of Tables 5.1 and 5.2 reveals that two factors that were

Table 5.1 Univariate associations between risk and aggravating factors and proven sexual reoffending in a two-year follow-up period for the RM2000S***

Variable	Barnett et al. (2010) X^2	Grubin (2011) X^2	d.f.
Step one: Risk Factors			
Age	2.41^{NS}	8.06*	2
Sexual Appearances (In court for sentencing)	76.8***	63.33***	3
Criminal Appearances (In court for sentencing)	12.43***	13.73***	1
Step two: Aggravating Factors			
Male Victim of Sexual Offence	0.02^{NS}	2.97^{NS}	1
Stranger Victim of Sexual Offence	16.60***	15.68***	1
Single (Never in Marital Type Relationship)	4.06*	0.76^{NS}	1
Non-Contact Sex Offence	34.78***	40.38***	1

Notes
* $p<0.05$;
*** $p<0.001$.

Violence risk: the actuarial illusion 81

Table 5.2 Final two-stage logistic regression model of risk and aggravating factors and proven sexual reoffending in a two-year follow-up period for the RM2000S***

Risk or aggravating factor	B	S.E.	Wald	d.f.	Exp(B)
Age	0.324***	0.135	5.79	1	1.38
Sexual Appearances	0.565***	0.106	28.47	1	1.76
Criminal Appearances					
Male Victim					
Stranger Victim	0.416*	0.207	4.04	1	1.52
Single					
Non-Contact Sex Offence	0.766***	0.213	12.89	1	2.15

Notes
* $p<0.05$;
** $p<0.01$;
*** $p<0.001$.

significant on univariate analyses were not significant in the logistic analysis, i.e. *number of criminal appearances* and *single (never married)*; also *age*, which was non-significant in the univariate analyses, was significant in the logistic analysis. This is not hard to understand. When age is entered on the first step it absorbs the variance associated with *number of criminal appearances* and *single (never married)* because being older provides more opportunities for both types of behaviour, i.e. criminal behaviour and getting married.

Were these poor findings the result of one poor study? Since publishing Cooke and Michie (2014) we have analysed another large and important RM2000S database. Grubin (2011) examined the performance of the RM2000S in a large cohort of Scottish prisoners convicted of a sexual offence and with a five-year follow-up period. This study has been used to support the use of the RM2000S throughout the criminal justice system in Scotland. Grubin's (2011) intent was to determine whether prior findings in England and Wales could generalise to another jurisdiction with a distinct legal code, i.e. Scotland. We carried out similar analyses to those above (Cooke & Michie, in prep) and our broad conclusions were the same, i.e. the risk factors and aggravating factors do not perform in the same manner as those in the developmental sample. Examination of Table 5.1 illustrates that once again only five out of the seven univariate comparisons demonstrated statistically significant relationships with outcome, i.e. recidivism. Of particular note, in this large sample different risk factors failed to show univariate associations with recidivism; *age* was significantly related but *being single* was not. As in the previous study having a *male victim of a sexual offence* was not associated with future recidivism. When logistic analysis was carried out to parallel the analysis of the previous data set, only three of the seven factors fitted the model, i.e. *age, sexual appearances* and *non-contact sex offence*. Once again good model fit was achieved but the variance explained by the model was very low (Pseudo R^2 estimated between 0.0.057 and 0.117).

Thus it would appear that when the appropriate analyses are carried out on large data sets the component factors of the RM2000 can be shown to have

82 D.J. Cooke

unreliable, weak or non-existent relationships with the outcome of concern – sexual recidivism. Clearly they are not as *reliably* or *correlated highly* with the outcome as the proponents of ARAIs claim (Barnett et al., 2010; Craig & Beech, 2009). In essence, only three variables are reliably related to recidivism in these studies, i.e. *age, sexual appearances* and *non-contact sex-offence*. If you are young and have committed sexual offences before then you have a somewhat increased likelihood of reoffending sexually in the future. It might well be asked: where is the psychological science in that finding? And critically, how useful is that finding when it comes to the single case?

Information about groups and information about individuals

At the heart of forensic practice are questions about the individual; should this man be given a preventative sentence, should he be released on parole, is he of sufficient risk to merit a place on a treatment programme? In recent years considerable debate has focused on whether accurate predictions can be achieved (Cooke & Michie, 2010b, 2012, 2014; Hanson & Howard, 2010; Hart & Cooke, 2013; Hart et al., 2007a; Skeem & Monahan, 2011). To some extent this debate has focused on arcane statistics; understandably this has resulted in many practitioners ignoring these arguments as being too complex or too far outside their knowledge base. This problem of confusion amongst practitioners has been described in other fields, e.g. medicine. Gigerenzer, Gaissmaier, Kurz-Milcke, Schwartz, and Woloshin (2008) argued that when single-event probabilities are being considered the most transparent method for presenting their precision – and hence their probative value – is the use of natural frequencies. These are just numbers and not arcane statistics; their interpretation is straightforward. Let us apply this method.

Data from the RM2000S study of Barnett et al. (2010) are displayed in Figure 5.1. This information informs us about the precision with which it is possible to predict that an individual will have a proven sex offence in the two-year

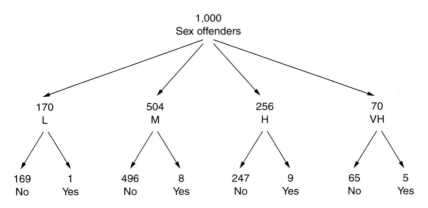

Figure 5.1 Natural frequency diagram of reoffending by RM2000S risk category data from Barnett et al. (2010).

Violence risk: the actuarial illusion 83

follow-up period. Following Gigerenzer (2002, p. 81 et seq.), for the ease of interpretation, the data are first standardised to 1,000 offenders. First, it will be observed that that the vast majority of offenders (977) do not reoffend in the follow-up period. Second, it will be observed that even in the *Very High* risk group the vast majority – 92.9% (65/70) – do not reoffend. Put bluntly, using this instrument, your prediction that an offender who is placed in the *Very High* risk group will offend would be incorrect 93% of the time: put another way you would need to lock up 14 (70/5) *Very High* risk prisoners to stop 1 reoffending. It will be observed that the imprecision is even greater when the *High Risk* or *Medium Risk* groups are considered.

When Gigerenzer's prescription is applied to the presentation of data it is self-evident that uncertainty abounds when it comes to predicting what any one individual will do. Should we be surprised? As is often the case in psychology the lessons of the past are forgotten. Allport (1940), in his presidential address to the American Psychological Association, pointed out the fallacious reasoning underpinning the actuarial approach to the individual.

> We find that 72 per cent of the men with John's antecedents make good, and many of us conclude that John, therefore, has a *72 per cent* chance of making good. There is an obvious error here. The fact that *72 per cent* of the men having the same antecedent record as John will make good is merely an actuarial statement. It tells us nothing about John.
>
> (Allport, 1940, pp. 16–17, original emphases)

Why is our interpretation of these two studies (i.e. Barnett et al., 2010; Grubin, 2011) so different from those of the authors (Cooke & Michie, 2014, in prep)? There are perhaps four reasons.

First, the authors of the two studies assumed – but did not evaluate – whether the RM2000S items were associated with recidivism in their samples. The original data on which the RM2000S was developed were collected on a sample of male sexual offenders released from prison in 1979. Changes in criminal justice practice, patterns of offending and societal mores mean that it is likely that the samples of Barnett et al. (2010) and Grubin (2011) will be rather different to the samples on which the RM2000S was developed.

Second, we were not surprised that the RM2000S items failed to predict for another more fundamental reason; the problems of model cross-validation and shrinkage. Cross-validation should be a fundamental feature of any statistical modelling: in essence it assesses whether the same patterns, and the same strength of relationships, emerge when the model is evaluated against another set of data. Cross-validation is a vital test of model utility because the original model will be optimised for the sample upon which it was developed; the model will inevitably do less well with new data. Gigerenzer and Brighton (2009) summarised the challenge: "achieving a good fit to observations does not necessarily mean we have found a good model, and choosing a model with the best fit is likely to result in poor predictions" (p. 118).

84   *D.J. Cooke*

Third, the authors of both studies based their judgements of the predictive validity of the RM2000S using an inappropriate statistic; the areas under the curve (AUC) of the receiver operator characteristic curve (ROC). The AUC can be defined as the probability that a randomly selected violent individual will be assessed as higher risk than a randomly selected non-violent individual by the scale under consideration (Swets, 1988). An AUC of 0.50 demonstrates that there is no relationship between the scale and outcome; values greater than 0.50 suggest a relationship. While the AUC statistic is popular amongst the adherents of ARAIs (e.g. Craig & Beech, 2009; Hanson, Helmus, & Thornton, 2010; Mossman, 1994) it is fundamentally uninformative for decisions about individuals (Cooke & Michie, 2014). A distinguished psychiatrist, and more importantly, two distinguished statisticians recently made the point trenchantly: "even a highly statistically significant AUC is of limited value in clinical practice" (Szmukler, Everitt, & Leese, 2012, p. 895).

It is perhaps unfortunate that the use of the AUC has become a statistical ritual (Cooke & Michie, 2014); such rituals are sanctioned by researchers, reviewers and editors and as Gigerenzer (2002) observed: "Their function is to make the final product, a significant result, appear highly informative, and thereby justify the rituals" (p. 594). Gigerenzer (2002) was referring to the inappropriate application of null hypothesis testing; however, the ritual of the ROC is a dangerous ritual in forensic practice because it can adversely affect judgements about offenders and their potential victims (Cooke & Michie, 2014).

Epidemiologists recognise two distinct applications of the AUC approach; diagnostic testing and prognostic modelling. The RM2000S is not a diagnostic test but rather it is concerned with prognosis, with claims that it can predict the likelihood that the offender will commit another sexual offence over the next 15 years. When the AUC is used to evaluate a diagnostic test the illness has already occurred but its presence is unknown to the clinician. When the AUC is used for a prognostic test the outcome has yet to occur and is thus unknown. The outcome is a stochastic process (i.e. not a deterministic process) and can thus only be expressed as a probability estimate. Cook (2007) showed that the AUC has little utility in the evaluation of a prognostic test because the AUC provides no indication of the probability that an individual will become a case (i.e. a recidivist); as the definition of the AUC (see above) indicates merely that the predicted risk for a case is higher than that for a non-case. Proponents of ARAI do not appear to appreciate, or perhaps they do not admit, that the maximum AUC of 1.00 could be achieved, if for example, the test predicted a reconviction rate of 0.45 for all cases and a rate of 0.44 for all non-cases. Such a difference would be irrelevant in, for example, decisions about release. Because the AUC is founded upon ranks, the magnitude of the AUC is influenced equally by trivial differences between two very low risk individuals (e.g. a 0.30% likelihood cf. a 0.31% likelihood) as between a *Medium Risk* and *High Risk* individual (e.g. 8% compared with 33%; RM2000S risk groups). Clearly separating the latter two individuals is more important that the former two but the size of the AUC cannot provide any useful information; it is absolute risk that is relevant not relative risk (Cook,

2007). The failure of Barnett et al. (2010) and Grubin (2011) to discover that the RM2000 model did not cross-validate may be attributed to an overdependence on the AUC statistic, a statistic which, although it has achieved totemic status amongst adherents of the ARAI approach, cannot provide useful information about the point probability for an individual offender.

Fourth, there appears to be a pervasive tendency, for whatever reason, to overstate the utility of the RM2000 and similar tools. For example, Barnett et al. (2010) stated: "The present study found the RM2000v scale to have very good accuracy as a predictor or relative risk of violent reoffending in this large sample of sexual offenders" (p. 468) and again "The odds of proven sexual offending over 2 years increased by 160% for those in the RM2000/s medium risk category compared with those in the low-risk category" (p. 455). This tendency to overstate is founded in part on the misinterpretation of the magnitude and relevance of AUC (Cooke & Michie, 2014) but is also underpinned by reliance – as illustrated in the two quotes above – on relative statements. When determining questions of release the key question must be the absolute risk that an individual might pose of future offending, not his risk relative to another offender. This use of relative statements is a common problem in other fields, for example, in the description of the efficacy of medication. Rather trenchantly, Gigerenzer and Gray (2001) indicated: "Framing benefits in terms of *relative risk* (20%) is a common way to mislead the public without actually lying" (p. 6, emphases added). A 50% reduction in mortality from 200 to 100 per 10,000 would be of greater interest than a reduction from 2 to 1 per 10,000.

Once again Gigerenzer's prescription of applying natural frequencies can cast light on the credibility and utility of such claims. Barnett et al.'s (2010) claim of a 160% increase in the odds of risk sounds impressive. However, it becomes less persuasive when it is considered that the claim is based on a rate of 6 per 1,000 in the *Low Risk* group compared with 16 per 1,000 in the *Medium Risk* group; in other words 994 in the *Low Risk* group do not reoffend compared with 984 in the *Medium Risk*; there is no meaningful way of distinguishing reoffenders from non-reoffenders so this is a claim of no practical utility. Barnett et al.'s (2010) claims that increased odds of 400% and almost increased odds of 300% for the RM2000V and the combination of the RM2000S and RM2000V have similar credibility. Indeed, using their data it is possible to demonstrate that the RM2000S can achieve 98% accuracy; this is achieved merely by predicting that everyone will fail to reoffend (i.e. 977/1,000, Figure 5.1).

In summary, studying data from these large studies can illustrate many of the ills that ARAIs are prone to suffer from. The proponents of the ARAI method failed to check whether the risk factors are associated with the outcomes of concern, they used statistics that cannot answer the key question about whether tests can provide useful and valid predictions for individual offenders, and finally, there is a pervasive tendency to upgrade evidence in attempts to prove the utility of the tests.

Thinking psychologically not statistically

Should we be surprised by these poor results? I would suggest not. First, consider the range of behaviour that the actuarialists are trying to predict; anything from viewing pornographic images on a screen, to the exposure of a private member, through child abuse to rape, or even sexual homicide. Even if only one legal category is considered – rape – the psychological processes underpinning that crime are diverse and complex. Second, consider the non-specific nature of the risk factors included in the RM2000S and cognate ARAIs; these variables are a long way from the causal nexus linking risk processes to sexual offending (Cooke, 2010b). This lack of saliency is unsurprising because these variables were chosen, not for their relevance to sexual offending, but rather because they were easily available in prison files.

The uncertain conceptual basis of the ARAI approach

The ills of the ARAI approach go far beyond empirical inadequacy; they are based on a faulty conception of the problem. Wittgenstein (1958) observed that in psychology "the existence of the experimental method makes us think we have the means of solving the problems which trouble us; though problem and method pass one another by" (p. 243). The literature on actuarial risk assessment is a clear example of this mismatch between method and problem. As Cohen (1990) observed, psychologists can become mesmerised by apparently "'objective' rituals in which we convert numbers into other numbers and get a yes-no answer, we have come to neglect close scrutiny of where the numbers came from" (p. 1310).

The violence risk assessment literature is replete with arcane discussions about probability theory; can point predictions be made with accuracy, should we use subjectivist or frequentist definitions of probability, will Bayesian methods reveal the true value of our approaches? Regrettably, while of intellectual interest these issues and approaches do not really assist us in the task at hand. Such a view may seem heretical to many in the risk assessment business. Clearly, probability theory has an important place in science but not necessarily in assessing the risk that an individual poses. As Gigerenzer (2014) indicates: "Probability theory provides the best answers only when the rules of the game are certain, when all alternatives, consequences, and probabilities are known or can be calculated" (p. 128). This is not the case with violence risk assessment. Games – dice, selecting balls from urns, roulette, even the Russian variant – do not provide appropriate analogues for risk assessment. Such thinking has been described as the *Ludic Fallacy* (Taleb, 2010): that is, the making of a false parallel between real-world risks with unknown outcomes and games of chance which are constructed to have known outcomes. Why is that the case? Scott (1977) makes clear that the processes underpinning risk assessment are complex, interactive, multiplicative, indeed, risk can be considered to be an emergent construct; that is, it is more than the sum of the underlying risk factors

Violence risk: the actuarial illusion 87

and not irreducible to the level of the risk factors. Even if strong risk factors could be identified for sexual offending (which despite the claims to the contrary is not the case), how they interact in any one individual – and in his particular circumstances – cannot be modelled using simple linear models of the type used to underpin ARAI. This problem has been recognised in other fields:

> The inherent complexity of biological (e.g., Noble, 2008) and economic (e.g., Beinhocker, 2006) systems show that they are not adequately described by deterministic or traditional probabilistic models. Yet the siren call of models is seductive and too easily they take on the status of false gods.
>
> (Taylor, 2011, p. 445)

There is a growing awareness in psychology that dominant empirical paradigms such as between-subject models (e.g. measures of individual differences) cannot test or support causal accounts (e.g. pertaining to violence) that are valid at the individual level (Borsboom, Mellenbergh, & van Heeran, 2003; Cooke & Michie, 2010a; Richters, 1997). With a between-subjects design it is possible to argue legitimately that within population differences in the prevalence of personality disorder, or the mean level of psychopathy as measured by, for example, the PCL-R (Hare, 1991), can account for differences in population variations in violent reoffending. However, this position cannot be defended at the level of the individual; this is because there is an unspoken – and unmerited – assumption that the mechanisms that operate at the level of the individual also explain variations *amongst* individuals. Richters (1997) clarified the fundamental nature of this problem:

> The extraordinary human capacity for equifinal and multifinal functioning, however, renders the structural homogeneity assumption untenable. Very similar patterns of overt functioning may be caused by qualitatively differing underlying structures both within the same individual at different points in time, and across different individuals at the same time (equi-finality). Conversely, different patterns of overt functioning may stem from very similar processes within the same individual over time, and across different individuals at the same time (multi-finality).
>
> (pp. 206–207)

Individuals are violent for different reasons: any one individual may be violent for different reasons on different occasions (Cooke, 2010b).

Let us consider how this might apply to sexual offending. Take one form of sexual offending, the viewing of images of abuse. Not unsurprisingly the primary function of such behaviour is to facilitate sexual arousal; images are frequently used to enhance masturbatory fantasies. This may be one stage in behavioural try-outs that ultimately lead to offending (MacCulloch, Snowden, Wood, &

88 *D.J. Cooke*

Mills, 1983). However, images of abuse may play other roles; they are used as collectibles with the collector deriving satisfaction from having a complete collection, or they may be used for trading, to establish on-line relationships and to gain status within the on-line community (Quayle, 2008; Wolak, Finkelhor, Mitchell, & Ybarra, 2008). This would be a form of equi-final behaviour; viewing images of abuse being driven by a range of different psychological processes. Similarly, multi-finality is likely to play a role in sexual offending. For example, having deviant sexual fantasies might result in different patterns of behaviour from reading pornographic literature, to viewing pornographic videos, through engaging in simulations with consenting partners to engaging in a contact sex offence with a non-consenting victim.

The unspoken assumption of the actuarial approach is that one process underpins sexual offending – there is structural homogeneity in the functioning of individuals in the sample – and that this is summarised by the constructing of a hypothetical individual who represents this process (Richter, 1997). This approach cannot work if members of the sample do not share the same process, if different structures and processes result in sexual offending then the model cannot work effectively. In the case of sexual offending the causal processes are complex, interacting and often unknown, and unknowable.

It is perhaps even more complex than that. Scott emphasises the interactive quality of risk; risk processes may interact with each other in complex, including synergistic, ways; risk processes centred in the individual may interact with situational or contextual factors; risk processes are not static but may evolve, increase or decline with time. Writing in the journal *Forecasting and Futurism*, Mills (2009) summed up the challenges created by complex systems:

> The key point about complex adaptive systems is that their behavior is not forecastable over more than a short time horizon. For example, we cannot forecast weather for more than 14 days, or even the trajectories of billiard balls on a table.... Even less can we forecast complex social systems where the vagaries of human desire are involved.
>
> (p. 27)

The pervasive practice of actuarial assessment

There can be little doubt that in the field of sexual offender assessment the use of ARAIs has become pervasive. They can impact important decisions. For example, in Scotland the application of the RM2000 has been approved by the Appeal Court:

> The Risk Matrix 2000 assessment tool is regularly and widely used for the purposes of assessing the risk presented by an offender to the public.... In our view she [the trial judge] was entitled to proceed upon the basis of the outcome of the risk assessment carried out using Risk Matrix 2000.
>
> (*HMA* v. *Thomas Russell Currie* [2008] HCJAC 67)

Violence risk: the actuarial illusion 89

So why have methods such as the RM2000 become so widely accepted? There are perhaps five reasons. First, in our increasingly risk aversive times, bureaucratic systems require risk assessment procedures to be in place; in my own experience these procedures are more to do with managing corporate risk than with effectively identifying the risk that individual patients pose to themselves or others.

Second, actuarial tools are cheap to implement; many staff can be trained quickly. Third, on the surface the actuarial approach has face validity. But this, as we have seen, is an illusion. The use of the term actuarial is misleading; it smacks of science and mathematics. The ARAIs are presented as being based on data and "science" and thus they are ascribed credibility.

Fourth, and related to the above, is the fact highlighted by commentators such as Ben Goldacre (2010) that one of the problems is that many of the decision makers are arts graduates who do not necessarily have a firm grasp of numerical reasoning, so they are thereby unable to properly evaluate the utility of ARAIs.

Fifth, in some cases there is a lack of independence – one of the tenets of science is that results should be subject to external review. Many of these tests have not been subject to proper peer review – requests for data for reanalysis are frequently turned down. It is concerning that access to raw data for legitimate reanalysis appears to be a problem in this field (e.g. Waggoner, Wollert, & Cramer, 2008). There are vested interests – not necessarily financial – in selling these procedures. Conflicts of interest can result in information being presented in non-transparent ways: such interests could range from the financial (Poythress & Petrila, 2010) through to the championing of a particular ideology by organisations endeavouring to be cost efficient. This championing may not be founded on any malicious intent but rather on ignorance; this is a common problem in the risk arena well summarised by Taleb (2010):

> The problem with experts is that they do not know what they do not know. Lack of knowledge and delusion about the quality of your knowledge come together – the same process that makes you know less makes you satisfied with your knowledge.
>
> (p. 147)

This chapter should not be read as an assault on research on the nature and relevance of risk factors to future violence. Nomothetic information is a fundamental anchor in the turbulent sea of violence risk management. However, the ultimate problem in violence risk assessment is idiographic: It is only the understanding of the unique and particular ways in which the risk factors – both psychological and contextual – are presented in real people that is ultimately of value. Fortunately, psychology is not constrained by one paradigm but has access to many paradigms and can choose an appropriate paradigm to match the problem. These paradigms would include clinical formulation, case-study methodology and structured professional judgement methods (e.g. Butler, 1998; Miller & Waller, 2003; Otto & Douglas, 2010; Richters, 1997; Yin, 2003). All these paradigms have developed methods for bringing nomothetic information to bear on the task of

90 *D.J. Cooke*

understanding the individual. They provide criteria for evaluating the quality of the inferences being made regarding individuals; these are not necessarily statistical criteria but rather qualitative criteria, and unsurprisingly there is consistency across paradigms in terms of these criteria. Richters (1997), from the perspective of developmental psychologist, observed: "In general judgments made at the individual level must be evaluated by qualitative criteria such as coherence, explanatory power and the ability to account for facts that are otherwise difficult to explain" (pp. 224–225). In a similar vein, discussing SPJ approaches to violence risk management, Hart (2009) argued that the plausibility of any explanation – formulation – of a case should be judged "to the extent it coheres with the fact of the case, common sense views of the world, and (where applicable) scientific research and theory" (p. 170). This strikes me as a more honest and transparent approach than the pretence that a simple algorithm, containing a few non-specific risk factors, can provide useful information regarding the likely behaviour of an individual.

In conclusion, psychology appears, at times, to forget the lessons of history (Allport, 1940; Richters, 1997) Trying to ape the physical sciences, by adopting the Humean principles of causation and reductionism around the time that those sciences were rejecting such approaches and embracing uncertainty, resulted in the values of idiographic approaches being forgotten (Allport, 1940; Peat, 2002). For some problems – and I would suggest violence risk management is one – we need to embrace methods that let us grasp the uncertainties inherent in complex emergent concepts such as violence risk. The problem of predicting the behaviour of individuals has been long known. The famous Belgian statistician Quetelet published many papers on the description of society, and indeed he was the first to describe the age-crime curve, one of the fundamental findings of criminology (Blonigen, 2010). Quetelet introduced the concept of "l'homme moyen" – the average man – but knew he did not exist; it was merely a hypothetical construct. As Siegfried (2006) observed:

> Quetelet also repeatedly emphasized that the statistical approach could not be used to draw conclusions about any given individual (another principle that is often forgotten by today's media philosophers). The insurance company's mortality tables cannot forecast the time of any one person's death, for instance.
>
> (p. 134)

It is regrettable that when violence risk is considered this insight from the nineteenth century appears to have been lost and replaced by the actuarial illusion.

References

Allport, G. (1940). The psychologist's frame of reference. *Psychological Bulletin, 37*, 1–28.

Altman, D. G., & Royston, P. (2000). What do we mean by validating a prognostic model? *Statistics in Medicine, 19*, 453–473.

Barnett, G. D., Wakeling, H. C., & Howard, P. D. (2010). An examination of the predictive validity of the Risk Matrix 2000 in England and Wales. *Sexual Abuse: A Journal of Research and Treatment*, 22, 443–470.

Blonigen, D. M. (2010). Explaining the relationship between age and crime: Contributions from the developmental literature on personality. *Clinical Psychology Review, 30*, 89–100.

Borsboom, D., Mellenbergh, G. J., & Van Heerden, J. (2003). The theoretical status of latent variables. *Psychological Review, 110*(2), 203.

Butler, G. (1998). Clinical formulation. In A. S. Bellack & M. E. Hersen (eds), *Comprehensive Clinical Psychology* (pp. 1–23). New York: Pergammon Press. (Reprinted from: IN FILE).

Cohen, J. (1990). Things I have learned (so far). *American Psychologist, 45*(12), 1304.

Cook, N. (2007). Use and misuse of the Receiver Operating Characteristic curve in risk prediction. *Circulation, 115*, 928–935.

Cooke, D. J. (2010a). More prejudicial than probative. *The Journal of the Law Society of Scotland, 55*(1), 20–23.

Cooke, D. J. (2010b). Personality disorder and violence: Understand violence risk: An introduction to the special section personality disorder and violence. *Journal of Personality Disorders, 24*(5), 539–550.

Cooke, D. J., & Michie, C. (2010a) Limitations of diagnostic precision and predictive utility in the individual case: A challenge for forensic practice. *Law and Human Behavior*, 34, 259–274.

Cooke, D. J., & Michie, C. (2010b). Violence risk assessment: Challenging the illusion of certainty. In B. McSherry & P. Keyser (eds), *Managing high-risk offenders: Policy and practice*. London: Routledge.

Cooke, D. J., & Michie, C. (2012). Violence risk assessment: From prediction to understanding, from what? to why? In C. Logan & E. Johnstone (eds), *Managing clinical risk: A guide to effective practice*. New York: Routledge.

Cooke, D. J., & Michie, C. (2014). The generalizability of the Risk Matrix 2000: On model shrinkage and the misinterpretation of the area under the curve. *Journal of Threat Assessment and Management, 1*(1), 42–55.

Craig, L., & Beech, A. R. (2009). Best practice in conducting actuarial risk assessments with adult sexual offenders. *Journal of Sexual Aggression, 15*(2), 193–211.

Douglas, K. S., Hart, S. D., Webster, C. D., & Belfrage, H. (2013). *HCR-20v3: Assessing risk for violence*. Burnaby, BC: Simon Fraser University.

Gigerenzer, G. (2002). *Reckoning with risk: Learning to live with uncertainty*. London: Penguin.

Gigerenzer, G. (2014). *Risk savvy: How to make good decisions*. London: Penguin.

Gigerenzer, G., & Brighton, H. (2009). Homo heuristicus: Why biased minds make better inferences. *Topics in Cognitive Science, 1*(1), 107–143.

Gigerenzer, G., Gaissmaier, W., Kurz-Milcke, E., Schwartz, L. M., & Woloshin, S. (2008). Helping doctors and patients make sense of health statistics. *Psychological Science in the Public Interest, 8*(2), 53–96.

Gigerenzer, G., & Gray, J. A. M. (2011). *Better doctors, better patients, better decisions: Envisioning health care 2020*: Cambridge, MA: MIT Press.

Goldacre, B. (2010). *Bad science: Quacks, hacks, and big pharma flacks*. London: McClelland & Stewart.

Grubin, D. (2011). A large-scale evaluation of Risk Matrix 2000 in Scotland. *Sexual Abuse: A Journal of Research and Treatment, 23*(4), 419–433.

92 D.J. Cooke

Hajek, A. (2007). The reference class problem is your problem too. *Synthese, 156*(3), 563–585.

Hanson, R. K., Helmus, L., & Thornton, D. (2010). Predicting recidivism amongst sexual offenders: A multi-site study of Static-2002. *Law and Human Behavior, 34*, 198–211.

Hanson, R. K., & Howard, P. D. (2010). Individual confidence intervals do not inform decision makers about the accuracy of risk assessment evaluations. *Law and Human Behavior, 34*, 275–281.

Hare, R. D. (1991). *The Hare Psychopathy Checklist – Revised.* Toronto, Ontario: Multi-Health Systems.

Hart, S. (2009). Evidence-based assessment of risk for sexual violence. *Chapman Journal of Criminal Justice, 1*, 143–165.

Hart, S. D., & Cooke, D. J. (2013) Another look at the (im-)precision of individual estimates made using actuarial risk assessment instruments. *Behavioral Sciences and the Law, 31*, 81–102.

Hart, S. D., Kropp, P. R., Laws, R., Klaver, J., Logan, C., & Watt, K. A. (2003). *The risk of sexual violence protocol (RSVP).* Burnaby, BC: Mental Health, Law, and Policy Institute, Simon Fraser University.

Hart, S. D., Michie, C., & Cooke, D. J. (2007a). Precision of actuarial risk assessment instruments: Evaluating the "margins of error" of group v. individual predictions of violence. *British Journal of Psychiatry, 190*, s60–s65.

Hart, S. D., Michie, C., & Cooke, D. J. (2007b). Authors' reply: Margins of error for individual risk estimates: Large, unknown, or incalculable [Letter]. *British Journal of Psychiatry, 191*, 561–562.

Khiroya, R., Weaver, T., & Maden, A. (2009). Use and perceived utility of structured violence risk assessments in English medium secure forensic units. *The Psychiatrist, 33*, 129–132.

MacCulloch, M., Snowden, P., Wood, P., & Mills, H. (1983). Sadistic fantasy, sadistic behaviour and offending. *The British Journal of Psychiatry, 143*(1), 20–29.

Meehl, P. E. (1954). *Clinical versus statistical prediction: A theoretical analysis and a review of the evidence* (Vol. 1). Minneapolis: University of Minnesota Press.

Miller, K. D., & Waller, G. H. (2003). Scenarios, real options and integrated risk management. *Long Range Planning, 36*, 93–107.

Mills, A. (2009). Should actuaries get another job? *Forecasting and Futurism*, 1, 22–30.

Mossman, D. (1994). Assessing predictions of violence: Being accurate about accuracy. *Journal of Consulting and Clinical Psychology, 62*(4), 783–792.

Murrie, D. C., Boccaccini, M. T., Turner, D., Meeks, M., Woods, C., & Tussey, C. (2009). Rater (dis)agreement on risk assessment measures in sexually violent predator proceedings: Evidence of adversarial allegiance in forensic evaluation. *Psychology, Public Policy and Law, 15*(1), 19–53.

Otto, R. K., & Douglas, K. S. (2010). *Handbook of violence risk assessment.* New York: Routledge.

Peat, F. D. (2002). *From certainty to uncertainty: The story of science and ideas in the twentieth century.* Washington, D.C.: Joseph Henry Press.

Poythress, N., & Petrila, J. P. (2010). PCL-R psychopathy: Threats to sue, peer review, and potential implications for science and law. A commentary. *International Journal of Forensic Mental Health, 9*(1), 3–10.

Quayle, E. (2008). The COPINE Project. *Irish Probation Journal, 5*, 65–83.

Quinsey, V. L., Harris, G. T., Rice, M. E., & Cormier, C. A. (1998). *Violent offenders: Appraising and managing risk.* American Psychological Association: Washington, DC.

Richters, J. E. (1997). The Hubble hypothesis and the developmentalist's dilemma. *Development and Psychopathology, 9*, 193–229.

Scott, P. D. (1977). Assessing dangerousness in criminals. *British Journal of Psychiatry, 131*, 127–142.

Siegfried, T. (2006). *A beautiful math: John Nash, Game Theory, and the modern quest for a code of nature.* Washington, D.C.: National Academies Press.

Skeem, J. L., & Monahan, J. (2011). Current directions in violence risk assessment. *Current Directions in Psychological Science, 20*(1), 38–42.

Sreenivasan, S., Wienberger, L. E., Frances, A., & Cusworth-Walker, S. (2010). Alice in acturarial-land: Through the looking glass of changing Static-99 norms. *The Journal of the American Academy of Psychiatry and the Law, 38*, 400–406.

Swets, J. A. (1988). Measuring the accuracy of diagnostic systems. *Science, 240*, 1285–1293.

Szmukler, G., Everitt, B., & Leese, M. (2012). Risk assessment and receiver operating characteristic curves. *Psychological Medicine, 42*(5), 895–898.

Taleb, N. N. (2010). *The black swan: The impact of the highly improbable fragility.* New York: Random House.

Taylor, P. R. (2011). The mismeasure of risk. In S. Roeser, R. Hillerbrand, P. Sandin & M. Peterson (eds), *Handbook of risk theory: Epistemology, decision theory, ethics, and social implications of risk* (pp. 441–475). Dordrecht, Netherlands: Springer.

The State of California State Authorized Risk Assessment Tool for Sex Offenders Review Committee (2015). www.saratso.org/index.cfm?pid=467.

Waggoner, J., Wollert, R., & Cramer, E. (2008). A respecification of Hanson's updated Static-99 experience table that controls for the effect of age on sexual recidivism among young offenders. *Law, Probability and Risk, 7*, 305–312.

Wittgenstein, L. (1958). *Philosophical investigations.* Oxford: Blackwell.

Wolak, J., Finkelhor, D., Mitchell, K. J., & Ybarra, M. L. (2008). Online "predators" and their victims: Myths, realities, and implications for prevention and treatment. *American Psychologist, 63*, 111–128.

Yin, R. K. (2003). *Case study research: Design and methods* (Vol. 3). Thousand Oaks, CA: Sage.

6 The psychopath: continuity or change?

Stability of psychopathic traits and predictors of stability

Henriette Bergstrøm, Adelle E. Forth and David P. Farrington

Psychopathic traits in children and adolescents

It has been argued that a thorough understanding of psychopathy is central for criminal justice professionals and their practice (Hare, 1998), because of the construct's strong relationship with serious criminal behaviour (Leistico, Salekin, DeCoster, & Rogers, 2008; Salekin, Rogers, & Sewell, 1996). While only approximately 0.6%–2% of the general population (Coid, Yang, Ullrich, Roberts, & Hare, 2009; Neumann & Hare, 2008) and 10–25% of prison populations (Hare, 2003), reach the criteria of psychopathy, psychopaths are some of the most predatory and highest risk criminals in our society (Blais, Solodukhin, & Forth, 2014; Woodworth & Porter, 2002). In adults, psychopathy is most commonly conceptualized as a four factor construct consisting of interpersonal, affective, lifestyle, and antisocial traits (Hare, 2003). The manifestations and treatment amenability[1] of psychopathic traits are well established in adults (Cleckley, 1941; Cooke, Hart, Logan & Michie, 2012; Hare, 1998, 2003; McCord & McCord, 1964; Rice et al., 1992).

The downward extension of psychopathic traits to children and adolescents is however less clear (Seagrave & Grisso, 2002). To the extent that psychopathic traits are stable throughout life, it is important to identify children and adolescents' early maladjustment and to design efforts to prevent the development and persistence of psychopathic traits (Forth, Kosson, & Hare, 2003; Salekin, 2008). One of the most central criteria for the validity of the downward extension of psychopathic traits is their stability (Andershed, 2010; Salekin, 2008), as transiency would cast doubt on the value of the construct of psychopathy (Seagrave & Grisso, 2002). Until the past decade, little was empirically known about this stability (Andershed, 2010).

The degree of stability is also important from a developmental perspective on psychopathic traits. Two main personality perspectives have been suggested as theoretical frameworks for stability, the trait and the contextual models respectively (Andershed, 2010; Lynam, 2002). The former, endorsed by Andershed (2010), Caspi (2000) and Lynam (2002), stipulates that personality traits are biologically based, static constructs, with limited flexibility (Clark & Watson, 2010;

The psychopath: continuity or change? 95

McCrae & Costa, 2010; McCrae et al., 2000; Roberts et al., 2001). From the presumed biological, deterministic, nature of traits, it also follows that any change will take place at a group level parallelling physiological maturation (Clark & Watson, 2010; McCrae et al., 2000; Roberts et al., 2001).

The trait perspective is in accordance with much of the research on the etiology of psychopathic traits. Traditionally, psychopathic traits have been found to have significant biological and genetic correlates and markers (De Oliveira-Souza et al., 2008; Fowler et al., 2009; Hare, Frazelle, & Cox, 1978; Intrator et al., 1997; Jutai, Hare, & Connolly, 1987; Kiehl et al., 2001; Kiehl et al., 2004; Larsson, Andershed, & Lichtenstein, 2006; Levenston, Patrick, Bradley, & Lang, 2000; Patrick, Bradley, & Lang, 1993; Taylor, Loney, Bobadilla, Iacono, & McGue, 2003; Tikkanen et al., 2011; Verona et al., 2004). Therefore, it is not an unreasonable tenet that psychopathic traits would be similar (Lynam, 2002). However, there are multiple competing perspectives.

In particular, Andershed (2010) is more supportive of contextual influences on personality development (Lewis, 1999, 2001a, 2001b). The latter framework directly contradicts the trait perspective because of its theoretical reliance on the impact of social context and social factors in the formation, development, and presumed *in*stability of personality traits (Andershed, 2010; Lewis, 1999, 2001a, 2001b). Despite the previously mentioned biological correlates, there is now also emerging evidence suggesting the effect of a wide range of social factors on the emergence of psychopathic traits (Farrington & Bergstrøm, in press; Farrington, Ullrich, & Salekin, 2010). Both proposed perspectives will have implications for the development and stability of psychopathic traits (Andershed, 2010; Lynam, 2002), yet the literature does not clearly indicate which perspective receives the most support. This might be linked to the quality of the studies on stability, which are discussed below.

Stability of psychopathic traits across the lifespan

Rank-order stability

The most common approach to assessing stability is through rank-order stability (Andershed, 2010; Roberts et al., 2001), also known as *relative* stability (Lynam & Gudonis, 2005). This is a group-level measure, where an individual's relative place is compared to that of others in the sample or population (Lynam & Gudonis, 2005; Roberts et al., 2001). The following section will focus on the findings on rank-order stability from the available studies. Table 6.1 presents an overview of studies investigating the rank-order stability of psychopathic traits. It appears that the degree of rank-order stability differs somewhat according to the developmental period. Andershed (2010) suggested that rank-order stability estimates in excess of 0.70 indicate very high trait stability between two time points. Conversely, results below 0.30 indicate low stability. Rank-order correlations in the range 0.50–0.69 reflect high stability, while a result in the range 0.30–0.49 is considered to indicate moderate stability between two time points.

Table 6.1 Overview of longitudinal studies investigating rank-order stability of psychopathic traits

Developmental period and study	Age at first assessment	Length of follow-up	Measure	Stability
Childhood				
Barry, Barry, Deming, and Lochman (2008)	9–12	2 years	APSD	0.72–0.89 (ICC)
Dadds, Fraser, Frost, and Hawes (2005)	4–9	1 year	APSD	0.60–0.70 (r)
Frick, Kimonis, Dandreaux, and Farrell (2003)	8	4 years	APSD	0.87–0.93 (ICC)
Lynam et al. (2009)	7	11 years	CPS	0.56–0.74 (average r)
Obradovic, Pardini, Long, and Loeber (2007)	8	8 years	CBCL	0.27–0.84 (latent factor correlations)
Van Baardewijk, Vermeiren, Stegge, and Doreleijers (2011)	9–12	1.5 years	YPI-CV	0.59–0.76 (ICC)
Adolescence				
Blonigen, Hicks, Krueger, Patrick, and Iacono (2006)	17	7 years	MPQ	0.61–0.75 (r corrected for attenuation)
Forsman, Lichtenstein, Andershed, and Larsson (2008)	16	3 years	YPI	0.43–0.61 (r)
Loney, Taylor, Butler, and Iacono (2007)	16	6 years	MTI	0.40–0.41 (average ICCs)
Lynam, Caspi, Moffitt, Loeber, and Stouthamer-Loeber (2007)	13	11 years	CPS PCL:SV	0.31 (r)
Munoz & Frick (2007)	13	2 years	APSD	0.43–0.84
Salihovic, Özdemir, and Kerr (2014)	13	4 years	YPI	0.36–0.66 (r)
Adulthood				
Rutherford, Cacciola, Alterman, McKay, and Cook (1999)	N/A	2 years	PCL-R	0.60–0.65 (ICC for total scores)

Notes
APSD = Antisocial Process Screening Measure (Frick & Hare, 2001). CBCL = Child Behavior Checklist (Achenbach, 1991). YPI-CV = Youth Psychopathic Traits Inventory – Child Version (Van Baardewijk et al., 2008). MPQ = Multidimensional Personality Questionnaire (Tellegen, unpublished manuscript from 1982), MTI = Minnesota Temperament Inventory (Loney et al., 2007), YPI = Youth Psychopathic Traits Inventory (Andershed, Kerry Stattin, & Levander, 2002), PCL:SV = Psychopathy Checklist: Screening Version (Hart, Cox, & Hare, 1995), PCL-R = Psychopathy Checklist-Revised (Hare, 2003).

The psychopath: continuity or change? 97

However, the current authors disagree somewhat with Andershed (2010). The guidelines set forth by Andershed (2010) are appropriate when the data is normally distributed and error free. However, this is rarely the case, especially with longitudinal studies spanning several decades. As a result, we suggest the following rank-order stability guidelines: <0.20 indicates low stability, 0.20–0.39 reflects moderate stability, 0.40–0.59 indicates high stability, and correlations above 0.60 indicate very high stability.

As can be seen from Table 6.1, studies targeting the developmental period of childhood and measuring psychopathic traits using the Antisocial Process Screening Device (APSD; Frick & Hare, 2001) show moderate to very high stability (0.36–0.93) according to our proposed guidelines. However, many studies (e.g. Barry et al., 2008; Dadds et al., 2005; Munoz & Frick, 2007; Pardini, Lochmann, & Powell, 2007; Van Baardewijk et al., 2011) use rather short follow-up periods (e.g. approximately one year), and many of the studies on rank-order stability only utilize two time points (e.g. Blonigen et al., 2006; Forsman et al., 2008; Loney et al., 2007; Neumann, Wampler, Taylor, Blonigen, & Iacono, 2011). It can be argued that such short time spans are not good tests of stability (Andershed, 2010). Lynam et al. (2009) found in their longitudinal study of psychopathic traits that shorter time spans compared to longer time between assessments yielded higher stability estimates. In adolescence, the available studies suggest that more fluctuation takes place during this developmental period. As can be seen from Table 6.1, the rank-order stability estimates range from moderate to high using Andershed's (2010) guidelines, and high to very highly stable using our recommendations. In adulthood, Rutherford et al. (1999) suggest that psychopathic traits only display moderate to high rank-order stability over a two year period. While Rutherford et al. (1999) used a well-known measure of psychopathic traits (i.e. PCL-R; Hare, 2003), the sample was limited to methadone patients, which limits generalizability to other samples.

Mean-level stability

Another commonly used way of assessing stability of psychopathic traits is through measuring stability and change in mean scores over time (Lynam & Gudonis, 2005; Roberts et al., 2001). To date, four published studies spanning substantial time periods have investigated the mean-level stability of psychopathic traits. Table 6.2 presents an overview of these studies. As the table highlights, the observed change, or lack thereof, indicates that psychopathic traits are stable across time. Of particular interest is the study by Harpur and Hare (1994), in light of the fact that very little attention has been paid to stability through adulthood (Barry et al., 2008). Harpur and Hare (1994) conducted a study of 889 prisoners and psychiatric patients assessed on the PCL-R. The sample was divided into seven age cohorts (16–20, 21–25, 26–30, 31–35, 36–40, 41–45, and 46–70), with the greatest number of participants in the age ranges of 21–25 and 26–30 ($n=244$ and $n=240$, respectively). A differential mean-level stability pattern emerged between the PCL-R factors. Factor 1, which measures

98   *H. Bergstrøm* et al.

Table 6.2 Overview of longitudinal studies investigating mean-level stability of psychopathic traits

Developmental period and study	Age at first assessment	Length of follow-up	Measure	Change (Cohen's d)
Childhood				
Lynam et al. (2009)	7	11 years	CPS	Effect sizes not provided
Adolescence				
Blonigen et al. (2006)	17	7 years	MPQ	−0.06; −0.99
Forsman et al. (2008)	16	3 years	YPI	−0.02; 0.47
Adulthood				
Harpur & Hare (1994)	16–70	Cross-sectional	PCL-R	Mean scores not provided

Notes
CPS = Child Psychopathy Scale (Lynam, 1997), MPQ = Multidimensional Personality Questionnaire (Tellegen, in press), YPI = Youth Psychopathic Traits Inventory (Andershed et al., 2002), PCL-R = Psychopathy Checklist-Revised (Hare, 2003).

interpersonal and affective traits, was stable across the age cohorts (no significant change detected). Factor 2, which compromises lifestyle and antisocial traits, did however decrease. While covering a wide age range, the design is, as pointed out by Blonigen et al. (2006), cross-sectional, and such a design limits any causal inferences (Andershed, 2010; Blonigen et al., 2006; Farrington et al., 2010).

Explanation of variability

There are a number of potential reasons for the variation in both rank-order and mean-level stability. First, it might be due to the natural and commonplace maturation and social changes that take place during the adolescent period (McCrae et al., 2000; Moffitt, 1993; Rindfuss, 1991; Roberts et al., 2001). However, it might also be due to methodological issues such as the use of non-validated measures of psychopathic traits (e.g. MPQ; Tellegen, in press; MTI; Loney et al., 2007), and the differential duration of the studies (Lynam et al., 2009; see also Forth, Bergstrøm & Clark (2015)). To date, there are only two published studies focused on the adult stability of psychopathic traits (see Tables 6.1 and 6.2).

Predictors of stability in psychopathic traits

In an effort to understand the stability and development of psychopathic traits, there has been an increased interest in investigating potential predictors of stability and change (Andershed, 2010; Barry et al., 2008; Frick et al., 2003; Lynam, Loeber, & Stouthamer-Loeber, 2008; Neumann et al., 2011). Multiple analytical approaches have been utilized to assess such predictors (e.g. moderation (Lynam

The psychopath: continuity or change? 99

et al., 2008), conditional latent growth curves (Salihovic, Kerr, Özdemir, & Pakalnieskene, 2012)). For the current discussion we will focus on the approach taken by Frick et al. (2003) as, mathematically speaking, predicting later psychopathic traits while controlling for earlier traits is equivalent to predicting changes in psychopathic traits.

Frick and his colleagues (2003) were some of the first researchers to investigate the longitudinal stability of psychopathic traits using a validated measure of child and adolescent psychopathic traits, and in addition their study was one of the first to assess predictors of stability and change. As previously mentioned, the authors utilised the Antisocial Process Screening Device (APSD; Frick & Hare, 2001) that measures psychopathy as a three factor construct, consisting of Callous-Unemotional (CU), Narcissism, and Impulsivity. In their study, Frick et al. (2003) established the importance of a wide range of individual and social factors that were predictive of later psychopathic traits when controlling for earlier manifestations of psychopathy. The results indicated that the importance of predictors of stability and change depends on type of risk factor and the APSD subscale in question.

Frick et al. (2003) found that conduct disorder (CD)/oppositional defiant disorder (ODD), and delinquency measured at the level of the individual child, were related to later psychopathic traits when controlling for earlier psychopathic traits. However, only CD and ODD were related to any of the APSD subscales, namely the Narcissism subscale. While positive parenting was not a protective factor, negative parenting was related to total psychopathic traits and all of the APSD subscales. Finally, socioeconomic status (SES) had a negative relationship with psychopathic traits, but only for the total APSD and the CU and the Narcissism subscales. This latter finding indicates that a low family SES is related to an increase in psychopathic traits, while a high SES might function as a protective factor as it might contribute to a decrease in psychopathic traits.

Considering the literature on predictors of psychopathic traits (see Farrington, 2007 for a more comprehensive discussion), it is rather surprising that more factors have not been found to influence stability. However, this might be because of methodological limitations, which the current study aims to address.

The current study

The current study is by far the longest investigation to date, spanning multiple developmental periods. The hypotheses guiding the current study are as follows: First, it was expected that stability across developmental periods would be in the moderate range, and second, that shorter time periods between assessment points would elicit higher stability estimates compared with longer ones. Third, and of a more exploratory nature, the study investigated factors that uniquely predict psychopathic traits, meaning that the interest is in social factors that predict psychopathic traits at a specific time point while controlling for earlier psychopathic traits. If none of the suggested predictors were related to an increase or decrease in psychopathic traits, this would not only provide support for the stability of

100 *H. Bergstrøm et al.*

psychopathic traits, but it would also have implications for the understanding of the development of psychopathic traits. Based on the three proposed hypotheses it was possible to make inferences about which, if any, of the proposed theoretical models of personality are most plausible.

Methodology

Design and sample

The current study is an analysis of data from the Cambridge Study in Delinquent Development (CSDD). The CSDD is a well renowned and thoroughly analysed 40 year prospective longitudinal study of 411 boys from childhood (approximate age of eight) to middle age (age 48) (Farrington, Ttofi, & Coid, 2009). Attrition was very low across adolescence (Farrington, Gallagher, Morley, St Ledger, & West, 1990). At age 48, 365 out of 394 who were still alive were interviewed (93%), and 304 of the remaining 365 (83%) completed the medical assessment that included the Psychopathy Checklist: Screening Version (PCL:SV; Hart et al., 1995). It has previously been hypothesized that it is the most antisocial males who would drop out of the study (Farrington et al., 1990), but comparisons of the level of psychopathic traits in the current study between those who dropped out and those who remained showed no significant differences.

Measures of psychopathic traits

Two developmentally appropriate measures were utilized in the current study.

Antisocial Process Screening Device (APSD; Frick & Hare, 2001)

To assess psychopathic traits in childhood and adolescence, the Antisocial Process Screening Device (APSD; Frick & Hare, 2001) was used. This measurement scale is a derivative of the PCL-R. The APSD consists of 20 developmentally appropriate items measured on an ordinal 3 point scale (0, 1, and 2). The maximum score obtainable is 40, while the minimum score is 0. Originally, the measure was designed to be rated by parents and/or teachers (Frick & Hare, 2001), but it has also been successfully utilized as a self-report scale (Lee, Hart & Corrado, 2003; Munoz & Frick, 2007; Silverthorn, Frick, & Reynolds, 2001).

Psychopathy Checklist: Screening Version (PCL:SV; Hart et al., 1995)

The PCL:SV is a shorter screening version of the more comprehensive PCL-R (Hare, 2003; Hart et al., 1995). As with the APSD (Frick & Hare, 2001) and the PCL-R (Hare, 2003), the 12 items on the PCL:SV (Hart et al., 1995) are measured on the same 3 point ordinal scale for a maximum score of 24. Originally, the PCL:SV reflected the two factor structure (Factor 1 (interpersonal/affective) and Factor 2 (lifestyle/antisocial)) of the psychopathy construct (Hart et al.,

The psychopath: continuity or change? 101

1995), but a number of recent studies (Dolan & Fullman, 2006; Guy & Douglas, 2006; Walters et al., 2007) have found evidence for the four facet structure as well: facet 1 (interpersonal), facet 2 (affective), facet 3 (lifestyle), and facet 4 (antisocial) (Hare, 2003). For the current study, only the two factor structure is utilized. The PCL:SV is used frequently in community samples to measure psychopathic traits and has shown high validity and reliability (Cooke, Michie, Hart, & Hare, 1999; Gray, Fitzgerald, Taylor, MacCulloch, & Snowden, 2007; Hastings, Tangney, & Stuewig, 2008).

Coding of psychopathic traits

Since the CSDD was started in the early 1960s, no validated measures of psychopathic traits were included in the original assessments as they were not available at this time. Salekin and Lynam (2010) suggest that, in cases such as these, this can be rectified by creating proxies from the original data. To ensure that such a proxy was based on as comprehensive information as possible, multiple data points were combined. The following presents the utilized time points and the specific information that the coding was based upon.

Time 1 (age 8–10) and Time 2 (age 12–14)

Psychopathic traits were coded for Time 1 and Time 2 by creating a proxy APSD score based on information from five main sources. These were indicators reflecting official records, interviews with parents, teacher-ratings, peer ratings, and self-reports from the boys themselves. The APSD total score at Time 1 had a Cronbach's α of 0.59, while the Time 2 Cronbach's α was 0.62.

Time 3 (age 16–18)

The APSD proxy measure at Time 3 differed somewhat from Time 1 and 2 as it was only based on official records and self-reports from the youths themselves. At this time point, Cronbach's α was 0.27. The APSD proxy measure had very low internal reliability. This has been a common issue with the APSD (Bijttebier & Decoene, 2009; Falkenbach, Poythress, & Heide, 2003; Lee et al., 2003; Munoz & Frick, 2007; Poythress, Dembo, Wareham, & Greenbaum, 2006a; Vitacco, Rogers, & Neumann, 2003), and could be linked to problems with establishing a clear factor structure of the measure (Dadds et al., 2005; Poythress et al., 2006a; Sijtsma, 2009). The especially low internal consistency at Time 3 (age 16–18) compared to the earlier time points might also be attributable to the less comprehensive information on which the coding was based.

Time 4 (age 48)

A measure of psychopathic traits (PCL:SV; Hart et al., 1995) was included at age 48 (Time 4) in the original assessment. There was therefore no need to create

102   H. Bergstrøm et al.

a proxy for this time point. The PCL:SV assessment was conducted by one trained and qualified rater. Cronbach's α for the total PCL:SV score was 0.72, while for Factor 1 it was 0.56 and Factor 2 it was 0.70 (Piquero et al., 2012).

APSD score proxy quality

In support of the quality of the proxy, it was created through a comprehensive process. The proxy was developed by the first author in close collaboration with the second author. The second author, Adelle Forth, is one of the leading experts on psychopathic traits in adolescence. In addition, a third qualified assessor provided feedback on the proxies. A confirmatory factor analysis was also conducted to ensure that all four time points loaded onto the same underlying latent factor. The results indicated a good fit $\chi^2(2, N=395)=2.96$, $p=0.23$, RMSEA$=0.04$, CFI$=0.99$, and TLI$=0.98$ (Wang & Wang, 2012).

Predictors of stability in psychopathy

As highlighted in Table 6.3, a wide range of social factors were measured in the current study. Because of the limited research in this area, composite measures were created based partly on the previous literature in the area and the indicators that were available in the CSDD. Low SES was conceptualized according to Mueller and Parcel (1981) and included indicators relating to social class, occupational prestige, and financial situation. Similarly complex is the negative parenting predictor consisting of multiple indicators such as neglect, physical abuse, and maternal attitude (Trocme et al., 2005). Antisocial family and antisocial peers were measured through reported criminal and antisocial acts in family members and peers respectively. Unfortunately it was not possible to assess the parents of the original boys' psychopathic traits (see Auty, Farrington, & Coid, 2015 for how the boys' psychopathic traits influence their children's psychopathic traits), so instead general parental psychopathology was measured using CSDD indicators such as parents' psychological health and if they have received psychological treatment in the past. Negative family functioning was conceptualized differently than negative parenting as it focused less on abuse related indicators, and more on the quality of the relationship between parents and with the youth.

Table 6.3 Overview of potential predictors/moderators and time of measurement

Predictor/moderators	Time 1 (8–10)	Time 2 (12–14)	Time 3 (16–18)
Low SES	X	X	
Negative Parenting	X	X	
Antisocial Family	X	X	
Antisocial Peers		X	X
Parental Psychopathology	X	X	
Negative Family Functioning	X	X	X

Analytical plan

Rank-order (relative) stability

Rank-order stability is measured through test-retest Pearson's correlations (r) (Roberts et al., 2001). Due to the rather low internal reliability of the measures, the correlations were corrected for attenuation in accordance with Olweus (1979).

Mean-level (absolute) stability

In accordance with Forsman et al. (2008), a repeated measures ANOVA was conducted in accordance to measure mean-level stability. To ensure that the APSD and PCL:SV mean scores could be compared, PCL:SV at 48 was prorated to reflect the same 0–40 scale as APSD.

Stability classification

Due to the lack of research on the stability of adult psychopathic traits (Andershed, 2010; Barry et al., 2008; Blonigen et al., 2006), the current study included a more in-depth look at the time period from 18 to 48 by classifying the boys as either high, middle, or low on psychopathic traits at the APSD at age 16–18 (Time 3) and on the prorated PCL:SV at age 48. Change scores were calculated, classified, and then compared with each other.

Partial correlations

Since the study is partly based on the Frick et al. (2003) study, their analytical strategy has also been followed. Separate regressions were conducted for each stability period and the corresponding predictors. Through the regressions, partial correlations were obtained. These partial correlations show the unique contribution of the predictor on psychopathic traits when controlling for earlier psychopathic traits (Frick et al., 2003).

Results

Descriptive statistics

The level of psychopathic traits across time points were within the low to average range, compared with other community samples (Frick & Hare, 2001; Hart et al., 1995). Time 1 (age 8–10) had a Mean score on the APSD of 14.10 with a *SD* of 4.45, while at Time 2 (age 12–14) the Mean was 10.79 with $SD=3.63$. At Time 3 (age 16–18) the level of psychopathic traits were $M=12.34$, $SD=3.40$. The PCL:SV's range is between 0 and 24 (the APSD range is between 0 and 40), and this is reflected in the low means at age 48 (Time 4). The *Mean*

104 *H. Bergstrøm* et al.

score for the total PCL:SV was 3.14 (SD=3.40), while the Factor 1 *Mean* was 1.00 (SD=1.32) and the Factor 2 *Mean* was 2.09 (SD=2.32).[2]

Correlations corrected for attenuation

As previously mentioned rank-order stability is assessed through test-retest correlations, and to limit measurement error it is common practice to correct these correlations for attenuation (Olweus, 1979; Roberts et al., 2001). The results are presented in Table 6.4.

According to the guidelines set forth by the current authors, all of the correlations were in the moderate to very high range. Table 6.4 also shows a trend where the shorter time spans yield higher rank-order stability estimates compared to the longer times between assessments. The strongest correlation was found between Time 3 psychopathic traits and Factor 2. The correlation of 0.84 shows remarkable stability over a 30 year period.

Mean-level stability

The results from the repeated measures ANOVA indicated that more change was taking place at the mean-level from Time 1 to prorated Time 4. Since the Mauchly's test of Sphericity was significant (χ^2=28.90, $d.f.$=5, $p<0.001$), the Greenhouser-Geiser correction was utilized. The overall effect was significant with F[2.77, 667.59]=299.28 ($p<0.001$) and a η^2=0.55, and the mean difference between each time point was significant ($p<0.05$) as well. Calculated effect sizes (Cohen's d) are presented in Table 6.5.

Stability classification

The results from the group classification indicate that the majority of participants in the sample remain stable from late adolescence to middle age. From age 16–18 (Time 3) to age 48 (Time 4), 24.9% decreased on psychopathic traits

Table 6.4 Correlations corrected for attenuation

Psychopathic traits	1	2	3
1 APSD age 8–10 (Time 1)			
2 APSD age 12–14 (Time 2)	0.61**		
3 APSD age 16–18 (Time 3)	0.58**	0.64**	
4 PCL:SV Total age 48 (Time 4)	0.40**	0.52**	0.66**
a Factor 1 age 48 (Time 4)	0.26*	0.42**	0.46**
b Factor 2 age 48 (Time 4)	0.48**	0.58**	0.84**

Notes
* $p<0.05$;
** $p<0.001$;
n=266–370.

The psychopath: continuity or change? 105

while only 4.1% increased. The majority of the sample remained constant from Time 3 to Time 4 (71%).

Predictors

The detailed findings for each stability period are presented in Tables 6.6 and 6.7. A wide range of predictors influence psychopathic traits in one time period when controlling for psychopathic traits at an earlier time.

When reviewing the partial correlations, some clear trends emerged. An antisocial family and antisocial peers were consistently uniquely predictive of increases in psychopathic traits across time. Low SES, parental psychopathology, and negative family functioning were less consistent across developmental periods, but they predict an increase in psychopathic traits over time.

Discussion

The current study is one of the longest investigations of the stability of psychopathic traits to date. While only using four time points, the study does span a total of 40 years. The main findings from this study are that at a rank-order level, psychopathic traits are moderately to very highly stable. This means that people keep their relative position on psychopathic traits within the sample over time (Roberts et al., 2001). These results are in accordance with previous findings from other longitudinal studies (e.g. Blonigen et al., 2006; Forsman et al., 2008; Lynam et al., 2007; Lynam et al., 2009). Since many of these prior studies have used different measures of psychopathic traits and targeted differential developmental periods, the congruency is quite remarkable (Andershed, 2010). However, different levels of analysis seem to provide different results (Andershed, 2010; Blonigen et al., 2006; Forsman et al., 2008; Roberts et al., 2001). Change is happening in accordance with previous studies (e.g. Blonigen et al., 2006; Forsman et al., 2008), but this appears to be mainly taking place at a mean, absolute level. This means that the sample as a whole is changing over time, rather than individuals having varying trajectories within the sample. This indicates that those who are the highest remain the highest on psychopathic traits, while those who are low on psychopathic traits tend to stay low. These results emphasize the importance of using different levels of analysis, and highlight that

Table 6.5 Mean level stability of psychopathic traits

	1	2	3	4
1 APSD age 8–10 (Time 1)	–			
2 APSD age 12–14 (Time 2)	−0.74	–		
3 APSD age 16–18 (Time 3)	−0.36	0.38	–	
4 Prorated PCL:SV age 48 (Time 4)	−1.56	−1.15	−1.48	–

Note
Effect sizes (Cohen's *d*) between each time point.

106 *H. Bergstrøm* et al.

Table 6.6 Partial correlations between predictors and psychopathic traits while controlling for time 1 psychopathic traits

Predictors	APSD age 12–14	APSD age 16–18	PCL:SV age 48
Predictors age 8–10			
Low SES	0.01 (0.05)	0.01 (0.07)	0.12 (0.20**)
Antisocial Family	0.12* (0.17**)	0.13* (0.19**)	0.21** (0.26**)
Negative Parenting	0.06 (0.16**)	−0.05 (−0.01)	0.06 (0.13*)
Parental Psychopathology	−0.05 (−0.02)	0.03 (0.06)	0.13* (0.16*)
Negative Family Functioning	0.01 (0.08)	−0.01 (0.02)	0.07 (0.14*)
Predictors age 12–14			
Low SES		−0.01 (0.06)	0.17** (0.23**)
Antisocial Family		0.12* (0.16**)	0.12* (0.18**)
Antisocial Peers		0.20***(0.25***)	0.24*** (0.29***)
Negative Parenting		0.05 (0.09)	0.01 (0.07)
Parental Psychopathology		0.17** (0.20***)	0.27*** (0.26***)
Negative Family Functioning		0.06 (0.11)	0.07 (0.14*)
Predictors age 16–18			
Antisocial Peers			0.31*** (0.36***)
Negative Family Functioning			0.22*** (0.22***)

Notes
Bivariate correlations in parentheses.
$n = 282–358$;
* $p < 0.05$;
** $p < 0.01$;
*** $p < 0.001$.

Table 6.7 Partial correlations between predictors and psychopathic traits while controlling for time 2 psychopathic traits

Predictors	APSD age 16–18	PCL:SV age 48
Predictors age 12–14		
Low SES	0.04 (0.06)	0.22** (0.23**)
Antisocial Family	0.12* (0.16**)	0.10 (0.18**)
Antisocial Peers	0.19** (0.25***)	0.20** (0.29***)
Negative Parenting	0.07 (0.09)	0.11 (0.07)
Parental Psychopathology	0.17** (0.20***)	0.26*** (0.26***)
Negative Family Functioning	0.08 (0.11)	0.14* (0.14*)
Predictors age 16–18		
Antisocial Peers		0.26*** (0.36***)
Negative Family Functioning		0.19** (0.22***)

Notes
Bivariate correlations in parentheses.
$n = 218–342$;
* $p < 0.05$;
** $p < 0.01$;
*** $p < 0.001$.

The psychopath: continuity or change? 107

results from one level cannot necessarily be generalized to another (Andershed, 2010; Roberts et al., 2001).

The stability results also indicate that psychopathic traits are more stable across short-term periods (e.g. approximate 2–4 years between assessments) compared to longer term periods (e.g. across multiple developmental periods) up to 30 years. As Lynam et al. (2009) and the current study show, using only short time spans is not sufficient to understand trajectories and stability of psychopathic traits. Both short-term (e.g. monthly or annually) and long-term assessments are needed that span developmental periods (Andershed, 2010; Lynam et al., 2009). The importance of this finding becomes evident when reviewing the findings on the development period where the greatest change takes place. The greatest change took place from late adolescence to middle age, which might be explained by the 30 year assessment span. However, when classifying the number of males who increased, decreased, or remained constant in this 30 year time period, it was clear that the majority actually remained constant from age 16–18 to 48. The rather large mean difference might actually reflect a difference in types of measurements used (APSD versus PCL:SV) than actual instability in traits. These results show for the first time the moderate to very high stability from childhood (age 8–10) to middle age (age 48), and as such the current study complements and extends prior studies and further enhances the understanding of stability.

Because of the previously mentioned lack of research on predictors of stability and change (Andershed, 2010), the current study is unique in its systematic investigation of predictive factors. In line with the risk factor literature and Frick et al. (2003), it seems that factors related to the immediate social environment of the child are crucial to the development and instability of psychopathic traits. It also appears that some factors, such as low SES and parental psychopathology, only have an effect on stability in certain developmental periods. The current study extends Frick et al. (2003) due to its longer assessment period, and the increased number of tested predictors. When comparing the predictors with and without controlling for psychopathic traits it becomes clear that this strategy is important when investigating predictors as earlier traits might contribute to inflated significant correlations. The most surprising finding is the lack of significance of negative parenting, as previous studies have established its importance as a factor that increases psychopathic traits (Farrington, 2007; Farrington et al., 2010; Frick et al., 2003; Krischer & Sevecke, 2008; Poythress, Skeem, & Lillienfeld, 2006b; Serin, 1991; Weiler & Widom, 1996).

A potential explanation for the differential findings between Frick et al. (2003) and the current study on negative parenting might be due to differences in samples. Frick et al.'s (2003) sample consisted of carefully matched groups while the current study utilized a comprehensive community sample. Another explanation might be based on how negative parenting was conceptualized in the current study. Negative parenting focused mostly on parenting techniques and discipline, while negative family functioning measured the more general functioning of the family. It might be that, for the current sample, the broad family functioning is more important for their development than physical discipline. If

108 *H. Bergstrøm et al.*

negative parenting and negative family functioning had been combined, the findings might have been more in line with Frick et al. (2003) as these variables would have measured a wider range of parenting behaviours. Different conceptualizations of risk factors might cloud the understanding of predictive factors, and future research should aim at being more consistent in their measures.

Implications

The findings on the rank-order and mean-level stability of psychopathic traits have several implications for research on psychopathy in childhood and adolescents. First and foremost, the rather high stability provides further evidence for the downward extension of psychopathic traits to childhood. The observed stability provides evidence that childhood and adolescent psychopathy are useful constructs that are not mere transient states that a person "grows out of" over time (Forth et al., 2003; Seagrave & Grisso, 2002). Therefore, psychopathic traits can be a feasible treatment target in children as young as eight years of age (Forth et al., 2003; Frick & Hare, 2001). It is generally recognized that treating adults with psychopathic traits is difficult and challenging (Rice et al., 1992; Salekin, 2010). By targeting psychopathic traits as early as childhood, timely interventions might prevent the development of negative trajectories (Forth et al., 2003, Salekin, 2007, 2008; Salekin, Rosenbaum, & Lee., 2008; Seagrave & Grisso, 2002). Based on the findings from the current study, the family context is a reasonable treatment and intervention target.

The lack of fluctuation over time and relatively high stability estimates indicate that the development of psychopathic traits adheres to the trait perspective of personality development as originally suggested by Andershed (2010), Caspi (2000) and Lynam (2002). This perspective proposes that psychopathic traits are formed early in development, and any observed change and discontinuity will be of a superficial and transient nature (McCrae et al., 2000). Since the personality trait perspective has received substantial support as a general model of personality (Kallasmaa, Allik, Realo, & McCrae, 2000; McCrae & Costa, 1987; McCrae, Costa, Del Pilar, Rolland, & Parker, 1998; Parker & Stumpf, 1998; Piedmont, 1994; Piedmont & Chae, 1997; Rozsa et al., 2008; Schinka, Kinder, & Kremer, 1997; Yang et al., 1999), it might not come as a surprise that psychopathic traits display characteristics according to this model over time. However, the number of significant predictors (partial correlations) does indicate that psychopathic traits are not necessarily as static as assumed by the personality trait perspective. The personality trait perspective itself has also been criticized for its focus on group level stability (Lewis, 1999, 2001a, 2001b).

Limitations

The current study has a number of limitations, but the main one is related to rank-order and mean-level stability, which provide information about the stability of psychopathic traits at a group level (Andershed, 2010; Lynam &

Gudonis, 2005; Roberts et al., 2001). While valuable in their own right, rank-order and mean-level stability does not provide information about individual trajectories within a group (Andershed, 2010; Roberts et al., 2001). According to Andershed (2010) future research should focus more on individual trajectories to truly understand how psychopathic traits develop over the life course.

Conclusion

The current study not only enhances the understanding of psychopathy and its development, but also provides further validation of the construct of psychopathy in children and adolescents. It appears that at a rank-order, group, level, psychopathic traits are moderately to highly stable across a 40 year long period. While change is taking place at a mean-level, especially from late adolescence to middle age, it appears that it is the group that changes together, rather than individuals within it. Such high stability indicates that psychopathic traits develop according to the trait perspective of personality development, but there might still be room for change based on the number of significant predictors.

Notes

1 Or lack thereof (Rice, Harris, & Cormier, 1992).
2 The Factor Means at age 48 do not add up to the Mean of the total score due to outlier corrections.

References

Achenbach, T. M. (1991). *Manual for the Child Behavioral Checklist/4–18 and 1991 profile.* Burlington: University of Vermont.
Andershed, H. (2010). Stability and change of psychopathic traits: What do we know? In R. T. Salekin & D. R. Lynam (eds), *Handbook of child and adolescent psychopathy* (pp. 233–250). New York: The Guilford Press.
Andershed, H., Kerr, M., Stattin, H., & Levander, S. (2002). Psychopathic traits in non-referred youths: A new assessment tool. In E. Blaauw & L. Sheridan (eds), *Psychopaths: Current international perspectives* (pp. 131–158). The Hague: Elsevier.
Auty, K., M., Farrington, D. P., & Coid, J. W. (2015). Intergenerational transmission of psychopathy and mediation via psychosocial factors. *British Journal of Psychiatry, 206,* 26–31.
Barry, T. D., Barry, C. T., Deming, A. M., & Lochman, J. E. (2008). Stability of psychopathic characteristics in childhood. The influence of social relationships. *Criminal Justice and Behavior, 35,* 244–262.
Bijttebier, P., & Decoene, S. (2009). Assessment of psychopathic traits in children and adolescents. Further validation of the Antisocial Process Screening Device and the Child Psychopathy Scale. *European Journal of Psychological Assessment, 25,* 157–163.
Blais, J., Solodukhin, E., & Forth, A. E. (2014). A meta-analysis exploring the relationship between psychopathy and instrumental versus reactive violence. *Criminal Justice and Behavior, 41,* 797–821.

110   *H. Bergstrøm et al.*

Blonigen, D. M., Hicks, B. M., Krueger, R. F., Patrick, C. J., & Iacono, W. G. (2006). Continuity and change in psychopathic traits measured via normal-range personality: A longitudinal-biometric study. *Journal of Abnormal Psychology, 115*, 85–95.

Caspi, A. (2000). The child is the father of the man: Personality continuities from childhood to adulthood. *Journal of Personality and Social Psychology, 78*, 158–172.

Clark, L. A., & Watson, D. (2010). Temperament: An organizing paradigm for trait psychology. In O. P. John, R. W. Robins, & L. A. Pervin (eds), *Handbook of personality: Theory and research* (Vol. 3, pp. 265–286). New York: The Guilford Press.

Cleckley, H. (1941). *The mask of sanity: An attempt to reinterpret the so-called psychopathic personality*. Oxford: Mosby.

Coid, J., Yang, M., Ullrich, S., Roberts, A., & Hare, R. (2009). Prevalence and correlates of psychopathic traits in the household population of Great Britain. *International Journal of Law and Psychiatry, 32*, 65–73.

Cooke, D. J., Hart, S. D., Logan, C. & Michie, C. (2012). Explicating the construct of psychopathy: Development and validation of a conceptual model, the Comprehensive Assessment of Psychopathic Personality (CAPP). *International Journal of Forensic Mental Health*, 11, 242-252.

Cooke, D. J., Michie, C., Hart, S. D., & Hare, R. D. (1999). Evaluating the screening version of the Hare Psychopathy Checklist-Revised (PCL:SV): An item response theory analysis. *Psychological Assessment, 11*, 3–13.

Dadds, M. R., Fraser, J., Frost, A., & Hawes, D. J. (2005). Disentangling the underlying dimensions of psychopathy in conduct problems in childhood: A community study. *Journal of Consulting and Clinical Psychology, 73*, 400–410.

De Oliveira-Souza, R., Hare, R. D., Bramati, I. E., Garrido, G. J., Ignacio, F. A., & Tovar-Moll, F. M. (2008). Psychopathy as a disorder of the moral brain: Fronto-temporo-limbic grey matter reduction demonstrated by voxel-based morphometry. *NeuroImage, 40*, 1202–1213.

Dolan, M., & Fullam, R. (2006). Face affect recognition deficits in personality-disordered offenders: Association with psychopathy. *Psychological Medicine, 36*, 1563–1569.

Falkenbach, D. M., Poythress, N. G., & Heide, K. M. (2003). Psychopathic features in a juvenile diversion population: Reliability and predictive validity of two self-report measures. *Behavioral Sciences and the Law, 21*, 787–805.

Farrington, D. P. (2007). Family background and psychopathy. In C. J. Patrick (ed.), *Handbook of psychopathy* (pp. 229–250). New York: The Guilford Press.

Farrington, D. P., & Bergstrøm, H. (in press). Family background and psychopathy. In C. J. Patrick (ed.), *Handbook of psychopathy* (2nd edn). New York: Guilford Press.

Farrington, D. P., Gallagher, B., Morley, L., St Ledger, R., & West, D. J. (1990). Minimizing attrition in longitudinal research: Methods of tracing and securing cooperation in a 24 year follow up study. In D. Magnusson & L. Bergman (eds), *Data quality in longitudinal research* (pp. 122–147). Cambridge: Cambridge University Press.

Farrington, D. P., Ttofi, M. M., & Coid, J. W. (2009). Development of adolescence-limited, late onset, and persistent offenders from age 8 to age 48. *Aggressive Behavior, 35*, 150–163.

Farrington, D. P., Ullrich, S., & Salekin, R. T. (2010). Environmental influences on child and adolescent psychopathy. In R. T. Salekin & D. R. Lynam (eds), *Handbook of child and adolescent psychopathy* (pp. 202–232). New York: The Guilford Press.

Forsman, M., Lichtenstein, P., Andershed, H., & Larsson, H. (2008). Genetic effects explain the stability of psychopathic personality from mid- to late adolescence. *Journal of Abnormal Psychology, 117*, 606–617.

The psychopath: continuity or change? 111

Forth, A. E., Bergstrøm, H., & Clark, H. J. (2015). Psychopathic traits in adolescence. In C. B. Gacano (ed.) *The clinical and forensic assessment of psychopathy: A practitioner's guide* (pp. 115-136). New York: Routledge.

Forth, A. E., Kosson, D. S., & Hare, R. D. (2003). *The Psychopathy Checklist: Youth Version manual.* Toronto: Multi-Health Systems.

Fowler, T., Langley, K., Rice, F., van den Bree, M. B. M., Ross, K., Wilkinson, L. S., Owen, M. J., O'Donovan, M. C., & Thapar, A. (2009). Psychopathy trait scores in adolescents with childhood ADHD: The contribution of genotypes affecting MAOA, 5HTT and COMT activity. *Psychiatric Genetics, 19,* 312–319.

Frick, P. J., & Hare, R. D. (2001). *Antisocial Process Screening Device: APSD.* Toronto: Multi-Health Systems.

Frick, P. J., Kimonis, E. R., Dandreaux, D. M., & Farrell, J. M. (2003). The 4 year stability of psychopathic traits in non-referred youth. *Behavioral Sciences and the Law, 21,* 713–736.

Gray, N. S., Fitzgerald, N., Taylor, J., MacCulloch, M. J., & Snowden, R. J. (2007). Predicting future reconviction in offenders with intellectual disabilities: The predictive efficacy of VRAG, PCL-SV, and the HCR-20. *Psychological Assessment, 19,* 474–479.

Guy, L. S., & Douglas, K. S. (2006). Examining the utility of the PCL:SV as a screening measure using competive factor models of psychopathy. *Psychological Assessment, 18,* 225–230.

Hare, R. D. (1998). The Hare PCL-R: Some issues concerning its use and misuse. *Legal and Criminological Psychology, 3,* 99–119.

Hare, R. D. (2003). *Manual for the Hare Psychopathy Checklist – revised* (2nd edn). Toronto: Multi-Health Systems.

Hare, R. D., Frazelle, J., & Cox, D. N. (1978). Psychopathy and physiological responses to threat of an aversive stimulus. *Psychophysiology, 15,* 165–172.

Harpur, T. J., & Hare, R. D. (1994). Assessment of psychopathy as a function of age. *Journal of Abnormal Psychology, 103,* 604–609.

Hart, S., Cox, D., & Hare, R. (1995). *Manual for the Psychopathy Checklist: Screening Version (PCL:SV).* Toronto: Multi-Health Systems.

Hastings, M. E., Tangney, J. P., & Stuewig, J. (2008). Psychopathy and identification of facial expressions of emotion. *Personality and Individual Differences, 44,* 1474–1483.

Intrator, J., Hare, R., Stritzke, P., Brichtswein, K., Dorfman, D., Harpur, T.,... Machhac, J. (1997). A brain imaging (single photon emission computerized tomogrophy) study of semantic and affective processing in psychopaths. *Biological Psychiatry, 42,* 96–103.

Jutai, J. W., Hare, R. D., & Connolly, J. F. (1987). Psychopathy and Event-Related Brain Potentials (ERPs) associated with attention to speech stimuli. *Personality and Individual Differences, 8,* 175–184.

Kallasmaa, T., Allik, J., Realo, A., & McCrae, R. R. (2000). The Estonian version of the NEO-PI-R: An examination of universal and culture-specific aspects of the Five-Factor Model. *European Journal of Personality, 14,* 265–278.

Kiehl, K. A., Smith, A. M., Hare, R. D., Mendrek, A., Forster, B. B., Brink, J., & Liddle, P. F. (2001). Limbic abnormalities in affective processing by criminal psychopaths as revealed by functional magnetic resonance imaging. *Biological Psychiatry, 50,* 677–684.

Kiehl, K. A., Smith, A. M., Mendrek, A., Forster, B. B., Hare, R. D., & Liddle, P. F. (2004). Temporal lobe abnormalities in semantic processing by criminal psychopaths as revealed by functional magnetic resonance imaging. *Psychiatry Research: Neuroimaging, 130,* 297–312.

112 H. Bergstrøm et al.

Krischer, M. K., & Sevecke, K. (2008). Early traumatization and psychopathy in female and male juvenile offenders. *International Journal of Law and Psychiatry, 31*, 253–262.

Larsson, H., Andershed, H., & Lichtenstein, P. (2006). A genetic factor explains most of the variation in the psychopathic personality. *Journal of Abnormal Psychology, 115*, 221–230.

Lee, Z. V., Hart, S. D., & Corrado, R. R. (2003). The validity of the Antisocial Process Screening Device as a self-report measure of psychopathy in adolescent offenders. *Behavioral Sciences and the Law, 21*, 771–786.

Leistico, A.-M. R., Salekin, R. T., DeCoster, J., & Rogers, R. (2008). A large scale meta-analysis relating the Hare measures of psychopathy to antisocial conduct. *Law and Human Behavior, 32*, 28–45.

Levenston, G. K., Patrick, C. J., Bradley, M. M., & Lang, P. J. (2000). The psychopath as observer: Emotion and attention in picture processing. *Journal of Abnormal Psychology, 109*, 373–385.

Lewis, M. (1999). On the development of personality. In L. A. Pervin & O. P. John (eds), *Handbook of personality theory and research* (2nd edn, pp. 327–346). New York: The Guilford Press.

Lewis, M. (2001a). Issues in the study of personality development. *Psychological Inquiry, 12*, 67–83.

Lewis, M. (2001b). Continuity and change: A reply. *Psychological Inquiry, 12*, 110–112.

Loney, B. R., Taylor, J., Butler, M. A., & Iacono, W. G. (2007). Adolescent psychopathy features: 6-year temporal stability and the prediction of externalizing symptoms during the transition to adulthood. *Aggressive Behavior, 33*, 242–252.

Lynam, D. R. (2002). Fledging psychopathy: A view from personality theory. *Law and Human Behavior, 26*, 255–259.

Lynam, D. R., Caspi, A., Moffitt, T. E., Loeber, R., & Stouthamer-Loeber, M. (2007). Longitudinal evidence that psychopathy scores in early adolescence predict adult psychopathy. *Journal of Abnormal Psychology, 116*, 155–165.

Lynam, D. R., Charnigo, R., Moffitt, T. E., Raine, A., Loeber, R., & Stouthamer-Loeber, M. (2009). The stability of psychopathy across adolescence. *Development and Psychopathology, 21*, 1133–1153.

Lynam, D. R., & Gudonis, L. (2005). The development of psychopathy. *Annual Review of Clinical Psychology, 1*, 381–407.

Lynam, D. R., Loeber, R., & Stouthamer-Loeber, M. (2008). The stability of psychopathy from adolescence into adulthood. The search for moderators. *Criminal Justice and Behavior, 35*, 228–243.

McCord, W., & McCord, J. (1964). *The psychopath: An essay on the criminal mind.* Princeton, NJ: Van Nostrand.

McCrae, R. R., & Costa, P. T. (1987). Validation of the five-factor model of personality across instruments and observers. *Journal of Personality and Social Psychology, 52*, 81–90.

McCrae, R. R., & Costa, P. T. (2010). The five-factor theory of personality. In O. P. John, R. W. Robins, & L. A. Pervin (eds), *Handbook of personality: Theory and research* (3rd edn, pp. 159–181). New York: The Guilford Press.

McCrae, R. R., Costa, P. T., Del Pilar, G. H., Rolland, J.-P., & Parker, W. D. (1998). Cross-cultural assessment of the Five-Factor Model. The revised NEO Personality Inventory. *Journal of Cross Cultural Psychology, 29*, 171–188.

The psychopath: continuity or change? 113

McCrae, R. R., Costa, P. T., Ostendorf, F., Angleitner, A., Hrebikova, M., Aviva, M. D.,… Sanchez-Bernardos, M. L. (2000). Nature over nurture: Temperament, personality and life span development. *Journal of Personality and Social Psychology, 78*, 173–186.

Moffitt, T. E. (1993). Life-course persistent and adolescent limited antisocial behavior: A developmental taxonomy. *Psychological Review, 100*, 674–701.

Mueller, C. W., & Parcel, T. L. (1981). Measures of socioeconomic status: Alternatives and recommendations. *Child Development, 52*, 13–30.

Munoz, L. C., & Frick, P. J. (2007). The reliability, stability, and predictive utility of the self-report version of the Antisocial Process Screening Device. *Scandinavian Journal of Psychology, 48*, 299–312.

Neumann, C., Wampler, M., Taylor, J., Blonigen, D. M., & Iacono, W. G. (2011). Stability and invariance of psychopathic traits from late adolescence to young adulthood. *Journal of Research in Personality, 45*, 145–152.

Neumann, C. S., & Hare, R. D. (2008). Psychopathic traits in a large community sample: Links to violence, alcohol use, and intelligence. *Journal of Consulting and Clinical Psychology, 76*, 893–899.

Obradovic, J., Pardini, D. A., Long, J. D., & Loeber, R. (2007). Measuring interpersonal callousness in boys from childhood to adolescence: An examination of longitudinal invariance and temporal stability. *Journal of Clinical Child and Adolescent Psychology, 36*, 276–292.

Olweus, D. (1979). Stability of aggressive reaction patterns in males: A review. *Psychological Bulletin, 86*, 852–875.

Pardini, D. A., Lochman, J. E., & Powell, N. (2007). The development of callous-unemotional traits and antisocial behavior in children: Are there shared and/or unique predictors. *Journal of Clinical Child and Adolescent Psychology, 36*, 319–333.

Patrick, C. J., Bradley, M. M., & Lang, P. J. (1993). Emotion in the criminal psychopath: Startle reflex modulation. *Journal of Abnormal Psychology, 102*, 82–92.

Parker, W. D., & Stumpf, H. (1998). A validation of the five-factor model of personality in academically talented youths across observers and instruments. *Personality and Individual Differences, 25*, 1005–1025.

Piedmont, R. L. (1994). Validation of the NEO PI-R observer form in college students: Toward a paradigm for studying personality development. *Assessment, 1*, 259–268.

Piedmont, R. L., & Chae, J.-H. (1997). Cross-cultural generalizability of the Five Factor Model of personality: Development and validation of the NEO-PI-R for Koreans. *Journal of Cross-Cultural Psychology, 28*, 131–155.

Piquero, A. R., Farrington, D. P., Fontaine, N. M. G., Vincent, G., Coid, J., & Ullrich, S. (2012). Childhood risk, offending trajectories, and psychopathy at 48 years in the Cambridge Study in Delinquent Development. *Psychology, Public Policy, and Law, 18*, 577–598.

Poythress, N. G., Dembo, R., Wareham, J., & Greenbaum, P. E. (2006). Construct validity of the Youth Psychopathic Traits Inventory (YPI) and the Antisocial Process Screening Device (APSD) with justice-involved adolescents. *Criminal Justice and Behavior, 33*, 26–55.

Poythress, N. G., Skeem, J. L., & Lilienfeld, S. O. (2006). Associations among early abuse, dissociation, and psychopathy in an offender sample. *Journal of Abnormal Psychology, 115*, 288–297.

Rice, M. E., Harris, G. T., & Cormier, C. A. (1992). An evaluation of a maximum security therapeutic community for psychopaths and other mentally disordered offenders. *Law and Human Behavior, 16*, 399–412.

114   *H. Bergstrøm* et al.

Rindfuss, R. R. (1991). The young adult years: Diversity, structural change, and fertility. *Demography, 28*, 493–512.

Roberts, B. W., Caspi, A., & Moffitt, T. E. (2001). The kids are alright: Growth and stability in personality development from adolescence to adulthood. *Personality Processes and Individual Differences, 81*, 670–683.

Rozsa, S., Rihmer, Z., Gonda, X., Szili, I., Rihmer, A., Ko, N.,… Akiskal, H. S. (2008). A study of affective temperaments in Hungary: Internal consistency and concurrent validity of the TEMPS-A against the TCI and NEO-PI-R. *Journal of Affective Disorders, 106*, 45–53.

Rutherford, M., Cacciola, J. S., Alterman, A. I., McKay, J. R., & Cook, T. G. (1999). The 2-year test-retest reliability of the Psychopathy Checklist-Revised in methadone patients. *Assessment, 6*, 285–291.

Salekin, R. T. (2007). Psychopathy in children and adolescents: Key issues in conceptualizations and assessment. In C. J. Patrick (ed.), *Handbook of psychopathy* (pp. 389–416). New York: The Guilford Press.

Salekin, R. T. (2008). Psychopathy and recidivism from mid-adolescence to young adulthood: Cumulating legal problems and limiting life opportunities. *Journal of Abnormal Psychology, 117*, 386–395.

Salekin, R. T. (2010). Treatment of child and adolescent psychopathy: Focusing on change. In R. T. Salekin & D. R. Lynam (eds), *Handbook of child and adolescent psychopathy* (pp. 343–373). New York: The Guilford Press.

Salekin, R. T., & Lynam, D. R. (2010). Child and adolescent psychopathy: An introduction. In R. T. Salekin & D. R. Lynam (eds), *Handbook of child and adolescent psychopathy* (pp. 1–14). New York: The Guilford Press.

Salekin, R. T., Rogers, R., & Sewell, K. W. (1996). A review and meta-analysis of the Psychopathy Checklist and Psychopathy Checklist-Revised: Predictive validity of dangerousness. *Clinical Psychology: Science and Practice, 3*, 203–215.

Salekin, R. T., Rosenbaum, J., & Lee, Z. (2008). Child and adolescent psychopathy: Stability and change. *Psychiatry, Psychology, and Law, 15*, 224–236.

Salihovic, S., Kerr, M., Özdemir, M., & Pakalnieskene, V. (2012). Directions of effects between adolescent psychopathic traits and parental behavior. *Journal of Abnormal Child Psychology, 40*, 957–969.

Salihovic, S., Özdemir, M., & Kerr, M. (2014). Trajectories of adolescent psychopathic traits. *Journal of Psychopathology and Behavioural Assessment, 36*, 47–59.

Schinka, J. A., Kinder, B. N., & Kremer, T. (1997). Research validity scales for the NEO-PI-R: Development and initial validation. *Journal of Personality Assessment, 68*, 127–138.

Seagrave, D., & Grisso, T. (2002). Adolescent development and the measurement of juvenile psychopathy. *Law and Human Behavior, 26*, 219–239.

Serin, R. C. (1991). Psychopathy and violence in criminals. *Journal of Interpersonal Violence, 6*, 423–431.

Sijtsma, K. (2009). On the use, misuse, and the very limited usefulness of Cronbach's alpha. *Psychometrika, 74*, 107–120.

Silverthorn, P., Frick, P. J., & Reynolds, R. (2001). Timing of onset and correlates of severe conduct problems in adjudicated girls and boys. *Journal of Psychopathology and Behavioral Assessment, 23*, 1717–181.

Taylor, J., Loney, B. R., Bobadilla, L., Iacono, W. G., & McGue, M. (2003). Genetic and environmental influences on psychopathy trait dimensions in a community sample of male twins. *Journal of Abnormal Child Psychology, 31*, 633–645.

The psychopath: continuity or change? 115

Tikkanen, R., Auvinen-Lintunen, L., Ducci, F., Sjöberg, R. L., Goldman, D., Tiihonen, J., Ojansuu, I., & Virkkunen, M. (2011). Psychopathy, PCL-R, and MAOA genotype as predictors of violent reconvictions. *Psychiatry Research*, 185, 382–386.

Trocme, N., Fallon, B., MacLaurin, B., Daciuk, J., Felstiner, C. B., Black, T., Tonmyr, L., Blackstock, C., & Barter, K. (2005). *Canadian Incidence study of reported child abuse and neglect 2003: Major findings.* Ottawa: Minister of Public Works and Government Services Canada.

Van Baardewijk, Y., Stegge, H., Andershed, H., Thomaes, S., Scholte, E., & Vermeiren, R. (2008). Measuring psychopathic traits through self-report: The development of the Youth Psychopathic traits Inventory – Child Version. *International Journal of Law and Psychiatry, 31*, 199–209.

Van Baardewijk, Y., Vermeiren, R., Stegge, H., & Doreleijers, T. (2011). Self-reported psychopathic traits in children: Their stability and concurrent and prospective association with conduct problems and aggression. *Journal of Psychopathology and Behavioral Assessment, 33*, 236–245.

Verona, E., Curtin, J. J., Patrick, C. J., Bradley, M. M., & Lang, P. J. (2004). Psychopathy and physiological response to emotionally evocative sounds. *Journal of Abnormal Psychology, 113*, 99–108.

Vitacco, M. J., Rogers, R., & Neumann, C. S. (2003). The Antisocial Process Screening Device. An examination of its construct and criterion-related validity. *Assessment, 10*, 143–150.

Walters, G. D., Gray, N. S., Jackson, R. L., Sewell, K. W., Rogers, R., Taylor, J., & Snowden, R. J. (2007). A taxometric analysis of the Psychopathy Checklist: Screening Version (PCL:SV): Further evidence of dimensionality. *Psychological Assessment, 19*, 330–339.

Wang, J. & Wang, X. (2012). *Structural equation modeling: Applications using Mplus.* Chichester: John Wiley & Sons Ltd.

Weiler, B. L., & Widom, C. S. (1996). Psychopathy and violent behaviour in abused and neglected young adults. *Criminal Behaviour and Mental Health, 6*, 253–271.

Woodworth, M., & Porter, S. (2002). In cold blood: Characteristics of criminal homicides as a function of psychopathy. *Journal of Abnormal Psychology, 111*, 436–445.

Yang, J., McCrae, R. R., Costa, P. T., Dai, X., Yao, S., Cai, T., & Gao, B. (1999). Cross-cultural personality assessment in psychiatric populations: The NEO-PI-R in the People's Republic of China. *Psychological Assessment, 11*, 359–368.

Part II
Policing and detecting deception

7 Questioning the interrogational practices of US law-enforcement officers

Legal and psychological perspectives

David Walsh, Sean O'Callaghan, and Rebecca Milne

Historical background

In the early years of the twentieth century the police, in the USA, interrogated suspects most commonly using a method known as the third degree (Hopkins, 1931; Kassin et al., 2010; Leo, 2004). This interrogative approach remained common practice in the United States until the mid-1930s (Leo, 1992). Leo (2004) identified seven general forms of the third degree found to be in use, namely: (i) brutal physical force; (ii) physical torture; (iii) deniable physical and physiological coercion; (iv) incommunicado interrogation; (v) physical duress; (vi) threats of harm; and (vii) prolonged detention and confinement. While some of these methods included the use of physical force, others such as incommunicado interrogation and threats of harm did not, but were still likely to be coercive because of the psychological implications. Moreover, Emanual Lavine, a former *New York Times* journalist, noted that these techniques were commonplace during police questioning and were not isolated occurrences (Lavine, 1930).

The publication of the Wickersham report in 1931, which exposed these coercive techniques, prompted a public uproar, enforcing a change in these police procedures (Wickersham, 1931). The report revealed to the public the brutality carried out at the hands of the police (Walker, 1980). Once known, the public began to insist on the disbandment of the third degree approach, enforcing a change to a more professional approach to police interviewing. This change was assisted by a number of legal decisions which made certain aspects of the third degree illegal (*Brown* v. *Mississippi*, 1936; *Miranda* v. *Arizona*, 1966). Along with these legal decisions, various law enforcement agencies began to make changes internally. Chiefs, sheriffs, and other law enforcement leaders began to enact and enforce departmental policies against the use of such brutal behaviour (Leo, 2004). Additionally, the Federal Bureau of Investigations (FBI) conducted investigations into such practices (Leo, 1992). While these actions helped speed up the removal of the old methods, it failed to provide police with an effective alternative. Consequently, departments and individuals began to construct their own training manuals in the hopes of developing a more effective (and acceptable) approach to the interrogation of criminal suspects. Probably the first of

120 *D. Walsh* et al.

these new methods was Kidd's police interrogation manual (Kidd, 1940). Developed by a Berkley police lieutenant, this 200 page training manual was significant because of its shift toward a more psychologically based method of interviewing (Leo, 2008). Various other manuals soon followed. Indeed, Kelly and Meissner (2016) advise that many training courses exist today, concerning a range of methods that include in-house training courses for officers in some of the larger cities in the USA, as well as other model-specific training programmes such as the Kinesic Interview (Walters, 2003), and the W-Z model (Zulawski, Wicklander, Sturman, & Hoover, 2001). However, none have been more significant than the Reid technique (Inbau, Reid, Buckley, & Jayne, 2013).

The emergence of psychological interrogation and the Reid technique

Developed by Fred Inbau and John Reid, the Reid interviewing manual remains one of the most influential texts concerning interrogation throughout the world (Kassin et al., 2007). Introduced in 1942, the Reid technique consisted of 19 'trial and error' tactics, each of which lacked either organisation or empirical foundation. Since its initial inception however, this technique has become more organised, consisting of a nine-step asocial psychological process designed to be used by investigators during police interrogations (Inbau et al., 2013). The technique is intended to gradually break down the suspect's defences, convincing him/her that it would be in his/her best interests to confess. Additionally, the Reid model makes a clear distinction between an interview and an interrogation, arguing that an interrogation should not be used until an individual's guilt is 'reasonably certain' (Inbau et al., 2013). This is because, while not explicitly stated by Reid, the purpose of an interrogation as defined by Reid is to obtain a confession. Use of the Reid model (or derivations thereof) is widespread throughout the USA and elsewhere (e.g. Canada, Slovenia, Japan). Indeed, Zalman and Smith (2007) found that two-thirds of US police officers stated that they had received training in the model, while the Reid website claims that over half a million people have received training in the model since 1974 (www. reid.com).

The model involves two phases; the first involves a claimed non-accusatory interview stage, known as the Behavioural Analysis Interview (BAI), whose purpose is to determine guilt or innocence by gathering information about the alleged crime in a 'free flowing and relatively unstructured' manner (Inbau et al., 2013). Indicators, as prescribed by Inbau et al., will lead the investigator to the conclusion that the suspect is either guilty or innocent. Horvath, Jayne, and Buckley (1994) suggest that those trained in the BAI can discriminate between these two outcomes at a very high rate, despite the fact that research has tended to show that investigation professionals regularly detect deception at rates only just above chance (Bond & DePaulo, 2006; Kassin & Fong, 1999; Vrij, Mann, & Fisher, 2006). Regardless, the BAI, containing a series of biographical, investigation-relevant, and behaviour-provoking questions, is argued to prompt

Interrogational practices in the US   121

indicators that reveal verbal and non-verbal behavioural signs of truth and deception (although Meissner & Kassin, 2002, found that officers tended to focus on identifying deception). That is, for example, suspects' reduced movements in the hands, feet, and legs, decreased eye contact, talking time, and speech rate, longer latency in responses to questions, lowering of voice pitch are all, according to the Reid technique, signals of deception. However, in a major meta-analysis of veracity/deception studies conducted by DePaulo et al. (2003) it was found that these indicators were not associated with those telling lies, and some (e.g. feet/ leg movements and pitch) were actually more associated with truth-tellers (Masip & Herrero, 2013; Masip, Herrero, Garrido, & Barba, 2010).

While evidence/information may well have been considered by investigators, assumptions of guilt are largely a result of interviewers' intuitive feelings and their reliance on unscientific guilt-based indicators (St-Yves & Tanguay, 2009). Notwithstanding these concerns, if those behavioural signals, following the Reid model, are present they are to be interpreted (when denials are received) as signals of guilt. As such the next phase of the Reid model (called the interrogation) commences.

The interrogation phase of the Reid model

The model's interrogation phase involves an array of persuasive tactics designed to socially influence people by increasing their anxieties that are associated with denials, yet underlay those that are associated with confessions (Davis & O'Donahue, 2003). Interrogation presumes guilt by its very definition. Its sole purpose is to gain a confession, from those who, after processing the BAI, are presumed guilty (and whose denials are deemed to be untrue ones). From previous research (e.g. Hill, Memon, & McGeorge, 2008; Kassin, Goldstein, & Savitsky, 2003) it has been found that if investigators believe that the suspect is guilty they will focus only on questioning and other tactics that are designed to prove guilt, setting aside any other possibility (including that of innocence).

Before the interrogation phase begins suspects are advised of their rights in the subsequent interrogation relating to their silence and legal representation (the so-called 'Miranda' warning). While the Miranda warning will be discussed later in the chapter here it will be mentioned that it is a matter of conjecture as to whether suspects (particularly vulnerable ones; e.g. those young in age) actually comprehend what these rights mean (see, for example, Grisso, 1980, 1997, 1998, 2003, who reported high levels of misunderstanding among juvenile suspects). Regardless of age, other studies have found very high rates of interviewees who waive their rights (Kassin & Nowick, 2004; Leo, 1996). According to White (2001) this is largely due to the police becoming rather skilled at persuading suspects that it is in their best interests to waive their rights.

After this phase, officers trained in the Reid model are expected to undertake a nine-step framework. The first step involves 'direct, positive confrontation' where an investigator is advised to utter an accusation (whether actual or contrived) that the suspect is unequivocally guilty and, further, impress upon the

122 *D. Walsh* et al.

suspect that any denials, in the face of such blatant culpability, would be a futile gesture. The Reid model suggests that using the first name of the suspect when being accusatory creates further psychological gain. Inbau et al. (2013, pp. 195–196) suggest that the interviewer should examine behavioural responses to the accusation, indicating that some (e.g. posture shifting, gaze aversion, etc.) will likely be indicators of guilt. As previously noted, the scientific evidence supporting these claims does not exist. However, such techniques may well increase the suspect's anxiety. After this first step the investigator is advised to evaluate the suspect's responses to the accusation, urging him/her to confess. Thereafter, the second step (i.e. 'theme development') involves the interviewer providing a 'moral excuse' for the suspect to explain his/her actions. By so doing, this step is intended to minimise the suspect's suggested criminality, acting either as a 'face-saving' technique (e.g. "anyone else would have done the same thing in those circumstances"), or portraying either the victim or any accomplice as the one really to blame. Such techniques may imply attitudes of sympathy and leniency by the investigator toward the suspect. The next step (Step Three) concerns the handling of denials, ensuring these are not given any accommodation, through investigator interruptions, which are intended to reinforce the investigator's belief in the suspect's guilt, whilst displaying that such denials will not be entertained.

Step Four, in turn, involves the interviewer overcoming any objections or explanations behind any denials from the suspect. As such, the interviewer is attempting to disarm the suspect and, thus, create further feelings of futility in any continual denial of their involvement in the crime. If multiple objections are received this is said to be a sign of probable guilt (Inbau et al., 2013, p. 281). Following this step, which may have led to the suspect becoming passive or withdrawn, the next two steps advise the interviewer to recognise such symptoms and deal with them in order to regain the participation of the suspect (for example, by moving nearer to the suspect, asking hypothetical questions, expressing empathy, sympathy, etc. in order to gain co-operation), before presenting the suspect with an alternative question (Step Eight). Here, the interviewer may present the suspect with two scenarios or reasons for committing the crime (one more attractive or reasonable than the other), in an attempt to prompt the suspect to choose the morally acceptable one, and confess to the crime. The officer should then convert that verbal confession into a written one (Step Nine).

Underpinning the Reid model are an array of techniques designed to create psychological domination over the suspect through accusation, bluff, veiled threats, isolation, providing face-saving rationales, minimisation (i.e. mitigating the offence, feigning friendship or sympathy, using flattery), and maximisation (i.e., exaggerating evidence strength or the consequences of not confessing) to overcome any denials and erode resistance in order to gain compliance, and ultimately a confession (Kassin & McNall, 1991). Other tactics to overcome resistance include the use of trickery and deception. For example, the police might state that they have found fingerprint evidence that matches that of the suspect at the crime scene when no such evidence exists (a matter of blatant lying).

Furthermore, implicit in much of the fundamentals of the Reid model is the notion that innocent people do not confess. However, people do falsely confess to crimes they have not committed, particularly when certain conditions are present in interviews (see Gudjonsson, 2003 for a review). The Reid technique appears to overlook another important matter; denials will be made by those who are innocent. However, since by this stage suspects will be viewed as guilty, innocence is insufficiently considered by Inbau et al. As such, investigators may view any denials as ones that indicate the suspect is lying about their involvement. Research shows that law enforcement officials invariably do not significantly outperform members of the public at being able to detect lies (even though they confidently believe they can regularly detect lies; Masip, Alonso, Garrido, & Herrero, 2009). As noted, prior research commonly finds them achieving rates of identification at just above those of chance (Kassin & Fong, 1999). This finding is further compounded by an absence of any training that would make investigators aware of the possibility of false confessions (Kassin, 2002).

The Reid model has been the subject of much criticism, despite its global reach and influence. Recently, a case involving Juan Rivera has been reported (Starr, 2015). Rivera was sentenced to life imprisonment for rape and murder in 1993. He had been, during the investigation, interrogated several times over four days, Some of this questioning was undertaken by both police officers, who had been trained in the Reid model, and also by an employee of the Reid organisation (who purportedly told Rivera that he had failed a polygraph test, and that this demonstrated his guilt). Rivera's conviction was eventually overturned in 2012 on appeal. Following the flawed investigation, and his subsequent false conviction, a civil lawsuit was settled in 2015, reckoned to amount to involve Rivera receiving over $20 million. The Reid organisation's share of this amount is reported as $2 million.

In light of such an experience it is not surprising that concerns have been raised that the Reid method of interrogation is as manipulative as the third degree (Kolker, 2010). While a number of ethical concerns have been raised, this assertion is primarily due to the research showing that many of the assumptions made by the Reid technique are flawed. One such assumption is that interviewers can utilise non-verbal clues to determine whether or not a suspect is lying (Horvath, Jayne, & Buckley, 1994; Inbau et al., 2013). The problem is, the Reid technique advises that all interviews with suspects be conducted in a small, soundproof, skeletally furnished room (Inbau et al., 2013). According to Jayne (1986) this environment can elicit feelings of social isolation, sensory deprivation, and helplessness which can lead a guilty person to confess. However, other authors (e.g. Kassin & Gudjonsson, 2004) assert that these are also the conditions which can lead to innocent people making false confessions.

While it is true that guilty people confess to crimes they did commit when interrogated by police officers using the above procedure, and it may well be that most people questioned by the police are guilty of the crimes for which they are being interrogated, it remains that false confessions occur. Indeed, over a quarter

124 *D. Walsh* et al.

of those cases reported by the Innocence Project in the USA, found that the miscarriages of justice were a consequence of a suspect making a false confession, as these confessions were later found to be untrue (see www.innocenceproject. org). Further, Drizin and Leo (2004) found that, where the suspect falsely confessed, interrogations were on average over eight times longer than the norm, indicating that being incommunicado for a prolonged period of time, with relentless questioning, and fatigue may be a probable cause for such outcomes.

Evaluations of the Reid model have largely concerned examinations of the principles of the model. There have been few evaluations through naturalistic studies. Indeed, despite the number of officers trained in the Reid model and, in turn, the huge number of interrogations they conduct annually there has been little awareness of how they actually perform in the field. A few studies, however, have been conducted that involve surveys of officers, examining their beliefs (e.g., Kassin et al., 2007; Meyer & Reppucci, 2007). Both studies found that officers fail to recognise that techniques they report as ones they regularly use may also cause false confessions. For example, in the study conducted by Kassin et al. law enforcement officers stated that, while they rarely used coercive techniques (such as using threats, anger, or lying about a failed polygraph evidence), they admitted to both regularly deceiving suspects about their supposed possession of other forms of evidence, and being presumptuous of the suspect's guilt.

Kassin et al. also found that officers said they used rapport on a frequent basis. More recently, Redlich, Kelly, and Miller (2014) in their survey of a range of law enforcement officers also found rapport being stated as a tactic they often used (alongside building a relationship with the suspect, and also provoking emotional reactions). In further self-report studies it has been found that most of the time investigators stated that they (i) observed suspects' body language or speech patterns in an attempt to detect deception; (ii) repeatedly asked the same question; and (iii) employed various minimisation techniques, while they (iv) lied to suspects about evidence supposedly held, a tactic still favoured by a third of survey participants (Meyer & Reppucci, 2007; Reppucci, Meyer, & Kostelnik, 2010).

More recently, O'Callaghan (in preparation) has undertaken a survey of US police officers ($N=116$). He found, in his self-report study (which included both police officers who had undergone training in the Reid model, and those who had not), that half of the officers felt it was acceptable to lie to suspects about the supposed available evidence (i.e. stating that it was at hand when it was not), while almost all of them felt they could identify deception when it occurred. Around a third felt the Miranda warning was not that important, believing that if a suspect was silent that they should be allowed to continue questioning (despite their being prohibited by law from so doing). However, in contrast, the majority felt that officers should remain 'neutral' during interrogations.

In two studies (i.e. Feld, 2013; Leo, 1996) observations were undertaken of officers' practice as they undertook their questioning of suspects. In Feld's study (where the suspects were juveniles, $N=307$) he found a tendency for officers to

Interrogational practices in the US   125

(i) ask leading questions; (ii) exploit suspects' anxieties; (iii) urge them to tell the truth; while (iv) maximisation techniques were evident in almost all of his sample; and (v) minimisation techniques were found in a third of the sample. Feld's findings largely replicated those of Leo (1996), whose field study also included adult populations. Although two thirds of the 182 suspects in Leo's study were below the age of 30, being largely representative of the criminal age range in police statistics (Newburn, 2013). Leo also found (i) the use of praise and flattery; (ii) stressing the importance of co-operation; (iii) appealing to the suspect's self-conscience; (iv) identifying contradictions in the suspect's story; and (v) the use of moral justifications frequently being undertaken. In interviews Leo characterised as accusatorial frequent incidence of both confronting suspects with evidence (actual or reported) and appealing to the suspect's self-interest occurred. Despite the matter that it was believed that the police officers were Reid-trained in these two studies no single officer was found to employ all the steps of the Reid model.

Walsh (2012) presented findings of a further small-scale field study of 35 US police interrogations (although none of the officers were believed to have undertaken training in the Reid model). He revealed that most interviews contained techniques such as (i) appeals to the suspects' self-interest; (ii) disclosing evidence (although almost always being stated as held rather than actually being presented during the interrogation); (iii) using leading questions; (iv) urging of suspects to state the truth; and (v) maximisation techniques. Similar to those aforementioned field studies, Walsh also found that rapport was frequently used, particularly in the initial phases of the interrogation. After receiving denials, Walsh then found officers turning more accusatorial and hostile, with any rapport that had been built being lost. From these few survey and observational studies it does appear that several of the techniques recommended by the Reid Model (and other ones) are both favoured by law enforcement officers, and find their way into practice. This is reinforced by the legal framework, the matter to which this chapter now turns.

The laws concerning interrogations in the USA

While the questioning of suspects has been commonly recognised as a necessary and valuable part of any criminal investigation, when conducting such questioning, the court must weigh the needs of the police against the rights of the accused. In the United States, and indeed in many other countries, this balancing act is settled through the use of laws, policies, and legal decisions, each acting to help define interviewing and interrogation.

In the United States this power, however, does not reside with one person or governmental body. Instead, the structure of the United States is more dispersed, in that there are multiple government agencies which can influence the way police conduct the questioning of suspects. On the federal level for example, this power is divided into four areas: (i) the US Constitution; (ii) the executive branch; (iii) the legislative branch; and (iv) the judicial branch. More commonly

126 *D. Walsh* et al.

known as the separation of powers, each has its own particular control over how the questioning of suspects is conducted. Thus, because of this complexity, it is important to understand what laws and legal decisions have an effect on police interviewing and interrogation procedures.

In the American criminal justice system it is the role of the investigator to collect evidence and relevant case information and then, without bias, determine whether or not a criminal case is present. In order for this task to be accomplished investigators question individuals in efforts to determine what actually occurred (and by whom). With regard to suspects, the most important issue is whether the interview/interrogation is classified as custodial or non-custodial, since many of the regulations governing interrogations only apply when they are classified as custodial ones. The US Supreme Court's definition of custody refers to whether the suspect's freedom is hindered due to "the degrees associated with formal arrest" (*Minnesota* v. *Murphy*, 1984). To accurately evaluate this, an objective standard was adopted, relying on what "a reasonable man in the suspect's position would have understood his situation" to mean (*Berkemer* v. *McCarty*, 1984). In order for the Court to conclude that a suspect is in a custodial interview the Court must evaluate the totality of the circumstances and conclude that a reasonable person would not feel like they had the right to leave. In order to ensure that the rights of the suspect are adequately protected, while still keeping in mind the goal of obtaining justice, the United States has instilled a number of laws in which police must follow during these custodial interrogations.

Laws governing arrest

The Fourth Amendment to the US Constitution guarantees all individuals, regardless of what crime has been committed, with the right to be secure both in their "persons" and in their "houses, papers, and effects" against "unreasonable" searches and seizures (U.S. Const. amend. IV). In other words, the government, namely the police, must obtain probable cause and a warrant before violating an individual's civil liberties. As such, before any interview can occur the suspect must be brought in for questioning and agree to participate. Over the course of time this process has moved from one of coercion and forcefulness to one of procedure and ethical consideration. This evolving situation began in 1979 with the US Supreme Court case of *Dunaway* v. *New York*, 1979). In this case, the Court ruled that a confession obtained after an arrest that had no probable cause could not be used as evidence against the suspect. Thus, based on this decision, whenever an investigator desires to question a suspect, there must be cause to warrant an arrest or the suspect must consent to being questioned and understand that they are *not* under arrest and can leave at any time. However, what constitutes probable cause for arrest is not a simple concept to objectify. The United States Supreme Court (in *Beck* v. *Ohio*, 1964) defines probable cause as "[W]hether at that moment the facts and circumstances within their knowledge and of which they had reasonably trustworthy information were sufficient to warrant a prudent man in believing that the petitioner had committed or was committing an offense" (*Beck* v. *Ohio*, 1964, p. 91).

While probable still remains a vague standard (McCauliff, 1982; Slobogin, 1998), it is clear that an investigator needs more than mere suspicion. In reality, the Court must balance the interests of law enforcement against the personal liberty of the individual. It is only once the interests of law enforcement finally outweigh probable cause that a warrant can be issued.

The 'Miranda' rights

Once probable cause has been obtained and the decision has been made to formally question a suspect, the next step is to ensure that a legal interview takes place. However, before any interviewing can occur the suspect must be advised of and read his/her Miranda rights. Established in 1966 as a result of the *Miranda* v. *Arizona* ruling these rights have now become the cornerstone of the rules governing suspect interviewing in the United States. In fact, in the Dickerson case (*Dickerson* v. *United States*, 2000) the Court refused to overturn Miranda stating that "Miranda has become embedded in routine police practice to the point where the warnings have become part of our national culture."

The road to the inception of the Miranda rights began in 1964 (*Escobedo* v. *Illinois*, 1964) where the Court began to extend rights originally reserved for the court room to all police interviews. Escobedo was repeatedly denied access to his lawyer. After 14 hours of interrogation Escobedo finally made a confession. However, the US Supreme Court later reversed his conviction on the grounds that the confession was illegally obtained. The Court held that because Escobedo was denied his sixth amendment right to counsel any statements obtained afterward were illegally obtained.

While a major step forward, the *Escobedo* decision failed to resolve the issue concerning the rights of suspects during police questioning. As such, these were once again addressed two years later with the *Miranda* decision. Ernesto Miranda had been arrested by the Phoenix Police for kidnapping and rape. After two hours of questioning he signed a confession in which he acknowledged that he did so "with full knowledge of [his] legal rights" (*Miranda* v. *Arizona*, 1966). Using this confession, Miranda was convicted and was given a lengthy prison sentence. Miranda subsequently appealed to the US Supreme Court claiming that he should have been informed of his rights prior to being questioned. The Court held that Miranda's rights were violated and that from that point on no statement would be valid unless the suspect was informed of their rights prior to any questioning being conducted. Additionally, then Chief Justice Earl Warren also stipulated that these rights must be presented in a "clear and unequivocal language" (*Miranda* v. *Arizona*, 1966) and that they must be understood before any questioning can begin. Furthermore suspects, who have waived their Miranda rights, can still invoke these rights at any later point in time. This process of informing the suspect of their rights, known as the Miranda warning, is now used by all law enforcement officers throughout the United States.

128   *D. Walsh* et al.

The premise of the Miranda warning was that a suspect would be "adequately and effectively apprised of their rights" and assured of a "continuous opportunity to exercise them" (*Miranda* v. *Arizona*, 1966). Investigators, following the Miranda ruling, prior to any interview had to inform a suspect about:

i   their right to remain silent and refuse to answer questions;
ii   the fact that anything they say can and will be used against them in court;
iii that they have the right to counsel, consult them prior to questioning, and to have them present during all subsequent questioning; and
iv   that if they cannot afford a lawyer, the court will appoint one for them prior to any questioning at no cost to them.

Defining coercion and cruel and unusual punishment

While much of the US Constitution highlights the rights of the individual, many parts also limit what the government can and cannot do in the pursuit of justice. The eighth amendment, for example, protects an individual from being subjected to "cruel and unusual punishment" (U.S. Const. amend. VIII). With regard to the interviewing of suspects, the US Supreme Court made direction in the landmark case in *Hopt* v. *Utah*, 1884, requiring all statements to be made voluntarily, while rendering statements induced by threats or coercion to be inadmissible. Despite this, as discussed earlier in the chapter, the police continued to act unethically by way of employing overtly coercive tactics in interrogations. In *Brown* v. *Mississippi*, 1936 where three suspects were each whipped and beaten over the course of several days until they confessed, all three men were subsequently convicted of murder and sentenced to death. Upon appeal to the US Supreme Court, their convictions were overturned because their confessions, which were the basis for their convictions, were obtained through the use of torture. Citing both the eighth and fourteenth amendments, the Court held that any statement obtained as a result of coercion or physical brutality violated the constitution.

The law also prohibits other forms of coercion, such as threats (whether explicit or implicit), physical distress or psychological maltreatment to convince a suspect to confess to a crime. In evaluating whether or not a method of interviewing is coercive the courts must consider (i) the conduct of the investigator; (ii) the environment in which the interview was conducted; and (iii) the suspect's mental and physical condition. Threats concern those made either directly to the suspect or to other individuals close to the suspect, such as their family (*Malinski* v. *New York*, 1945; *Stein* v. *New York*, 1959). In the case of physical mistreatment, any information obtained from an individual who is interviewed for a prolonged period of time without intervals of sleep, rest, or food and water cannot be used against them (*Brooks* v. *Florida*, 1961). Additionally, if the interview lasts an 'overly exorbitant' amount of time even with these breaks the information can be deemed inadmissible (*Ashcraft* v. *Tennessee*, 1944; *Lyons* v. *Oklahoma*, 1944; *Reck* v. *Pate*, 1961). As such, the Supreme Court has limited what investigators can and cannot do during a lawful police interrogation and

Interrogational practices in the US   129

thus any techniques used by police to obtain information must be considered ethical by the Court before any information can be deemed admissible.

Permissible tactics and techniques

Despite these stated restrictions certain controversial tactics and techniques are still permitted, most notably the use of deception to try to convince a suspect to talk and confess. In 1969, following the US Supreme Court ruling of *Frazier* v. *Cupp*, the use of deception was officially ratified as a permissible technique to be used where the suspect, having been (falsely) told that his accomplice had confessed to the crime, confessed. The police, as a result of this ruling, began to experiment with different forms of deception (such as minimisation or maximisation) with the intention of obtaining confessions (Inbau et al., 2013). However, since this decision, the Court has put a number of restrictions on how the police can and cannot use deception. For example, the Court acknowledged (*Moran* v. *Burbine*, 1986) that some forms of police deception might be considered "egregious" and could rise to the "level of a due process violation". One such restriction is the use of false documents and evidence while interviewing a suspect stated by the Court as an unacceptably high risk that could lead to false confessions, as well as the added risk that the false evidence would be mistakenly considered as true by the Court.

Individual differences between states

In addition to federal laws and policies governing police interviewing, each state has the power to add additional laws. That said, while a number of differences may exist (e.g. recording of interviews), there are few disparities across the major laws concerning the way in which interviews are carried out throughout the United States. The most notable exception, however, concerns the mandatory recording of suspect interviews. In 1985 in the case of *Stephan* v. *State*, Alaska became the first state to require the recording of all custodial interrogations by way of a State Supreme Court ruling. Then, in 2003, Illinois became the first state to enact law requiring such action (725 ILCS 5/103–2.1) and was quickly followed by Maine (ME. REV. STAT. ANN. 15§ 801) and the District of Columbia (D.C. CODE ANN. § 5–133.20) that same year. Today, 20 states and the District of Columbia now require some form of mandatory electronic recording with regards to custodial interrogations (although a number of states have legislative bills pending). These different laws create a disparity between how interviews are conducted in each state.

The second difference among states with regards to interviewing concerns the interviewing of juvenile suspects. While the Supreme Court case of *In re Gault* held that the Miranda rule also applied to the interviewing of juvenile offenders, it failed to apply any safeguards beyond this point. As a result many states made their own interpretations in applying such safeguards, utilising two tests. Most commonly used is the Totality of the Circumstances test, which requires that the

130   *D. Walsh* et al.

police should consider such factors as the juvenile's "age, intelligence, maturity, and prior experience in criminal proceedings" when determining if a juvenile suspect is capable of waiving their rights and agreeing to participate in an interview. The Supreme Court affirmed this approach (*Fare* v. *Michael C.*, 1979) and set it as the federal constitutional standard for which all courts must follow. The Court further determined that the voluntariness of the waiver should not be based solely on a particular procedure employed in obtaining the waiver or on a specific characteristic of the accused juvenile, but rather on all the circumstances of the particular case put together. Consequently, since the *Fare* case, nine factors are generally considered when evaluating a juvenile interview:

  i the age of the juvenile;
  ii the current or perceived educational level of the child;
  iii the juvenile's knowledge of the "substance of the charge and nature of his right to consult with an attorney";
  iv whether the child was or is being held incommunicado;
  v whether the child was "interrogated before or after formal charges had been filed";
  vi method and techniques used during the interview;
  vii length of interview;
  viii whether the accused previously refused to give voluntary statements; and
  ix whether the juvenile recanted his "extrajudicial statement" at a later date

(*West* v. *United States*, 1968)

While most states have kept with this standard, 15 states have contended that the Totality of the Circumstances test is too vague and, as such, does not sufficiently safeguard juveniles. As a result, these states have instituted policies, either by legislation or court decisions, requiring that juvenile suspects be interviewed in the presence of an "interested adult". Known as the per se rule, this presence of an adult, usually a parent, automatically invalidates a Miranda waiver made by a juvenile arguing that "the spirit of Miranda is violated by the giving of a warning, intended for an adult, to a child who cannot reasonably be expected to give an informed response or appreciate the consequences of his decision" (Bailey, 1983, p. 740).

Discussion and future implications

A major and oft-repeated concern is that the psychological tactics employed by police officers (such as those recommended by the Reid model) are likely to produce false confessions (Drizin & Leo, 2004). Indeed, in cases which have involved exonerating once convicted suspects, over a quarter were found to be as a result of false confessions (DeClue, 2006). From the consistent experiences of the past it might be suggested that interrogational practice is likely to remain confession focused, using an array of tactics based upon unscientific

Interrogational practices in the US 131

foundations, and being largely based on intuition concerning the suspect's guilt. As such, false confessions may also be viewed as a continuing concern.

It remains surprising (or may be possibly not) that proponents of interrogational models, such as those covered in this chapter, have not commissioned or funded independent research that would examine their favoured approaches. Such research may actually examine whether such models of interrogation actually do succeed in commonly achieving their aims in practice. Cases exonerating wrongly convicted people continue to provide doubts as to whether such practices are effective. However, there are some early signs of change. Research that has been conducted in the USA in the last five years or so suggests that information gathering approaches may be more effective in establishing if a crime has been committed. For example, Kelly and Meissner (2016) report that the US government has funded a multi-agency group research project (the High-Value Detainee Interrogation Group), with the aim of developing a more scientific and more ethical model of interrogation using both experimental and applied research methodologies (see for example, Evans, Meissner, Brandon, Russano, & Kleinman, 2010; Evans et al., 2013; Kelly, Abdel-Salam, Miller, & Redlich, 2015). Increasingly, more states are recording their interviews.

It must, however, be cautioned that the recording of interviews alone, while providing greater transparency as to what actually happens when suspects are interrogated, is unlikely to prompt change. Just as important are both changes in legislation (that outlaw unethical practices) and in police culture, which embrace more ethical techniques (where the aim of the interview is not to simply gather a confession, but a reliable account). Further, it is encouraging to see recent developments where researchers and investigators are keen to collaborate (joint research endeavours are known to be a contributory feature of transforming practice elsewhere in the world; see for example, Clarke & Milne, 2001; Walsh & Bull, 2010, 2012a, 2012b; Walsh & Milne, 2008). Overarching these developments in the United States has been the publication of an official report that condemns the use of torture as a means of gathering reliable information, detailing the risks involved in such unethical practices (Senate Committee on Intelligence, 2014). As such, it is hoped that interrogational practices as we currently know them (along with false confessions) may in time be consigned to history.

References

Bailey, A. (1983). Waiver of Miranda rights by juveniles: Is parental presence a necessary safeguard? *Journal of Family Law, 21*(4), 725–743.

Bond, C. F., & DePaulo, B. (2006). Accuracy of deception judgments. *Personality and Social Psychology Review, 10*, 214–234.

Clarke, C., & Milne, R. (2001). *National evaluation of the PEACE investigative interviewing course.* Police Research Award Scheme Report No. PRAS/149. London: Home Office.

Davis, D., & O'Donahue, W. (2003). The road to perdition: Extreme influence tactics in the interrogation room. In W. O'Donahue (ed.), *Handbook of forensic psychology* (pp. 897–996). San Diego, CA: Academic Press.

132 *D. Walsh* et al.

DeClue, G. (2006). The psychology of interrogations and confessions. *Florida Psychologist, 57*, 17–18.

DePaulo, B. M., Lindsay, J. J., Malone, B. E., Muhlenbruck, L., Charlton, K., & Cooper, H. (2003). Cues to deception. *Psychological Bulletin, 129*, 74–118.

Drizin, S., & Leo, R. A. (2004). The problem of false confessions in the post-DNA world. *North Carolina Law Review, 3*, 891–1008.

Evans, J. R., Meissner, C. A., Brandon, S. E., Russano, M. B., & Kleinman, S. M. (2010). Criminal versus HUMINT interrogations: The importance of psychological science to improving interrogative practice. *Journal of Psychiatry and Law, 38*, 215–249.

Evans, J. R., Meissner, C. A., Ross, A. B., Houston, K. A., Russano, M. B., & Horgan, A. (2013). Obtaining guilty knowledge in human intelligence interrogations: Comparing accusatorial and information gathering approaches with a novel experimental paradigm. *Journal of Applied Research in Memory and Cognition, 2*, 83–88.

Feld, B. (2013). *Kids, cops, and interrogation: Inside the interrogation room.* New York: New York University Press.

Grisso, T. (1980). Juveniles' capacities to waive Miranda rights: An empirical analysis. *California Law Review, 68*, 1134–1166.

Grisso, T. (1997). The competence of adolescents as trial defendants. *Psychology, Public Policy, and Law, 3*, 3–32.

Grisso, T. (1998). *Instruments for assessing understanding and appreciation of Miranda rights.* Sarasota: Professional Resource Press/Professional Resource Exchange.

Grisso, T. (2003). *Evaluating competencies: Forensic assessments and instruments* (2nd ed.). New York: Kluwer Academic/Plenum Press.

Gudjonsson, G. (2003). *The psychology of interrogations and confessions.* Chichester: Wiley.

Hill, C., Memon, A., & McGeorge, P. (2008). The role of confirmation bias in suspect interviews: A systematic evaluation. *Legal and Criminological Psychology, 13*, 357–371.

Hopkins, E. (1931). *Our lawless police: A study of the unlawful enforcement of the law.* New York: Viking Press.

Horvath, F., Jayne, B., & Buckley, J. (1994). Differentiation of truthful and deceptive criminal suspects in behavior analysis interviews. *Journal of Forensic Sciences, 39*(3), 793–807.

Inbau, F. E., Reid, J. E., Buckley, J. P., & Jayne, B. C. (2013). *Criminal interrogation and confessions* (5th edn). Burlington, MA: Jones and Bartlett Learning.

Jayne, B. (1986). The psychological principles of criminal interrogation. An appendix. In F. E. Inbau, J. E. Reid, & J. P. Buckley, *Criminal interrogation and confessions* (3rd edn) (pp. 327–347). Baltimore: Williams & Wilkins.

Kassin, S. (2002) Human judges of truth, deception, and credibility: Confident but erroneous, *Cardozo Law Review*, 809–814.

Kassin, S., & Fong, C. (1999) "I'm innocent!": Effects of training on judgments of truth and deception in the interrogation room. *Law and Human Behavior, 23*, 499–516.

Kassin, S., & Norwick, R. (2004). Why people waive their Miranda rights: The power of innocence. *Law and Human Behavior, 28*, 211–221.

Kassin, S. M., Drizin, S. A., Grisso, T., Gudjonsson, G. H., Leo, R. A., & Redlich, A. D. (2010). Police-induced confessions: Risk factors and recommendations. *Law and Human Behavior, 34*, 3–38.

Kassin, S. M., Goldstein, C. J., & Savitsky, K. (2003). Behavioral confirmation in the interrogation room: On the dangers of presuming guilt. *Law and Human Behavior, 27*, 187–203.

Kassin, S. M., & Gudjonsson, G. H. (2004). The psychology of confession evidence: A review of the literature and issues. *Psychological Science in the Public Interest, 5*, 35–69.

Kassin, S. M., Leo, R. A., Meissner, C. A., Richman, K. D., Colwell, L. H., & Leach, A.-M. (2007). Police interviewing and interrogation: A self-report survey of police practices and beliefs. *Law and Human Behavior, 31*, 381–400.

Kassin, S. M., & McNall, K. (1991). Police interrogations and confessions: Communicating promises and threats by pragmatic implication. *Law and Human Behavior, 15*, 233–251.

Kelly, C., & Meissner, C. (2016). Interrogation and investigative interviewing in the United States: Research and practice. In D. Walsh, G. Oxburgh, A. Redlich, & T. Myklebust (eds). *Contemporary developments and practices in investigative interviewing and interrogation: An international perspective*. London: Routledge.

Kelly, C. E., Abdel-Salam, S., Miller, J. C., & Redlich, A. D. (2015). Social identity and the perception of effective interrogation methods. *Investigative Interviewing: Research and Practice, 7*, 1–19.

Kidd, W. R. (1940). *Police interrogation*. New York: Basuino.

Kolker, R. (October 3, 2010). "I did it." Why do people confess to crimes they didn't commit? *New York Magazine*. Retrieved from http://nymag.com/news/crimelaw/68715.

Lavine, E. (1930). *The third degree: A detailed and appalling expose of police brutality*. New York: Garden City Publishing.

Leo, R. (1992). From coercion to deception: The changing nature of police interrogation in America. *Crime, Law and Social Change, 18*, 35–59.

Leo, R. (2004) The third degree and the origins of psychological interrogation in the United States. In D. Lassiter (ed.), *Interrogations, confessions and entrapment* (pp. 37–84). Athens, OH: Springer.

Leo, R. (2008) *Police interrogation and American justice*. Cambridge, MA: Harvard University Press.

Leo, R. A. (1996). Inside the interrogation room. *Journal of Criminal Law and Criminology, 86*, 266–303.

Masip, J., Alonso, H., Garrido, E., & Herrero, C. (2009). Training to detect what? The biasing effects of training on veracity judgments. *Applied Cognitive Psychology, 23*, 1282–1296.

Masip, J., & Herrero, C. (2013). What would you say if you were guilty? Suspects' strategies during a hypothetical behaviour analysis interview concerning a serious crime. *Applied Cognitive Psychology, 27*, 60–70.

Masip, J., Herrero, C., Garrido, E., & Barba, A. (2010) Is the behaviour analysis interview just common sense? *Applied Cognitive Psychology, 25*, 593–604.

McCauliff, C. (1982) Burdens of proof: Degrees of belief, quanta of evidence, or constitutional guarantees? *Vanderbilt Law Review, 35*, 1293–1335.

Meissner, C. A., & Kassin, S. M. (2002). "He's guilty!": Investigator bias in judgments of truth and deception. *Law and Human Behavior, 26*, 469–480.

Meyer, J. R., & Reppucci, N. D. (2007). Police practices and perceptions regarding juvenile interrogation and interrogative suggestibility. *Behavioral Sciences and the Law, 25*, 757–780.

Newburn, T. (2013). *Criminology*. London: Routledge.

O'Callaghan, S (in preparation). Interviewing in the United States. Doctoral thesis, University of Portsmouth.

134   D. Walsh et al.

Redlich, A. D., Kelly, C. E., & Miller, J. C. (2014). The who, what, and why of human intelligence gathering: Self-reported measures of interrogation methods. *Applied Cognitive Psychology, 28*, 817–828.

Reppucci, N. D., Meyer, J., & Kostelnik, J. (2010). Police interrogation of juveniles: Results from a national survey of police. In G. D. Lassiter & C. Meissner (eds), *Interrogations and confessions: Current research, practices, and policy*. Washington, DC: American Psychological Association.

Senate Select Committee (2014). *Report of the Senate Select Committee on intelligence; Committee study of the Central Intelligence Agency's detention and interrogation program*. Washington: United States Government.

Slobogin, C. (1998) Let's not bury Terry: A call for rejuvenation of the proportionality principle. *St John's Law Review, 72*, 1053–1085.

Starr, D. (2015, May 22). Juan Rivera and the dangers of coercive interrogation. *The New Yorker*.

St-Yves, M., & Tanguay, M. (2009). The psychology of interrogation: A quest for a confession or a quest for the truth? In M. St-Ybes and M. Tanguay (eds), *The psychology of criminal investigations: The search for the truth* (pp. 9–40). Toronto: Cornwell.

Vrij, A., Mann, S., & Fisher, R. (2006). Information-gathering vs accusatory interview style: Individual differences in respondents' experiences. *Personality and Individual Differences, 41*, 589–599.

Walker, S. (1980). *Popular justice: A history of American criminal justice*. New York: Oxford University Press.

Walsh, D. (2012). *Interrogating suspects in the United States: Introducing a field study*. 21st Conference of the European Association of Psychology and Law, Nicosia, 13–16 April 2012.

Walsh, D., & Bull, R. (2010). The interviewing of suspects by non-police agencies: What's effective? What is effective! *Legal and Criminological Psychology, 15*, 305–321.

Walsh, D., & Bull, R. (2012a) How do interviewers attempt to overcome suspects' denials? *Psychiatry, Psychology, and Law, 19*, 151–168.

Walsh, D., & Bull, R. (2012b). Examining rapport in investigative interviews with suspects: Does its building and maintenance work? *Journal of Police and Criminal Psychology, 27*, 73–84.

Walsh, D., & Milne, R. (2008) Keeping the P.E.A.C.E.? An analysis of the taped interview performance of benefit fraud investigators within the DWP. *Legal and Criminological Psychology, 13*, 39–57.

Walters, S. B. (2003). *Principles of kinesic interview and interrogation*. Boca Raton, FL: CRC Press.

White, W. S. (2001). *Miranda's waning protections: Police interrogation practices after Dickerson*. Ann Arbor, MI: University of Michigan Press.

Wickersham, G. (1931). Program of the Commission on Law Observance and Enforcement. *The ABA Journal, 16*, 654.

Zalman, M., & Smith, B. W. (2007) Attitudes of police executives toward Miranda and interrogation policies. *Journal of Criminal Law and Criminology, 97*, 873–942.

Zulawski, D. E., Wicklander, D. E., Sturman, S. G., & Hoover, L. W. (2001). *Practical aspects of interview and interrogation* (2nd edn). Boca Raton, FL: CRC Press.

Cases

Ashcraft v. *Tennessee*, 322 U.S. 143 (1944).
Beck v. *Ohio*, 379 U.S. 89 (1964).
Berkemer v. *McCarty*, 468 U.S. 420 (1984).
Brooks v. *Florida*, 389 U.S. 413 (1961).
Brown v. *Mississippi*, 297 U.S. 278 56 S. Ct. 461, 80 L. Ed. 682 (1936).
Dickerson v. *United States*, 530 U.S. 428, 444 (2000).
Dunaway v. *New York*, 442 U.S. 200 (1979).
Escobedo v. *Illinois*, 378 U.S. 478 (1964).
Fare v. *Michael C.*, 442 U.S. 707 (1979).
Frazier v. *Cupp*, 394 U.S. 731 (1969).
Hopt v. *Utah*, 110 U.S. 574 (1884).
In re Gault, 387 U.S. 1 (1967).
Lyons v. *Oklahoma* (1944).
Malinski v. *New York*, 324 U.S. 401 (1945).
Minnesota v. *Murphy*, 465 U.S. 420, 430–431 (1984).
Miranda v. *Arizona*, 384 U.S. 436, 444–445, 467–468, 469, 471, 479, 499–555 (1966).
Moran v. *Burbine*, 475 U.S. 412, 432 (1986).
Reck v. *Pate*, 367 U.S. 433 (1961).
Stein v. *New York*, 346 U.S. 156, 182 (1959).
Stephan v. *State*, 711 P.2d 1156 (1985).
U.S. Const. amend. IV.
U.S. Const. amend. VIII.
West v. *United States*, 399 F.2d 467(1968).

Websites

www.reid.com/success_reid/r_success.html.
www.innocenceproject.org/.

8 Police interviews of sexually abused children

The state of the art in differentiating truthful and false accounts

Marilena Kyriakidou

Uncommonness of false sexual abuse allegations by children

Individuals 17 years old or younger do not usually wake up one day in their childish routine and think, '*Oh! Let's make up a lie that X touched my boobies and his penis penetrated my vagina and imprison him!*' Generally speaking, to have such a thought, a child must reason and comprehend sexual abuse as well as the legal consequences for the accuser. This may be challenging for young individuals as children have difficulties perceiving what legal personnel expect from them and have unrealistic perceptions of legal procedures, such as the illusion that they will go to jail if they lie (Saywitz & Nathanson, 1993). A child must also perceive that intercourse with an adult is wrong and therefore it is an abuse; a realisation that is not easily reached by child victims. Sas and Cunningham's (1995) qualitative study analysed 500 data files and conducted 135 interviews with children involved in sexual abuse cases that were prosecuted in Middlesex County in England between 1988 and 1993. The outcomes revealed that four out of ten children did not identify their sexual experience as wrong. The year after this study was published sexual education courses were introduced in UK schools and children today are much more likely to classify these acts as wrong. However, recent studies show that children still have difficulty in understanding what sexual abuse is (Paine & Hansen, 2002).

Consequently, it should not come as a surprise to the reader that false sexual allegations by children are uncommon. The first national study in Canada documenting the proportions of false child allegations included 7,672 suspected child abuse cases between October and December 1998 (Trocmé & Bala, 2005). These cases were reported to child welfare authorities as suspected child abuse incidents. From these cases, not a single case of false sexual abuse was attributed to a child. The false allegations of sexual abuse were attributed mostly to a custodial parent (19%). False sexual abuse reports represented 14% of the sample with 48% being neglect, 31% being physical abuse and 7% emotional maltreatment.

Turning back to our example thought, '*Oh! Let's make up a lie that X touched my boobies and his penis penetrated my vagina and imprison him!*', prior to such a thought we usually observe an analogy of Newton's third law of action-reaction applied here, which is a stimulus (=action) to trigger the child's

Police interviews of sexually abused children 137

motivation to arouse this thought (=reaction). In those rare cases in which false sexual accounts do occur they are usually accompanied by stimulus such as parental separation and mass hysteria. Starting with parental separation as a stimulus, a plethora of studies has provided evidence that false sexual abuse allegations greatly increase due to a divorce (Bala & Schuman, 2000; Gardner, 1992, 1998; Trocmé & Bala, 2005). However, a study by Thoennes and Tjaden (1990), which was a large-scale study of 9,000 separation or divorce cases, identified only 196 incidents (2%) of false sexual abuse reports. This is a surprisingly low figure compared with earlier studies. The different studies' methodologies could have resulted in the dissimilar figures and make it difficult to have a common level of comparison. Relying on the majority of studies which show the increase of false sexual allegations during divorce cases, a strong motive for such acts is the custody of the child. With such allegations, 90% of the time the allegation comes from the child's mother with the accused being the child's father (Gardner, 1992).

Moving on to mass hysteria as a stimulus for false sexual accounts parallels can be drawn with ethylene's effects on a bowl full of fruit. Ethylene is the ripening hormone and fruit produce ethylene gas when they ripen. As a result, in a bowl full of fruit, one overripe fruit will lead to the ripening of the other fruit. In an environment such as a nursery or a small village (=bowl), one false sexual allegation by a child (=one overripe fruit), is likely to cause further false reports (=ripening of other fruit). One example of the 'ripened fruit' situation took place in Little Rascals Day Care Center in Edenton in the United States. In January 1989, one child testified that he was sexually abused by one of the two owners of the centre. The next month, three more children testified that they had been sexually abused. The total number of children from the centre that eventually made allegations of sexual abuse reached 90. Most of the children that testified against the suspects were interviewed repeatedly by their parents or therapists concerning potential abuse. Parents and therapists' interviews were characterised as suggestive and inappropriate to elicit accurate accounts from children. This resulted in the accusation of 20 adults with 429 incidents of sexual abuse. The police interviews, prosecutions and trials that arose from this 'ripened fruit' situation cost more than $1.2 million and resulted in the convictions and, finally, the acquittals of all the suspects who were charged.

Sadly the consequences of such allegations, depending on the background laws and historical era in which they occurred, serviced to incommode the public economically, as in the 1600s the offenders were required to pay the expenses of their trials and imprisonment (Hill & Armstrong, 2002). Additionally, forensic premises' income was misspent, which caused further difficulties in the early twenty-first century economic recession, and wasted the time of legal personnel, which has been considered a crime since the 1960s. Most importantly innocent people were imprisoned and executed and 'real' offenders (in case we had 'real' offenders) were allowed to reoffend.

It can be seen that false sexual allegations made by children require children to consciously make sense of what sexual abuse is and what the legal consequences

138 M. Kyriakidou

of such an accusation may be. Such allegations are uncommon. In cases where they do occur they are usually made by parents during divorce cases and attributed to children during mass hysteria crises. False sexual allegations have cost people's lives in the past, placed innocent people in jail and caused unnecessary inconvenience to a lot of individuals, communities and legal personnel as well as to economic systems. Being able to distinguish between children's true and false accounts of sexual abuse would be an asset in forensic investigations. But can researchers or legal personnel spot a false sexual abuse allegation by a child?

Instruments and software for differentiating false accounts

Features of false accounts

The discussion that follows excludes people who lie without being aware of it because they have adopted a false memory. A challenging question is how to distinguish between accounts of intentional liars and truthful children. If a 17-year-old or someone younger consciously decides to provide a false testimony to fabricate sexual abuse, an effort should be made to justify this accusation. The individual in our example is about to intentionally lie during police interviews and in court. So the example thought, '*Oh! Let's make up a lie that X touched my boobies and his penis penetrated my vagina and imprison him!*' should now be turned into an action description, a story such as 'X_1 *touched my boobies and penetrated my vagina with his penis and he has to go to jail*'. These two details (touch and penetration) are the foundation of the story. Our intentional liar would need much more detail than these two aspects in order to prosecute the accuser. He or she would need to provide and support extensive details such as the time of the alleged abuse, a description of the accused's genitals, words exchanged during the abuse, etc. Based on simple mathematical logic, these two false details would need to be supported by further false details leading to a network of lies. If one false detail contradicts another detail then the liar is caught out. However, one contradiction can be covered with further lies making the detection of lying difficult. The child's process of formal logic to build up a false network of details is the key process that helps researchers to set up the boundaries between true and false accounts of children's sexual abuse.

One of these boundaries comes from capturing brain activity during intentional lying and truthful accounts. Brain waves provide indications that true and false memories can be distinguished via gamma neural oscillation (Sederberg et al., 2007). Neuroimaging techniques, event-related potentials (ERPs) and functional magnetic resonance imaging (fMRI) studies show that true and false memories' formal logic to construct a story comes from different brain areas. For instance, sensory activity is higher during the recall of true memory than false memory (Schacter & Slotnik, 2004). This activation could be because true accounts are gained from the outside, from the environment, via the sensory system (e.g. vision, auditory, olfaction/smell). The formal logic of recalling a true memory is linked to descriptions of smells or tastes because this is where it came from. In opposition, a false account is constructed from the inside, from the child's already existing cognitive schemata of the environment. Therefore, far less sensory activity is required to recall a false account as most of the formal logic of the account is based on imagination. This background setting of different brain activities between true and false memories leads to another boundary between true and false accounts, which is the content of the story. The formal logic of true accounts is signified by significantly more sensory and conceptual details as, for example, spatial, temporal and olfactory details compare with false accounts (Suengas & Johnson, 1988). Moreover, true accounts usually have, on average, much more detail of the described incident than a false description (Schooler, Gerhard, & Loftus, 1986). The features of false accounts provide clues for researchers to develop instruments to detect them. Prior to elaborating on these instruments below, the reader should be warned of the absence of a widely accepted 'Pinocchio' test. In other words, currently, there is no single test providing clear evidence on how to differentiate between true and false accounts. Placing this disappointment aside, the next section highlights the artistry of researchers to form a 'Pinocchio' test. Statement Validity Assessment (SVA) and the Reality Monitoring (RM) approach are two popular instruments aiming to assess the authenticity of an account.

Instruments to distinguish false accounts

SVA was labelled as one of the most widespread instruments used to identify children's false accounts of sexual abuse incidents (Vrij, 2000). In the 1950s the Supreme Court of Germany and Sweden called upon psychologists to determine the credibility of children making sexual abuse allegations. The principles behind Statement Reality Analysis lay in the 'Undeutch hypothesis' (Steller, 1989) that true testimonies are different in quality compared with false testimonies. The Statement Reality Analysis was partially based on psychological research. Later work produced the SVA in 1985 (Raskin & Esplin, 1991; Steller, 1989) which assesses how valid a child's testimony is and not whether the testimony is true or false (see Kapardis, 2014, pp. 280–284 for detailed discussion of SVA accuracy). There are three stages of SVA. First is the necessity of a structured interview with the child and second is the content analysis of the structured interview based on 18 content criteria, which is known as the Criterion-Based Content Analysis (CBCA). Over time, different versions of CBCA were produced with different numbers of criteria. CBCA evaluated, among other criteria, the logical coherence of the child's account, which is how logical the construction of the account is, the organisation of the account and the number of details provided. The third stage combines the CBCA outcomes with a Validity Checklist which is a questionnaire reviewing interviewee and interview characteristics, motives and the account's consistency (Steller, 1989). CBCA distinguishes true accounts from false ones based on the presence or absence of the criteria; the higher the scores on CBCA, the more likely the child's testimony is to be valid. Training is required prior to the application of CBCA.

140   M. Kyriakidou

In a study by Roma, Martini, Sabatello, Tatarelli, and Ferracuti (2011), the CBCA scores were compared between confirmed and unconfirmed (or doubtful) cases of child sexual abuse. The hypothesis was that children's testimonies from confirmed cases would result in higher CBCA scores. This was a field study with a sample of 60 confirmed and 49 unconfirmed cases. Children's average age on the confirmed cases was 9.21 years and in the unconfirmed cases was 7.81 years. There was a statistically significant difference ($p < 0.001$) between the CBCA scores on children's testimonies from confirmed and unconfirmed cases. CBCA scores for confirmed cases was 7.63 and for unconfirmed cases was 4.08. The CBCA criterion that clarified best between the two conditions was the quantity of details. Following this outcome the authors proposed that CBCA could be a useful tool for forensic investigations of child sexual abuse allegations.

Another study, Hershkowitz (2001), used CBCA to evaluate one ten-year-old child's testimony that intentionally provided a false allegation of sexual abuse to the police. The child first provided a false testimony to the police because she claimed the abuse was taking place on the shortcut in the woods that her mother had forbidden her to use. To support this lie, the child provided further lies that were not confirmed via medical examination. As a result the child provided a second testimony describing the true event. CBCA was conducted on the first and second testimony of the child. The CBCA scores were not able to provide any significant differences and the author suggested the avoidance of CBCA as a scientific tool for forensic investigations. Vrij (2005) reviewed 37 studies. The review explored the accuracy of CBCA and found that the criterion that best distinguished true accounts from false ones in most studies was the amount of detail provided. However, Vrij's (2005) review suggests that SVA cannot be safely used as a scientific tool for police investigations and by criminal courts due to the frequent inaccuracies reported in the majority of studies. Further studies show CBCA scores are sensitive and therefore easily affected by the familiarity of the person with an event (Blandon-Gitlin, Pezdek, Rogers, & Brodie, 2005; Pezdek et al., 2004) as well as guidance or coaching on the person's account (Vrij, Akehurst, Soukara, & Bull, 2004). As children's false sexual accounts may be accompanied by guidance from a parent or therapist, extra caution is warranted in using CBCA.

Another approach developed is the Reality Monitoring (RM) instrument. This approach was first published in *Psychological Review Journal* in 1981. The paper of Johnson and Raye (1981) reviewed the outcomes of studies that ended up forming the model of reality monitoring. The hypothesis here is that accounts come either from external or internal sources. Accounts that are the result of external sources would include far more perceptual details such as visual, smells, sounds. Accounts that are the result of internal sources would include far more cognitive processes such as reasoning, imagination and thought. RM aims to identify whether an account is coming from external or internal sources (Johnson & Raye, 1981). The assumption is that accounts from external sources are much more truthful than accounts from internal sources. The basic idea here is that memories from external sources or perceived events are retrieved more quickly

Police interviews of sexually abused children 141

and almost automatically with fewer decision processes compared with memories coming from internal sources. A primary question of interest in this context is what are the differences between memories coming from external sources and memories coming from internal sources? Memories that we have experienced and which came from external sources would be richer on perceptual (e.g. sounds), contextual (e.g. when, where, who) and affective (e.g. reactions) information compared with memories coming from internal sources. With Johnson and Raye's (1981) paper as a starting point, later researchers (Vrij, Mann, Kirsten, & Fisher, 2007) developed six RM criteria to discriminate true accounts from false ones. These criteria are visual, temporal, spatial, auditory, cognitive and affective details. The higher the scores obtained on these six RM criteria, the more likely it is that the statement is true.

The first study exploring RM validity was published in 1986 by Schooler, Gerhard, and Loftus. The study indicated that the descriptions of incidents that were attributed to the adult participants had significantly fewer references to sensory qualities than the true memories and that there was an accurate categorisation into true and suggested accounts of participants' memories based on RM criteria. In this study, participants had imposed memories and therefore they were not intentionally lying. Studies also applied RM onto children's accounts. Otgaar, Candel, Memon, and Almerigogna (2010) aimed to evaluate RM credibility for distinguishing children's true accounts from false ones. Two judges were trained to use RM. The judges were asked to rate 190 transcripts of children's true and false memories. The children had an average age of 9.13 years. Based on RM's six criteria, children's descriptions of true memories concerning visual details scored on average 12.26 compared with the false memories average score on the same criterion, which was 9.46. This was the only statistical ($p < 0.001$) difference of the six criteria. The remaining five RM criteria (temporal, spatial, auditory, cognitive and affective) were almost equal between children's true and false accounts. It is important to note that this study suggested false memories to children and that the children were not intentionally lying during data collection.

In contrast with the studies conducted with CBCA, the studies of RM presented here analysed participants' accounts of false memories and memories that were imposed on them. This different methodological approach makes comparison difficult. A study by Masip, Sporer, Garrido, and Herrero (2005) reviewed virtually all empirical studies that used RM. The review study provided contradictory evidence on RM's applicability. However, recent studies in the review analysis seem to suggest that RM can discriminate above chance just as CBCA.

It would be unfair for the reader to assume that these instruments are impractical. It is important to note that using CBCA and RM to detect children's false accounts is a much safer approach than relying on laypersons' judgements (people without any special knowledge of these two instruments). Strömwall and Granhag (2005) provided evidence that adults can distinguish between children's true and false accounts just above chance with 59% accuracy. In contrast with this, CBCA reached 65–90% accuracy in distinguishing children's accounts

142 *M. Kyriakidou*

(Vrij, 2005) and RM reached 64–85% accuracy rates (Masip et al., 2005). Increasing our chances within a range of 5–31% to detect a false allegation made by a child is an immediate and respectful result of researchers' efforts for our 'Pinocchio' test. Of course, research is driven by a desire to achieve more and these earlier studies inspired researchers' artistry into computerising the distinction of false accounts. The software techniques have increased our accuracy level to a range of between 67% and 72.4%.

Software to distinguish false accounts

Limitations of CBCA and RM include the extended training required prior to their applications (especially for CBCA) (Akehurst, Bull, Vrij, & Köhnken, 2004; Vrij et al., 2004; Sporer, 1997). Automatising the application of CBCA and RM via software would only require the pressing of a few buttons with no time 'wasted' on long training courses. Moreover, inter-rater reliability is required for two coders to jointly decide which details from the child's testimonies will be scored on CBCA and RM criteria. Therefore, the scores of CBCA and RM would be subject to change due to the changeability of inter-rater reliability (Sporer, 1997; Vrij, 2000). Computer software could be programmed to detect the details consistently and would not be subject to any variability. Building on CBCA and RM instruments, researchers combined linguistics involved in true and false accounts and developed programmes to analyse peoples' statements automatically (Bond & Lee, 2005; Newman, Pennebaker, Berry, & Richards, 2003).

Linguistic Inquiry Word Count (LIWC) software analyses the text of a document in terms of words and expressions used. Its database includes more than 2,000 words divided into 82 language dimensions. It was mentioned earlier that true accounts are much more likely to include perceptual details such as visual and auditory information. This assumption framed RM criteria. CBCA also relied on the number of details provided in an account. LIWC software can help researchers to analyse a child's testimony more quickly and much more accurately to detect the CBCA and RM criteria. The use of LIWC allows a much more comprehensive analysis of individuals' accounts. In Newman et al.'s study (2003), students were asked to either tell a lie or to tell the truth on a variety of themes. LIWC analysis showed that liars used fewer cognitively complex words, fewer self-referencing words (e.g. my), stated more negative emotions (e.g. hate, enemy) and used more motion verbs (e.g. move) than truth-tellers. The distinction between liars and truth-tellers was on a rate of 67%. Another study provided evidence that the accuracy rate of LIWC was 71.1% compared with RM's accuracy rate, which was 69.7% (Bond & Lee, 2005). LIWC was also applied to a study with children.

A study by Williams, Talwar, Lindsay, Bala, and Lee (2014) analysed the accounts of 47 children and 28 adults of true and false memories. Children were invited to testify in a mock court. Half of the children were advised by their parents to provide a false account on a choice of topics including birthday parties and vacations. The other half of the children were advised by their parents to

Police interviews of sexually abused children   143

describe a real experience again from the same choice of topics. The adults were also instructed to tell a true or a false story in a mock courtroom setting. The participants' accounts were analysed by LIWC and laypersons. LIWC accurately distinguished true from false accounts on a rate of 72.4% for both children and adults combined, reaching 86.8% accuracy in detecting true statements. Layperson estimates were 65% for true testimonies and 45% for false testimonies. Children's false accounts contained significantly more first person words, something that contrasts with Newman et al.'s (2003) findings that adults' false accounts have far fewer self-references. The authors attribute this to the children's egocentric nature compared with adults. Children also used many more spatial words in their true accounts, something that replicates RM's theory and that of earlier studies (Bond & Lee, 2005). LIWC has made advances on earlier instruments for detecting false accounts in terms of speech and accuracy but still is not the perfect 'Pinocchio' test. It is, however, a promising approach to detecting children's false accounts.

In summary, the formal logic to construct a lie takes a different path from the logic to describe a true event. The different paths begin from different brain activities for the two scenarios and as a result different contextual details are given in the accounts. These dissimilarities enable instruments such as CBCA, which is part of SVA, and RM to be frequently used to distinguish true accounts from false ones above chance level. Recent software (e.g. LIWC) offers new avenues for researchers to analyse children's accounts in order to establish their credibility more reliably.

Details provided so far can be compared with the field of the construction engineering of infrastructures. A simplistic analogy would place LIWC as a decorating tool within a property; something like the walls' colour. SVA and RM can represent the walls. Brain activities and contextual descriptions given during true and false accounts are similar to materials used to build the property. If we get the brain activities and contextual details wrong, this will send the rest of the construction process on a critical path of collision. It is not a random choice that a structured interview is the first stage of SVA. Getting the right details is the foundation of our construction. Police interviews are positioned on this chain as the central key to detecting false accounts. The next section explores police questioning.

Police interviews of sexually abused children: unfolding the truth

Memory is vulnerable and relatively 'weak' and police questioning can be so controlling and powerful. The aim of interviewers is to get accurate accounts. However, each interviewer utterance can increase or decrease the possibility of obtaining accurate details on sexual abuse allegations. The truthfulness of each detail given by the child depends on the interviewer's approach. If we follow our example thought, '*Oh! Let's make up a lie that X touched my boobies and his penis penetrated my vagina and imprison him!*' this child walks into a police

144   *M. Kyriakidou*

department and says, 'X_1 *touched my boobies and penetrated my vagina with his penis and he has to go to jail*', then the police would likely investigate the case. We need to pause our discussion here and introduce a new example. A second child named Y_2 also walks into the police department and tells exactly the same story as our first child (named Y_1), 'X_1 *touched my boobies and penetrated my vagina with his penis and he has to go to jail*', but in this case, Y_2 is telling the truth. Both sexual abuse allegations would be scrutinised by police interviewers. Y_1's false allegation would need to be creative and absolutely consistent to stand up to police interrogation. Both children need to provide enough reliable evidence for prosecution.

Before taking our two children into the police interview room, reasons will be provided to explain why memory is vulnerable by exploring its mental process. Pure or uncontaminated memories do not exist. Memory is not a clear reflection of our experiences but a 'constructive' process of them. Encoding, the first phase of our memory system, is the process where an experience is recorded or encoded into our brain. Encoding is affected by each person's cognitive abilities. The more familiar a person is with an event, the more possible it is that it will be encoded accurately. Stress also influences encoding. Children's sexual experiences are limited and are accompanied by stress, factors that may affect encoding. Storage is the second phase of our memory system where encoded memories are stored into short-term memory and if they survive they proceed into long-term memory. Our self-image, motives and expectations are just a few of the factors that can reconstruct stored memories. The passage of time can also weaken the authenticity of the memory. Retrieval is the final phase of our memory system. This is the phase where Y_2 would reveal her/his memories of the sexual abuse experience. Police questioning has the privilege of 'controlling' the retrieval process. Like a remote control, police questions can increase the possibility of gaining accurate details from a child's memory or lead the child to false accounts. Interviewers' approaches in combination with children's accounts will end up determining the quality of the child's testimony. There are two main categories of police approaches, the appropriate approach and the inappropriate approach. Appropriate approaches are techniques likely to retrieve accurate memories from children. Inappropriate approaches have the potential to mislead children's retrieval processes and provide false details of an event. The two examples will be temporarily set aside and attention will now turn to the description of appropriate interview techniques.

Appropriate interviewing techniques: *'well begun is half done'*

There are disagreements among researchers on how to define appropriate and inappropriate approaches and as a consequence on how to analyse them (for a comprehensive review please see Oxburg, Myklebust, & Grant, 2010). It is, however, generally accepted that facilitators and echoes are two of the safest approaches to be used during police questioning of allegedly abused children.

Facilitators encourage children to talk further, e.g. 'Go on' without affecting a child's recall. Echoes also catalyse the conversation; here the interviewer repeats a word or words from the child's earlier account. As with a facilitator, echoes stimulate a child's retrieval process by increasing the possibility of gaining a reliable testimony. Following the agreement among researchers that facilitators and echoes are safe interviewing approaches, the next agreement on what clarifies an appropriate approach are utterances such as, '*Explain to me*', '*Tell me more about this*' and '*Describe this*'. These utterances (explain, tell, describe) access what is known as recall memory. Freely recalling an event is a much safer retrieval route than sharing an event via recognition memory (e.g. Akehurst, Milne, & Köhnken, 2003). Recognition memory is less accurate when it comes to re-accessing an event through our memory (Lamb & Fauchier, 1999). '*Explain*', '*tell*' and '*describe*' utterances rarely contaminate a child's testimony. The next safest approach is the so-called wh-questions (what, why, when, where and who). This is where some disagreements start to emerge between researchers. Some studies' methodologies have five wh-questions and some have six wh-questions where 'how' is also included (Oxburg et al., 2010). Another point of disagreement is whether to define wh-questions as an open questioning technique (ones that access recall memory) or as a focused questioning technique (ones that access recognition memory). Some researchers suggest that wh-questions should be listed within open questions (Centrex, 2004) but other researchers argue they are not open questions but focused questions (Loftus, 1982). So if an interviewer says, '*Explain to me what happened*', this is considered to be a safe approach but not as safe as saying, '*Explain to me*'. Emphasising the importance of details in this context is important because details can make a difference to a court verdict about the conviction of a person or being sentenced to death in jurisdictions where such a sentence is still possible. These details are what define the state of the art on police interviews in eliciting truthful accounts from children.

There is another significant detail here which is nicely captured by Aristotle's quote, '*Well begun is half done*'. The position of appropriate approaches within an interview can influence children's accounts. Appropriate approaches are essential to the starting point of the questioning process and the very first utterances of the interviewer. Police interviews should offer as many opportunities as possible to children via open questions (explain, tell, describe), and facilitators and echoes at the early stages of the interview (Bull, 1995). Placing appropriate questions at the interview's beginning offers children a chance to practice their descriptions and leads to the production of more positive responses (Sternberg, Lamb, Davies, & Westcott, 2001). A high frequency of open-ended questions in the rapport phase can produce more accurate information from children in the following phases of the interview (Warren & Lane, 1995). The importance of the appropriate approaches' position in an interview led to the progression of suitable interview structures. Most guidelines, such as Achieving Best Evidence (2011) and P.E.A.C.E (which stands for: Preparation and Planning; Engage and Explain; Account, Clarify and Challenge; and Closure and Evaluation (Clarke &

146　*M. Kyriakidou*

Milne, 2001)) describe the importance of the very first interaction of the child with the interviewer, called the rapport phase. From the early 1980s, researchers argued that a well-constructed rapport phase facilitates retrieving information, just as poor rapport phases are more likely to influence negatively a child's account (Walsh & Bull, 2011; Walsh & Milne, 2007). Interviewers using appropriate techniques and positioning them well in an interview with a child assist the child to provide reliable details against the suspect. Conversely, there are approaches that interviewers should avoid as they are likely to contaminate children's recollections.

Inappropriate interviewing techniques

There are a variety of approaches that are considered inappropriate during police questioning of children. Inappropriate approaches are considered inappropriate because they can contaminate the retrieval process and lead children to provide false testimonies. Inappropriate approaches vary from interviewers' behaviours to interviewers' utterances. Based on Westcott and Kynan (2006) some inappropriate interviewers' behaviours include offering bribes to the child (e.g. *'If you answer this question I will give you colours'*), showing disbelief in the child's account (e.g. *'That cannot be true'*) and making inappropriate comments about the suspect (e.g. *'She was awful'*). Offering bribes is considered a serious leading technique (Ceci & Friedman, 2000) that can manipulate children's behaviour (Ettinger, Crooks & Stein, 1994) or generate inaccurate details (Garven, Wood, & Malpass, 2000). Furthermore, describing an alleged perpetrator in negative terms can also influence children's reactions (Leichtman & Ceci, 1995) and, as a result, the quality of details shared.

Turning to interviewers' inappropriate utterances we come across utterances that focus the child's attention on a specific issue by minimising the answer's length or requesting recognition of something, as well as confirmation or denial. These are generally known as focused questions. Relying on the England and Wales guidelines on questioning, focused questions are divided into specific questions (e.g. why, what, who, when, where, how), yes/no (where the answer is yes or no) and closed or choice questions (where the question offers a choice, e.g. *'Was he wearing a black or blue t-shirt?'*) (Ministry of Justice, 2011). Choice and yes/no questions are considered to be two of the least reliable interview approaches. This could be due to children's cognitive schemata on authority figures. Children assume that they have to answer police officers' or lawyers' choice questions or yes/no questions even if they do not know the answer (Poole & Lamb, 1998). In most cases children may answer choice or yes/no questions even if they do not make sense to them (or anybody) (Hughes & Grieve, 1980). Choice and yes/no questions exacerbate children's false responses. It is better to use wh-specific questions with young children rather than yes/no questions as their accounts are more easily influenced by the latter (Peterson & Biggs, 1997). Focused questions (wh-questions, choices and yes/no questions) access recognition memory which is a much less reliable source to retrieve memories from.

Police interviews of sexually abused children 147

Therefore, focused questions are likely to increase children's false accounts. Another type of inappropriate approach is repeating questions. Children in their everyday experiences in schools have learnt that when a teacher repeats a question it is usually because the child has provided the wrong answer. The teacher then repeats the question to offer another opportunity to the child to change her/his answer in order to learn (Kucuktepe, 2010). This experience is passed into children's cognitive schemata and children are likely to assume an interviewer repeats a question because they gave the wrong answer earlier. In a forensic setting, if the child changes his or her answer, they would be challenged as an inconsistent interviewee. As a result, repeating questions are likely to cause children to change their original answers (Krähenbühl & Blades, 2006). It would be ideal to have a testimony without any inappropriate questions but it seems that there is a kind of necessity to use inappropriate questions during police interviews with children.

Appropriate interviewing approaches offer us a powerful tool to elicit truthful and reliable details from children. They do, however, come at a price. As children are not familiar with sexual experiences they may rely on interviewers' cues to recall an event. A cue could be *'Compared with me, how tall was he?'* These cues are typically phrased as focused questions. So in a way, focused questions may be more developmentally appropriate for questioning children and can result in the provision of important information for a criminal investigation that children might not have recalled otherwise. This can be challenging for legal personnel to handle during questioning as ascertaining what happened, by whom, how, where and when in an interview is crucial for forensic investigations (Milne & Bull, 2006). Studies found that when children were asked open-ended questions to describe their visit to a medical doctor, they only provided 10% (Saywitz, Goodman, Nicholas, & Moan, 1991) and 25% (Steward et al., 1996) of details of all the body touches. Further studies supported the theory that children will not reveal any vital abuse details after the first few open-ended questions but only do so after focused questions (DeVoe & Faller, 2002). This wave of studies provides strong indications that focused questions are essential to help children describe alleged sexual abuse. After defining the most and least appropriate approaches for police questioning of children, we need to acknowledge the emphasis given to them by police guidelines and legislations.

Police guidelines

Guidelines have been influenced by researchers whose aim has been to increase the extent and accuracy of children's accounts. Guidelines in Cyprus, England, Sweden, Norway and Finland emphasise the superiority of open-ended questions as well as the recommendation that focused questions should be used later in an interview (Ministry of Justice, 2011). Guidelines also suggest that in case a focused question needs to be asked it should be immediately followed with open ended questions. For example, *'Was she eating a pizza or a burger? Describe to me what she was eating'*.

148 *M. Kyriakidou*

Researchers' clarification of appropriate and inappropriate interviewing approaches led to the construction of police guidelines as well as to police training courses. Field studies investigated whether these scientific suggestions are applied by police interviewers in different countries. Evidence shows that interviewers do not merely rely on appropriate approaches to interview children. Inappropriate interviewing approaches have been found to dominate forensic interviews with children in countries such as Cyprus (Kyriakidou, 2011), England and Wales (Sternberg et al., 2001), Finland (Korkman, Santtila, & Sandnabba, 2006), Norway (e.g. Lønnum, Thoresen, Melinder, Stridbeck, & Magnussen, 2006), USA (Craig, Scheibe, Raskin, Kircher, & Dodd, 1999), Sweden (Cederborg, Orbach, Sternberg, & Lamb, 2000), and Israel (Lamb et al., 1996). In all of these studies interviewers were relying heavily on focused questions to gain details on alleged abuse resulting sometimes in up to half of children's accounts coming from focused questions. A further point of concern is the interview structure with the rapport phase frequently being absent or too brief during forensic interviews with children (e.g. Westcott & Kynan, 2004). Moreover, most interviewers start their interviews with focused questions (e.g. Cederborg et al., 2000). It seems that important guidelines are omitted during interviewing and this omission can challenge the decision to proceed with the testimony to a trial.

Judging children's testimonies in court

Returning to our examples, Y_1 walked into the police interviewing room and intentionally provided a false testimony of a sexual abuse incident, Y_2 provided a truthful testimony. The next step is for legal personnel to determine whether these two testimonies will proceed to prosecution and to a trial. The primary criterion would be the number of details provided in the testimony. If a testimony has a lot of detail (or evidence) against the suspect it is likely that the case will be taken to court. In addition to this, the testimony should also demonstrate competency and credibility. Combining our knowledge on the different characteristics of true and false accounts, it would be expected that Y_1's false accusation would have far less chance of proceeding to trial. This would be because Y_1's account would have far fewer details and, most likely, less consistency. This is a hypothesis and not a fact; as discussed earlier, there are a number of false testimonies which have resulted in convictions in the past. The testimonies from Y_1 and Y_2 would be judged on another factor beyond the child's control. This is the interviewer's performance. Researchers have asked adults to judge the quality of testimonies and the outcomes provide evidence that adults often characterise a child's testimony as less convincing when inappropriate questions have been used (Lindsay & Lamb, 2010). So if an interviewer's performance is extremely poor this may cost the prosecution the case.

If the cases of both children from our example proceed to trial their testimonies of sexual abuse will finally be judged in a court of law. All themes discussed so far (e.g. motivations, contextual details, instruments used, police

Police interviews of sexually abused children 149

questioning) would be comprehensively elaborated upon between two parties, the prosecution (the child's lawyer) and the defence (the suspect's lawyer/s). In adversarial legal systems, the two opposite parties would present their positions in an attempt to contradict each other's evidence. In child abuse cases unambiguous evidence (like medical evidence) does not usually exist. For example, of all cases investigated by the Cyprus police that required a child's testimony between 2004 and 2009, two-thirds did not have any other evidence available except for the child's testimony (Kyriakidou, 2011). Lack of other evidence such as medical records or third party testimonies is common in child sexual abuse cases. Consequently, the key strategy for the defence party is to prove that the child's testimony is too unreliable to convict the suspect. As a result, judges in trials without juries (bench trials) and the juries, where they are present, are heavily dependent on the police questioning to determine the outcome of a trial (Porter & Brinke, 2009). Defence lawyers will pick up focused questions by interviewers and each inconsistency of a child's account to characterise the police interview as misleading and the child as an unreliable witness. Interviewers' inappropriate approaches and children's inconsistencies would be the focus of attention in court (Wood & Garven, 2000). Children can be susceptible to courtroom interrogation as one party will aim to prove them wrong. There are procedures here that can assist children to provide accurate evidence.

Attention should be given to these procedures as defence lawyers will take advantage of memory's 'weakness' and the powerful tool of questioning to prove the child is an unreliable witness. Defence lawyers use mostly inappropriate questioning approaches like repeating questions and multiple questions (Back, Gustafsson, Larsson, & Bertero, 2011) because these questions reduce the accuracy of children's accounts. One of these procedures is part of a judge's duties in an adversarial system and is to ensure that both the alleged victim and the suspect receive a fair trial and are treated with respect during the trial. For example, judges can interrupt lawyers' questioning and stop inappropriate behaviour. At this point police interviewing is often challenged during defence and prosecution lawyers' arguments under the 'supervision' of judges. The judge's 'supervision' is an indirect process that assists children. More direct processes that can help children are the opportunity to testify via a video link and to familiarise themselves with the trial procedures via pre-trial preparation. Such procedures reduce stress during a child's testimony in court and increase the possibility of children resisting leading questions by defence lawyers (e.g. Cashmore, 2002). The comprehensive and complex interviewing techniques used in a court environment will use all information for and against Y_1 and Y_2's accounts. It is expected that such a detailed interrogation will help the justice system to reach the right decision, which is convicting the offender involved in Y_2's sexual abuse.

In summary, memory is vulnerable to various cognitive processes, making it sometimes unreliable. In contrast, police questioning can influence the accuracy of memories recalled by children based on the use of appropriate and inappropriate approaches. Facilitators, echoes and utterances such as 'tell', 'explain' and

150   M. Kyriakidou

'describe to me' are considered to be the safest approach to elicit reliable evidence. It is advisable to use these safe approaches at the early stages of police interviews to further assist the possibility of gaining reliable evidence. Inappropriate behaviours mainly consist of offering bribes to children, showing disbelief and making unsuitable comments about the suspect. Inappropriate utterance are wh-questions (these are also considered appropriate by some researchers), yes/no questions and choice questions. Police guidelines highlight these questioning techniques and advise interviewers to base their interviews on appropriate approaches. These guidelines are not widely followed by practitioners, resulting in most police interviews having mostly inappropriate utterances within them. Courtroom procedures such as testifying from a video link and pre-trial preparation can help children to provide much more accurate information during their testimonies in trials.

Conclusions

False sexual abuse allegations by children are rare. When they do occur, usually by the guidance of divorced parents or therapies during mass hysteria, they end up causing serious inconveniences for individuals and the society. Since the 1950s, researchers have been invited to distinguish false accusations. The need to distinguish such accusations has resulted in the development of instruments such as Criteria-Based Content Analysis (CBCA), Reality Monitoring (RM) and recently the use of Linguistic Inquiry Word Count (LIWC). Today, we are in an advanced position to conduct carefully structured police interviews with children to gain the best out of such accusations. Police questioning as well as children's accounts are challenged in court for justice to prevail. The state of the art in differentiating false accounts lies in unifying fabrication characteristics into testing instruments and, importantly, police interviewing approaches. The research presented in this chapter documents the progress that has been made by researchers that provides the knowledge, tools and interviewing techniques necessary to meet this challenge.

References

Akehurst, L., Bull, R., Vrij, A., & Köhnken, G. (2004). The effects of training professional groups and lay person to use criteria-based content analysis to detect deception. *Applied Cognitive Psychology, 18*(7), 877–889.

Akehurst, L., Milne, R., & Köhnken, G. (2003). The effects of children's age and delay on recall in a cognitive or structured interview. *Psychology Crime and Law, 9*, 97–107.

Back, C., Gustafsson, P. A., Larsson, I., & Bertero, C. (2011). Managing the legal proceedings: An interpretative phenomenological analysis of sexually abused children's experience with the legal progress. *Child Abuse & Neglect, 35*, 50–57.

Bala, N., & Schuman, J. (2000). Allegations of sexual abuse when parents have separated. *Canadian Family Law Quarterly, 17*, 191–241.

Blandon-Gitlin, I., Pezdek, K., Rogers, R., & Brodie, L. (2005). The effects of event familiarity on Criteria-Based Content Analysis ratings: An experimental study. *Law and Human Behavior, 29*, 187–197.

Police interviews of sexually abused children 151

Bond, G. D., & Lee, A. Y. (2005). Language of lies in prison: Linguistic classification of prisoners' truthful and deceptive natural language. *Applied Cognitive Psychology, 19*(3), 313–329.

Bull, R. (1995). Innovative techniques for the questioning of child witnesses, especially those who are young and those with learning disability. In M. Zaragoza, G. Graham, G. Hall, R. Hirschman, & Y. Ben-Porath (eds), *Memory and testimony in the child witness* (pp. 179–194). Thousand Oaks, CA: Sage.

Cashmore, J. (2002). Innovative procedures for child witnesses. In G. M. Davies & R. H. Bull (eds), *Children's testimony: A handbook of psychological research and forensic practice* (pp. 203–217). West Sussex, England: John Wiley and Sons.

Ceci, S. J., & Friedman, R. D. (2000). The suggestibility of children: Scientific research and legal implications. *Cornell Law Review, 86*, 34–108.

Cederborg, A., Orbach, Y., Sternberg, K. L., & Lamb, M. E. (2000). Investigative interviews of child witnesses in Sweden. *Child Abuse & Neglect, 24*, 1355–1361.

Centrex (2004). *Practical Guide to Investigative Interviewing*. London: Central Police Training and Development Authority.

Clarke, C., & Milne, R. (2001). *National evaluation of the PEACE investigative interviewing course*. Police Research Award Scheme Report No. PRAS/149. London: Home Office.

Craig, R. A., Scheibe, R., Raskin, D. C., Kircher, J. C., & Dodd, D. H. (1999). Interviewer questions and content analysis of children's statements of sexual abuse. *Applied Developmental Science, 3*, 77–85.

DeVoe, E. R., & Faller, K. C. (2002). Questioning strategies in interviews with children who may have been sexually abused. *Child Welfare, 81*, 5–32.

Ettinger, R. H., Crooks, R. L., & Stein, J. (1994). *Psychology: Science, behavior and life*. Fort Worth, TX: Harcourt Brace.

Gardner, R. (1992). *True and false accusations of child sex abuse*. Cresskill, NJ: Creative Therapeutics.

Gardner, R. (1998). *The parental alienation syndrome* (2nd ed.). Cresskill, NJ: Creative Therapeutics.

Garven, S., Wood, J. M., & Malpass, R. (2000). Allegations of wrongdoing: The effects of reinforcement on children's mundane and fantastic claims. *Journal of Applied Psychology, 85*, 38–49.

Hershkowitz, I. (2001). A case study of child sexual false allegation. *Child Abuse & Neglect, 25*, 1397–1411.

Hill, F., & Armstrong, K. (2002). *A delusion of Satan: The full story of the Salem witch trials*. Boston, MA: Da Capo Press.

Hughes, M., & Grieve, R. (1980). On asking children bizarre questions. *First Language, 1*, 149–160.

Johnson, M. K., & Raye, C. L. (1981). Reality Monitoring. *Psychological Review, 88*(1), 67–85.

Kapardis, A. (2014). *Psychology and law: A critical introduction* (4th edn). Cambridge, England: Cambridge University Press.

Korkman, J., Santtila, P., & Sandnabba, N. K. (2006). Dynamics of verbal interaction between interviewer and child interviews with alleged victims of child sexual abuse. *Scandinavian Journal of Psychology, 47*, 109–119.

Krähenbühl, S., & Blades, M. (2006). The effect of question repetition within interviews on young children's eyewitness recall. *Journal of Experimental Child Psychology, 94*, 57–67.

152   *M. Kyriakidou*

Kucuktepe, C. (2010). Examination of question types used by elementary school teachers in the process of teaching and learning. *Procedia Social and Behavioral Sciences, 2,* 5190–5195.

Kyriakidou, M. (2011). *Evaluation of children's testimonies in the Republic of Cyprus: Implications for criminal and legal procedures.* PhD Thesis, Sheffield University.

Lamb, M. E., & Fauchier, A. (1999). *The effects of question type on the accuracy of children's responses in forensic interviews.* Unpublished manuscript, National Institute of Health and Human Development, Bethesda, MD.

Lamb, M. E., Hershkowitz, I., Sternberg, K. J., Esplin, P. W., Hovav, M., Manor, T., et al. (1996). Effects of investigative utterance types on Israeli children's responses. *International Journal of Behavioral Development, 19,* 627–637.

Leichtman, M. D., & Ceci, S. J. (1995). The effects of stereotypes and suggestions on preschoolers' reports. *Developmental Psychology, 31,* 568–578.

Lindsay, C. M., & Lamb, M. E. (2010). Biases in judging victims and whose statements are inconsistent. *Law and Human Behavior, 34,* 46–48.

Loftus, E. (1982) Interrogating eyewitnesses – good questions and bad. In R. Hogarth (ed.), *Question framing and response consistency* (pp. 51–63). San Francisco: Jossey-Bass.

Lønnum, K., Thoresen, C., Melinder, A., Stridbeck, U., & Magnussen, S. J. (2006). Theory and practice in interviewing young children: A study of Norwegian police interviews 1985–2002. *Psychology, Crime and Law, 12,* 629–640.

Masip, J., Sporer, S., Garrido, E., & Herrero, C. (2005). The detection of deception with the reality monitoring approach. A review of the empirical evidence. *Psychology, Crime & Law, 11,* 99–122.

Ministry of Justice (2011). *Achieving best evidence in criminal proceedings: Guidance on interviewing victims and witnesses, and guidance on using special measures.*

Milne, R., & Bull, R. (2006) Interviewing victims of crime, including children and people with intellectual difficulties. In M. R. Kebbell & G. M. Davies (eds), *Practical psychology for forensic investigations* (pp. 7–23). Chichester, England: Wiley.

Newman, M. L., Pennebaker, J. W., Berry, D. S., & Richards, J. M. (2003). Lying words: Predicting deception from linguistic styles. *Personality and Social Psychology Bulletin, 29*(5), 665–675.

Otgaar, H., Candel, I., Memon, A., & Armerigogna, J. (2010). Differentiating between children's true and false memories using reality monitoring criteria. *Psychology, Crime, & Law, 16,* 555–566.

Oxburgh, G., Myklebust, T., & Grant, T. (2010) The question of question types in police interviews: A review of the literature from a psychological and linguistic perspective. *International Journal of Speech Language and the Law, 17,* 45–66.

Paine, M. L., & Hansen, D. (2002). Factors influencing children to self-disclose sexual abuse. *Clinical Psychology Review, 22,* 271–295.

Peterson, C., & Biggs, M. (1997). Interviewing children about trauma: Problems with "specific" questions. *Journal of Traumatic Stress, 10,* 279–290.

Pezdek, K., Morrow, A., Blandon-Gitlin, I., Goodman, G. S., Quas, J. A., Saywitz, K. J., et al. (2004). Detecting deception in children: Event familiarity affects Criteria-Based Content Analysis ratings. *Journal of Applied Psychology, 89,* 119–126.

Poole, D. A., & Lamb, M. E. (1998). *Investigative interviews of children: A guide for helping professionals.* Washington, DC: American Psychological Association.

Porter, S., & Brinke, L. (2009). Dangerous decisions: A theoretical framework for understanding how judges assess credibility in the courtroom. *Legal and Criminological Psychology, 14,* 119–134.

Police interviews of sexually abused children 153

Raskin, D. C., & Esplin, P. W. (1991). Statement validity assessment: Interview procedures and content analysis of children's statements of sexual abuse. *Behavioral Assessment, 13*, 265–291.

Roma, P., Martini, P. S., Sabatello, U., Tatarelli, R., & Ferracuti, S. (2011). Validity of Criteria-Based Content Analysis (CBCA) at trial in free-narrative interviews. *Child Abuse & Neglect, 35*, 613–620.

Sas, L. D., & Cunningham, A. H. (1995). *Tipping the balance to tell the secret: The public discovery of child sexual abuse.* London, Ontario, Canada: London Family Court Clinic.

Saywitz, K., Goodman, G., Nicholas, E., & Moan, S. (1991). Children's memory for a genital examination: Implications for child sexual abuse cases. *Journal of Consulting and Clinical Psychology, 59*, 682–691.

Saywitz, K., & Nathanson, R. (1993). Children's testimony and their perceptions of stress in and out of the courtroom. *Child Abuse & Neglect, 17*, 613–622.

Schacter, D. L., & Slotnik, S. D. (2004). The cognitive neuroscience of memory distortion. *Neuron, 44*, 149–160.

Schooler, J. W., Gerhard, D., & Loftus, E. F. (1986). Qualities of the unreal. *Journal of Experimental Psychology: Learning, Memory, and Cognition, 12*, 171–181.

Sederberg, P. B., Schulze-Bonhage, A., Madsen, J. R., Bromfield, E. B., Litt, B., Brandt, A., & Kahana, M. J. (2007). Gamma oscillations distinguish true from false memories. *Psychological Science, 18*, 927–932.

Sporer, S. L. (1997). The less travelled road to truth: Verbal cues in deception detection in accounts of fabricated and self-experienced events. *Applied Cognitive Psychology, 11*(5), 373–397.

Steller, M. (1989). Recent development in statement analysis. In J. C. Yuille (ed.), *Credibility assessment* (pp. 135–154). Dordrecht, Netherlands: Kluwer.

Sternberg, K. J., Lamb, M. E., Davies, G. M., & Westcott, H. L. (2001). The memorandum of good practice: Theory versus application. *Child Abuse & Neglect, 25*, 669–681.

Steward, M. S., Steward, D. S., Farquhar, L., Myers, J. E., Reinhart, M., & Welker, J. J. (1996). Interviewing young children about body touch and handling. *Monographs of the Society for Research in Child Development, 57*, 1–232.

Strömwall, L. A., & Granhag, P. A. (2005). Children's repeated lies and truths: Effects on adults' judgments and reality monitoring scores. *Psychiatry, Psychology and Law, 12*(2), 345–356.

Suengas, A. G., & Johnson, M. K. (1988). Qualitative effects of rehearsal on memories for perceived and imagined complex events. *Journal of Experimental Psychology: General, 117*, 377–389.

Thoennes, N., & Tjaden, P. (1990). The extent, nature, and validity of sexual abuse allegations in custody/visitation disputes. *Child Abuse & Neglect, 14*, 151–163.

Trocmé, N., & Bala, N. (2005). False allegations of abuse and neglect when parents separate. *Child Abuse & Neglect, 29*, 1333–1345.

Vrij, A. (2000). *Detecting lies and deceit: The psychology of lying and its implications for professional practice.* Chichester, England: Wiley.

Vrij, A. (2005). Criteria-Based Content Analysis: A qualitative review of the first 37 studies. *Psychology, Public Policy, and Law, 11*(1), 3–41.

Vrij, A., Akehurst, L., Soukara, S., & Bull, R. (2004). Let me inform you how to tell a convincing story: CBCA and reality monitoring scores as a function of age, coaching, and deception. *Canadian Journal of Behavioral Science, 24*, 239–263.

154 *M. Kyriakidou*

Vrij, A., Mann, S., Kirsten, S., & Fisher, R. P. (2007). Cues to deception and ability to detect lies as a function of police interview styles. *Law and Human Behavior, 31*, 499–518.

Walsh, D., & Bull, R. (2011). Benefit fraud investigative interviewing: A self-report study of investigation professionals' beliefs concerning practice. *Journal of Investigative Psychology and Offender Profiling, 8*, 131–148.

Walsh, D. W., & Milne, R. (2007). Giving P.E.A.C.E. a chance: A study of DWP investigators' perceptions of their interviewing practices. *Public Administration, 25*, 525–540.

Warren, A., & Lane, P. (1995). Effects of timing and type of questioning on eyewitness accuracy and suggestibility. In M. Zaragoza, J. R. Graham, G. C. Hall, R. Hirschman, & Y. S. Ben-Porath (eds), *Memory and testimony in the child witness* (pp. 23–46). Thousand Oaks, CA: Sage.

Westcott, H., & Kynan, S. (2006). Interviewer practice in investigative interviews for suspected child sexual abuse. *Psychology, Crime and Law, 12*, 367–382.

Westcott, H. L., & Kynan, S. (2004). The application of a "story telling" framework to investigative interviews for suspected child sexual abuse. *Legal and Criminological Psychology, 9*(1), 37–56.

Williams, S. M., Talwar, V., Lindsay, R. C. L., Bala, N., & Lee, K. (2014). Is the truth in your words? Distinguishing children's deceptive and truthful statement. *Journal of Criminology*, 1–9.

Wood, J. M., & Garven, S. (2000). How sexual abuse interviews go astray: Implications for prosecutors, police, and child protection services. *Child Maltreatment, 5*, 109–129.

9 Psychophysiological detection of deception

A review of detection methods, recent research and potential forensic applications

Gershon Ben-Shakhar

Deception is a frequent, perhaps essential, feature of human behavior, which may be expressed in a variety of situations (e.g., Saxe, 1991). The frequent use of deception in social contexts highlights the importance of detecting deception. Indeed, scientists, forensic experts and law enforcement agencies have attempted for many years to develop methods and instruments for detecting deception. However, since research on perceivers' ability to differentiate between truthful and deceptive messages has indicated that, in most cases, people, including professionals whose tasks involve detection of deceit, perform this task not much better than chance levels (see DePaulo, 1994; DePaulo et al., 2003; Ekman and O'Sullivan, 1991; Vrij, 2008), it is not surprising that the idea of using physiological measures for detecting deception has been very appealing to law-enforcement agencies (e.g., Larson, 1932; Marston, 1917, 1938; Reid, 1947; Reid & Inbau, 1977). Indeed, several psychophysiological methods (popularly labeled, "polygraph techniques") have been developed since the beginning of the twentieth century and the study of psychophysiological detection of deception has attracted a great deal of interest among researchers as well as practitioners and has become an important area of applied psychology (e.g., Ben-Shakhar & Furedy, 1990; Lykken, 1998; National Research Council, 2003; Raskin, 1989; Reid & Inbau, 1977). This interest has considerably increased since the September 11th terror attack in the United States and the subsequent terror activities in Europe (for a review of recent research, see Ben-Shakhar, 2012; Rosenfeld, Ben-Shakhar, & Ganis, 2012; Verschuere, Ben-Shakhar, & Meijer, 2011). Furthermore, the increased need to detect suspects involved in planning and executing terror activities has raised new questions that require new research directions (see a review in Ben-Shakhar, 2012).

Unfortunately, the literature dealing with psychophysiological detection of deception is clouded by lack of conceptual clarity and a host of methodological problems (see Ben-Shakhar & Meijer, 2012). These problems are not unique to any specific physiological measure, but relate to the research paradigms that have been adopted to study deception and its detection. Various recent publications, including the National Research Council report (National Research Council, 2003), fail to make proper distinctions between the various paradigms

156   *G. Ben-Shakhar*

used to study psychophysiological detection and lump them together under the misleading term "polygraph". For example, Sip, Roepstorff, McGregor, and Frith (2007, p. 50) write that "traditional paradigms used to detect deceptive behavior, such as the polygraph has many disadvantages." However, the term polygraph merely refers to the device used to record the physiological measures. It becomes a potentially diagnostic tool only when used in combination with a paradigm and a set of inference rules that specify how diagnostic decisions are made. It should be emphasized that all the shortcomings of what has been termed "traditional polygraph tests" are related to weaknesses of the paradigms used, rather than to the reliability and validity of autonomic nervous system (ANS) measures.

In this chapter, I will describe and compare the two prevalent paradigms of psychophysiological detection, focusing on their underlying rationales, their scientific validity and their potential usage as forensic tools. I will also point out several recent developments that may enhance the forensic applicability of psychophysiological detection methods.

Methods of psychophysiological detection

The various psychophysiological detection methods that have been developed can be broadly classified into two categories: (1) Methods designed to detect deception, which rely on physiological responses to direct questions (e.g., "did you break into the Jewelry store on Thursday night?"); and (2) methods designed to detect concealed knowledge (e.g., "was the stolen jewel, a golden watch?", "was it a diamond ring?"). The detection method, most closely associated with the first category, has been labeled the Control (or more recently, comparison) Questions Technique (CQT). The CQT has been the preferable detection method used by law enforcement agencies in the United States and subsequently in various other countries. Yet, the scientific foundation and the validity of the CQT have been debated and nowadays it is considered by most researchers as lacking scientific foundation (e.g., Ben-Shakhar, 2002; Honts, Raskin, & Kircher, 2002; Iacono & Lykken, 2002; National Research Council, 2003). The method designed to detect concealed knowledge was traditionally labeled The Guilty Knowledge Test (GKT, see Lykken, 1959, 1960), but more recently it has been referred to as The Concealed Information Test (CIT, see Verschuere et al., 2011). Although the CIT does have a solid rationale, theoretical basis and empirical support (e.g., Lykken, 1974; Meijer, Klein Selle, Elber, & Ben-Shakhar, 2014; Verschuere & Ben-Shakhar, 2011), it has been rarely implemented as an aid in criminal investigations and it is extensively applied only in Japan (Osugi, 2011).

The CQT

The CQT was developed in the United States during the 1940s by practitioners (e.g., Reid, 1947; Reid & Inbau, 1977) and its development was not guided by research and theory. However, it was apparent from the outset that analyzing physiological responses of an examinee to relevant questions would be meaningless unless these responses could be compared to some baseline response measure of this examinee. Thus, the CQT includes control questions, now referred to as comparison questions. These questions relate to general, nonspecific misconducts, of a nature as similar as possible to the issue under investigation (e.g., "Have you ever taken something that did not belong to you?").

The CQT is administered in several stages: First, the examiner becomes familiar with the facts of the case by reading the written report and by speaking directly to the police investigator who ordered the examination. Typically, relevant background information, such as the suspect's past criminal record, is made available to the examiner. During the next stage the examiner conducts a pre-test interview, in which the examinee is given the opportunity to talk about the offense and present his or her version of the case. The series of questions, to be asked later in the actual examination stage, is formulated during this pre-test interview through an examiner-examinee interaction. The examiner discusses the formulation of the questions with the examinee and ensures that he or she understands them and can give a direct "yes" or "no" answer to each question. The examiner explains the testing procedure and informs the examinee that the examination is voluntary. The next stage is the actual examination stage during which the examinee is attached to the polygraph. Typically, the examiner will attempt to convince the examinee that the polygraph is highly accurate. For this purpose a rigged card-test is usually administered either before conducting the CQT, or during an intermission between CQT sessions (for a more detailed description of this procedure, see Ben-Shakhar & Furedy, 1990; Saxe, 1991).

During the examination stage a series of questions is presented to the examinee while continuously measuring several physiological reactions. Typically, at least three physiological indices are used: Changes in respiration, obtained from a tube attached around the thorax and abdomen; changes in electrodermal activity, obtained from two electrodes placed on the palm surface of two fingers; and changes in relative blood pressure, obtained from a partially inflated cuff placed around the upper arm. The questions are of three general types and in addition to the relevant and comparison questions described above, several irrelevant questions focusing on completely neutral issues (e.g., are you sitting on a chair?) are presented to absorb the initial orienting response evoked by any opening question, and to enable rest periods between the more loaded questions. Typically, the whole question series includes about ten questions and is repeated at least three times.

The inference rule used to derive the outcomes of the test (i.e., the rule underlying inferences from a given pattern of physiological responding to a conclusion of guilt versus innocence, or truth versus deception) is based on a comparison of the responses evoked by the relevant and the control questions. Deceptive individuals are expected to show more pronounced responses to the relevant questions, whereas truthful individuals are expected to show the opposite response pattern (i.e., more pronounced responses to the control questions). Thus, a pattern of consistently larger responses to the relevant than to the control questions is taken as an indication of deception ("deception indicated"); whereas a consistent pattern of larger responses to the control questions will lead to a conclusion that the examinee is answering truthfully ("no deception indicated"). An inconsistent pattern of responding or a pattern of no differences in the responses to the two types of questions will lead to an inconclusive decision.

The CIT

The CIT (see Verschuere et al., 2011) is not a deception test, but rather designed to detect whether an examinee possesses certain information. It can be used as an aid to law enforcement agencies because discriminating between suspects who possess crime-related information and those who are unaware of this information, may indicate involvement in a crime. In the CIT, examinees are presented with a series of multiple-choice questions, each having one relevant alternative (e.g., a feature of the crime under investigation) and several neutral (control) alternatives, chosen so that an innocent suspect would not be able to discriminate them from the relevant alternative. On the other hand, a guilty suspect who is familiar with the details of the crime would be able to discriminate between the relevant and the neutral, control items. Furthermore, the familiar, relevant alternative is of great significance for the guilty suspect.

Unlike deception tests (e.g., the CQT), the development of the CIT was based on research and theory (e.g., Ben-Shakhar & Elaad, 2003; Lykken, 1974; Verschuere & Ben-Shakhar, 2011) and the CIT effect (enhanced responses to the relevant items among knowledgeable examinees) can be accounted for by the well established observation that rare and significant stimuli elicit enhanced physiological responses, either with ANS measures (e.g., Sokolov, 1963) or event-related potentials (ERPs) (Donchin, 1981). Thus, this effect does not reflect deception, although a deceptive response may increase the CIT effect (e.g., Horneman & O'Gorman, 1985). The CIT has been studied extensively with both ANS measures (see Gamer, 2011a for a review) and in the last two decades with ERP measures (see Rosenfeld, 2011 for a review). Recently, several CIT studies using brain imaging techniques have been published (see reviews by Gamer, 2011b and Rosenfeld, Ben-Shakhar, & Ganis, 2012).

A comparison of the two psychophysiological detection paradigms

In this section I will compare the CQT and the CIT. This comparison will be conducted along several critical factors that are essential for any scientifically based technique.

Theoretical basis and underlying rationale: An essential requirement of any technique, derived from scientific principles, is that it would be linked to a theory that can be tested and validated. Indeed, modern views of the concept of validity (e.g., Messick, 1995) include the theoretical foundation as an essential element. This implies that in order to validate a test or a method, it is not

Psychophysiological detection of deception 159

sufficient to demonstrate that its results correlate with a relevant criterion (i.e., predictive, or criterion validity). A theoretical foundation is particularly important for validating psychophysiological detection methods because we need to generalize from experimental situations to realistic settings and this is virtually impossible without a theory.

Saxe and Ben-Shakhar (1999) analyzed the CQT, in light of Messick's (1989, 1995) approach and showed that it cannot be regarded as a valid test of deception. Specifically, there is no theory that can establish the relationships between the physiological changes measured in the CQT and deception. Thus, Saxe and Ben-Shakhar (1999) argued that the two major sources of invalidity noted by Messick (1995) affect CQT polygraph testing. First, the construct of deception is underrepresented by the CQT results, because there is neither a theoretical rationale, nor empirical evidence to support the relationship between the physiological measures monitored during the CQT examination and deceptive behavior. Second, CQT results may reflect other constructs, such as surprise, mental effort, anxiety and stress. Consequently, it suffers from the second major threat to validity suggested by Messick, namely "construct-irrelevant variance" – the assessment is too broad, and contains excess reliable variance associated with other distinct constructs.

Recently, Palmatier and Rovner (2014) have proposed that the preliminary process theory (PPT), proposed by Barry (2006, 2009) can account for the outcomes of the CQT. However, they completely failed to show how the PPT is related to the CQT. Particularly, the assumption that innocent suspects will be more concerned with the control than with the relevant questions cannot be accounted for by any known theory, including the PPT (see a critique by Ben-Shakhar, Gamer, Iacono, Meijer, & Verschuere, 2014).

Indeed, many CQT proponents (e.g., Raskin, 1986) have abandoned the notion of "a specific lie response", but argued that inferences about truth or deception could be made by comparing the relative strength of the subject's responses to relevant and control questions. However, no convincing rationale for such inferences has been given so far. The major problem stems from the nature of the control questions used in the CQT. The phrase "Control Questions" gives the impression that true controls are being exercised. From a logical perspective, true controls require a perfect match between all factors other than the factor being tested (in this case, the factor of deception or involvement in a crime). Hence, the control questions ought to be just like the relevant questions in all details, though only the relevant questions should tie the suspect to the crime. In other words, from the perspective of an innocent suspect there ought to be no differences whatsoever between the two types of questions. Whereas this kind of control is exercised in the CIT, it does not exist in the CQT. The relevant CQT questions relate directly to the specific event being investigated, while the control questions relate to general, non-specific crimes. Clearly, one cannot assume that these questions are equivalent. The differences between the two types of questions are obvious, and even an innocent suspect can easily distinguish between a question that relates directly to the focal event around which the

160   *G. Ben-Shakhar*

investigation revolves and general questions related to hypothetical events from the examinee's past. Moreover, once examinees become aware of the CQT's rationale and inference rule, it is quite obvious to them that only the relevant questions pose a real threat. It should be stressed that the problematic nature of the control questions is not merely semantic, and calling these questions "comparison questions", as has been proposed by many CQT proponents, would not make the CQT's inference rule more reasonable and would not provide better protection against false-positive outcomes.

Supporters of the CQT claim that a skilled interrogator is capable of choosing control questions, while interviewing the suspect and of creating an atmosphere that leads innocent examinees, who believe in the veracity of their answers, to be more concerned with the control than the relevant questions, while guilty suspects become more concerned with the relevant than the control questions (see, e.g., Honts & Perry, 1992). Unfortunately, other than the polygraphists' strong belief in this assumption, it has no grounding in psychological or psychophysiological research, nor is it convincing in its inner logic. Honts and Perry's reasoning rests on the assumption that "belief in the veracity of their answers to the relevant questions" *is sufficient* to guarantee that innocent suspects will show larger physiological responses to the control questions. This might have made sense, if such beliefs were the only factor determining physiological reactions. But as indicated earlier, many other factors affect physiological responsivity. Particularly, fear of being falsely classified as guilty and bearing the consequences of such an error is one salient factor that may cause strong reactions to the relevant, crime-related, questions among innocent suspects, even if they believe in the veracity of their answers to the relevant questions. Indeed, numerous researchers (e.g., Ben-Shakhar & Furedy, 1990; Lykken, 1974, 1998) have expressed a concern that this technique is biased against the innocent suspect, because relevant questions could be readily perceived as more threatening and agitating than control questions to all examinees.

As indicated above the CIT is not a test of deception, but can only connect suspects with a crime through their possession of crime-related information. Consequently, the CIT overcomes many of the weaknesses associated with the CQT, mainly because as long as critical information has not been leaked to innocent suspects, the test has proper control questions and thus provides appropriate protection for the innocent suspect. In addition, when innocent suspects cannot discriminate between the relevant and the control items, their differential responses to the relevant items cannot be affected by factors such as stress and motivation to avoid detection. In addition, the CIT does rest on sound theoretical foundations (for a review of theoretical accounts for the CIT, see Verschuere & Ben-Shakhar, 2011). Specifically, as the autonomic measures used in the CIT are components of the orienting response (OR) (see Lynn, 1966; Sokolov, 1963), it is not surprising that this concept has been proposed to account for the CIT effect (e.g., Ben-Shakhar, 1977; Gati & Ben-Shakhar, 1990; Lieblich, Kugelmass, & Ben-Shakhar, 1970; Lykken, 1974). Furthermore, Sokolov (1963) and his followers noted that significant stimuli ("signal-value stimuli", to use

Sokolov's terminology) elicit enhanced ORs with slower habituation and this can account for the enhanced responses to the crime-relevant stimuli observed among knowledgeable (guilty) individuals. The relationship between the CIT effect and OR was highlighted by Lykken (1974) who wrote that, "for the guilty subject only, the 'correct' alternative will have a special significance, an added 'signal value' which will tend to produce a stronger orienting reflex than that subject will show to other alternatives" (p. 728). There is ample evidence supporting the OR account for the CIT effect (for a more detailed description, see Verschuere & Ben-Shakhar, 2011).

However, the CIT depends on two major assumptions which are essential for a successful application of this technique. First, it is assumed that individuals committing a crime will be aware of a sufficient number of critical crime details and will remember them during the test. Thus, although controlled laboratory studies typically demonstrated impressive validity estimates for the CIT (Ben-Shakhar & Elaad, 2003; Meijer et al., 2014), it is highly questionable whether these results can be generalized to realistic situations. Only recently a few studies examined the role of memory for critical items on the CIT's outcomes (Carmel, Dayan, Naveh, Raveh, & Ben-Shakhar, 2003; Gamer, Kosiol, & Vossel, 2010; Nahari & Ben-Shakhar, 2011) and revealed that when the CIT is administered one or two weeks after the mock crime, certain critical items are not recalled and don't elicit differential responses. However, memory loss occurs mostly with peripheral items (features that are not directly related to the execution of the crime, such as a picture on the wall of the crime scene) whereas central features, such as type of weapon used, are capable of eliciting large responses even when the test is delayed.

Second, it is assumed that only the guilty suspects have knowledge of the critical items. Unfortunately, in realistic criminal investigations it is very difficult to guarantee that critical items will not leak out either through the media or during the course of police investigation. Several studies examined the effects of information leakage on the CIT's outcomes and although their results are not entirely consistent, it seems that leakage of information to innocent suspects may significantly increase the rate of false-positive outcomes (for a review of leakage studies, see Bradley, Barefoot, & Arsenault, 2011).

Standardization: A review of the scientific literature dealing with psychological testing reveals that standardization is a basic requirement of a "test". This requirement is essential to guarantee that all examinees undergo the same experience. Only when this requirement is fulfilled, the resulting scores (or evaluations) have a uniform meaning, allowing comparisons between different people who took the test. Furthermore, standardization is essential for obtaining a sufficient level of reliability of the test's results. Unfortunately, the CQT procedure is poorly standardized. The pretest interview, which is an essential part of every CQT examination, is completely subjective, but it plays a major role because the control questions, which later form the basis of the CQT's inferences, are determined during this interview through the examiner-examinee interaction.

162　*G. Ben-Shakhar*

In addition, the testing conditions may also be a function of the examiner and the relationship he or she forms with the examinee. For example, an examiner may present the questions in a different manner when he believes that the examinee is deceptive than when he believes he is testing a truthful suspect. This feature of the CQT has been acknowledged even by supporters of this technique. For example, Honts and Perry (1992, p. 372) wrote that,

> an examiner who was motivated to produce a deceptive result might ask over-general or provocative relevant questions, and spend a great deal of time on their review and presentation. Subsequently, this unethical examiner could ask very narrow, specific, or inappropriate control questions and spend very little time on their review and presentation. An examiner predisposed to produce a truthful result could take the opposite approach, over-emphasizing the control questions and minimizing the relevant questions.

Honts and Perry (1992) raised this possibility in relation to an unethical and dishonest examiner, but decades of research in social psychology teaches us that honest persons could be unintentionally affected by their prior beliefs (e.g., Chapman & Chapman, 1982; Klayman & Ha, 1987). This citation highlights the implications of the unstandardized nature of the CQT. It is therefore clear that, by and large, polygraph examinations conducted by different interrogators (even for a given case and suspect) are liable to be quite different from each other.

Lack of standardization characterizes not only the choice and presentation of the CQT questions, but also the measurement and quantification of the physiological responses. This is rather surprising because all the physiological responses monitored during a typical CQT test can be easily measured in an objective manner, using computerized procedures. Such an objective quantification is a routine procedure in psychophysiological experiments, and computer algorithms have been developed for measuring the responses in the CQT (e.g., Kircher & Raskin, 1988). However, objective, quantified measurement procedures are rare in CQT practice. Some polygraph agencies rely on an overall evaluation of the polygraph charts, which is clearly impressionistic and subjective, and as such, vulnerable to various judgment biases. Other polygraph examiners use the semi-objective procedure proposed originally by Backster (1963) and described in details in Ben-Shakhar (2002). While this procedure is certainly an improvement over the overall evaluation approach, it is still subjective because it is based on the examiner's subjective judgment as to whether a given pair of responses reflects a large, medium or small difference. Thus, this approach too, may be vulnerable to judgment biases.

The CIT, on the other hand, does not require a pre-test interview or any pre-test interaction with the examinee. The CIT questions are derived from an observation of the crime scene and the equivalence between the relevant (crime-related) and the neutral items can be pretested using known innocent subjects. The questions can be presented by "a blind examiner" who is unaware of the nature of the various items, thus avoiding the potential biases raised above regarding the CQT.

Contamination and the confirmation bias: Judgments made on the basis of the CQT are based on more information than is contained in the physiological measures alone, such as the examinee's criminal record and the information contained therein, the opinion of previous investigators and impressions formed during the pretest interview. In addition, the polygraphist is in the position to watch and monitor during the investigation the totality of a suspect's behavior, and not just his physiological changes. While such rich information could affect the accuracy of the polygraphist's final judgment, it also contaminates the physiological evidence with other sources of information. This implies that it would be impossible to attribute the final judgment made by a CQT examiner to the physiological data. The distinction between an objective lie detector based on physiological responses and the subjective impressions of human investigators must not be blurred. If we confuse the validity of the polygraphist's judgment with the validity of the polygraph, we are liable to overestimate the validity of the machine. Furthermore, contamination may introduce a confirmation bias into the polygraph examiner's final judgment (e.g., Ben-Shakhar, Bar-Hillel, & Lieblich, 1986). Specifically, the knowledge gathered prior to the polygraph investigation may induce certain expectations in the examiner and the polygraph investigation and chart interpretation may be biased in favor of these prior expectations. This potential bias is exuberated by the unstandardized nature of the CQT discussed above. An interesting and impressive demonstration of the effect of contamination on CQT results and the confirmation bias to which it could lead, was presented in a television program produced by CBS in 1986 (see a description in Ben-Shakhar, 2002). Furthermore, the effect of confirmation bias on CQT's chart interpretation was experimentally demonstrated by Elaad, Ginton, and Ben-Shakhar (1994).

As indicated above, the CIT does not require any prior information about the examinee and it can be implemented in a standardized fashion, thus avoiding the risk of contamination and the resulting bias.

Countermeasures: Countermeasures are deliberate techniques that might be used by suspects to alter their physiological reactions. Since detection decisions are always based on contrasting the individual's responses to the relevant vs. control questions (or items in the CIT), countermeasures can be employed in an attempt either to inhibit responses to the relevant questions or create excitation to the controls. Since learning to inhibit one's responses to significant stimuli seems to be an extremely difficult task, almost all documented attempts to study countermeasures, used various techniques to enhance responses to the control questions. In general, there are two types of countermeasure techniques: (1) Physical countermeasures – physical activities performed by examinees during presentation of the control questions (e.g., examinees may try to inflict pain upon themselves by biting their tongue); (2) Mental countermeasures – any mental activity the examinee performs to create or enhance physiological responding to the comparison questions (or neutral items). Clearly, both types of countermeasures require some sophistication and certain knowledge (e.g., knowing the distinction between the relevant and comparison questions in the CQT or

164   G. Ben-Shakhar

between the relevant and neutral CIT items). However, by now there is an extensive literature in which polygraph procedures including effective countermeasure techniques are described in great detail. Thus, the danger that interested individuals might gain the necessary understanding in order to use countermeasures is a real one.

Several studies that focused on the effects of various countermeasure techniques on the outcomes of both the CIT and the CQT have been reported since the early 1960s (e.g., Ben-Shakhar & Dolev, 1996; Honts, Devitt, Winbush, & Kircher, 1996; Honts, Raskin, & Kircher, 1994). These studies demonstrated that both the CIT and the CQT are highly vulnerable to countermeasures (for a review see Ben-Shakhar, 2011). Countermeasures were effective not only when applied against the autonomic measures, but also when detection was based on event-related potentials. Specifically, initial CIT studies that used the p-300 component demonstrated that both physical and mental countermeasures were effective (Mertens & Allen, 2008; Rosenfeld, Soskins, Bosh, & Ryan, 2004).

As indicated above countermeasures present serious threat to the validity of all psychophysiological detection methods. However, more recent studies conducted by Rosenfeld and his colleagues suggest that a modified version of the standard protocol typically used in p-300 based CIT studies, labeled "the complex trial protocol" (see Rosenfeld, 2011 for a review), may be countermeasure resistant (e.g., Rosenfeld, Hu, Labkovsky, Meixner, & Winograd, 2013; Rosenfeld et al., 2008). Thus, it seems that this development introduces a detection method with great potential for application in criminal investigations.

Criterion validity: The validity of the CQT based on ANS measures has been studied (e.g., Bersh, 1969; Podlesny, & Raskin, 1977) but this research suffered from a host of methodological problems (see e.g., Ginton, Dai, Elaad, & Ben-Shakhar, 1982; Iacono, 1991; National Research Council, 2003) and consequently it is impossible to draw meaningful generalizations from this research. The most severe methodological problem is reflected by an inherent conflict between internal and external validity. While in realistic contexts, no verified criterion exists, experimental studies lack the emotional-motivational factors that characterize criminal investigations and are particularly crucial for the CQT (for a more thorough discussion of these problems, see Ben-Shakhar, 2002; Ginton et al., 1982; Iacono, 1991). In principle, the CQT can also be applied with ERP and fMRI, but no systematic attempts to validate the use of the CQT with brain measures have been made.

The validity of the CIT has been extensively studied in a controlled laboratory environment, using either simulated, mock-crimes or autobiographical information. These studies typically produced impressive levels of validity (for reviews and meta analyses, see Ben-Shakhar & Elaad, 2003; MacLaren, 2001; Meijer et al., 2014). While the bulk of CIT research rests on more solid methodological grounds as compared with CQT research, due to the proper control questions used in the CIT, the external validity of this research is questionable (e.g., Carmel et al., 2003). Unfortunately, very few attempts have been made to examine the validity of the CIT in realistic criminal investigations. Two field

Psychophysiological detection of deception 165

CIT studies, based on criminal cases investigated by the Israeli Police (Elaad, 1990; Elaad, Ginton, & Jungman, 1992) showed that while the rates of false-positive errors were as low as those reported in laboratory experiments (2% in the former study, which relied only on the electrodermal measure, and 5% in the latter study, which utilized a combination of electrodermal and respiration measures), the rates of false-negative errors were much larger (42% in the former study and 20% in the latter). This may imply that CIT experiments have a weak external validity, but it should be noted that the mean number of questions used in these field studies (2 and 1.8 in Elaad, 1990 and Elaad et al., 1992, respectively) was much smaller than recommended. In addition, the two field studies were based on CITs that were administered immediately after a CQT, and this might have attenuated the sensitivity of the physiological measures due to habituation. Thus, it is possible that the relatively high rates of false-negative errors and lower detection efficiency obtained in these field studies resulted from a non-optimal usage of the CIT.

Conclusions and recommendations

This chapter focused on a comparison of the two methods of psychophysiological detection of deception. This comparison revealed that only the CIT has a potential as a scientifically valid technique. However, it is clear that this method has several limitations and that current research does not supply sufficient information about its validity in the realistic forensic arena. Thus, in this final section I will list several recommendations that may enhance the applicability of the CIT.

1 *Identifying a sufficient number of salient crime-features.* Recent research suggested that the CIT performs best with central features of the crime, especially when the test is delayed (Carmel et al., 2003; Gamer et al., 2010; Nahari & Ben-Shakhar, 2011). This poses a great challenge because it has been suggested that at least five different CIT questions should be formulated (Ben-Shakhar & Elaad, 2003; Lykken, 1988). Two approaches may be offered to overcome this difficulty. First, although multiple questions are definitely desired, two studies demonstrated that the CIT can be successfully used with many fewer questions provided that questions are repeated several times and that a combination of several physiological measures is used (Ben-Shakhar & Elaad, 2002; Elaad & Ben-Shakhar, 1997). Second, the criminal investigation process should be modified, such that polygraph examiners would be able to inspect the crime scene soon after a crime was committed, as practiced by the Japanese National Police.

2 *Protecting critical items and preventing leakage.* Although the results of the field studies reported by Elaad and his colleagues (Elaad, 1990; Elaad et al., 1992) suggest that leakage of crime-related information did not affect the results of CITs administered by the Israeli police, preventing leakage is essential for a wide application of the CIT. Some research results described

166 *G. Ben-Shakhar*

earlier (Ben-Shakhar, Gronau, & Elaad, 1999; Bradley, MacLaren, & Carle, 1996) offered methods to reduce the effects of information leakage. However, even with these methods false-positive outcomes among knowledgeable innocent subjects were too high to tolerate. Thus, it seems that the only solution to this problem is to modify police practices, such that critical features of the event are identified and concealed at the outset of the investigation and that the CIT questions will be previewed by the suspects (see Verschuere & Crombez, 2008).

3   *Dealing with countermeasures.* A possible approach for dealing with countermeasure manipulations is the use of the CIT with ERPs, rather than autonomic measures. Although initial studies suggested that ERPs are vulnerable to countermeasures (Mertens & Allen, 2008; Rosenfeld et al., 2004), more recent studies using the complex trial protocol showed impressive detection efficiency both when participants applied physical and mental countermeasures and under a non-countermeasure codition (Meixner & Rosenfeld, 2010; Rosenfeld & Labkovsky, 2010; Rosenfeld et al., 2008). In addition, it is important to note that detection efficiency with ERP measures have been demonstrated to be better than that obtained with ANS measures (Meijer et al., 2014). A different approach for dealing with countermeasures was adopted by Elaad and his colleagues who examined several covert respiration measures, assuming that examinees who are unaware of the fact that they are connected to a polygraph will not be motivated to apply countermeasures (e.g., Elaad & Ben-Shakhar, 2008). However, this idea raises ethical questions that may severely limit or even prohibit its use (for a review of research on covert measures, see Elaad, 2011). More recently, two studies examined whether the CIT can be applied when the questions are presented subliminally and masked (Lui & Rosenfeld, 2009; Maoz, Breska, & Ben-Shakhar, 2012). The rationale is similar to the use of covert measures, but it is unclear whether the potential advantage of using invisible stimuli in combating countermeasures, outweighs the cost of reducing detection efficiency as observed in Maoz et al. (2012) under subliminal presentation conditions.

4   *Future research directions.* Clearly, all the above recommendations require additional research. For example, the complex trial protocol should be further examined in various laboratories. Similarly, the idea that memory of central crime details is stable over time and unaffected by emotional stress needs further research. Finally, it is essential to examine these factors under realistic conditions, with real criminal suspects.

References

Backster, C. (1963). Polygraph professionalization through technique standardization. *Law and Order, 11*, 63–64.

Barry, R. J. (2006). Promise versus reality in relation to the unitary orienting reflex: A case study examining the role of theory in psychophysiology. *International Journal of Psychophysiology, 62*(3), 353–366.

Psychophysiological detection of deception 167

Barry, R. J. (2009). Habituation of the orienting reflex and the development of preliminary process theory. *Neurobiology of Learning and Memory, 92*(2), 235–242.

Ben-Shakhar, G. (1977). A further study of the dichotomization theory in detection of information. *Psychophysiology, 14,* 408–413.

Ben-Shakhar, G. (2002). A critical review of the Control Questions Test (CQT). In M. Kleiner (ed.), *Handbook of polygraph testing* (pp. 103–126). Cambridge, MA: Academic Press.

Ben-Shakhar, G. (2011). Countermeasures. In B. Verschuere, G. Ben-Shakhar, & E. Meijer (eds), *Memory detection: Theory and application of the Concealed Information Test*. Cambridge, UK: Cambridge University Press.

Ben-Shakhar, G. (2012). Current research and potential application of the Concealed Information Test: An overview. *Frontiers in Psychology, 3,* September, 342.

Ben-Shakhar, G., Bar-Hillel, M., & Lieblich, I. (1986). Trial by polygraph: Scientific and juridical issues in lie detection. *Behavioral Sciences and the Law, 4,* 459–479.

Ben-Shakhar, G., & Dolev, K. (1996). Psychophysiological detection through the guilty knowledge technique: Effects of mental countermeasures. *Journal of Applied Psychology, 81,* 273–281.

Ben-Shakhar, G., & Elaad, E. (2002). Effects of questions' repetition and variation on the efficiency of the guilty knowledge test: A reexamination. *Journal of Applied Psychology, 87,* 972–977.

Ben-Shakhar, G., & Elaad, E. (2003). The validity of psychophysiological detection of deception with the Guilty Knowledge Test: A meta-analytic review. *Journal of Applied Psychology, 88,* 131–151.

Ben-Shakhar, G., & Furedy, J. J. (1990). *Theories and applications in the detection of deception: A psychophysiological and international perspective*. New York: Springer-Verlag.

Ben-Shakhar, G., Gamer, M., Iacono, W., Meijer, E., & Verschuere, B. (2014). Preliminary Process Theory does not validate the Comparison Question Test: A comment on Palmatier and Rovner (2014). *International Journal of Psychophysiology, 95,* 16–19.

Ben-Shakhar, G., Gronau, N., & Elaad, E. (1999). Leakage of relevant information to innocent examinees in the GKT: An attempt to reduce false-positive outcomes by introducing target stimuli. *Journal of Applied Psychology, 84,* 651–660.

Ben-Shakhar, G., & Meijer, E. (2012). Conceptual and methodological considerations in current research on (psychophysiological) detection of deception. The 16th World Congress of Psychophysiology, Pisa, Italy, September, 2012. *International Journal of Psychophysiology, 85,* 305.

Bersh, P. J. (1969). A validation study of polygraph examiner judgment. *Journal of Applied Psychology, 53,* 399–403.

Bradley, M. T., Barefoot, C. A. & Arsenault, A. M. (2011). Leakage of information to innocent suspects. In B. Verschuere, G. Ben-Shakhar, & E. Meijer (eds), *Memory detection: Theory and application of the Concealed Information Test* (pp. 187–199). Cambridge, UK: Cambridge University Press.

Bradley, M. T., MacLaren, V. V., & Carle, S. B. (1996). Deception and nondeception in guilty knowledge and guilty action polygraph tests. *Journal of Applied Psychology, 81,* 153–160.

Carmel, D., Dayan, E., Naveh, A., Raveh, O., & Ben-Shakhar, G. (2003). Estimating the validity of the guilty knowledge test from simulated experiments: The external validity of mock crime studies. *Journal of Experimental Psychology-Applied, 9,* 261–269.

168 G. Ben-Shakhar

Chapman, L. J., & Chapman, J. P. (1982). Test results are what you think they are. In D. Kahneman, P. Slovic, & A. Tversky (eds), *Judgment under uncertainty: Heuristics and biases* (pp. 239–248). New York: Cambridge University Press.

DePaulo, B. M. (1994). Spotting lies: Can humans learn to do better? *Current Directions in Psychological Science, 3*, 83–86.

DePaulo, B. M., Lindsay, J. J., Malone, B. E., Muhlenbruck, L., Charlton, K., & Coope, H. (2003). Cues to deception. *Psychological Bulletin, 129*, 74–118.

Donchin, E. (1981). Surprise!... surprise? *Psychophysiology, 18*, 493–513.

Ekman, P., & O'Sullivan, M. (1991). Who can catch a liar? *American Psychologist, 46*, 913–920.

Elaad, E. (1990). Detection of guilty knowledge in real-life criminal investigations. *Journal of Applied Psychology, 75*, 521–529.

Elaad, E. (2011). New and old covert measures in the concealed information test. In B. Verschuere, G. Ben-Shakhar, & E. Meijer (eds), *Memory detection: Theory and application of the Concealed Information Test*. Cambridge, UK: Cambridge University Press.

Elaad, E., & Ben-Shakhar, G. (1997). Effects of items' repetitions and variations on the efficiency of the guilty knowledge test. *Psychophysiology, 34*, 587–596.

Elaad, E., & Ben-Shakhar, G. (2008). Covert respiration measures for the detection of concealed information. *Biological Psychology, 77*, 284–291.

Elaad, E., Ginton, A., & Ben-Shakhar, G. (1994). The effects of prior expectations and outcome knowledge on polygraph examiners' decisions. *Journal of Behavioral Decision Making, 7*, 279–292.

Elaad, E., Ginton, A., & Jungman N. (1992). Detection measures in real-life criminal guilty knowledge tests. *Journal of Applied Psychology, 77*, 757–767.

Gamer, M. (2011a). Detecting concealed information using autonomic measures. In B. Verschuere, G. Ben-Shakhar & E. Meijer (eds), *Memory detection: Theory and application of the Concealed Information Test* (pp. 27–45). Cambridge, UK: Cambridge University Press.

Gamer, M. (2011b). Detecting of deception and concealed information using neuroimaging techniques. In B. Verschuere, G. Ben-Shakhar & E. Meijer (eds), *Memory detection: Theory and application of the Concealed Information Test*. Cambridge, UK: Cambridge University Press.

Gamer, M., Kosiol, D., & Vossel, G. (2010). Strength of memory encoding affects physiological responses in the Guilty Action Test. *Biological Psychology, 83*, 101–107.

Gati, I., & Ben-Shakhar, G. (1990). Novelty and significance in orientation and habituation: A feature-matching approach. *Journal of Experimental Psychology: General, 119*, 251–263.

Ginton, A., Daie, N., Elaad, E., & Ben-Shakhar, G. (1982). A method for evaluating the use of the polygraph in a real life situation. *Journal of Applied Psychology, 67*, 131–137.

Honts, C. R., Devitt, M. K., Winbush, M., & Kircher, J. C. (1996). Mental and physical countermeasures reduce the accuracy of the concealed knowledge test. *Psychophysiology, 33*, 84–92.

Honts, C. R., & Perry, M. V. (1992). Polygraph admissibility: Changes and challenges *Law and Human Behavior, 16*, 357–379.

Honts, C. R., Raskin, D. C., & Kircher, J. C. (1994). Mental and physical countermeasures reduce the accuracy of polygraph tests. *Journal of Applied Psychology, 79*, 252–259.

Psychophysiological detection of deception 169

Honts, C. R., Raskin, D. C., & Kircher, J. C. (2002). The scientific status of research on polygraph techniques: The case for polygraph tests. In D. L. Faigman, D. H. Kaye, M. J. Saks & J. Sanders (eds), *Modern scientific evidence: The law and science of expert testimony* (Vol. 2, pp. 446–483). St. Paul, MN: West Publishing.

Horneman, C. J., & O'Gorman, J. G. (1985). Detectability in the card test as a function of the subject's verbal response. *Psychophysiology, 22*, 330–333.

Iacono, W. G. (1991). Can we determine the accuracy of polygraph tests? In P. K. Ackles, J. R. Jennings and M. G. H. Coles (eds), *Advances in psychophysiology* (pp. 201–201). Greenwich, CT: JAI Press.

Iacono, W. G., & Lykken, D. T. (2002). The scientific status of research on polygraph techniques: The case against polygraph tests. In D. L. Faigman, D. H. Kaye, M. J. Saks & J. Sanders (eds), *Modern scientific evidence: The law and science of expert testimony* (Vol. 2, pp. 483–538). St. Paul, MN: West Publishing.

Kircher, J. C., & Raskin, D. C. (1988). Human versus computerized evaluations of polygraph data in a laboratory setting. *Journal of Applied Psychology, 73*, 291–302.

Klayman, J., & Ha, Y. W. (1987). Confirmation, disconfirmation, and information in hypothesis testing. *Psychological Review, 94*, 211–228.

Larson, J. A. (1932). *Lying and its detection: A study of deception and deception tests.* Chicago, IL: University of Chicago Press.

Lieblich, I., Kugelmass, S., & Ben Shakhar, G. (1970). Efficiency of GSR detection of information as a function of stimulus set size. *Psychophysiology, 6*, 601–608.

Lui, M., & Rosenfeld, P. J. (2009). The application of subliminal priming in lie detection: Scenario for identification of members of a terrorist ring. *Psychophysiology, 46*, 889–903.

Lykken, D. T. (1959). The GSR in the detection of guilt. *Journal of Applied Psychology, 43*, 385–388.

Lykken, D. T. (1960). The validity of the guilty knowledge technique: The effects of faking. *Journal of Applied Psychology, 44*, 258–262.

Lykken, D. T. (1974). Psychology and the lie detector industry. *American Psychologist, 29*, 725–739.

Lykken, D. T. (1988). Detection of guilty knowledge: A comment on Forman and McCauley. *Journal of Applied Psychology, 73*, 303–304.

Lykken, D. T. (1998). *A tremor in the blood: Uses and abuses of the lie detector.* New York: Plenum Trade.

Lynn, R. (1966). *Attention, arousal and the orienting reaction.* New York: Pergamon.

MacLaren, V. V. (2001). A quantitative review of the guilty knowledge test. *Journal of Applied Psychology, 86*, 674–683.

Maoz, K., Breska, A., & Ben-Shakhar, G. (2012). Orienting response elicitation by personally significant information under subliminal stimulus presentation: A demonstration using the concealed information test. *Psychophysiology, 49*, 1610–1617.

Marston, W. M. (1917). Systolic blood pressure changes in deception. *Journal of Experimental Psychology, 2*, 143–163.

Marston, W. M. (1938). *The lie detector test.* New York: Smith.

Meijer, E. H., Klein-Selle, N., Elber, L., & Ben-Shakhar, G. (2014). Memory detection with the Concealed Information Test: A meta analysis of skin conductance, respiration, heart rate, and P300 data. *Psychophysiology, 51*, 879–904.

Meixner, J. B., & Rosenfeld, J. P. (2010). Countermeasure mechanisms in a P300-based Concealed Information Test. *Psychophysiology, 47*, 57–65.

170 G. Ben-Shakhar

Mertens, R., & Allen, J. J. (2008). The role of psychophysiology in forensic assessments: Deception detection, Event-Related Potentials, and virtual reality mock crime scenarios. *Psychophysiology, 45*, 286–298.

Messick, S. (1989). Validity. In R. L. Linn (ed.), *Educational Measurement* (3rd ed., pp. 13–103). New York: Macmillan.

Messick, S. (1995). Validity of psychological assessment: Validation of inferences from persons' responses and performances as scientific inquiry into score meaning. *American Psychologist, 50*, 741–749.

Nahari, G., & Ben-Shakhar, G. (2011). Psychophysiological and behavioral measures for detecting concealed information: The role of memory for crime details. *Psychophysiology, 48*, 733–744.

National Research Council (2003). *The Polygraph and Lie Detection.* Committee to review the scientific evidence on the Polygraph. Division of Behavioral and Social Sciences and Education. Washington, DC: The National Academies Press.

Osugi, A. (2011). Daily application of the Concealed Information Test: Japan. In B. Verschuere, G. Ben Shakhar & E. Meijer (eds), *Memory detection: Theory and application of the concealed information test* (pp. 253–275). Cambridge, UK: Cambridge University Press.

Palmatier, J. J., & Rovner, L. (2014). Credibility assessment: Preliminary process theory, the polygraph process and construct validity. *International Journal of Psychophysiology*, in press.

Podlesny, J. A., & Raskin, D. C. (1977). Physiological measures and the detection of deception. *Psychological Bulletin, 84*, 782–799.

Raskin, D. C. (1986). The polygraph in 1986: Scientific, professional, and legal issues surrounding applications and acceptance of polygraph evidence. *Utah Law Review, 60*, 29–74.

Raskin, D. C. (1989). Polygraph techniques for the detection of deception. In D. C. Raskin (ed.), *Psychological methods in criminal investigation and evidence.* New York: Springer.

Reid, J. E. (1947). A revised questioning technique in lie-detection tests. *Journal of Criminal Law and Criminology, 37*, 542–547.

Reid, J. E., & Inbau, F. E. (1977). *Truth and deception: The polygraph ("lie detector") technique* (2nd ed.). Baltimore: Williams & Wilkins.

Rosenfeld, J. P. (2011). P300 in detecting concealed information. In B. Verschuere, G. Ben-Shakhar & E. Meijer (eds), *Memory detection: Theory and application of the concealed information test* (pp. 63–89). Cambridge, UK: Cambridge University Press.

Rosenfeld, J. P., Ben-Shakhar, G., & Ganis, G. (2012). Detection of concealed stored memories with psychophysiological and neuroimaging methods. In L. Nadel & W. Sinnott-Armstrong (eds), *Memory and law* (pp. 263–303). Oxford, UK: Oxford University Press.

Rosenfeld, J. P., Hu, X., Labkovsky, E., Meixner, J., & Winograd, M. R. (2013). Review of recent studies and issues regarding the P300-based complex trial protocol for detection of concealed information. *International Journal of Psychophysiology, 90*, 118–134.

Rosenfeld, J. P., & Labkovsky, E. (2010) New P300-based protocol to detect concealed information: Resistance to mental countermeasures against only half the irrelevant stimuli and a possible ERP indicator of countermeasures. *Psychophysiology, 47*, 1002–1010.

Rosenfeld, J. P., Labkovsky, E., Winograd, M., Lui, M. A., Vandenboom, C., & Chedid, E. (2008). The Complex Trial Protocol (CTP): A new, countermeasure-resistant, accurate P300-based method for detection of concealed information. *Psychophysiology, 45,* 906–919.

Rosenfeld, J. P., Soskins, M., Bosh, G., & Ryan, A. (2004). Simple, effective countermeasures to P300-based tests of detection of concealed information. *Psychophysiology, 41,* 205–219.

Saxe, L. (1991). Lying: Thoughts of an applied social psychologist. *American Psychologist, 46,* 409–415.

Saxe L., & Ben-Shakhar, G. (1999). Admissibility of polygraph tests: The application of scientific standards post-Daubert. *Psychology, Public Policy and Law, 5,* 203–223.

Sip, K. E., Roepstorff, A., McGregor, W., & Frith, C. D. (2007). Detecting deception: The scope and limits. *Trends in Cognitive Sciences, 12,* 48–53.

Sokolov, E. N. (1963). *Perception and the conditioned reflex.* New York: Macmillan.

Verschuere, B., & Ben-Shakhar, G. (2011). Theory of the concealed information test. In B. Verschuere, G. Ben-Shakhar & E. Meijer (eds), *Memory detection: Theory and application of the Concealed Information Test* (pp. 128–148). Cambridge, UK: Cambridge University Press.

Verschuere, B., Ben-Shakhar, G., & Meijer, E (eds). (2011). *Memory detection: Theory and application of the Concealed Information Test.* Cambridge, UK: Cambridge University Press.

Verschuere, B., & Crombez, G. (2008). Déjà vu! The effect of previewing test items on the validity of the Concealed Information polygraph Test. *Psychology, Crime and Law, 14,* 287–297.

Vrij, A. (2008). *Detecting lies and deceit: Pitfalls and opportunities.* Chichester: John Wiley and Sons.

Part III
Courts and sentencing

10 Wrongful convictions

Psychological and criminal justice system contributors

C. Ronald Huff

Innocent but convicted: the nature and scope of the problem

Recent decades have seen increasing scholarly and public interest in the problem of wrongful convictions. For purposes of this chapter, "wrongful convictions" will be understood to mean the convictions of individuals who are factually innocent of the crimes for which they were convicted. In part, the increasing awareness of and attention to this problem is due to the increasing use of DNA profiling since its first use in criminal cases in the mid-1980s (first in England, then in the U.S.) to free the innocent and convict the guilty and the widespread media attention that has developed around this issue. On the scholarly side, scores of journal articles and two recent books (Cutler, 2012; Simon, 2012) exemplify the important contributions of psychological science in developing greater insights into the causes of such errors of justice. The Innocence Project, based in New York City, recently issued its annual report, showing that there have been 325 post-conviction exonerations based on DNA evidence in the United States since 1989 (Innocence Project, 2015a). The National Registry of Exonerations' most recent report included a total of 1,535 known exonerations (DNA and non-DNA) in the U.S. in the same time period, including 125 during 2014. The National Registry includes in its tally both DNA exonerations and those "declared to be factually innocent by a government official or agency with the authority to make that declaration" or those individuals "relieved of all the consequences of the criminal conviction by a government official or body with the authority to take that action" (National Registry of Exonerations, 2015a).

It is important to note that official counts of exonerations, while useful, represent only the proverbial "tip of the iceberg" of wrongful conviction. It is not possible to know with certainty how many individuals have been wrongfully convicted (Huff et al.,1996; Gross, 2013). By comparison, it is much easier to estimate how much crime there is, since we have developed crime victimization surveys that can help us extrapolate from official arrest data to get a better idea of how much crime actually occurs. But a similar survey of prisoners asking them if they are innocent would not be regarded as credible. We don't find out that someone was wrongfully convicted until convincing evidence surfaces that proves actual innocence, and for most of those who are innocent but convicted,

176 C.R. Huff

such evidence is never produced. One important source of such evidence is DNA, but biological evidence is found in less than 10 percent of criminal cases and many times, even when it is available, it is not retained long enough for testing following a conviction. That is even more true in many European nations, where final adjudication is less subject to appeals (most appeals are appeals of sentences, rather than convictions) and biological evidence is often discarded after conviction, since the issue of guilt is deemed to have been resolved. Also, the criminal justice system, especially in the United States, is resistant at many points to revisiting a case after a verdict. Finally, each exoneration requires the expenditure of enormous human and financial resources, far beyond the reach of nearly all of those who are convicted but innocent. Even a small error rate generates a large number of wrongful convictions in nations like the United States, where there are millions of criminal cases each year. Therefore, many more – likely tens of thousands – of innocent persons have been wrongfully convicted in the United States, along with others in Europe, and they may never have the opportunity to prove their innocence.

While wrongful convictions can and do occur anywhere, the frequency of wrongful convictions appears to vary considerably, both within the same nation (National Registry of Exonerations, 2015b) and across different nations. Zalman (2012) has shown how difficult it is to estimate the odds of wrongful conviction in a given case, but previous research appears to show that this is much more frequent in the United States, compared to Europe. Huff and Killias (2013), using exoneration data provided by Gross et al. (2005) for those sentenced to death or very long prison terms in the United States over a period of 15 years, concluded that those data would yield about 20 exonerations per year in the U.S. and when translated into the relative proportions in Germany, that would mean that about seven exonerations should be expected each year for inmates serving life or very long sentences; about five in France; and roughly one every second year in Switzerland. But the actual figures for those three countries fall far short of those expected proportions (Dongois, 2008; Huff and Killias, 2008; Kessler, 2008). The lower frequency of exonerations in Europe may be related to a number of characteristics of continental criminal justice systems, especially those with inquisitorial systems. While adversarial systems, such as that in the United States, emphasize procedural justice, continental inquisitorial systems focus on a search for truth; generally utilize less aggressive forms of police interrogation; place far less emphasis on confessions; and do not typically use plea bargaining to induce guilty pleas, although the increasing use of summary proceedings in many European nations may increase wrongful convictions (Gillieron, 2013). Of course, all systems are vulnerable to errors committed by forensic experts, eyewitness testimony, and, most of all, the ever-increasing use of plea bargains and summary proceedings.

Factors contributing to wrongful conviction

The main factors contributing to wrongful conviction, based on the Innocence Project's database, are eyewitness misidentification, unvalidated or improper forensics, false confessions, government misconduct, the use of informants ("snitches"), and bad lawyering (inadequate counsel) (Innocence Project, 2015b). The National Registry of Exonerations utilizes essentially the same list of factors and adds perjury/false accusation (National Registry of Exonerations, 2015b). Each of these factors will be discussed below, with government misconduct being discussed under both the investigation stage (police interrogations designed to extract confessions and police misconduct) and the prosecution stage (prosecutorial misconduct). In most cases, more than one of these factors is present, and they interact to lead to the wrong outcome. They are not usually due to *intentional* errors, but reflect a misguided attempt to protect the public by convicting someone who may *seem* to be guilty. A useful analogy is the conclusion reached by Diane Vaughan in her important study of NASA's *Challenger* disaster in 1986, when that space ship exploded after 73 seconds in flight and disintegrated over the Atlantic Ocean, killing all seven astronauts. After a lengthy study of the organizational factors at NASA that contributed to that tragedy, Vaughan concluded that the decisionmaking process represented an incremental descent into poor judgment (Vaughan, 2009). There was organizational pressure to launch and the decision to do so reflected a type of confirmation bias that we see all too often in cases of wrongful conviction.

More on that will follow below but first, let's look at the stages that occur in known cases involving wrongful conviction that have resulted in exoneration. The process includes investigation, prosecution, conviction, and post-conviction exoneration. Since this chapter is concerned with psychological and legal factors that contribute to wrongful convictions, it will focus on the first two of these three stages: investigation and prosecution.

The investigation stage

Eyewitness misidentification

There is a vast psychological literature on this problem (see, for example, Loftus, 1996; Wells, 2006). The testimony of an eyewitness is, for most jurors, very compelling because they assume that since the witness was there and saw what happened, they must know. But that assumption is often flawed, and many innocent persons are incorrectly identified by mostly well-intentioned witnesses whose perceptions may have been adversely affected by such factors as fear, especially when facing a weapon; stress; anxiety; trauma; difficulties associated with cross-racial identification; poor lighting; poor eyesight; and other factors. In addition, human memory can be adversely affected by leading questions or suggestions by police, for example, who believe they are just "helping the witness along," by the passage of time ("memory decay"), and other factors.

178 C.R. Huff

Forensic errors and incompetence

There may also be forensic evidence. That evidence could be compromised by a flawed chain of evidence, improper handling of evidence, mixing of samples, or even outright fraud. It may also depend on unreliable "junk science" that masquerades as science but is not empirically valid, such as the use of bite marks and some cases involving burn patterns in fires (see National Research Council, 2009, for a comprehensive assessment of forensic sciences). The forensic scientist may also be influenced, consciously or otherwise, by information s/he has that there is other compelling evidence allegedly showing that the suspect is guilty and the police simply need the forensic scientist to "strengthen the case a bit." Since forensic labs are typically part of law enforcement organizations, the organizational culture can sometimes exert undue influence on forensic examiners.

Cole and Thompson (2013), in their excellent discussion of the role of forensic science in helping produce or reverse wrongful convictions, list among the forensic contributions to wrongful convictions the following factors: incompetent/corrupt analysts, overclaiming (exaggerating the strength of the evidence), biased interpretations, lack of basic validation research, poor regulation, and inadequate oversight by the courts. While flawed forensics has been an important factor in the U.S., some European nations place even more weight on scientific testimony and, while scientific testimony is to be preferred over relying solely on eyewitness statements, it does make those European justice systems vulnerable if there are forensic errors as, for example, occurred in the recent case of Amanda Knox in Italy, as reported by independent analysts (see Vuille et al., 2014, for an excellent discussion of the forensic aspects of the Knox case).

False confessions, police interrogations, and police misconduct

According to the National Registry of Exonerations, there were 60 guilty-plea exonerations in the U.S. from 2009 through 2013 – an average of 12 a year, an increase from an average of 4 a year from 1989 through 2008. Through 2008, guilty-plea cases made up 8 percent of known exonerations; from 2009 to 2013 they constituted 16 percent. This may reflect greater willingness by authorities to reconsider the guilt of innocent defendants who accepted plea bargains rather than risk higher penalties at trial (National Registry of Exonerations, 2015c).

Why would an innocent person confess? This seems incomprehensible to the average person, but it happens fairly often (see Kassin, 2012 regarding how confessions can overcome the presumption of innocence). Certain kinds of people are more likely to give a false confession: young people; people with mental illness; those with a low IQ who may be easily led by interrogators; people who have various cognitive impairments and are easily influenced and/or confused; and guilt-ridden "compulsive confessors" who might confess to having committed acts that they did not, in fact, commit. Modern interrogations often use

Wrongful convictions 179

sophisticated psychological techniques, such as making the suspect believe that there is no realistic option other than confessing and pleading guilty (see Kassin et al., 2010, for a comprehensive discussion of police-induced confessions). The suspect may be confronted with evidence that is circumstantial (or told that there is powerful evidence against him) and may be subjected to prolonged interrogation with, perhaps, deprivation of sleep, water, or food. In some places, this has occurred fairly often. Many European nations are less subject to this problem simply because they often do not assign as much weight to a confession as happens in the U.S. In the continental/inquisitorial system's mandate to "search for the truth," greater emphasis is placed on obtaining corroborating evidence and, if such evidence is not forthcoming, the confession is not taken as seriously.

Since many exonerations in the U.S. over the last 20 years involved convictions that were obtained after false confessions, this in itself may help explain the higher rate of exonerations in the United States. The problem is exacerbated by the role confessions play under the adversarial, compared to the inquisitorial, system. Certainly, there are examples of false confessions and their fatal role in Europe as well (see, for example, Brants, 2008), but overcoming a false admission of guilt is far more complicated under the American system. The American plea bargaining system is based on the admission of guilt which, in the daily routine, is not questioned any further by the court. Many of the important reforms brought about by the U.S. Supreme Court in the 1960s were motivated, in part, by the important role of confessions in the American system. Finally, although Aebi and Campistol (2014) found no evidence to support the allegation that members of ETA in Spain had falsely confessed in order to protect others in that organization, it is nonetheless possible that placing great emphasis on confessions could backfire and compromise public safety if the confessor is, say, a member of a terrorist group who simply wants to take responsibility by pleading guilty, thereby protecting other members of the terrorist group. Similar behavior has occurred when junior organized crime figures "took the rap" and "did time" for more senior members at times in the U.S., thus earning more respect from their peers upon their release from prison.

Finally, there are too many instances of unethical and unprofessional conduct by law enforcement officers, usually officers who are convinced of the suspect's guilt (see the discussion of tunnel vision below) and who believe that their actions are helping protect public safety by getting the suspect off the streets. Some law enforcement units seem especially prone to such unethical behavior. These include "elitist" units that tend to operate with more independence from the rest of the organization, such as elite narcotics enforcement and street gang units. For example, in the highly publicized scandal involving the Rampart Division of the Los Angeles Police Department (subsequently depicted in the movie, "Rampart"), an excerpt from one officer's own testimony illustrates the problem:

> Well, sir, make no bones about it, what we did was wrong – planting evidence ... fabricating evidence, perjuring ourselves – but our mentality was us against them.... We knew that Rampart's crime rate, murder rate, was the

180   *C.R. Huff*

highest in the city.... (L)ieutenants, captains, and everybody else would come to our roll calls and say this has to end and you guys are in charge of things. Do something about it. That's your responsibility.... And the mentality was, it was like a war, us against them...

(McDermott, 2000: A22)

Use of informants/"snitches"

The misuse of confidential informants, or "snitches," has also been an important factor in the U.S. and has been among the leading causes of wrongful conviction in capital cases (see Natapof, 2009, for an comprehensive overview of this problem). Especially egregious have been the incidents involving the use of "jailhouse snitches" who testify, often more than once, against accused persons in return for favorable considerations, such as dropped or reduced charges or favorable sentencing recommendations in their own cases. It is, at the very least, ironic that these same people, when they were coming before the court as defendants in their own cases, would never have been believed by the prosecutors, but now that they say they can help convict someone else, they are suddenly transformed into credible witnesses. That's an amazing transformation to behold, and yet this has happened repeatedly, resulting in scandals involving hundreds of wrongful convictions in the U.S., as well as the well-known case of Thomas Sophonow in Canada, involving three jailhouse informants who provided false evidence against Sophonow, implicating him in a homicide. That case involved undisclosed incentives for informant testimony; an informant with a prior conviction for perjury, and obvious signs of unreliability. The Sophonow case became the basis for important reforms, including limits on the use of such informant testimony. The report concluded, in part, "Jailhouse informants comprise the most deceitful and deceptive group of witnesses known to frequent the courts ... They must be recognized as a very great danger to our trial system" (Manitoba Justice, 2001).

Inadequate counsel (bad lawyering)

Another factor that contributes to wrongful convictions is inadequate counsel. This has been the basis of appeal in the U.S. since the infamous Scottsboro Boys case (*Powell* v. *Alabama*, 1932), but it is often unsuccessful because the bar has been set so high by appeals courts. Many public defenders in the U.S. have very high caseloads and have few resources and little time for independent investigations. Therefore, they tend to rely heavily on police investigations. The defendant may also be represented by private counsel, rather than a public defender. In that case, the private attorney may be inexperienced in the criminal courts. S/he may also take on a large caseload, since each case may pay very little money, and thereby earn a higher income. If the attorney then decides simply to encourage plea bargaining without independently verifying the police investigation, s/he can become what we called "guilty plea wholesalers" in an earlier book (Huff et al., 1996).

Wrongful convictions 181

In European nations utilizing the inquisitorial system, rather than the adversarial system, far less responsibility is placed on the defense attorney to discover facts that support his/her client's innocence. In the inquisitorial system, there is an emphasis on balanced fact finding, and the investigation is intended to discover the facts whether they support or help disprove the allegations. The defense also has far greater access to the prosecutor's case file ("open file discovery"), since the objective is to discover the truth rather than for either the prosecution or the defense to "win" the case. Therefore, such systems appear to be less vulnerable to errors that are purely due to inadequate defense counsel representation.

Perjury/false accusations

The National Registry of Exonerations (2015d) reports that between 1989 and 2012, 27 percent of the U.S. exonerations in its database included deliberate misidentifications, wherein one or more witnesses falsely claimed to have witnessed the defendant committing a crime. In addition, another 11 percent of the exonerations involved cases in which crimes were completely fabricated; that is, a crime was alleged when, in fact, no crime had occurred. The latter category often included cases in which child sexual abuse was alleged by someone who knew the accused. In fact, fully three-fourths of all exonerations involving allegations of child sex abuse included perjury or false accusations, mostly by alleged eyewitnesses. And in homicide cases that resulted in exonerations, two-thirds involved perjury and other lies, including many by jailhouse snitches, law enforcement officers, and forensic witnesses.

The prosecution stage

Prosecutorial misconduct

The Innocence Project has identified prosecutorial misconduct in many forms. Examples include, but are not limited to, coercing witnesses; allowing perjured testimony; rewarding snitches and informants for testimony without revealing the consideration provided; deliberately placing the defendant in a jail cell with a known frequent informant; relying on fraudulent forensic testimony; destroying or withholding exculpatory evidence; and, in opening or closing statements, referencing evidence not introduced or misrepresenting evidence so as to overstate its probative value. The organization reported that 65 of the first 255 DNA-exonerated persons claimed prosecutorial misconduct in appeals or civil suits, and in 18 percent of the cases, the error was significant enough to be acknowledged by the courts, resulting in reversal of the conviction (West, 2010). This is similar to the 17.6 percent harmful error rate determined in a larger study in 2003 that included non-innocence cases by the Center for Public Integrity (2003).

Among the most egregious examples of prosecutorial misconduct is withholding from the defense evidence supporting a defendant's innocence. *Brady* v.

182   *C.R. Huff*

Maryland (1963) requires prosecutors to disclose to the defense any "exculpatory evidence," an obligation that continues from indictment through the post-conviction appeal process. Failure to do so can be reversible error.

In a recent dissenting opinion that was so strongly worded that it attracted widespread attention throughout the U.S. legal community, federal appellate judge Alex Kozinski (9th Circuit Court of Appeals) observed the following:

> There is an epidemic of *Brady* violations abroad in the land. Only judges can put a stop to it.... A robust and vigorously enforced *Brady* rule is imperative because all the incentives prosecutors confront encourage them not to discover or disclose exculpatory evidence. Due to the nature of a *Brady* violation, it's highly unlikely wrongdoing will ever come to light in the first place. This creates a serious moral hazard for those prosecutors who are more interested in winning a conviction than serving justice.
>
> (*United States* v. *Olsen*, 2013)

To place prosecutorial abuses in a comparative context, consider that the legal concepts of *mens rea* and *actus reus* have been central to the determination of criminal culpability in many nations for centuries. In establishing guilt, it has been essential to prove that both a mental element (*mens rea*, commonly understood as "intent") and a physical element (*actus reus*, referring to the act itself) existed with respect to the conduct at issue. When we consider the documented cases of prosecutors who have *intentionally* withheld from the defense evidence that could prove exculpatory and (under current criteria for establishing *Brady* violations), which the defense could not have discovered on its own, as well as other *intentional* misconduct, it is clear that both *mens rea* and *actus reus* exist in those cases. We now know that some prosecutors have withheld such evidence in cases that have resulted in multiple wrongful convictions, suggesting, to carry this analogy further, that there are some "recidivist prosecutors" who have violated legal and ethical standards repeatedly in the pursuit of convictions rather than justice (Ridolfi and Possley, 2010). As noted above, in the United States such prosecutors have rarely been subjected to sanctions. The absence of such sanctions makes it very difficult to deter such behavior.

When comparing different systems of justice in the U.S. and many European nations, Martin Killias and I concluded that such prosecutorial misconduct appears to be less frequent in European nations with the continental/inquisitorial system than in the U.S. (Huff and Killias, 2013). This may be due in part to the volume of cases and the "caseload pressures" to come to closure. One key factor differentiating U.S. prosecutors from most European prosecutors is that U.S. prosecutors are elected, which introduces a strong political element in their motivations, and the fact that sanctions for such behavior are extremely rare, as noted above. Also, in the U.S., the volume of cases places more emphasis on the practice of entering into negotiated guilty pleas, or "plea bargains," which account for more than 90 percent of convictions in most American jurisdictions. Such plea agreements are, of course, far more restricted in the continental/inquisitorial

Wrongful convictions 183

system (but see Gillieron, 2013, regarding the increasing use of summary proceedings in Europe), and are often limited to cases involving sentences of less than a year. In such jurisdictions, it is far more common to ask for a reduced sentence after being convicted. And the adversarial system in the U.S. and some other nations places greater emphasis on a competition between the prosecution and the defense, rather than a bilateral search for the truth, with a (theoretically, at least) impartial investigation. However, neither system is perfect, as shown in the research of Chrisje Brants in the Netherlands, for example, who argues that the Dutch inquisitorial system, in practice, has two weaknesses:

1   Truth finding depends on having impartial investigations under the supervision of the prosecutor, but recently, public dissatisfaction with public safety has brought increased pressure on prosecutors who, she argues, then behave more like adversarial prosecutors bent on convictions, and since the defense is not expected to conduct its own investigations, this does not make for a level playing field; and
2   Courts can also become victims of confirmation bias, especially if judges are much closer, professionally, to the prosecutors and the procedures do not allow for adversarial debate.

Similar concerns have been noted with respect to France, where the proportion of decisions overturned is quite small in comparison to many other nations, suggesting the possibility that many errors go undetected due to the very strict rules governing petitions of revision, thus protecting final decisions as really "final" (Dongois, 2008).

Tunnel vision: a pervasive psychological factor

Based on a large, and growing, body of research it is clear that tunnel vision is a problem that is pervasive at all stages of the criminal justice process. In fact, it may be the single most important problem in producing wrongful convictions because it cuts across every stage of the criminal justice process. It is a normal human occurrence, but one that must be recognized and corrected whenever possible if we are to reduce these errors. In an excellent analysis of tunnel vision as it relates to wrongful conviction, Findley and Scott (2006) discuss two major cognitive components of tunnel vision: confirmation bias and belief perseverance:

Confirmation bias refers to our tendency to seek or interpret evidence in ways that support existing beliefs, expectations, or hypotheses. People not only seek and are more likely to accept confirming information, but research shows that they also tend to recall that information in a biased manner. People also tend to assign greater weight to positive (confirmatory) evidence and assign less weight to negative (disconfirming) evidence.

Belief perseverance (or belief persistence) refers to the fact that we tend to resist changing our beliefs, even when faced with new evidence that is completely inconsistent with our initial belief (for example, some prosecutors, when presented with clear DNA-based evidence of innocence, continue to argue that the defendant/inmate is nonetheless guilty).

Just as Vaughan (2009) concluded that the decisionmaking process in the *Challenger* disaster represented an incremental descent into poor judgment, so too do most instances of wrongful conviction. It is not usually the case that authorities set out to convict an innocent person. What is much more common, at every stage of the process, is that cognitive factors – especially tunnel vision – impact perceptions, beliefs, and judgments that result in identifying the wrong suspect and then refusing to accept alternative theories of crimes that could lead to the identification of the actual offender. In most cases, there are "interaction effects" when more than one of the factors discussed above come into play in an interactive way to result in a wrongful conviction. What do these factors have in common? In many cases, it is clear that tunnel vision was the single unifying factor that cut across the various errors that occurred. For example, a wrongful conviction might begin with an eyewitness who is convinced of the suspect's guilt but whose perception and memory may have been impacted by tunnel vision. That mistake might, in turn, be compounded by overzealous law enforcement officers who, convinced of the suspect's guilt, may set out to extract a confession via highly aggressive and/or psychologically sophisticated interrogation techniques; prosecutors who believe that withholding exculpatory evidence is justified since it helps remove a suspected criminal from the street (while, of course, allowing the actual offender to remain free); forensic analysts, usually working in a law enforcement context, who may overstate or occasionally falsify their conclusions to support the prosecution's theory of the case; defense attorneys who, faced with large caseloads and meager compensation, may believe their client is guilty and can therefore rationalize spending little time defending him/her; and judges who often are former prosecutors and who may more easily favor the prosecution's case and overlook errors.

A lot of times, mistakes in the investigative stage boil down to the decision to use deductive logic instead of inductive logic; that is, to start with a theory, or conclusion, about the crime and then defend that theory or conclusion, even against contradictory information, as opposed to following the facts wherever they may lead. So powerful is tunnel vision that it helps police, prosecutors, and even defense attorneys rationalize unethical and even illegal behavior, all for the sake of convicting someone who, they are certain, is guilty. And, as noted above, even when confronted with DNA evidence showing that a convicted person did not commit the crime, many prosecutors have engaged in denial based on tunnel vision (belief perseverance). So strong is this denial that in many cases in which DNA evidence has proved the innocence of the person whom they helped convict, prosecutors have failed to use that DNA evidence to try to identify the real offender by utilizing existing DNA databases, thus compromising public safety for a second time in the same case.

Finally, the reduction of wrongful convictions is an important societal goal. Such miscarriages of justice represent a dual threat:

1 They are injustices that undermine the legitimacy of and respect for the criminal justice system, and
2 They threaten public safety by allowing the actual offenders to remain free while the innocent are convicted and incarcerated.

Reducing these errors will depend heavily on our ability to (1) recognize and help neutralize the negative effects of tunnel vision by insisting on investigations and prosecutions that proceed according to inductive logic and balanced fact finding; and (2) increase the detection of and sanctioning of unethical behavior.

References

Aebi, M. F. and Campistol, C. (2014). "Voluntary" false confessions as a source of wrongful convictions: The case of Spain. Pp. 193–208 in C. R. Huff and M. Killias (eds.), *Wrongful Convictions & Miscarriages of Justice: Causes and Remedies in North American and European Criminal Justice Systems*. New York and London: Routledge.

Brants, C. (2008). The vulnerability of Dutch criminal procedure to wrongful conviction. Pp. 157–182 in C. R. Huff and M. Killias (eds.), *Wrongful Conviction: International Perspectives on Miscarriages of Justice*. Philadelphia, PA: Temple University Press.

Center for Public Integrity (2003, June 26). *Prosecutorial Misconduct*. Retrieved from www.publicintegrity.org/news/Prosecutorial-misconduct.

Cole, S. A. and Thompson, W. C. (2013). Forensic science and wrongful convictions. Pp. 111–135 in C. R. Huff and M. Killias (eds.), *Wrongful Convictions & Miscarriages of Justice: Causes and Remedies in North American and European Criminal Justice Systems*. New York and London: Routledge.

Cutler, B. L. (ed.) (2012). *Conviction of the Innocent: Lessons from Psychological Research*. Washington, DC: American Psychological Association.

Dongois, N. (2008). Wrongful convictions in France: The limits of "*pourvoi en revision.*" Pp. 249–261 in C. R. Huff and M. Killias (eds.), *Wrongful Conviction: International Perspectives on Miscarriages of Justice*. Philadelphia, PA: Temple University Press.

Findley, K. A. and Scott, M. S. (2006). The multiple dimensions of tunnel vision in criminal cases. *Wisconsin Law Review*, 2: 291–397.

Gillieron, G. (2013). The risks of summary proceedings, plea bargains, and penal orders in producing wrongful convictions in the U.S. and Europe. Pp. 237–258 in C. R. Huff and M. Killias (eds.), *Wrongful Convictions & Miscarriages of Justice: Causes and Remedies in North American and European Criminal Justice Systems*. New York and London: Routledge.

Gross, S. R. (2013). How many false convictions are there? How many exonerations are there? Pp. 45–59 in C. R. Huff and M. Killias (eds.), *Wrongful Convictions & Miscarriages of Justice: Causes and Remedies in North American and European Criminal Justice Systems*. New York and London: Routledge.

Gross, S. R., Jacoby, K., Matheson, D. J., Montgomery, N., and Patil, S. (2005). Exonerations in the United States, 1989 through 2003. *Journal of Criminal Law & Criminology*, 95 (2): 523–560.

Huff, C. R. and Killias, M. (2008). Wrongful conviction: Conclusions from an international overview. Pp. 287–300 in C. R. Huff and M. Killias (eds.), *Wrongful Conviction: International Perspectives on Miscarriages of Justice*. Philadelphia, PA: Temple University Press.

186   C.R. Huff

Huff, C. R. and Killias, M. (eds.) (2013). *Wrongful Convictions & Miscarriages of Justice: Causes and Remedies in North American and European Criminal Justice Systems*. New York and London: Routledge.

Huff, C. R., Rattner, A., and Sagarin, E. (1996). *Convicted but Innocent: Wrongful Conviction and Public Policy*. Thousand Oaks, CA: Sage Publications.

Innocence Project (2015a, January 23). Retrieved from www.innocenceproject.org/know/.

Innocence Project (2015b, January 23). Retrieved from www.innocenceproject.org/understand/.

Kassin, S. M. (2012). Why confessions trump innocence. *American Psychologist* 67 (6): 431–445.

Kassin, S. M., Drizin, S. A., Grisso, T., Gudjonsson, G. H., Leo, R. A., and Redlich, A. D. (2010). Police-induced confessions: Risk factors and recommendations. *Law and Human Behavior*, 34: 3–38.

Kessler, I. (2008). A comparative analysis of prosecution in Germany and the United Kingdom: Searching for truth or getting a conviction? Pp. 213–247 in C. R. Huff and M. Killias (eds.), *Wrongful Convictions & Miscarriages of Justice: Causes and Remedies in North American and European Criminal Justice Systems*. New York and London: Routledge.

Loftus, E. F. (1996). *Eyewitness Testimony*. Cambridge, MA: Harvard University Press.

Manitoba Justice (2001). *The Inquiry Regarding Thomas Sophonow*. Retrieved from www.gov.mb.ca/justice/publications/sophonow/toc.html on February 24, 2014.

McDermott, T. (2000, December 31). "Perez's Bitter Saga of Lies, Regrets, and Harm." *Los Angeles Times*, A1, A22–24.

Natapof, A. (2009). *Snitching: Criminal Informants and the Erosion of American Justice*. New York and London: New York University Press.

National Registry of Exonerations (2015a, January 23). Retrieved from www.law.umich.edu/special/exoneration/Pages/about.aspx.

National Registry of Exonerations (2015b, January 23). Retrieved from www.law.umich.edu/special/exoneration/Pages/detaillist.aspx.

National Registry of Exonerations (2015c, January 23). Retrieved from www.law.umich.edu/special/exoneration/Documents/Exonerations_in_2013_Report.pdf.

National Registry of Exonerations (2015d, January 23). Retrieved from www.law.umich.edu/special/exoneration/Documents/exonerations_us_1989_2012_full_report.pdf.

National Research Council (2009). *Strengthening Forensic Science in the United States: A Path Forward*. Washington, DC: National Academies Press. Available online at https://www.ncjrs.gov/pdffiles1/nij/grants/228091.pdf.

Ridolfi, K. M. and Possley, M. (2010) *Preventable Error: A Report of Prosecutorial Misconduct in California 1997–2009*. Santa Clara, CA: Northern California Innocence Project, Santa Clara University School of Law.

Simon, D. (2012). *In Doubt: The Psychology of the Criminal Justice Process*. Cambridge, MA and London: Harvard University Press.

Vaughan, D. (2009). *The Challenger Launch Decision: Risky Technology, Culture, and Deviance at NASA*. Chicago: University of Chicago Press.

Vuille, J., Biedermann, A., and Taroni, F. (2014). The importance of having a logical framework for expert conclusions in forensic DNA profiling: Illustrations from the Amanda Knox case. Pp. 137–159 in C. R. Huff and M. Killias (eds.), *Wrongful Convictions & Miscarriages of Justice: Causes and Remedies in North American and European Criminal Justice Systems*. New York and London: Routledge.

Wells, G. L. (2006). Eyewitness identification: Systemic reforms. *Wisconsin Law Review*, 2006 (2): 615–643.

West, E. (2010). *Court Findings of Prosecutorial Misconduct Claims in Post-Conviction Appeals and Civil Suits Among the First 255 DNA Exoneration Cases*. New York: Innocence Project. Retrieved from www.innocenceproject.org/docs/Innocence_Project_Pros_Misconduct.pdf on February 1, 2014.

Zalman, M. (2012). Qualitatively estimating the incidence of wrongful convictions. *Criminal Law Bulletin*, 48 (2): 221–277.

Cases cited

Brady v. *Maryland*, 373 U.S. 83 (1963).
Powell v. *Alabama*, 287 U.S. 45 (1932).
United States v. *Olsen*, 704 F.3d 1172, 1177 (9th Cir. 2013; Dissenting opinion).

11 The English jury
Issues, concerns and future directions

Nicola Padfield

Introduction

This chapter arose out of a conference at which I knew there would be a predominance of psychologists over lawyers. I wanted to raise some questions for psychologists, but from a lawyer's perspective. There has been a certain amount of research carried out into jury decision-making, some by psychologists, using 'mock' juries (see, by way of example, in England and Wales, McCabe, 1972; McCabe and Purves, 1974; and Hastie, 1983). This chapter raises some basic questions about trial by jury in order to challenge the utility of some of this research where the focus is on experiments – I would argue that the role and function of the jury has to be examined in the context, the real life situation, in which it functions. My views are coloured by my own experiences: both as an academic lawyer but also as a part-time judge.[1] The chapter seeks to provoke interest, and indeed research.

The role of the jury

We start with a conundrum. The jury is said to have many functions, and of course our evaluation of it depends in large measure on what we think it is designed to achieve. In criminal cases, the jury's role is limited to determining guilt, and they have no role in sentencing. Juries have to decide issues of fact, and on those facts decide whether or not the defendant is guilty of the crime charged. In the English system, they give no reasons for their decisions, with the result that it is extremely difficult to challenge a verdict.[2] If it is designed to decide who is guilty of a certain crime, or whether someone is guilty of a certain crime, it is a curious body. It sits back and listens – it does not investigate.

If the jury's role is to decide whether someone's guilt is proved beyond reasonable doubt, it is perhaps a little better equipped for the task. A group of people may weigh up the evidence, and decide together whether they are convinced to the appropriate standard of proof of someone's guilt. But it is often said that the jury represents something much more than simply a method of fact-finding. Do they have an additional function of introducing 'lay values' into the administration of justice (see Andrews, 1978)? Is it part of their function to

The English jury   189

prevent the unjust use of the criminal law, exercising what is sometimes called 'jury equity', their own sense of justice? Some people go much further: Lord Devlin famously commented that trial by jury is the "lamp that shows that freedom lives", not just a barometer of public opinion (see Devlin, 1956). I listened with some humility to a debate some years ago between a group of Botswanan and South African judges about whether their jurisdictions could support trial by jury, the implication being that only 'strong' democracies could enjoy the privilege of trial by jury. Am I hasty in my criticisms, in danger of throwing out something which reflects very well on our democratic form of governance? . Lord Devlin argued that the jury exhibits "the element of popularity that is appropriate in a democracy; it will be a long time before the judiciary ceases to be associated in the public mind with the upper classes" (Devlin, 1991, p. 402).

But this 'sentimental' attachment to the symbol of the jury is itself dangerous. As Darbyshire argues,

> adulation of the jury is based on no justification or spurious justification. It has fed public complacency with the English legal system and distracted attention from its evils; a systematic lack of due process pre-trial and post-trial and certain deficiencies in the trial process itself. It has distorted the truth.
>
> (Darbyshire, 1991, p. 741)

There has been a host of rather shocking tales escaping from juries about malpractice: in both press[3] and law reports.[4] We need to question the function of the jury, and whether it is fit for purpose.

It is perhaps also worth noting at the outset what is not the jury's function: in England and Wales they have no function in relation to sentencing. Why not? There is much divide about public opinion and sentencing, and I suspect (but cannot prove) that juries might be often more lenient and/or merciful than judges (on which see fascinating research conducted with real juries in Tasmania: Warner *et al.*, 2011). Would it be a 'good thing' to involve juries in sentencing? One of my favourite books on the jury is Vidmar (2000) – he gives an overview (at one point in history, sadly) of world jury systems, and of course different jurisdictions use the jury very differently. My opinions are shaped by the criminal justice system in England and Wales (a jury is still summoned in some inquests in coroners' courts, particularly where there has been a death in custody, and occasionally in civil justice). This chapter is concerned only with juries in criminal trials: it begs the question of the role of the jury in civil matters or elsewhere (see *H* v. *Ministry of Defence* [1991] 2 QB 103 for a fascinating case which decided that a jury was no longer available in a civil personal injuries case).

Trial by jury in England and Wales

The jury is summoned from a random selection of people registered on the electoral role. The basic rules governing juries are found in the Juries Act 1974,

190 N. Padfield

though the Criminal Justice Act 1988, s 119 raised the maximum age of jurors to 70 (jury service is voluntary after the age of 65) and both the Criminal Justice and Public Order Act 1994 and the Criminal Justice Act 2003 dramatically amended the rules on disqualification and excusal. Nowadays few people are exempt: judges and police officers, for example, may well find themselves summoned for jury service. (For a study of whether juries are 'representative': see Thomas, 2008).

There is no questioning of the jury to explore their prejudices (a sharp contrast with the US system, which astonishes the English spectator). 'Peremptory' challenges have long since been abolished (see section 118 of the Criminal Justice Act 1988), and since potential jurors cannot be questioned, challenges 'for cause' are very rare. The prosecution can ask a potential juror to stand by, and clearly there are occasionally some unusual practices. Thus, for example, in *Jalil* [2008] EWCA Crim 2910, [2009] Crim LR 442 about 90 potential jurors were summoned. The judge agreed that they should be asked questions to elicit connections or interests which might form the basis of challenge for cause. The panel was then reduced to 14: some were released as a result of questions, others because it was impracticable for them to sit for the length of time anticipated. The defence submitted that two of the 14 should be excluded on the basis of some connection to army and/or the metropolitan police. The judge ruled that they were not to be excluded, but was sympathetic to the defence's wishes to achieve a jury without the complication of such connections if it could be done, so he encouraged the prosecution to stand these two jurors by, if they were selected in the ballot. The prosecution agreed. The jurors were selected, and the prosecution did stand them by. So the defendant was tried by 12 jurors "against whom no possible complaint of unsuitable connection is made". An appeal against on the ground that there was no proper ballot because in effect there were only 12 "eligible" jurors, not surprisingly, failed.

They are given very little guidance at the beginning of their jury service: a straight-forward video is shown to them which explains procedures, and details like how to claim their expenses. Once they have been empanelled (a process which usually happens very quickly), they will be given a copy of the indictment which summarises the counts on which the defendant or defendants stand trial. There is no opening speech from the judge on the subject matter of the trial. The judge at this stage simply warns the jury that they shouldn't discuss the case outside court with those who are not a member of the jury, that they should raise with the judge any concerns that they may have about the behaviour of others, and will add a warning of the dangers of inappropriate jury behaviour, and indeed the possibility of prosecution for contempt of court.

It is prosecuting counsel who outlines the facts of the cases and tells the jury that later on 'Her Honour the judge' will explain the relevant law. So the jury just listens, and take notes (or not according to their choice). Since the Royal Commission of 1993's sensible recommendation that the provision of writing materials should be standard, juries are provided with pen and paper. But, in my

The English jury 191

experience, they vary enormously (as individuals and as juries) in the use they make of this facility.

The prosecution opens the case, and calls witnesses. Each witness is examined by the lawyer (counsel) who calls them, cross-examined by the lawyer for the other side, and then re-examined by the first lawyer. At the end of the examination of the witness, the lawyer will ask: "Does your honour have any questions?". I learnt quite early in my judicial career not to say, "Yes, I have lots ... why didn't anyone ask the witness...". There was usually a good reason why neither side had chosen to open that particular can of worms.... Occasionally, though, I would ask a question if I felt it clarified an important matter for the jury. This raises important questions about the relative position of judge and jury. No-one asks the jury, "Do you have any questions?". I suspect that it would lead to chaos: "Yes, of course, we do". The jury is entitled to ask questions: they do it by way of written note to the judge, which the judge then shares with counsel, in the absence of the jury. It can be a cumbersome procedure: judge gets note; sends jury out of the court so that he/she can discuss an appropriate response to the jury with counsel, then gets jury back in and answers, perhaps, "Members of the jury that was a very good question, prosecuting counsel will put it to the officer in the case tomorrow morning"; or "I'm afraid you will not be hearing any medical evidence in this case; counsel have decided which witnesses they want you to hear from and you will not be hearing from any doctor"; or "I'm afraid that Mr Jones has now left court and it is impossible/inappropriate to call him back at this stage in proceedings".

Once the prosecution has called all its witnesses, presented all the evidence, then it is the defence's turn to present its case. Then counsel for both sides have the opportunity to make a closing speech to the jury. Then FINALLY the judge sums up. What does she/he say? Judges are given some training, and of course most have sat through many summings up as practicing lawyers. But not all. I suspect that most have created their own template which they then vary from case to case. The Judicial Studies Board (now known as the Judicial College) has produced some very helpful books. Thus the *Crown Court Bench Book: Directing the Jury* (see Judicial Studies Board, 2010) gives clear guidance on the 'Structure and Content of the Summing Up':

- introductory words at commencement of trial;
- Preliminary Directions of Law (which include issues such as burden and standard of proof; separate consideration of counts and/or defendant; alternative verdicts);
- the prosecution case and principles of criminal liability;
- (special) measures for witnesses;
- identification evidence;
- cross-admissibility;
- bad character;
- hearsay;
- the defendant's statements and behaviour, etc. etc.

192   *N. Padfield*

The Judicial Studies Board began to publish 'Specimen Directions' in the 1970s. As the Lord Chief Justice said in his 2010 Foreword to the Directions,

> the JSB has never claimed legal infallibility and aspired only to give advice. The authors of the Specimen Directions presented models which could be adapted to any factual context but, on appeal, variation from the JSB model was liable to attract criticism from the appellant advocate or the Court. As a result, the temptation was to take the 'safe' option of reading the specimen into a summing up without sufficient adaptation to the requirements of the case.

So, in 2009, the Bench book was re-designed as an electronic reference work. It is meant to be used more as a reference guide than as a hard and fast 'model'.

There have, as far as I know, been no studies in England of the words judges actually use. It is quite extraordinary that some issues of evidence may get lengthy comment, for example, a jury will be warned at some length when someone has lied, or may have lied in the police station, that people lie for many reasons, frequently innocent reasons. The usual guidance on when a jury may draw 'adverse inferences' from the defendant's failure to tell the police some fact which they later rely on at trial is so complex that I would be surprised if most jurors really understand the implications of what the judge is actually counselling. When it comes to summarising the facts of the case (which I believe that American judges do not do), the jury has more freedom. Although the judge will stress, "that when it comes to the facts, members of the jury, it is your opinion, and yours alone which counts", he or she is still free to comment, and indeed it is difficult to summarise the evidence without appearing to emphasise some points of evidence over others. There is much debate as to how best to summarise the evidence: a chronological narration may well be better than a summary witness by witness, but again this is a matter which is not, to my knowledge, discussed in the literature.

An interesting feature of the English system is the search for unanimity. The jury will be told that they have to reach a unanimous verdict, although they may well know that eventually a majority verdict may be permitted. At the end of the summing up they retire to a jury room to consider their verdict, and will then be kept together privately until either they reach a verdict or they are discharged because they find themselves unable to do so. Sometimes jurors wish to ask the judge questions or be reminded of a piece of evidence, in which case they will be brought back into open court. Occasionally, when the jury have been unable to reach a verdict swiftly, it has been necessary to keep them in a hotel overnight, but nowadays they will usually be permitted to separate for the night, even once they have retired to consider their verdict, and reconvene the following morning.

It is an interesting question to ask how far the jury must agree among themselves as to the grounds upon which the conviction is based. It is a surprisingly difficult question to answer in law, if not in practice. If they are all sure that he did it, either this way, or if not this way, then that way, then they should convict:

Staplyton v. *O'Callaghan* [1973] 2 All ER 782, [1974] Crim L R 64; *Giannetto* [1997] 1 Cr App R 1. But if half are sure that he did it X way (and no other), and half are sure that he did Y way (and no other), they should not in this case convict: *Brown* (1984) 79 Cr App R 115. The case law here is very complex: perhaps because the Court of Appeal is rightly keen to uphold the convictions of guilty people (or people who have been convicted by a jury), and because they don't want to uncover unnecessary 'cans of worms'. In *Carr* [2000] 2 Cr App R 149 where the question was whether the defendant killed the victim by a kick (as to which there was an issue of identification – who really was it who kicked him?) or by a punch (as to which there was an issue of self-defence – how hard did he hit him, etc.), the Court of Appeal held that the trial judge should have taken the initiative and told the jury that they must be agreed on which one it was. But of course, the inscrutable nature of the jury's verdict normally covers up this sort of issue.[5]

Are juries fair?

This seems to me to be a pretty basic question, but how do we answer it? In an important study carried out for the Ministry of Justice, Thomas (2010) concluded that there was "little evidence that juries are not fair". Is that good enough? She also identified several areas where the criminal justice system should and could better assist jurors in performing their role. The study used a variety of methods to examine these issues: case simulation with real juries at Crown Courts (involving 797 jurors on 68 juries); analysis of all actual jury verdicts in 2006–08 (over 68,000 verdicts); and post-verdict survey of jurors (668 jurors in 62 cases). Interestingly Thomas points out that section 8 of the Contempt of Court Act 1981 does not prevent comprehensive research about how juries reach their verdicts and that research from other jurisdictions should not be relied upon to understand juries in this country.

One question rarely asked is whether jury service is fair on the jurors. I have come across a number of people over the years who have been deeply affected by their jury service: both young and old, male and female, people who remain deeply troubled by their experience, often years later. Perhaps it is a simple question of distaste for the job. One woman told me:

> I hate thinking about the seamy side of life: why should I have to sit for several days hearing evidence about the unspeakable things that some people do to each other. Jury service should be optional – there would be plenty of volunteers.

Others are deeply traumatised by the sorts of decisions they are forced to make, in the company of 11 strangers. You might be the minority of one, who hangs out for an acquittal but fails to persuade your colleagues. You might have been unanimous in your decision to acquit, but deeply uncomfortable since you thought he was probably guilty but couldn't be sure. Did you let down the

194   *N. Padfield*

complainant? There have been complainants who have committed suicide after the jury acquitted. A famous case was that of a professional violinist who killed herself after giving evidence at the trial of her former music teacher, who was later found guilty of several counts of indecent assault.[6] In a case where the jury acquits, they may well have been quite right to do so: it is often difficult to be sure in a rape case, or in a sexual assault case, when it is only his word against hers. But it is a major burden on them to have to live with the realisation that their decision drove her to suicide.

Court facilities are often inadequate. Both the Royal Commission on *Criminal Justice* (1993) and Lord Justice Auld's *Review of the Criminal Courts* (2001) raised important questions about remuneration, financial loss allowances and general conditions. All these questions might usefully be explored, but perhaps this is unlikely at a time of massive cuts in spending on criminal justice?

Are juries effective?

This may be an even more difficult question to answer, because as we have already said, we can only measure effectiveness if we know what we want the jury to effect or to achieve. It is very difficult to assess the jury. Are they too easily swayed, susceptible to rhetoric? Are they prone to leniency? Are they too doubtful or too accepting of police evidence? There are many famous acquittals: some more or less 'political' (one might cite Clive Ponting's acquittal in 1985 of offences under the Official Secrets Act after he had disclosed documents about the sinking of an Argentine navy warship in the Falklands war of 1982 to a Labour MP; or the cases of 'mercy killing' doctors who have been acquitted of 'murdering' their patients: Dr Arthur Cox in 1981 or Dr David Moor in 1999). These can be seen as inappropriate – the proper means for amending the Official Secrets Act 1911 or the law on mercy killing is through the ballot box, not via the jury room – and one has to remember that in all 'miscarriage of justice' cases it was the jury who decided to convict. What does this say about 'effectiveness'?

Defendants and their legal advisers may prefer trial by jury and consider it fairer than trial by magistrates. But is this belief justified? Zander and Henderson (1993) asked the various participants in the trial process whether they were surprised by the jury's verdict. Prosecution barristers were surprised in 15 per cent of cases, defence barristers and judges in 14 per cent, defence solicitors in 18 per cent, police in 25 per cent and CPS in 27 per cent of cases. They were not necessarily surprised by the same verdicts, and acquittals gave rise to surprise more frequently than convictions. The police and CPS were surprised by 44–47 per cent of acquittals. Judges were surprised by 25 per cent of acquittals, though most of these were 'understandable in the light of the evidence'. However, according to judges, 29 per cent of all acquittals were against the weight of the evidence, against the judge's direction on the law or simply inexplicable to judges. The number of 'problematic acquittals', according to prosecution barristers, was 31 per cent, and for defence barristers the figure was 16 per cent. Does this suggest that a quarter of all acquittals are wrong (see Padfield, 2008)?

Questions for psychologists

The previous discussion should suggest that I am troubled by the system of trial by jury. And I have a number of questions which perhaps the psychologists might like to answer. Here I offer five. The first question: should juries get a pre-trial summary of issues? I think that Darbyshire, in her wonderful book which results from her sitting over a long period of time with judges at every level in the criminal court system, puts the point very clearly: "in other contexts it would seem unthinkable to present information to a group of decision-makers and tell them afterwards what they were expected to do with it" (Darbyshire, 2011, p. x). Why not give the jury a better briefing?

My second question is, when does the jury need the help of an expert (the judge or someone else?)? There are many limbs to this question. Let us question when the jury needs the expertise of the judge. It is extraordinary that we have decided in England and Wales today that some words need complex definitions, and others none at all. On the meaning of the word 'dishonest', the judge merely says something like "members of the jury, you all know what it is to be honest; dishonest is the opposite of that". Other words may be explained in detail. The meaning of an ordinary word may not be a question of law, but the proper construction of a statute clearly is. The criminal law reflects an ambivalence: some words – such as, for example, 'insulting' or 'dishonest' – are left for the jury to interpret according to their common sense, while others – such as 'intention', 'recklessness' or 'provocation' – have been rigidly judicially defined such that, at times, as a matter of law, they no longer mean what ordinary English suggests.

Then there are the current controversies concerning the need for the judge to dispel 'rape myths'. Should a judge explain that women in mini-skirts or those who hitch hike are not inviting rape? Or more difficult – should a judge explain that women react to trauma in different ways? As the *Crown Court Bench Book* (Judicial Studies Board, 2010) puts it (pp. 353 and 356),

> The experience of judges who try sexual offences is that an image of stereo-typical behaviour and demeanour by a victim or the perpetrator of a non-consensual offence such as rape held by some members of the public can be misleading and capable of leading to injustice. That experience has been gained by judges, expert in the field, presiding over many such trials during which guilt has been established but in which the behaviour and demeanour of complainants and defendants, both during the incident giving rise to the charge and in evidence, has been widely variable. Judges have, as a result of their experience, in recent years adopted the course of cautioning juries against applying stereotypical images how an alleged victim or an alleged perpetrator of a sexual offence ought to have behaved at the time, or ought to appear while giving evidence, and to judge the evidence on its intrinsic merits. This is not to invite juries to suspend their own judgement but to approach the evidence without prejudice...

196   *N. Padfield*

Research by those who are expert in the subject[7] discloses several subjects for stereotyping which could lead the jury to approach the complainant's evidence with unwarranted scepticism. They include but are not limited to:

- The complainant wore provocative clothing; therefore he/she must have wanted sex.
- The complainant got drunk in male company; therefore he/she must have been prepared for sex An attractive male does not need to have sex without consent.
- A complainant in a relationship with the alleged attacker is likely to have consented.
- Rape takes place between strangers.
- Rape does not take place without physical resistance from the victim.
- If it is rape there must be injuries.
- A person who has been sexually assaulted reports it as soon as possible.
- A person who has been sexually assaulted remembers events consistently.

The role of the 'expert witness' may be even more challenging. When does the jury need the help of an expert? This is another complex area of law, where the judge has to decide not only who is an expert (and to guard against bogus experts or 'junk science'), but also to work out whether and how a jury should get 'help' (see Criminal Procedure Rules, Part 33 – revised version, October 2014[8]).

My third question(s) concern the summing up. Should a judge sum up orally or in writing? Do the suggested directions on e.g. silence in the police station or on the risks of mistaken identity confuse jurors? How should judges guide juries in relation to contentious evidence? The fourth question is perhaps a subset of the third. Does the distinction between questions of law (which are for the judge) and questions of fact (which are for the jury) work in practice? For example, let us choose just two difficult areas of law. The first is the definition of causation. For example, is the word 'causes' in the Water Act 1989, s 107(1)) a question of fact or law? The section provides that: 'a person contravenes this section if he causes or knowingly permits (a) any poisonous, noxious or polluting matter or any solid waste matter to enter any controlled waters…'. In *National Rivers Authority* v. *Yorkshire Water Services Ltd* [1995] 1 AC 444 the Divisional Court held that whether or not Yorkshire Water was causing pollution was a question of fact for the jury, not a matter of law for the judge as the Crown Court had suggested. The House of Lords later allowed a final appeal by the sewage company. Does the distinction between law and fact in this context make sense, or is it just a technique that allows judges to avoid ruling on difficult questions? Here the important issue is whether a sewage company which unknowingly caused pollution, because an unauthorised person had dumped iso-octanol into the sewers, should be convicted of a criminal offence as defined in Act. Is this the function of judge or jury? Is the jury or the judge better equipped to deal with the meaning of ordinary words (or the ordinary meaning of words, as Guest (1986) prefers to put it).

The English jury   197

Another example of the fourth question is section 4(3) of the Criminal Attempts Act 1981, which leaves the jury with a wide, largely uncontrolled, discretion:

> Where, in proceedings against a person for the offence under section 1 above, there is evidence sufficient in law to support a finding that he did an act falling within subsection (1) of that section, the question whether or not his act fell within that subsection is a question of fact.

Does that make sense as a distinction? Is it helpful?

My fifth question concerns court architecture. Has anyone ever studied the impact on jury decision-making of their position within the courtroom? Modern courts in England usually, and shockingly to my eye, place the defendant in a glass box at the very back of the court room. I find that shocking as it appears to a large extent to exclude the defendant from his or her trial. As a judge I had occasion several times to say to the lawyer in front of me, "excuse me, Mr Jones, but your client obviously disagrees with the way you put that point". Only the judge is facing the defendant. The jury may be facing the public gallery, or simply sitting sideways to the rest of the court. Does it make a difference? I think as judge I was affected in some subtle way by whether, for example, there was a journalist in court, or whether the victim or the defendant's girlfriend were sitting sobbing in court. Presumably the jury is similarly affected, and where people sit in the court room must have an impact.

Finally, my sixth question: has the time come to allow the judge to retire with the jury? My view is that we should at least experiment with this possibility. Many years, ago, an experienced judge, Eric Stockdale, questioned why judge and jury are kept so rigorously separated 'and free to make their own mistakes' (see Stockdale, 1967). And Jackson and Doran (1997) argued that the traditional division of labour between judges and juries should be redrawn in order to enable judges to take greater responsibility for areas where their fact-finding strengths are located (for example, identification and scientific evidence). Most colleagues with whom I have discussed this idea appear wary of mixing judge and jury. They suggest that the judge would dominate. I don't see why. I would have thought it was perfectly sensible to have the judge as chairman of the discussion, and as the person who should facilitate debate. That raises too the question of whether 12 people are really necessary. Would a jury made up of nine, or even six, people be as satisfactory? Interestingly, since the decision of the Grand Chamber of the European Court of Human Rights ruled in *Taxquet* v. *Belgium* (2010) striking down the then Belgium system, the Belgium judge now includes the judge retiring with the jury, but only after they have reached their verdict, in order to help them formulate their reasons.[9] I don't know very much about this, and how this new system is being assessed. It seems to me to be deeply problematic: what happens if the judge discovers when helping the jury to formulate their reasons that they hadn't really agreed their verdict on the proper grounds?

Conclusion

The late Professor Sir John Smith was one of my academic heroes, but I was deeply frustrated by his article entitled, "Is ignorance bliss?". Professor Sir John Smith warns (1998, p. 105):

> Much of our law of evidence is based on assumptions about the behaviour of juries which are mere guesswork and, of course, I recognise that it is highly desirable that we should know whether these assumptions are well founded or not. But I fear that there is a price to be paid – namely the revelation that many cases are decided in consequence of material irregularities in the jury room with the consequent undermining of public confidence in jury trial. If we are to keep jury trial – and there is an overwhelming sentiment in favour of doing so – it is perhaps better not to know. Is this a case where ignorance is bliss?

I find it hard to accept that ignorance is bliss. In any case, we are not entirely ignorant. I have cited quite a lot in this chapter from research carried out decades ago (e.g. Zander and Henderson's Crown Court study (1993) which looked at real juries, but without going behind the 'veil'). Readers will not be surprised that I end this chapter with a plea for much more 'real world' research, and for psychologists to work more closely with lawyers.

Notes

1 I have taught law at the University of Cambridge since 1991, and sat as a Recorder (part-time trial judge) in the Crown Court for a few weeks every year between 2002 and 2014.
2 Perhaps surprisingly, this has withstood challenge before the European Court of Human Rights: see *Taxquet* v. *Belgium*, (Grand Chamber) 16 November 2010; (2012) 54 EHRR 26; [2011] Crim LR 236; [2011] Camb LJ 14; *Judge* v. *UK*, 8 February 2011, (2011) 52 EHRR SE17.
3 A dramatic example was at the end of the first trial of Vicky Pryce, the ex-wife of an MP, on a charge relating to speeding points she took for her ex-husband in 2013, where the trial judge, a very senior and experienced judge, described the jury, who had asked a series of very basic questions, as having a "fundamental deficit in understanding": see www.bbc.co.uk/news/uk-21516473.
4 See by way of examples: *Young* (1995) 2 Cr App R 379 (the infamous case of the jury which chose to use a ouija board to decide guilt or innocence); *Qureshi* [2002] 1 WLR 518, (2002) CLJ 291; *Mirza* [2004] UKHL 2, [2004] 2 WLR 201, (2004) CLJ 314 (NB Lord Steyn's dissent:

> "[W]here there is cogent evidence demonstrating a real risk that the jury was not impartial and that the general confidence in jury verdicts was in the particular case ill reposed, what possible public interest can there be in maintaining a dubious conviction?");

Smith and Merceica [2005] UKHL 12; [2005] 2 Cr App R 10; *Thompson etc.* [2010] EWCA Crim 1623: CA guidance in relation to jury irregularities including use of the internet, bringing extraneous material into the jury room and letters from jurors doubting the safety of the verdicts. Convictions upheld except for one; *Mears* [2011] EWCA Crim 2651 (juror in mobile contact with boyfriend in public gallery); *Hewgill* [2011] EWCA Crim 1778; [2012] Crim LR 134 (inappropriate conversations in pub); *AG* v. *Fraill* [2011] EWCA Crim 1570, [2012] Crim L.R. 286 (8 months imprisonment for a Facebook juror); *A-G* v. *Dallas* [2012] EWHC 156 (Admin); [2012] Crim LR 694; *Pardon* [2012] EWHC 3402 (Admin), *AG* v. *Davey*; *Beard* [2013] EWHC 2317 (Admin), where two jurors were prosecuted by the AG for contempt: one had posted on Facebook the following message: "Woooow I wasn't expecting to be in a jury Deciding a paedophile's fate, I've always wanted to Fuck up a paedophile & now I'm within the law!". The other had been 'surfing' the internet. The legal questions arise in two very different contexts: is the conviction safe? And should the juror be punished by the criminal law?

5 I am grateful to Professor Spencer for his lecture notes on this subject, from which I have borrowed; see also *Boreham* [2000] 2 Cr App R 17; and articles by J. C. Smith, at [1988] Crim LR 335, and Richard Taylor, *Jury Unanimity in Homicide* at [2001] Crim LR 283.

6 www.theguardian.com/uk/2013/feb/08/sexual-abuse-victim-killed-herself-trial.

7 E.g. Dr Fiona Mason's paper 'The Psychological Effects of Serious Sexual Assault: A Guide' and Powerpoint Seminar November 2008, JSB training website; Home Office Research Study 237 'Rape and sexual assault of women', March 2002 (www.home office.gov.uk/rds/pdfs2/hors237.pdf); Temkin and Krahe, *Sexual Assault and the Justice Gap: A Question of Attitude* (www.hartpub.co.uk); Ellison and Munro, 'React-ing to rape: Exploring mock jurors' assessments of complainant credibility', Br J Crim-inol. 2009; 49: 202–219 (http://bjc.oxfordjournals.org/cgi/reprint/azn077?iijkey=FFeru z5D5tBKVOz&keytype=ref). Some jurisdictions have already legislated for jury direc-tions based on such research.

8 See www.justice.gov.uk/courts/procedure-rules/criminal.

9 Personal communication.

Bibliography

Andrews, J. A. (1978). Uses and abuses of the jury. In P. R. Glazebrook (ed.), *Reshaping the Criminal Law*. London: Sweet & Maxwell.

Auld, R. (2001). *Review of the Criminal Courts*. London: Royal Courts of Justice (http://webarchive.nationalarchives.gov.uk/+/www.criminal-courts-review.org.uk/).

Baldwin, J. and McConville, M. (1979). *Jury Trials*. Oxford: Clarendon.

Cornish, W. R. (1968). *The Jury*. London: Allen Lane.

Darbyshire, P. (1991). The lamp that shows that freedom lives – is it worth the candle? *Criminal Law Review*, 740–752.

Darbyshire, P. (2011). *Sitting in Judgment: The Working Lives of Judges*. Oxford: Hart.

Denning, Lord (1982). *What Next in the Law?* London: Butterworths.

Devlin, P. (1956). *Trial by Jury*. London: Stevens.

Devlin, P. (1991). The conscience of the jury. *Law Quarterly Review*, 107, 398–404.

Enright, S. and Morton, J. (1990). *Taking Liberties: The Criminal Jury in the 1990s*. London: Weidenfeld & Nicolson.

Findlay, M. and Duff, P. (eds) (1998). *The Jury under Attack*. London: Butterworths.

Griew, E. (1985). Dishonesty: Objections to *Feely* and *Ghosh*. *Criminal Law Review*, 341–354.

Guest, S. (1986). Law, fact and lay questions. In I. H. Dennis (ed.), *Criminal Law and Justice*. London: Sweet & Maxwell.

Hans, V. P. and Vidmar, N. (1986). *Judging the Jury*. New York: Plenum Press.

200   N. Padfield

Hastie, R. (1983). *Inside the Juror: The Psychology of Juror Decision Making.* Cambridge: Cambridge University Press.

Jackson, J. and Doran, S. (1995). *Judge without Jury: Diplock Trials in the Adversary System.* Oxford: Clarendon.

Jackson, J. and Doran, S. (1997). Judge and jury: Towards a new division of labour in criminal trials. *Modern Law Review*, 60, 759–778.

Judicial Studies Board (2010). *Crown Court Bench Book: Directing the Jury* (www.judiciary.gov.uk/wp-content/uploads/JCO/Documents/Training/benchbook_criminal_2010.pdf).

McCabe, S. (1972). *The Jury at Work.* Oxford: Oxford University Penal Research Unit, Paper No. 4.

McCabe, S. and Purves, R. (1974). *The Shadow Jury at Work.* Oxford: Oxford University Penal Research Unit, Paper No. 8.

Padfield, N. (2008). *Text and Material on the Criminal Justice Process.* Oxford: Oxford University Press, 4th edn.

Roberts, J. and Hough, M. (2011). Public attitudes to the criminal jury: A review of recent findings. *Howard Journal*, 247–261.

Smith, J. C. (1998). Is ignorance bliss? Could jury trial survive investigation? *Medical Science and Law*, 38, 98.

Stockdale, E. (1967). *The Court and the Offender.* London: Gollanz.

Thomas, C. (2008). Exposing the myths of jury service. *Criminal Law Review*, 415–430.

Thomas, C. (2010). *Are Juries Fair?.* London: Ministry of Justice Research Series 1/10 (www.justice.gov.uk/downloads/publications/research-and-analysis/moj-research/are-juries-fair-research.pdf).

Thomas, C. (2013). Avoiding the perfect storm of juror contempt. *Criminal Law Review*, 483–503.

Vidmar, N. (ed.) (2000). *World Jury Systems.* Oxford: Oxford University Press.

Warner, K., Davis, J., Walter, M., Bradfield, R. and Vermey, R. (2011). *Public Judgement on Sentencing: Final Results from the Tasmanian Jury Sentencing Study.* Canberra: Australian Institute of Criminology (www.aic.gov.au/publications/current%20series/tandi/401-420/tandi407.html).

Zander, M. and Henderson, P. (1993). *The Crown Court Study.* Royal Commission on Criminal Justice Research Study 19. London: HMSO.

12 Extra-legal factors that impact on sentencing decisions[1]

Andreas Kapardis

Introduction

Since time immemorial crime and punishment has been a topic that arouses great interest and, not surprisingly, conflicting views have been expressed about sentencing. As Ashworth and Roberts (2012, p.866) remind us, 'The passage of a sentence on an offender is the most public stage of the criminal justice process'. Sentencing has also been termed 'the punch-line of the criminal justice system; (Sallmann and Willis 1984, p.157). The fact is, however, that a lot of negotiation precedes a guilty plea, sometimes even during the trial. The reader should also note in this context that: (a) plea-bargaining is a practice that is more prevalent in the United States than in the United Kingdom, Australia or New Zealand; and (b) in the last three decades or so in western countries there has been enormous growth in non-court penalties. Decisions by courts affect large numbers of people in society and in imposing sentences such as terms of imprisonment, judges and magistrates inevitably make policy and can become prison reformers.

In some countries legislation rigidly prescribes penalties for offences whereas the judiciary in common law jurisdictions enjoy a great deal of discretion in deciding the type and severity of sentence. However, their discretion is not unfettered because: statutes normally provide a maximum sentence for a given offence; there are mandatory and minimum sentences for certain offences; courts in common law countries are obliged to adhere to certain principles of sentencing; there are guidelines issued by dedicated bodies, including numerical guidelines which constrain judges even more;[2] available precedent (that is, case law) points to 'acceptable' sentences for crimes of a given seriousness; and they can and must take into account mitigating and aggravating features of the case in order to achieve a certain degree of consistency in sentencing; in Magistrates' Courts in England and Wales the court clerk plays an important role by giving advice to the bench of lay magistrates;[3] members of the judiciary in various jurisdictions participate in sentencing conferences aimed at reducing unjustifiable inconsistencies; and there is the possibility of appeal against the sentence.

Furthermore, there is guidance for judges regarding the proportionality principle (i.e. that the severity of the penalty imposed should be proportionate to the

202   *A. Kapardis*

seriousness of the crime and the culpability of the defendant) and the use of imprisonment as a last resort. US judge Alex Kozinski (1993) proposed two more constraints on judicial excesses: (a) self-respect, which he considers the most significant constraint; and (b) the political system: in the United States judges are often elected.[4] Finally, a court in England and Wales, as elsewhere, when passing sentence, has a duty to give reasons for, and explain to the defendant in ordinary language, the effect of the sentence on him or her and the effect of non-compliance with any other order that forms part of the sentence.[5] It should be noted in this context that the quality of the judgements that judges make[6] impacts on the institutional legitimacy of the judiciary.

One of the aims of the Sentencing Council is to promote a clear, fair and consistent approach to sentencing. However, as Padfield (2012), herself an ex-Circuit judge, has pointed out, 'consistency itself is a fluid and slippery concept. Are we seeking consistent outcomes, or simply consistent approaches to the sentencing process? More importantly, are we seeking consistency or some other measure?' Padfield goes on to argue that 'promoting' a consistent approach to sentencing is a modest aim of the Sentencing Council, and easier to achieve than actual 'consistency', and to point out that there is a limit to how much the Sentencing Council can realistically be expected to achieve. Regarding Sentencing Guidelines in the United States, the Supreme Court in 2005[7] ruled that in order to be constitutional, the federal guidelines must be advisory rather than prescriptive. Federal judges' discretion was expanded in subsequent decisions.[8] Interestingly, Ulmer *et al.* (2011) argued that extra-legal disparity and between-district variation in the effects of extra-legal factors on sentencing did not increase as a result of the 'liberation' of federal judges' discretion.

The concept of 'sentence'

An interesting question is whether the concept of 'sentence' is a unitary concept. In an interesting study of magistrates' decisions to impose fines, Raine and Dunstan (2009) measured the 'quality' of the decision in terms of equity (equality of impact), proportionality (the extent to which the size of the fine was commensurate with the seriousness of the offence) and consistency (the extent to which the sentences were predictable and reproducible or achieved minimal disparities in the fines imposed on similar cases) and concluded that the three 'measures' did not correlate with each other.

A term of imprisonment is considered the most severe sentence that a court can impose in jurisdictions where the death penalty has been abolished. However, differences between countries notwithstanding, as Nicola Padfield (2016 in this volume) and Padfield *et al.* (2012, p. 955) remind us, what constitutes 'sentencing' has been changing in many western countries and a sentence is rarely what a judge says in court that it will be, because of the importance of both 'front door' and 'back door' sentencing. The former refers to the initial sentence imposed by a court within a number of constraints while the latter refers to such strategies as remission for good behaviour, release on parole,

Extra-legal factors and sentencing 203

amnesties, release into community supervision programmes, etc. that aim to reduce the prison population. As Padfield *et al.* (2012) state, the concern here is that out-of-court sanctions 'raise important questions about transparency, fairness, and accountability of the quasi-judicial decisions that significantly affect the lives of both offenders and victims' (p. 956). Padfield also poses the question whether all penalties imposed after conviction are part of the 'sentence' and goes on to list 13 court orders that are often an integral part of a sentence package imposed by a court in England and Wales. Padfield (2016) maintains, and argues a convincing case for it, that all these orders should be considered as part of the 'sentence'. Finally, Padfield argues that conceptualising 'sentence' as an ongoing process not only draws attention to 'hidden' sentences but, also, it would: (a) inform the debate about the aims and purposes of sentencing; lead to greater understanding of the real meaning of the 'sentence'; and, finally, (c) lead to a 'more credible, orderly and efficient system'.

A difficulty which researchers and the judiciary alike confront is that there is no consensus on what is 'good judging' (see Wistrich 2010) or a 'right' sentence. Taking an empirical approach to the latter question, Farrington (1978) suggested that the 'right sentence' is the one that achieves a given penal aim for a given type of offender most effectively and efficiently. From a traditional, narrow (and cynical) legal point of view, the 'right' sentence is the one given by the judicial authority that spoke last and highest on the matter.

Judicial discretion and the existence of conflicting sentencing objectives[9] mean that, inevitably, sentencing is problematic, and full of unjustified disparities. Disparities in sentencing criminal defendants are endemic in the system. Indeed one of the main criticisms levelled against judicial discretion diachronically is that it often results in these disparities (Galton 1885; Skyrme 1979).

Disparity in sentencing is a ground for appeal. But when is 'disparity' justified? Drawing on Archbold (2012), regarding the meaning of 'disparity', imposing different sentences on two co-defendants is not considered an unjustified disparity if: one is amenable to a particular form of sentence and the other is not;[10] their roles in the offence are different; one is significantly younger than the other; one has a significantly less serious criminal record; some mitigating circumstance is available to one that is not available to the other; and where the power of the court to sentence one is restricted because of his or her age.

The findings of a Spanish experimental simulation study illustrate disparity in sentencing. A random sample of 52 judges in Spain, each with a minimum of one year's experience in the Appeal and High Court and with an average age 34.6 years, were given a detailed written transcript of a real trial where the defendant was to be sentenced for raping a woman. Half the judges were against incarceration, 40 per cent were in favour of incarceration and 10 per cent did not respond. Finally, the length of the sentence proposed varied from five to 25 years (Arce *et al.* 2001). Such disparities are understandably a cause for concern, especially when, as stated above, sentencing has been termed the 'cornerstone of the criminal justice system'.

204 *A. Kapardis*

The nature of the sentence decision-making process

Drawing on van Koppen (2002) as far as changes in judicial decision-making are concerned, the mechanical view of legal decision-making (better known as 'legal formalism') was not seriously questioned until the latter part of the nineteenth century. A judge would decide sentence in four stages: find out what the facts are, find the relevant law, apply the rule to the facts, and decide what the consequences should be. The mechanical view of legal decision-making came under attack by the proponents of 'legal realism', such as the pioneer US Supreme Court Justice Oliver Wendell Holmes (1881), who stated that 'the life of the law has not been logic; it has been experience'. Legal realists maintain that judicial decisions are the result of the rational application of legal reasons and of psychological, political and social factors. Pioneer thinker Justice Cardozo (1921) argued for judges to play a more creative role in law so that the law does not remain static but reflects the times we live in. Later on, legal realists such as Llewellyn and Hoebel (1941) and Jerome Frank (1950) shifted the focus to more pragmatic aspects, paving the way for research into social and psychological factors that impact on legal decision-making.

A question of interest to the judiciary worldwide is whether sentencing is an art or a science.[11] Some judges[12] like to describe what they do as a 'balancing act' between the often conflicting interests of the community, the offender and the victim. Mackenzie (2005) points out that the 'instinctive synthesis' perspective has been criticised by Ashworth (2000) and Tonry (1996) because it seems to assume that judges are the only ones who can know what is the 'right' sentence and sentence in a just way.

If we believe that judicial decision-making cannot be taught, then sentencing inconsistencies cannot be reduced by training judges. Most of the 31 judges interviewed in Mackenzie's (2005) study of sentencing in Queensland preferred to think of sentencing in terms of 'balancing'. According to Mackenzie, there is good case law[13] evidence in various jurisdictions in Australia, and from her own study, to indicate that Australian judges consider sentencing more of an 'art', a view also expressed by many Canadian judges (Canadian Sentencing Commission 1987). Interestingly, only a minority of judges in Ashworth's (1984) Crown Court study opted for 'intuitive process' in describing the nature of sentencing decision-making.[14]

Studying variations in sentencing

Examination of the literature on judicial decision-making[15] in chronological sequence shows a shift from the legal model (based on legal positivism) and from what judicial decision-making ought to include to the more substantial question of what is judicial decision-making, employing large-scale quantitative analysis of decisions (Goldman 1975), attitudinal research (Knight 2009) and analysis of correspondence between judges (Feeley and Rubin 1998). In recent years, the aim of sentencing researchers has been not only to understand judges'

Extra-legal factors and sentencing 205

and magistrates' decision-making, but also to create a legal system with less bias and more diversity.[16] The discussion of empirical evidence that follows concentrates on studies of actual sentencers.

There is a large amount of empirical literature on inconsistencies in sentencing and the importance of both legal and extra-legal factors in accounting for such inconsistencies. The early literature review of sentencing studies by Kapardis (1984) identified 11 'important' legal variables, namely: type of charge; defendant's criminal record; recency of last conviction; past interaction with the criminal justice system; type of plea; age; gender; community ties; provocation by the victim; whether a court is in an urban or rural area; and the probation officer's recommendation about sentence. Such a literature review today would also need to include some courts' use of Victim Impact Statements (VISs) when considering a sentence. The victim personal statement scheme in England and Wales started on 1 October 2001. In *Payne* v. *Tennessee*[17] the US Supreme Court allowed the admission of VISs during capital sentencing proceedings.

The extra-legal factors identified by Kapardis (1984) were: a defendant's pretrial status, socioeconomic status, race and attractiveness; the victim's race; and a sentencer's age, religion, education, social background, cognitive complexity, constructs, politics and penological orientation (that is, whether offence- or offender-focused).

There is no doubt that it is the interaction of both specific legal and extra-legal factors that best explains disparities in sentencing. Given regional differences in sentencing legislation and the large number of factors that have been found to have the potential to impact on sentence choice and severity, no generalisations are possible, especially not across jurisdictions or over time.[18] The sentencing stage in the criminal justice process provides a goldmine of opportunities for psychologists interested in decision-making.

Seven research methods have been used by studies of sentencing variations. They can be grouped as follows:[19] (a) crude comparison studies that compared sentences passed by different courts in the same region, by judges in different regions or by different judges in the same court and between sentences imposed for the same offence; (b) assumed-random-sample studies;[20] (c) matching-by-item studies;[21] (d) prediction studies;[22] (e) observational studies;[23] (f) experimental simulation studies: the great majority of experimental simulation studies in the United States have used student subjects and suffer from low external validity, whereas the few British studies have used real sentencers; and (g) interviewing judges: judges worldwide have traditionally been very reluctant to be interviewed about their sentencing behaviour. As Mackenzie (2005, p. 11) has put it: 'The voices of those who actually sentence offenders are very rarely heard, despite the fact that they have much to add to the knowledge and debate in the area.'

A researcher would be well-advised to combine different methods in researching sentencing such as using data from court records to match cases and compare sentences, make systematic observations in court, and interview judges or magistrates in order to identify the factors that are important in accounting for

206   *A. Kapardis*

inconsistencies in sentencing. One of the first to interview judges[24] in Britain was Ashworth (1984). Unfortunately, the then Chief Justice of England and Wales did not allow the study to proceed, so it was never finished. Of course magistrates and judges can also be 'interviewed' by means of a structured questionnaire.[25]

A number of penalties are available to judges. Therefore, in studying sentencing, there is a need for a scale to measure sentence severity. Such a scale was reported in the English study by Kapardis and Farrington (1981), who found significant consistency within and between 168 magistrates in their ranking of 12 different disposals across nine cases.

Some extra-legal factors that influence sentences

In considering the empirical evidence for extra-legal factors, we must not lose sight of the fact that the very same factors (e.g. defendant's gender and/or race) influence decision-making earlier in the criminal justice process, through, *inter alia*, differential access to private legal representation and the existence of stereotypes within the community and among law-enforcement personnel (for example, that a particular minority is more violence prone than others),[26] factors that can be expected to influence, for example, help-seeking behaviour of ethnic battered women (Raj and Silverman 2007), the charges laid against a defendant and/or a defendant's ability to bargain his/her plea for fewer and/or less serious charges. Let us next take a close and critical look at the empirical evidence for the importance of a few interesting non-legal factors in sentencing disparities.

Defendant's gender

As Nagel and Johnson (1994, p. 181) reminded their readers, 'Historically, female offenders have been at the margins of the criminal justice system'. The fact that a defendant is a woman is not in itself a ground for discrimination.[27] In addition to significant gender differences in offending that partly explain differences in the sentences imposed, a magistrate or judge may impose a more lenient sentence on a female than on a male defendant because she is perceived as 'troubled', while a male defendant is perceived as 'troublesome', as Hedderman and Gelsthorpe (1997) found when they interviewed 189 lay magistrates and eight stipendiary magistrates.

A number of explanations have been put forward for gender differences at sentencing. First, as Otto Pollak (1950) argued in his book *The Criminality of Women*, female offenders were preferentially treated by the criminal justice system because it was made up predominantly of men, who, not surprisingly, were characterised by male notions of chivalry. Gender bias, of course, is endemic in many societies and their criminal justice systems.[28] A case in point is India, with its gender asymmetry and its long-term grim record of female infant killings (because families have to pay expensive dowries at the time of their marriage). Second, gender differences in offending are well-established in

Extra-legal factors and sentencing   207

criminology:[29] in fact, women's offending tends to be less serious than men's and women are less likely to commit violent crime. Third, examination of police, court and prison statistics in English-speaking western common law countries shows that women are more likely to be granted bail than to be remanded in custody awaiting trial,[30] are treated more leniently by the courts and, if incarcerated, serve shorter terms of imprisonment than their male counterparts.[31] As Gelsthorpe and Loucks (1997) found, courts may be reluctant to fine female defendants because it would make their child-care responsibilities more difficult and they are not likely to have independent means to pay a fine.

In an interesting early study of judges' verbal statements in real courtroom settings by Fontaine and Emily (1978) it was found that judges gave reasons for their choice of sentence more often and focused on the crime (rather than on the defendant's circumstances) more often in the case of male than female defendants, an indication, perhaps, that the judges considered offending by females as out-of-role and, consequently, focused more on the type of woman the defendant was and her motives.[32] With one exception (Farrington and Morris 1983), British studies of gender differences in sentencing by Magistrates' Courts and Crown Courts have reported that female defendants receive more lenient sentences.[33] Wilczynski and Morris (1993) analysed data on 474 cases in which a child had been killed by a parent and found that labelling such women's killings as 'abnormal' behaviour which contradicts sentencers' perception of women as 'inherently passive, gentle and tolerant ... nurturing, caring and altruistic' and that a woman 'must have been "mad" to kill her own child', results in significantly lenient treatment by the courts.

Studies of the importance of gender at the sentencing stage in the United States have reported contradictory findings. Some researchers[34] have reported that female defendants are treated more leniently by the courts while others[35] reported no significant gender differences in sentencing. However, the weight of evidence documents American courts' lenient treatment of female defendants (see also Daly and Bordt's (1995) meta-analytic assessment) but, as we shall see below, some intervening variables complicate this conclusion. Feely's 1979 study in Connecticut, like Hampton's (1979) in New Zealand, reported that female offenders were given harsher sentences. As Steffensmeir and Demuth (2006) emphasised, however, a single characteristic's main effect may be much smaller than an interaction effect (gender and race/ethnicity) in this context, and statistically insignificant. For example, Tillyer *et al.* (2015) documented an interaction effect between gender and length of criminal history; they found that female defendants with lower criminal history scores received more lenient treatment relative to males (thus supporting the chivalry hypothesis) whereas those females with higher criminal history received severe sentences (supporting the evil woman hypothesis).

Similarly, Doerner and Demuth (2014) reported that the presence of mental illness in a case tended to increase the length of sentence for male defendants convicted for violent offences whereas the same factor decreased the sentence severity for such female defendants. Doerner and Demuth go on to conclude that

208   *A. Kapardis*

the context of a violent conviction may be interpreted as evidence of diminished responsibility for females but future dangerousness for males. Finally, a Texas study by Rodriguez *et al.* (2006) documented lenient treatment of female defendants (less likely to be sent to prison and to receive shorter terms of imprisonment) by the courts when convicted of drug offences whereas if convicted of violent offences female defendants were as likely to be sent to prison as their male counterparts but, nevertheless, received significantly shorter terms of imprisonment than males. Spohn *et al.* (1985) found that African American women were sentenced more leniently than African American men but were given sentences that were comparable to those of white men. Utilising US Sentencing Commission data, Doerner and Demuth (2010) reported an interaction effect between a defendant being male, young, Hispanic or black African American and receiving the harshest imprisonment sentences.

In Australia, Naylor's (1992) observational study of 1301 cases dealt with by the Victorian Magistrates Court in Melbourne and Jefffries and Bond's (2010–11) analysis of data from South Australia's higher courts reported that, controlling for legal variables, women were sentenced more leniently. Jeffries and Bond's results indicate that for judges, different factors may be important in determining the sentencing outcome for men and women. The study of gender and sentencing outcomes by the higher courts in the State of Victoria by the Sentencing Advisory Council (2010, p. 7) concluded that the disparities identified 'are likely to be a reflection not of bias, but of legitimate yet gender-linked characteristics' such as women's greater likelihood of having a history of psychiatric illness, physical or sexual traumatisation in childhood or early adulthood and a history of substance abuse.

As pointed out by Victoria's Sentencing Advisory Council (2010, p. 11), inconsistent findings about gender and sentencing 'are partly due to differences in the sophistication of the methodology employed, the factors examined in the analysis and the data from which the samples were drawn'. What can be concluded is that the tendency is for women offenders in the United Kingdom, the United States and New Zealand to receive downward departures from sentencing guidelines (Lindholm and Cederwall 2010). The weight of the empirical evidence shows that the effect of gender on sentencing is indirect; it is attributable to gender differences in offending behaviour and to a constellation of characteristics which create legitimate mitigating circumstances for female defendants – which, in turn, lead to justifiable inconsistencies in sentencing (Sentencing Advisory Council 2010). Finally, theoretical explanations[36] for gender differences in the courts have included paternalism/chivalry,[37] social control arguments (Kruttschnitt 1984), and feminist explanations (Daly 1994; Gelsthorpe 2004). Studies of the importance of gender in sentencing have focused on the gender of offenders. Curry *et al.* (2004) found in their study of offenders convicted of violent crimes in Texas that male offenders who victimised females received the longest sentence. The effect of the victim's gender on sentence severity warrants more attention by researchers.

Defendant's race and ethnicity

The clearest application of the principle of equality before the law means, *inter alia*, that no person should be sentenced more severely by virtue of race[38] or colour. African Americans, of course, are more likely to be unemployed, a factor that correlates with sentence severity (Nobiling *et al.* 1998). Racial discrimination also occurs earlier on in the criminal justice process. Some minorities are disproportionately represented in criminal statistics,[39] and are differentially treated by the criminal justice system in terms of:[40] stop-and-search police practices,[41] how effective a police investigation of a racist murder is,[42] and the decision to arrest, to charge, and to grant or not grant bail (Lichtblaum 2005). There are also differences in perceived culpability as a function of race or ethnicity. Lindholm and Christianson (1998) reported an experimental study in which Swedish subjects rated an immigrant offender who stabbed a victim in the face with a knife more culpable than a Swedish offender, while the opposite was found for subjects in the experiment from an immigrant background, confirming the evidence for 'similarity bias' found with jurors.

Research into race/ethnicity and sentencing has been reported in Canada,[43] Australia,[44] New Zealand,[45] Sweden and Denmark. Regarding the treatment of Aborigines in Australia by the criminal justice system, Indigenous status was found to be a predictor of imprisonment in New South Wales (Snowball and Weatherburn 2007) and for Indigenous males but not females in Western Australia (Bond and Jeffries 2011), whereas in South Australia Jeffries and Bond (2010) reported that Indigenous offenders were treated more leniently than non-Indigenous offenders by higher courts. How does indigeneity impact on sentencing? Jeffries and Bond (2010) examined the 'narratives of mitigation' and found that the sentencing stories of Indigenous and non-Indigenous defendants differed in ways that may have reduced assessments of blameworthiness (and, thus, culpability) and risk for Indigenous defendants. Furthermore, judges highlighted a number of Indigenous-specific constraints that could result in judges seeing incarceration as an excessively harsh and costly sentence for Indigenous offenders.

British researchers did not start looking into the possibility of racial discrimination at the sentencing stage until the late 1970s. Most of the published empirical studies have failed to find a positive relationship between a defendant's race and penalty severity.[46] Mair (1986) did find, however, that blacks were less likely to be given probation than whites, most likely because of black defendants' greater likelihood of being unemployed at the time of the trial (see Halevy 1995).

Taking into account 16 factors related to both the offences and the offenders' criminal records, Hood's (1992) study of 3317 cases tried at five Crown Courts in the West Midlands found that black men were 5–8 per cent more likely to be sentenced to a term of imprisonment than white men with similar antecedents convicted of the same crimes; Asian men were slightly less likely to be incarcerated than similarly placed whites. Blacks and Asians were more likely than

210   *A. Kapardis*

whites to have pleaded not guilty, and both groups were given significantly greater terms of imprisonment than whites in similar circumstances who had also pleaded not guilty.[47] Hood also compared the five Crown Court centres and found that discrimination against blacks, in terms of the rate of custodial sentences, was much higher at three of them – Dudley, Warwick and Stafford. In her review of studies of discrimination against ethnic minorities in the criminal justice system in England and Wales for the Royal Commission on Criminal Justice, Fitzgerald (1994) pointed out that: (a) researchers have tended to include people from the Indian subcontinent (Indians, Pakistanis and Bangladeshis) as a single 'Asian' group; and (b) that small direct and indirect racial discrimination effects at various stages in the criminal justice system can have a significant cumulative impact.

Finally, racial discrimination by British magistrates has been reported by Gelsthorpe and Loucks (1997) as being attributable to magistrates being influenced by the defendant's demeanour in court: they misinterpret the body language of black defendants as 'arrogance' and respond in an unsympathetic way.

Evidence of racially based discrimination has been reported in various domains in US society, including the criminal justice system. African Americans and Latinos have been found to be four times more likely than whites to be searched in traffic stops, twice as likely to be arrested and three times more likely to be handcuffed and to have excessive force used against them (Lichtblaum 2005). Research into racial discrimination at the sentencing stage has a much longer history in the United States, where some jurisdictions still provide for the death penalty for certain crimes. Since the mid-1980s,[48] a number of researchers[49] have reported evidence suggesting racial discriminatory practices against African Americans and Hispanics.[50] Some authors, however, reported no significant effects of race on sentence severity.[51] Mustard's (2001) study of 77,235 offenders sentenced under the 1984 *Federal Reform Act* (US)[52] controlled for a number of relevant variables and found that, contrary to the Sentencing Guidelines and Policy Statements of the *Sentencing Reform Act* of 1984 which was introduced to eliminate sentencing disparities, Hispanics and African Americans received significantly longer terms of imprisonment.

More recent work on the effects of race/ethnicity on sentencing outcomes in US federal courts by Doerner and Demuth (2010) has provided support for Spohn and Holloran's (2000) finding that unemployed African American or Hispanic males aged 21–29 were more likely to be imprisoned. Similarly, controlling for offence severity and criminal history, they reported that young Hispanic male defendants had the highest odds of incarceration and young male African American defendants received the longest sentences. Doerner and Demuth have suggested that researchers examine the combined effect on sentencing of multiple defendant statuses because joint effects are considerably larger than the effects of any single defendant characteristic.

Focusing on within-race sentencing disparities, Steen *et al.* (2005) found that in Washington State white offenders who most resemble the stereotype of a dangerous offender are sentenced more harshly by the court than other white

Extra-legal factors and sentencing   211

offenders, while for African American defendants, those who least resemble dangerous drug offenders are given more lenient sentences. As Blair _et al._ (2004) remind us, the potential effects of race may be subtle and invidious. Eberhardt _et al._ (2006) controlled for a number of sentencing-relevant factors and found that in cases involving a white victim, the more stereotypically African American a defendant is perceived to be, the more likely that person is to be sentenced to death. The whole notion of someone 'looking deathworthy' is a very worrying one indeed. The Blair _et al._ analysis of a random sample of 100 African American and 116 white prison inmates in Florida found that African Americans who were rated as having the most African features had received significantly longer sentences, controlling for offence seriousness and prior criminal record. Such unacceptable human error would not, of course, be corrected by sentencing guidelines. As Vidmar (2011) points out, the subtle effects of race may well operate in and be attributable to how such offenders are described in pre-sentence reports, the decision to grant them bail and with what conditions and, finally, to whether they are legally represented and the quality of that representation.

The reader may be surprised to read that minority members in Sweden (Lindholm and Cederwall 2010) and Denmark (Holmberg 2003) have also been shown to be given severer sentences for some offences than majority group members, controlling for many sentencing-relevant variables (Lindholm and Cedewall 2010). The empirical studies mentioned in this chapter show that minority defendants in the United States, and to a lesser extent in the United Kingdom and Sweden, are the object of discriminatory practices by the judiciary.

Ashworth (2000) advocates the following four measures in order to reduce racial discrimination in sentencing:[53] (a) increase the proportion of people from ethnic minorities who work in the police, the courts and the probation service; (b) increase relevant training to criminal justice personnel; (c) increase racial awareness training for the judiciary; and (d) monitor sentencing decisions more closely.[54]

Defendant's attractiveness

Defendants are often advised by the lawyers to look 'presentable' when appearing in court. People are generally given the same advice when going for a job interview. The assumption is that magistrates', judges' and jurors' decision-making, like that of members of the public, is influenced by a person's appearance. From a legal point of view, of course, such considerations are irrelevant to decisions about guilt and sentence. It is well established in social psychology that physical attractiveness: (a) is the characteristic that most determines whether a person will be liked by another; (b) is equally important to men and women; and (c) is assumed by most people to be highly correlated with such other desirable traits as sociability, extroversion, popularity, sexuality, happiness and assertiveness.[55]

212   *A. Kapardis*

In other words, there is a stereotype that 'what is attractive is good'. However, that stereotype does not include the same traits across cultures (Wheeler and Kim, 1997). The term 'attractive' can refer to physical appearance, likeability, the appeal of one's personality, or all of those. Social psychologists have also established that physical appearance is an important factor in impression formation. According to Bull (1974), people behave differently in the presence of a well-dressed, as opposed to a poorly dressed, individual. A respectable appearance can act as a buffer against imputations of deviance (Steffensmeier and Terry, 1973). But does a defendant's appearance impact significantly on the sentence he or she receives? Mazzella and Feingold (1994) suggested that attractive defendants may be held to higher standards for judgement and behaviour and thus may be treated more harshly when they do not live up to those standards. The experimental study by Abwender and Hough (2001) found that female subjects sentenced the unattractive female defendant to more years in prison than the attractive female defendant, while the male subjects showed the opposite tendency (see also 'Gender of sentencer' below).

A number of studies of real sentencers[56] also suggest that highly physically attractive/socially respectable defendants promote sympathy and attract more lenient sentences. The available evidence indicates that an attractive physical appearance is an asset for an offender at the sentencing stage. Future research with real sentencers should explore further the female same-sex punitiveness finding in relation to a defendant's attractiveness.

The sentencer

Internationally, a number of concerns have been expressed about judicial officers. A concern with the judiciary in the United States who, apparently, are held in low esteem and are paid low salaries,[57] is that some of them behave badly. According to an article in *The Economist*[58] a judge in New York was censored for jumping down from the Bench during a trial, taking off his robes and challenging a defendant to a fist-fight.[59] In Colorado, a male judge resigned after admitting having sex with a female prosecutor in his chambers, and in Oklahoma a judge with more than 20 years on the Bench was sent to prison for 4 years for indecent exposure and for masturbating during trials. The same article discusses more serious cases of judicial misbehaviour (involving corruption), and argues that low pay and partisan elections of judges in the United States are not conducive for judicial integrity.[60]

Another serious concern of the judiciary stems from the debates surrounding judicial diversity. The need for a more representative judiciary and the benefits this guarantees in terms of legitimacy and accountability have been the subject of academic debates for decades.[61] In the UK, the most senior female Supreme Court justice, Baroness Hale, argues that 'difference makes a difference',[62] agreeing with the statement by Benjamin Cardozo, former US Supreme Court Justice, that 'out of the attrition of diverse minds there is a beaten something which has a constancy and uniformity and average value greater than its

Extra-legal factors and sentencing 213

component merits'.[63] These debates have added another layer to the criticism that judges as individuals, and not supra-humans (Rackley, 2002), can be guided – or rather misguided – by theirs own biases and prejudices.

The fact that sentencing is influenced by judges' own prejudices is another serious concern in a number of jurisdictions.[64] In fact, Dowsett (2010) has argued that we cannot hope to form an accurate picture of how a judge's background may influence his or her approach to a particular case; at best, we can only guess, because prejudice can be conscious or unconscious. The importance of sentencer characteristics in sentencing was emphasised long ago by Everson (1919, p. 98), who concluded in his study of 28 Magistrates' Courts in New York that 'justice is a very personal thing, reflecting the temperament, the personality, the education, environment and personal traits of the magistrate'. A relationship between sentencer and sentence severity was also claimed by Palys and Divorski (1986). A few researchers, however, have reported negative findings (Konečni and Ebbesen 1979; Rhodes 1977). The role of the sentencer as a determinant of sentence has also received a great deal of attention by Australian researchers, who have reported a positive relationship between the two.[65]

Sentencer characteristics and sentence severity

In recent years we have witnessed an increase in the number of women in the legal profession and on the Bench in western countries. Feminist legal scholars have argued that the law's gendered (male-dominated nature) is undesirable and must be changed, and that men and women tend to approach and resolve moral problems in different ways because of their socialisation. Consequently, such authors have argued strongly that appointing women to the Bench will help to overcome the law's gender bias and change the content of substantive law and the nature of legal processes. According to Heidensohn (1992), women judges appear to face the dilemma of 'defeminisation or deprofessionalisation' and, consequently, try to neutralise themselves and their personal style. As far as the demographic composition of the judiciary is concerned, an argument has been put forward by Malleson (2006) in favour of an affirmative action policy in England and Wales in order to remedy the lack of diversity. She also argues that such policies are not incompatible with appointment to the Bench on merit.[66] What, then, is the evidence for a relationship between a sentencer's *gender* and his/her decision-making about sentence?

The early experimental simulation study by Kapardis (1985) used nine real cases with 168 lay magistrates/Justices of the Peace (JPs) deciding in 'benches' of three (as they most often do in real life) and found that women justices were significantly more likely to imprison the male defendant in an indecent assault on a female victim than their male colleagues, who were more likely to impose a severe fine. Female JPs were also significantly more likely in an assault case to rate the defendant's criminal record as serious than their male colleagues, and to impose a custodial sentence. In the same study, the female defendant in a theft case was significantly more likely to be given a less severe sentence by female

214   *A. Kapardis*

than male JPs: the former placed more emphasis on the social enquiry report and perceived the female defendant as in need of 'support'.

Bogoch (1999) examined all cases that were decided in the district and magistrates' courts in Israel in 1988 and 1993, with a sample consisting of 868 defendants involved in 747 cases in five different areas, and found that: (a) female judges were significantly more lenient than male judges; (b) panels that included women were more likely to impose harsher sentences than men-only panels; (c) when a man was judging, whether alone or in a panel, the sentence imposed on those convicted of sexual offences was significantly higher than that imposed on those convicted of bodily harm offences; but (d) when a woman was judging, especially in a panel, the sentence for sexual offences was lower than that handed down in bodily harm offences.

Bogoch concluded that if women have a different voice, it is muted in the role of judge. While the leniency of women judging alone may be explained by a gender-related rehabilitative rather than a punitive approach, it may also derive from her still relatively marginalized position in the profession.

As mentioned above, Kapardis' (1985) experimental simulation study with lay magistrates in England found that female magistrates sentenced a female defendant more leniently. But what have researchers reported on this who have used different methodologies and have focused on judges? Do female judges sentence female defendants more leniently? A survey of 10,500 felony cases in California reported that male judges imposed less harsh sentences on female offenders than on their male counterparts.[67] However, it was female rather than male judges who sentenced female offenders more leniently in Mulhausen's 2004 study in Pennsylvania. Clearly, the literature on gender biases in judges' sentencing provides an inconsistent picture.[68]

Concerning judicial officers' *age*, older JPs (50 years of *age* and older) in Kapardis (1985) were significantly more likely than younger JPs to commit to the Crown Court for sentence a male defendant who had committed unlawful sexual intercourse with a 14-year-old female. The same study reported inconsistent findings regarding the relationship between a magistrate's *social class* and their sentencing. Lay magistrates from small *rural* towns in England were found to be more punitive than their *urban* counterparts (Hood 1972), while *legally trained*, as opposed to lay, magistrates in Canada took a more flexible approach to law and focused on the offender in deciding on sentence (Hogarth 1971). The sentencer having been *victim of a crime* was found by Kapardis (1985) to correlate with a tendency to impose a severer sentence by JPs in England, contrary to what Tyler (1990) had reported. However, as the studies of sentence characteristics cited are relatively old, there is a need for more research in this area before conclusions can be drawn about the importance of sentence characteristics in sentencing disparities.

Extra-legal factors and sentencing 215

The demographic composition of the Bench

Using data from 56 'benches' of three JPs, Kapardis (1985) reported that a Bench consisting of three '*more experienced*' (with over four years' experience) was significantly more likely to impose a severer sentence in common assault cases.[69] Regarding magistrates' *educational standard*, Kapardis (1985) reported a tendency of a 'less educated' Bench (all with less than tertiary education) to decide on a harsher sentence in an indecent assault case.

Finally, no consistent associations between English magistrates' social background characteristics (that is, *gender, social class and political party affiliation*) and their sentencing behaviour were reported by Henham (1988) on the basis of his experimental simulation study. One limitation of Henham's otherwise interesting study is that he only investigated associations between two variables at a time; he ignored the importance of intervening variables and failed to take into consideration magistrates' age and education.

Regarding the importance of a judge's *race*,[70] an early study in a large northeastern community by Welch *et al.* (1988) of whether being a Black judge impacts on sentence severity reported that the impact of Black judges is mixed but in the crucial decision to imprison having more black judges increases equality of treatment. Mulhausen (2004) found that African American judges imposed harsher sentences on African American defendants than did white judges. Steffensmeier and Brit (2001) analysed data on sentencing outcomes in Pennsylvania in the early 1990s and found that African American and white judges weighted case and offender information in similar ways in deciding what sanction to impose. However, African American judges were more likely to send African American defendants to prison. Steffensmeier and Brit said their finding may be attributable to African American judges' greater sensitivity to the cost of crime, especially in African American communities. They concluded that it is the job, and not so much the individual, that apparently makes the judge. In an interesting study in Israel, Gazal-Eyal and Sulitzeanu-Kenan (2010) examined the decisions of Jewish and Arab judges in first bail hearings of Arab and Jewish suspects. They found evidence of same-ethnic group bias in detention decisions, but not in the length of detention. Regarding the effect of judicial diversity on sentencing, a study by Cameron and Cummings (2003) of all affirmative action cases from 1971 to 1999 in the US Court of Appeal reported that adding a single non-white judge to a three-judge panel changed the behaviour of the other judges on the panels significantly, and indicated that racial diversity improved the judicial panel's adjudication.

Inconsistent findings have been reported by American researchers concerning not only sentencers' gender but also their religion,[71] politics,[72] penal aims,[73] and sentencing decisions. In considering the relationship between judges' political affiliation and their decision-making, it should be noted that by appointing two young, bright and conservative judges to the Supreme Court, President Bush succeeded in shifting the court significantly to the right; this impacted on domestic policy for years because of the Supreme Court's response to reform of

216   *A. Kapardis*

immigration and social security.[74] Studies of the US Supreme Court have reported that judges appointed during the Carter Administration were likely to grant standing to sue to such 'underdog' plaintiffs as employees, plaintiff unions, minorities, aliens and criminals, whereas judges appointed during the Nixon Administration seemed to favour 'upperdog' plaintiffs such as corporations and governmental litigants (Rowland and Todd 1991). Evidence that judges appointed by a Democrat President were more likely to decide in favour of plaintiffs has also been reported by Kulik *et al.* (2003).

Finally, examination of Britain's *Industrial Relations Act 1971* and the correspondence between the President of the National Industrial Relations Court and members of the Conservative Cabinet led Spencer and Spencer (2006) to conclude that constitutional law scholars have ignored the extent to which judges may secretly influence politicians because they have concentrated on researching how the executive influences the judiciary.

Whether and when judges have a break from mentally demanding decision-making

An interesting but disturbing study of extraneous factors has been reported by Danziger *et al.* (2011) in Israel. They analysed court rulings by eight experienced judges in 1112 parole applications for release from prison or to have incarceration conditions changed. Controlling for offence seriousness, months spent in prison, recidivism and whether a rehabilitation programme would be available to the prisoner if released, it was found that: (a) favourable rulings declined significantly as time passed within each of the three decision sessions; (b) clemency shot up after each of two daily breaks during which judges retired for food; and (c) favourable decisions (for the prisoner) took less time to decide and more words to write. Also, it was the number of cases a judge had heard since his/her last break, not the number of cases he/she had been sitting for that correlated significantly with the type of decision made. It was concluded that judicial decision-making is mentally demanding and, when tired, the easy option is to opt for the status quo and deny the application. Danziger *et al.* concluded that their findings cast doubt on the view held by proponents of legal formalism that court rulings are based solely on laws and facts, and provide support for legal realists, who claim that judicial rulings can be swayed by extraneous variables that should have no bearing on them.

Concluding the discussion of sentencing as a human process, we can see that the available empirical evidence shows that magistrates and judges themselves play an important role as a determinant of sentence and that a number of defendant characteristics, such as gender, race/ethnicity and attractiveness, impact on sentence severity. The empirical evidence discussed here does not justify the conclusion that judicial decision-making can be explained largely by frivolous factors.[75] What the weight of the empirical evidence discussed shows is that judges apply the law to the facts in a logical mechanical way (as the formalists maintain), but they also follow an intuitive process to arrive at a decision which they later rationalise with deliberative reasoning, as the realists argue. Thus, as Guthrie *et al.* (2001) found, neither model is satisfactory because judges rely on intuition but sometimes override that intuition with deductive reasoning; in other words, they use two cognitive systems for making judgements. Some policy implications that seem to follow from the findings reported about the sentencer as a source of disparities are: (a) educate sentencers about this knowledge; and (b) actively involve them in realistic sentencing exercises aimed at achieving uniformity of approach.

Dowsett (2010), himself a judge, emphasises a number of defences against judicial prejudice, namely: the selection process; knowing how an appointee has performed in similar circumstances (in the practising profession); having an adequately resourced judiciary; providing adequate reasons for decisions made; safeguarding judicial independence within the court structure; maintaining the right court ethos; and ensuring that judges have sufficient insight into themselves and a degree of scepticism about their own motivation and capacity for self-delusion – that is, avoiding inflated egos. Regarding models of judicial decision-making, a variety of models has been proposed for judicial information-processing and decision-making by both psychologists and non-psychologists, but there is not one that is widely accepted. Discussion of such models is beyond the scope of the present chapter.[76]

Conclusions

Since the 1960s sentencing has attracted the interest of a plethora of researchers on both sides of the Atlantic and in the Antipodes. Furthermore, the concept of 'sentence' itself has come under close scrutiny and there have been strong arguments in favour of recasting it. Disparity in sentencing is an issue of public concern and has attracted considerable research. The available empirical evidence shows that a criminal defendant's race, gender and, to a lesser extent, attractiveness (in terms of appearance), and the sentencer him/herself, impact on sentence severity. Both legal and extra-legal factors influence the sentencing decision and contribute to disparities. Educating sentencers about sources of disparity – by focusing, perhaps, on how they perceive defendants and their circumstances, how they integrate a range of sources of information, how they attribute motives and traits to defendants in order to select a particular sentence – and training them in how to achieve uniformity of approach by using realistic sentencing exercises, appear promising avenues in the search for a reduction in disparity. There is already ample empirical evidence that Justice herself is not as effectively blindfolded as some conservative lawyers and judges would have us believe. Finally, research is needed on the concept of 'disparity' (i.e. unjustifiable inconsistency) in the light of Padfield's (2016) strong argument that we should distinguish 'front door' and 'back door' sentencing and a sentence should be seen as a process. The changed concept of 'sentence' means that the concept of 'disparity' needs to be revamped, rendering future research into 'sentencing disparities' very challenging indeed.

218   *A. Kapardis*

Notes

1 This chapter is an abbreviated, adapted and updated version of pages 177–203 from my book *Psychology and Law: A Critical Introduction* (4th edition), Cambridge: Cambridge University Press.

2 As has been the case for years in the state of Minnesota with the use of a sentencing grid (see Minnesota Sentencing Guidelines Commission 2010). For England and Wales see Ashworth and Roberts 2012, Roberts 2011 and Wasik 2008.

3 Kapardis 1985; Corbett 1987.

4 Kozinski mentions the removal of three justices of the California Supreme Court by the voters.

5 *Legal Aid, Sentencing and Punishment of Offenders Act 2012* (UK), Part 3, chapter 1, s.64(2), (3).

6 Guthrie *et al.* 2001.

7 In *States* v. *Booker and Fanfan* 543 US 220 (2005).

8 See especially *Gall* v. *United States* 128 S. Ct. 586 (2007).

9 These are identified in s.142(1) of the *Criminal Justice Act* 2003 as being: punishment, the reduction of crime, rehabilitation, protection of the public, and reparation. For a different taxonomy of sentencing objectives see s.718 of the Criminal Code of Canada and the federal sentencing guidelines in the United States.

10 *R* v. *Berry* 7 Cr.A.R.(S) 392, CA.

11 See Adam and Crocket JJ in *Willicroft* [1975] VR 292 at 300, subsequently quoted with approval in *R* (1993) 71 A CrimR 95 at 112 by Sully J for the notion of a sentencing decision as 'instinctive synthesis'.

12 For example, by more than one-third of the District and Supreme Court judges interviewed in Mackenzie's 2005 study in Queensland, Australia.

13 For example, in *Jurisic* (1998) 45 NSWLR 209 at 215 per Spigelman CJ; *Hayes* (1987) ACrimR 452 at 468 per Kirby J; and *Gooch* (1989) 43 ACrimR 382 (WA CCA) per Brinsden J.

14 See Sherwin 2010 on features of judicial reasoning.

15 Discussion of studies of the US Supreme Court is beyond the scope of this chapter. See Lovegrove 1997 for a discussion of theoretical and methodological issues in the psychological study of judicial sentencing. See Kapardis 1985 for a detailed discussion of the various methods used to study variations in sentencing, and early studies that have utilised each of the methods.

16 See Thomas 2005 for detailed discussion of judicial diversity in the United Kingdom and other jurisdictions.

17 501 US 808 (1991).

18 Freiberg 1999 explores the question of whether the sentencing policies of one country or jurisdiction can be said to be more or less severe than that of another and argues that one needs to distinguish sentence severity from the broader concept of 'penal severity'.

19 See Kapardis 1984 for a discussion of the merits and limitations of the different methods.

20 Chiricos and Waldo 1975; Everson 1919; Frankel 1940–41; Patchett and McClean 1965.

21 See Hedderman and Gelsthorpe 1997; Hood 1962; Mannheim *et al.* 1957; Nagel 1961; Wolfgang and Riedel 1975.

22 See also Baab and Furgeson 1967; Fitzmaurice *et al.* 1996; Hogarth 1971; Naylor 1992; Sutton 1978.

23 See also Carlen 1976; Darbyshire 1980; Konečni and Ebbesen 1979; Stewart 1980.

24 See Henham 1990 and Hedderman and Gelsthorpe 1997 on magistrates; McCormick and Greene 1990 in Canada and the Australia Law Reform Commission's national survey of magistrates and judges in the 1970s (see Cashman 1979). However, the judges in Victoria refused to take part in the national survey.

Extra-legal factors and sentencing   219

25 See Kapardis 1984; Guthrie *et al*. 2001.
26 See Biafora and Warheit 2007 for a study that demolishes a popular myth about race/ ethnicity and violence in the United States.
27 See *R* v. *Okuya and Nwaobi* 6 Cr.Ap.R(S) 253, CA, cited in Archbold (2012, p. 608.
28 See Logan 2008, for a historical perspective on feminism and criminal justice in Britain. See Odgers *et al*. 2010, for a study of the poor health of incarcerated female juveniles in the US.
29 Belknap 2001; Daly and Tonry 1997; Steffensmeier and Allan 1996.
30 Gelsthorpe and Loucks 1997; Spohn 1998; Spohn and Spears 1997; Starr 2012.
31 Sentencing Advisory Council 2010.
32 See also Hogarth 1971; Kapardis 1984; Oswald 1992.
33 Allen 1987; Casburn 1979; Hedderman 1994; Hedderman and Gelsthorpe 1997; Hood 1992; Kapardis and Farrington 1981; Mackay 1993; Mawby 1977; Phillpots and Lancucki 1979; Wilczynski and Morris 1993.
34 Atkinson and Neuman 1970; Doerner and Demuth, 2010, 2014; Feely, 1979; Mustard, 2001; Pope 1975; Starr, 2012.
35 Carter and Clelland 1979; Clarke and Koch 1976.
36 Discussion of these theoretical perspectives is beyond the scope of this chapter.
37 Alozie and Johnson, 2000; Daly and Tonry 1997; Moulds 1980; Warner 2002.
38 See Ansel 2013 for key concepts in race and ethnicity.
39 See Phillips and Bowling 2012 for detailed discussion.
40 See Elion and Megargee 1979; Forslund 1970; Goldman 1963; Jefferson and Walker 1992; Landau and Nathan 1983; Piliavin and Briar 1964; Stevens and Willis 1979.
41 See Scarman 1981 and Chapter 11 in this volume.
42 See Macpherson 1999 for the report into the Stephen Lawrence case. Eventually, in August 2012, two men were given life sentences for the Stephen Lawrence murder in 1993.
43 Hagan 1975, 1977; Rector and Bagby 1995.
44 Bond and Jeffries 2011; Eggleston 1976; Snowball and Weatherburn 2007; Walker and McDonald 1995.
45 Mugford and Gronfors 1978.
46 Brown and Hullin 1992; Crow and Cove 1984; Hudson 1989; Jefferson and Walker 1992; Kapardis and Farrington 1981.
47 See also Gelsthorpe and McWilliam 1993; Smith 1997.
48 See Kapardis (1984) for an early literature review of 37 studies.
49 Chiricos and Crawford 1995; Doerner and Demuth 2010; Spohn 2000; Zatz 2000. See, also, DeLone 2000.
50 Nelson 1992, in New York State; Walsh 1991, in Ohio; Sweeney and Haney's 1992 and meta-analytic review of the literature of 19 experimental simulation studies.
51 Engen and Gainey 2000; Miethe and Moore 1986.
52 Its purpose was to reduce sentence disparity between races, ethnic background and gender.
53 Also, see Aboud and Levy 1999 for a detailed discussion of various measures to reduce racial prejudice and discrimination in society.
54 This reform was also suggested in 2001 by the Auld Committee.
55 See Dion *et al*. 1972; Goldman and Lewis 1977; Miller 1970.
56 Douglas *et al*. 1980 in Melbourne, Australia; Finegan 1978 in Ontario, Canada; Stewart 1980 in Philadelphia, US.
57 *Economist*, 30 June 2007.
58 Ibid.
59 Further examples also given by Maroney 2012.
60 Interesting instances of judicial misbehaviour also depicted in Graeme Williams' *A Short Book of Bad Judges* (2013).
61 Rackley 2014.

220   *A. Kapardis*

62 https://kar.kent.ac.uk/23864/1/Hale-Hunter_interview.pdf.
63 www.lawgazette.co.uk/analysis/barriers-make-diversity-of-minds-in-the-legal-profession-impossible/62734.fullarticle.
64 See Dowsett 2010 for a discussion of judicial prejudice, its sources and manifestations, and defences against it.
65 Anderson 1987; Douglas 1989; Grabosky and Rizzo 1983; Lawrence and Homel 1987; Lovegrove 1984; Polk and Tait 1988.
66 See Cooney 1993 and Hale 2001 for arguments about why it is important that women be appointed to the judiciary.
67 Associated Press 1984, cited by Goodman-Delahunty *et al.*, 2005.
68 See also Ho and Venus 1995; Rose 1965; Solimine and Wheatley 1995.
69 See Martinek 2010 for judges as members of small groups.
70 See Davis and Vennard 2006 for a study of racism and stereotyping in 14 Magistrates' Courts in England.
71 See Bowen 1965; Gibson 1978; Hogarth 1971.
72 See Schubert 1959; Walker 1972.
73 See Hogarth 1971; Kapardis 1984, 1985; Spreutels 1980.
74 *Economist*, 7 July 2007, p. 49.
75 See also Kozinski 1993 on this.
76 See Klein and Mitchell 2010, and chapter 6 in Kapardis (2014) for discussion of such models.

References

Aboud, F. E. and Levy, S. R. (1999). Introduction: are we ready to translate research into programmes? *Journal of Social Issues*, 55 (4), 621–625.
Abwender, D. A. and Hough, K. (2001). Interactive effects of characteristics of defendant and mock juror on U.S. participants' judgement and sentencing recommendations. *Journal of Social Psychology*, 141 (5), 603–615.
Allen, H. (1987). The logic of gender in psychiatric reports to the courts. In D. C Pennington and S. Lloyd-Bostock (eds), *The Psychology of Sentencing: Approaches to Consistency* (pp. 104–116). Oxford: Centre for Socio-Legal Studies.
Alozie, N. and C. W. Johnston (2000). Probing the limits of the female advantage in criminal processing: pretrial diversion of drug offenders in an urban country. *Justice System Journal* 21 (3), 239.
Anderson, K. (1987). Sentencing in magistrates' courts. In I. Potas (ed.), *Sentencing in Australia: Issues, Policy and Reform* (pp. 191–206). Canberra: Australian Institute of Criminology.
Ansel, A.E. (2013). *Race and Ethnicity: The Key Concepts*. London, New York: Routledge.
Arce, R., Farina, F., Novo, M. and Seijo, D. (2001). Judges decision making from within. In R. Roesch, R. R. Corrado and R. Dempster (eds), *Psychology in the Courts: International Advances in Knowledge* (pp. 195–205). London and New York: Routledge.
Archbold (2012). *Criminal Pleading, Evidence and Practice*. London: Sweet & Maxwell.
Ashworth, A. (1984). Sentencing in the Crown Court: report of an exploratory study. Occasional Paper no. 10, Centre for Criminological Research, University of Oxford.
Ashworth, A. (2000). *Sentencing and Criminal Justice* (3rd ed.). London: Butterworths.
Ashworth, A. and Roberts, J. (2012). Sentencing: theory, principle, and practice. In M. Maguire, R. Morgan and R. Reiner (eds), *The Oxford Handbook of Criminology* (5th edn, pp. 866–894). Oxford: Oxford University Press.

Extra-legal factors and sentencing 221

Atkinson, D. N. and Neuman, D. A. (1970). Judicial attitudes and defendant attributes: some consequences of municipal court decision-making. *Journal of Public Law*, 19, 69–87.

Auld, Lord Justice (2001). *Review of the Criminal Courts of England and Wales* [The Auld Report]. London: HMSO.

Baab, G. W. and Furgeson, W. R. (1967). Texas sentencing practices: a statistical study. *Texas Law Review*, 472–503.

Belknap, J. (2001). *The Invisible Woman: Gender, Crime and Justice*. Belmont, CA: Thomson Wadsworth.

Biafora, F. and Warheit, G. (2007). Self-reported violent victimization among young adults in Miami, Florida: immigration, race/ethnic and gender contrasts. *International Review of Victimology*, 14, 29–55.

Blair, I. V., Judd, C. M. and Chapleau, K. M. (2004). The influence of Afrocentric facial features in criminal sentencing. *Psychological Science*, 15, 674–679.

Bogoch, B. (1999). Judging in a 'different' voice: gender and the sentencing of violent offences in Israel. *Journal of the Sociology of Law*, 27, 51–78.

Bond, C. E. W. and Jeffries, S. (2011). Indigeneity and the judicial decision to imprison: a study of Western Australia's higher courts. *British Journal of Criminology*, 51, 256–277.

Bowen, R. A. (1965). The explanation of judicial voting behavior from sociological characteristics of judges. Unpublished doctoral dissertation, Yale University. Cited by J. B. Grossman (1966). Social backgrounds and judicial decision-making. *Harvard Law Review*, 79, 1551–1561, at 1561.

Brown, I. and Hullin, R. (1992). A study of sentencing in the Leeds magistrates' courts: the treatment of ethnic minority and white offenders. *British Journal of Criminology*, 32, 41–53.

Bull, R. (1974). The importance of being beautiful. *New Society*, 30, 412–414.

Cameron, C. and Cummings, C. (2003). Diversity and judicial decision-making: evidence from affirmative action cases in the federal courts of appeal 1971–1999. Paper presented at the 2003 meeting of the of the Midwest Political Science Association.

Canadian Sentencing Commission. (1987). *Sentencing Reform: A Canadian Approach*. Canadian Government Publishing Center.

Cardozo, B.N. (1921). *The Nature of the Judicial Process*. New Haven, CT: Yale University Press.

Carlen, P. (1976). The staging of magistrates' justice. *British Journal of Criminology*, 161 (1), 48–55.

Carter, T. and Clelland, D. (1979). A neo-marxian critique, formulation and test of juvenile dispositions as a function of social class. *Social Problems*, 27 (1), 96–108.

Casburn, M. (1979). *Girls will be Girls: Sexism and Juvenile Justice in a London Borough*. London: Women's Research and Resources Centre.

Cashman, P. (1979). *Sentencing Reform: A National Survey of Judges and Magistrates: Preliminary Report*. Sydney: Law Foundation of New South Wales.

Chiricos, T. G. and Crawford, C. (1995). *Race and Imprisonment: A Contextual Assessment of the Evidence*. Albany, NY: State University of New York Press.

Chiricos, T. G. and Waldo, G. P. (1975). Socio-economic status and criminal sentencing: an empirical assessment of a conflict proposition. *American Sociological Review*, 40, 753–772.

Clarke, S. H. and Koch, G. G. (1976). The influence of income and other factors on whether criminal defendants go to prison. *Law and Society Review*, 11, 57–92.

222 *A. Kapardis*

Cooney, S. (1993). Gender and judicial selection: should there be more women on the courts? *Melbourne University Law Review*, 19, 20–44.

Corbett, C. (1987). Magistrates' and court clerks' sentencing behaviour: an experimental study. In D. C. Pennington and S. M. A. Lloyd-Bostock (eds), *The Psychology of Sentencing: Approaches to Consistency* (pp. 204–216). Oxford: Centre for Socio-Legal Studies.

Crow, I. and Cove, J. (1984). Ethnic minorities and the courts. *Criminal Law Review*, 413–417.

Curry, T. R., Lee, G. and Rodriguez, S. F. (2004). Does victim gender increase sentence severity? Further explorations of gender dynamics and sentencing outcomes. *Crime and Delinquency*, 50, 319–343.

Daly, K. (1994). *Gender, Crime, and Punishment*. New Haven, CT: Yale University Press.

Daly, K. and Bordt, R. (1995). Sex effects and sentencing: an analysis of the statistical literature. *Justice Quarterly*, 12 (1), 141ff.

Daly, K. and Tonry, M. (1997). Gender, race, and sentencing. *Crime and Justice*, 22, 201ff.

Danziger, S., Levav, J. and Avnaim-Pesso, L. (2011). Extraneous factors in judicial decisions. *Proceedings of the National Academy of Sciences*, 108 (17), 6889–6892.

Darbyshire, P. (1980). The role of the magistrates' clerk in summary proceedings. *Justice of the Peace*, 144, 186–188, 201–213, 219–221.

Davis, G. and Vennard, J. (2006). Racism in court: the experience of ethnic minority magistrates. *Howard Journal*, 45 (5), 485–501.

DeLone, M. (2000). When does race matter? An analysis of the conditions under which race affects sentence severity. *Sociology of Crime, Law and Deviance*, 2, 3–37.

Dion, K. E., Berscheld, E. and Walster, E. (1972). What is beautiful is good. *Journal of Personality and Social Psychology*, 24, 285–290.

Doerner, J. K. and Demuth, S. (2010). The independent and joint effects of race/ethnicity, gender, and age on sentencing outcomes in U.S. federal courts. *Justice Quarterly*, 27 (1), 1–27.

Doerner, J. K. and Demuth, S. (2014). Gender and sentencing in the federal courts: are women treated more leniently? *Criminal Justice Policy Review*, 25 (2), 242–269.

Douglas, R. (1989). Does the magistrate matter? Sentencers and sentence in the Victorian magistrates' courts. *Australian and New Zealand Journal of Criminology*, 22, 40–59.

Douglas, R., Weber, T. and Braybrook, E. K. (1980). *Guilty, Your Worship: A Study of Victoria's Magistrates' Courts*. Occasional Monograph no. 1, Legal Studies Department, La Trobe University, Melbourne, Australia.

Dowsett, J. A. (2010). Prejudice – the judicial virus. *Australian Journal of Forensic Sciences*, 42 (1), 37–40.

Eberhardt, J. L., Davies, P. G., Purdie-Vaughns, V. J. and Johnson, S. L. (2006). Looking death worthy: perceived stereotypicality of black defendants predicts capital sentencing outcomes. *Psychological Science*, 17, 383–386.

Eggleston, E. (1976). *Fear, Favour or Affection: Aborigines and the Criminal Law in Victoria, South Australia and Western Australia*. Canberra: Australian National University.

Elion, V. H. and Megargee, E. I. (1979). Racial identity, length of incarceration, and parole decision-making. *Journal of Research in Crime and Delinquency*, 16, 232–245.

Engen, R. J. and Gainey, R. R. (2000). Modelling the effects of legally relevant and extralegal factors under sentencing guidelines: the rules have changed. *Criminology*, 38 (4), 1207–1230.

Extra-legal factors and sentencing 223

Everson, G. (1919). The human element in justice. *Journal of Criminal Law and Criminology*, 10, 90–99.

Farrington, D. P. (1978). The effectiveness of sentences. *Justice of the Peace*, 4 February, 68–71.

Farrington, D. P. and Morris, A. (1983). Sex, sentencing and reconviction. *British Journal of Criminology*, 23, 229–248.

Feely, M. M. (1979). *The Process is the Punishment: Handling Cases in a Lower Criminal Court*. London: Russell Sage Foundation.

Feeley, M. and Rubin, L. R. (1998). *Judicial Policy Making and the Modern State: How the Court Reformed America's Prisons*. Oxford: Oxford University Press.

Finegan, J. (1978). The effects of non-legal factors on the severity of sentence in traffic court. Unpublished MA thesis, University of Toronto.

Fitzgerald, M. (1994). Ethnic minorities and the criminal justice system. *Research Bulletin*, no. 35, 49–50.

Fitzmaurice, C., Rogers, D. and Stanley, P. (1996). Predicting court sentences: a perilous exercise. In G. Davies, S. Lloyd-Bostock, M. McMurran and C. Wilson (eds), *Psychology, Law and Criminal Justice: International Developments in Research and Practice* (pp. 305–313). New York: de Gruyter.

Fontaine, G. and Emily, C. (1978). Causal attribution and judicial discretion: a look at the verbal behavior of municipal court judges. *Law and Human Behavior*, 2, 323–337.

Forslund, M.A. (1970). A comparison of negro and white crime rates. *Journal of Criminal Law, Criminology and Police Science*, 61, 214–217.

Frank, J.N. (1950). *Courts on Trial: Myths and Reality in American Justice* (2nd edn). Princeton, NJ: Princeton University Press.

Frankel, E. (1940–41). The offender and the court: a statistical analysis of the sentencing of delinquents. *J. Criminal Law, Criminology and Police Science*, 31, 448–456.

Freiberg, A. (1999). What's it worth? A cross-jurisdictional comparison of sentence severity. Paper presented at the Sentencing and Society Conference, University of Strathclyde, Glasgow, Scotland, 24–26 June.

Galton, Sir F. (1885). Terms of imprisonment. *Nature*, 20 June, 174–176.

Gazal-Eyal, O. and Sulitzeanu-Kenan, R. (2010). Let my people go: ethnic in-group bias in judicial decisions: evidence from a randomized natural experiment. *Journal of Empirical Legal Studies*, 7, 403–428.

Gelsthorpe, L. (2004). Back to basics in crime control: weaving in women. *Critical Review of International Social and Political Philosophy*, 7 (2), 76–103.

Gelsthorpe, L. and Loucks, N. (1997). Magistrates' explanations of sentencing decisions. In C. Hedderman and L. Gelsthorpe (eds), *Understanding the Sentencing of Women*. Home Office Research Study 170. London: Home Office.

Gelsthorpe, L. and McWilliam, W. (eds). (1993). *Minority Ethnic Groups and the Criminal Justice System*. Cambridge: Institute of Criminology, University of Cambridge.

Gibson, J.L. (1978). Race as a determinant of criminal sentences: a methodological critique and a case study. *Law and Society Review*, 12 (3), 455–478.

Goldman, N. (1963). The differential selection of juvenile offenders for court appearances. National Council on Crime and Delinquency – cited by C. E. Frazier (1979). Appearance, demeanor, and backstage negotiations: basis of discretion in a first appearance court. *International J. Sociology*, 7, 197–209.

Goldman, S. (1975). Voting behaviour on the U.S Courts of Appeal revisited. *American Political Science Review*, 69 (2), 491–506.

224   A. Kapardis

Goldman, W. and Lewis, P. (1977). Beautiful is good: evidence that the physically attractive are more socially skilful. *Journal of Experimental Social Psychology*, 13, 125–130.

Goodman-Delahunty, J., ForsterLee, L. and ForsterLee, R. (2005). Dealing with the guilty offender. In B. Brewer and K. D. Williams (eds), *Psychology and Law: An Empirical Perspective* (pp. 445–482). New York and London: Guildford Press.

Grabosky, P. and Rizzo, C. (1983). Dispositional disparities in courts of summary jurisdiction: the conviction and sentencing of shoplifters in South Australia, 1980. *Australian and New Zealand Journal of Criminology*, 16, 146–162.

Guthrie, C., Rachlinski, J. J. and Wistrich, A. J. (2001). Inside the judicial mind. *Dispute Resolution Alert*, 1 (7), 1–4.

Hagan, J. (1975). Law, order and sentencing: a study of attitude in action. *Sociometry*, 38, 374–384.

Hagan, J. (1977). Finding discrimination: a question of meaning. *Ethnicity*, 4, 167–176.

Hale, B. (2001). Equality and the judiciary: why should we want more women judges? *Public Law*, 489–504.

Halevy, T. (1995). Racial discrimination in sentencing? A study with dubious conclusions. *Criminal Law Review*, 267–271.

Hampton, R. E. (1979). Sexual sentencing in children's court. *Australian and New Zealand Journal of Criminology*, 12, 24–32.

Hedderman, C. (1994). Decision-making in court: observing the sentencing of men and women. *Psychology, Crime and Law*, 1, 165–173.

Hedderman, C. and Gelsthorpe, L. (1997). *Understanding the Sentencing of Women*. London: Home Office Research and Statistics Directorate.

Heidensohn, F. M. (1992). *Women in Control? The Role of Women in Law Enforcement*. Oxford: Oxford University Press.

Henham, R. (1988). The importance of background variables in sentencing behavior. *Criminal Justice and Behavior*, 15 (2), 255–263.

Henham, R. (1990). *Sentencing Principles and Magistrates' Sentencing Behaviour*. Aldershot: Avebury.

Ho, R. and Venus, M. (1995). Reactions to a battered woman who kills her abusive spouse: an attributional analysis. *Australian Journal of Psychology*, 47, 153–159.

Hogarth, J. (1971). *Sentencing as a Human Process*. Toronto: University of Toronto Press.

Holmberg, L. (2003). *Policing Stereotypes: A Qualitative Study of Police Work in Denmark*. Berlin: Galda & Wilch Verlag.

Holmes, O.W. (1881). *The Common Law*. Boston: Little, Brown.

Hood, R. (1962). *Sentencing in Magistrates' Court*. London: Stevens.

Hood, R. (1972). *Sentencing the Motoring Offender: A Study of Magistrates' Views and Practices*. London: Heinemann.

Hood, R. (1992). *Race and Sentencing: A Study in the Crown Court. A Report for the Commission for Racial Equality*. Oxford: Oxford University Press.

Hudson, B. (1989). Discrimination and disparity: the influence of race on sentencing. *New Community*, 16, 23–34.

Jefferson, T. and Walker, M. A. (1992). Ethnic minorities in the criminal justice system. *Criminal Law Review*, 83–95.

Jeffries, S. and Bond, C.E.W. (2010). Narratives of mitigation: sentencing indigenous criminal defendants in South Australia's higher courts. *Journal of Sociology*, 46 (3), 219–237.

Extra-legal factors and sentencing 225

Kapardis, A. (1984). *A Psychological Study of Magistrates' Decision Making*. Doctoral dissertation, Institute of Criminology, Cambridge University.

Kapardis, A. (1985). *Sentencing by English Magistrates as a Human Process*. Nicosia, Cyprus: Asselia Press.

Kapardis, A. (2014). *Psychology and Law* (4th ed.). Cambridge University Press.

Kapardis, A. and Farrington, D. P. (1981). An experimental study of sentencing by magistrates. *Law and Human Behavior*, 5, 107–121.

Klein, D. E. and Mitchell, G. (2010). *The Psychology of Judicial Decision-Making*. New York: Oxford University Press.

Knight, J. (2009). Are empiricists asking the right questions about judicial decision making? *Duke Law Journal*, 1531–1556.

Konečni, V. J. and Ebbesen, E. B. (1979). External validity of research in legal psychology. *Law and Human Behavior*, 3, 39–70.

Kozinski, A. (1993). What I ate for breakfast and other mysteries of judicial decision making. *Loyola of Los Angeles Law Review*, 26 (4/5), 993.

Kruttschnitt, C. (1984). Sex and criminal courts dispositions: the unresolved controversy. *Journal of Research in Crime and Delinquency*, 21 (3), 213ff.

Kulik, C., Perry, E. and Pepper, M. (2003). Here comes the judge: the influence of judge personal characteristics on federal sexual harassment case outcomes. *Law and Human Behaviour*, 27 (1), 69–86.

Landau, D. and Nathan, G. (1983). Selecting delinquents for cautioning. *British Journal of Criminology*, 23, 28ff.

Lawrence, J. and Homel, R. (1987). Sentencing in magistrates' courts: the magistrate as professional decision maker. In I. Potas (ed.), *Sentencing in Australia: Issues, Policy and Reform* (pp. 151–190). Canberra: Australian Institute of Criminology.

Lichtblaum, E. (2005). Profiling report leads to a demolition. *New York Times*, 24 August. Retrieved 28 March 2009 from: www.nytimes.com, cited by T. Lindholm and J. Y. Cederall (2010).

Lindholm, T. and Cederwall, J. Y. (2010). Ethnicity and gender bias in the courtroom. In P. A. Granhag (ed.), *Forensic Psychology in Context: Nordic and International Approaches.* (pp. 229–246). Cullompton: Willan.

Lindholm, T. and Christianson, S.A. (1998). Gender effects in eyewitness accounts of a violent crime. *Psychology, Crime and Law*, 4, 323–329.

Llewlyn, K. N. and Hoebel, E. A. (1941). *The Cheyenne Way: Conflict and Case Law in Primitive Jurisprudence*. Norman, OK: Oklahoma University Press.

Logan, A. (2008). *Feminism and Criminal Justice: A Historical Perspective*. London: Palgrave Macmillan.

Lovegrove, A. (1984). An empirical study of sentencing disparity among judges in an Australian criminal court. *International Review of Applied Psychology*, 33, 161–176.

Lovegrove, A. (1997). *The Framework of Judicial Sentencing*. Cambridge: Cambridge University Press.

Mackay, R.D. (1993). The consequences of killing very young children. *Criminal Law Review*, 21–30.

Mackenzie, G. (2005). *How Judges Sentence*. Sydney: Federation Press.

Macpherson of Cluny, Sir W. (1999). *The Stephen Lawrence Inquiry*. Cmnd: 4262–1. London: HMSO.

Mair, G. (1986). Ethnic minorities, probation and the courts. *British Journal of Criminology*, 26, 147–155.

226 *A. Kapardis*

Malleson, K. (2006). Rethinking the merit principle in judicial selection. *Journal of Law and Society*, 33 (1), 126–140.

Mannheim, H., Spencer, J. and Lynch, G. (1957). Magisterial policy in the London courts. *British Journal of Delinquency*, 8, 13–33, 119–139.

Maroney, T. (2012). Angry judges. *Vanderbilt Law Review*, 65, 1207–1286.

Martinek, W.L. (2010). Judges as members of small groups. In D. E. Klein and G. Mitchell (eds), *The Psychology of Judicial Decision-Making*. New York: Oxford University Press.

Mawby, R.I. (1977). Sexual discrimination and the law. *Probation Journal*, 24, 38–43.

Mazzella, R. and Feingold, A. (1994). The effects of physical attractiveness, race, socio-economic status, and gender of defendants and victims on judgments of mock jurors: a meta-analysis. *Applied Social Psychology*, 24, 1315–1344.

McCormick, P. and Greene, I. (1990). *Judges and Judging*. Toronto: Lorimer and Company.

Miethe, T. and Moore, G. (1986). Racial differences in criminal processing: the consequences of model selection on conclusions about differential treatment. *Sociological Quarterly*, 27, 217–237.

Miller, A.G. (1970). Role of physical attractiveness in impression formation. *Psychonomic Science*, 19, 241–243.

Minnesota Sentencing Guidelines Commission (2010). Sentencing Guidelines and Commentary. Available at: www.msgc.state.mn.us/.

Moulds, E. (1980). Chivalry and paternalism: disparities of treatment in the criminal justice system. In S. Datesman and F. Scarpitti (eds), *Women, Crime and Justice*. New York: Oxford Press.

Mugford, S. and Gronfors, M. (1978). Racial and class factors in the sentences of first offenders. *Australian and New Zealand Journal of Sociology*, 14, 58–61.

Mulhausen, D. B. (2004). *The Determination of Sentencing in Pennsylvania: Do the Characteristics of Judges Matter?* Washington. D.C: The Heritage Foundation.

Mustard, D. B. (2001). Racial, ethnic, and gender disparities in sentencing: evidence from the U.S. federal courts. *Journal of Law and Economics*, XLIV, 285ff.

Nagel, I. H. and Johnson, B. J. (1994). The role of gender in a structured sentencing system: equal treatment, policy choices, and the sentencing of female offenders under the United States sentencing guidelines. *Journal of Criminal Law and Criminology*, 85 (1), 181–221.

Nagel, S. S. (1961). Political party affiliation and judges' decisions. *American Political Science Review*, 55, 844–850.

Naylor, B. (1992). *Gender and Sentencing in the Victorian Magistrates' Court: A Pilot Project*. Report to the Criminology Council. Melbourne: Law Faculty, Monash University, Clayton, Victoria, Australia. Available at www.criminologyresearchcouncil.gov. au/reports/42-90.pdf.

Nelson, J. F. (1992). Hidden disparities in case processing: New York State, 1986–1986. *Journal of Criminal Justice*, 20, 181–200.

Nobiling, T., Spohn, C. and DeLone, M. (1998). A tale of two counties: unemployment and sentence severity. *Justice Quarterly*, 15 (3), 459–485.

Odgers, C., Robins, S. and Russell, M. (2010). Morbidity and mortality risk among the 'forgotten few': why are girls in the justice system in such poor health. *Law and Human Behavior*, 34 (6), 429–444.

Oswald, M. E. (1992). Justification and goals of punishment and the attribution of responsibility in judges. In F. Lösel, D. Bender and T. Bliesener (eds), *Psychology and Law: International Perspectives* (pp. 424–434). New York: Walter de Gruyter.

Padfield, N. (2012). Sentencing in England and Wales: too much law and not enough psychological research? Paper presented at the European Association of Psychology and Law conference in Nicosia, Cyprus, 10–13 April.

Padfield, N. (2016). Reflection on sentencing in England and Wales. In A. Kapardis and D. P. Farrington (eds), *Psychology, Crime, Policing and the Courts*. London: Routledge.

Padfield, N., Morgan, R. and Maguire, M. (2012). Out of court, out of sight? Criminal sanctions and non-judicial decision-making. In M. Maguire, M. Morgan and R. Reiner (eds), *The Oxford Handbook of Criminology* (5th edn, pp. 955–985). Oxford: Oxford University Press.

Palys, T. S. and Divorski, S. (1986). Explaining sentencing disparity. *Canadian Journal of Criminology*, 28, 347–362.

Patchett, K. W. and McClean, K. D. (1965). Decision-making in juvenile cases. *Criminal Law Review*, December, 699–710.

Phillips, C. and Bowling, B. (2012). Ethnicities, racism, crime, and criminal justice. In M. Maguire, M. Morgan and R. Reiner (eds), *The Oxford Handbook of Criminology* (5th edn, pp. 370–397). Oxford: Oxford University Press.

Phillpots, G. J. and Lancucki, L. B. (1979). *Previous Convictions, Sentence and Reconviction: A Statistical Study of a Sample of 5000 Offenders Convicted in January 1971*. London: Home Office, Research Study no. 53.

Piliavin, I. and Briar, S. (1964). Police encounters with juveniles. *American Journal of Sociology*, 70, 206–214.

Polk, K. and Tait, D. (1988). The use of imprisonment by the magistrates' courts. *Australian and New Zealand Journal of Criminology*, 21, 31–44.

Pollak, O. (1950). *The Criminality of Women*. New York: A.S. Barnes.

Pope, C. E. (1975). *Sentencing of California Felony Offenders*. Utilization of Criminal Statistics Project. Analytic report 6, US Department of Justice Law Enforcement Assistance Administration.

Rackley, E. (2002). Representations of the (woman) judge: Hercules, the little mermaid and the vain and naked emperor. *Legal Studies*, 22 (4), 602–624.

Rackley, E. (2014). *Women, Judging and Judiciary: From Difference to Diversity*. London: Routledge.

Raine, J.W. and Dunstan, E. (2009). How well do sentencing guidelines work? Equity, proportionality and consistency in the determination of fine levels in the magistrates' courts of England and Wales. 48 *Howard Journal* 13.

Raj, A. and Silverman, J. G. (2007). Domestic violence help-seeking behaviors of South Asian battered women residing in the United States. *International Review of Victimology*, 14, 143–170.

Rector, N. A. and Bagby, R. M. (1995). Criminal sentence recommendations in a simulated rape trial: examining juror prejudice in Canada. *Behavioural Sciences and the Law*, 13, 113–121.

Rhodes, W. M. (1977). A study of sentencing in the Hennepin County and Ramsay County District Courts. *Journal of Legal Studies*, 6, 333–353.

Roberts, J. V. (2011). Sentencing guidelines and judicial discretion: evolution of duty of courts to comply in England and Wales. *British Journal of Criminology*, 51, 997–1013.

Rodriguez, S. F., Curry, T. R. and Lee, G. (2006). Gender differences in criminal sentencing: do effects vary across violent, property, and drug offenses? *Social Sciences Quarterly*, 87 (2), 318–339.

Rose, G. (1965). An experimental study of sentencing. *British Journal of Criminology*, 5, 314–319.

228   *A. Kapardis*

Rowland, C. K. and Todd, B. J. (1991). Where you stand depends on who sits: platform promises and judicial gatekeeping in the federal district courts. *Journal of Politics*, 53, 175–185.

Sallmann, P. and Willis, J. (1984). *Criminal Justice in Australia*. Melbourne: Oxford University Press.

Scarman, Rt Hon., Lord. (1981). *The Scarman Report*. The Brixton Disorders 1–12 April 1981: Report of an Enquiry by Rt Hon. Lord Scarman. Cmnd. 8427. London: HMSO.

Schubert, G. (1959). *Quantitative Analysis of Judicial Behavior*. Glencoe, IL: The Free Press.

Sentencing Advisory Council. (2010). *Gender Differences in Sentencing Outcomes*. Melbourne, Victoria, Australia.

Sherwin, E. (2010). Features of judicial reasoning. In D. E. Klein and G. Mitchell (eds), *The Psychology of Judicial Decision-Making*. New York: Oxford University Press.

Skyrme, T. Sir. (1979). *The Changing Image of the Magistracy*. London: Macmillan.

Smith, D. (1997). Race, crime and criminal justice. In M. Maguire, R. Morgan and R. Reiner (eds), *The Oxford Handbook of Criminology*. Oxford: Clarendon Press.

Snowball, L. and Weatherburn, D. (2007). Does racial bias in sentencing contribute to indigenous overrepresentation in prison? *Australian and New Zealand Journal of Criminology*, 40 (3), 272–290.

Solimine, M. E. and Wheatley, S. E. (1995). Rethinking feminist judging. *Indiana Law Journal*, 70, 891–920.

Spencer, M. and Spencer, J. (2006). The judge as 'political advisor': behind the scenes at the National Industrial Relations Court. *Journal of Law and Society*, 33 (2), 199–220.

Spohn, C. (1998). Gender and sentencing of drug offenders: is chivalry dead? *Criminal Justice Policy Review*, 9 (3), 365ff.

Spohn, C. C. (2000). Thirty years of sentencing reform: the quest for a racially neutral sentencing process. In National Institute of Justice (ed.), *Criminal Justice*, 2000, 3, 427–501. Washington, DC: National Institute of Justice.

Spohn, C. C. and Spears, J. (1997). Gender and case processing decisions: a comparison of case outcomes for male and female defendants charged with violent felonies. *Women and Criminal Justice*, 8 (3), 29ff.

Spohn, C. C. and Holloran, D. (2000). The imprisonment penalty paid by young, unemployed Black and Hispanic male offenders. *Criminology*, 38 (1), 281–306.

Spohn, C. C., Welch, S. and Gruhl, J. (1985). Women defendants in court: the interaction between sex and race in convicting and sentencing. *Social Sciences Quarterly*, 66 (1), 178–185.

Spreutels, J. P. (1980). Giving reasons for sentence at the Crown Court. *Criminal Law Review*, 486–495.

Starr, S. B. (2012). Estimating gender disparities in federal criminal cases. *University of Michigan Law and Economics Research Paper Series* No. 12–018.

Steen, S., Engen, R. L. and Gainey, R. R. (2005). Images of danger and culpability: racial stereotyping, case processing, and criminal sentencing. *Criminology*, 43 (2), 435–468.

Steffensmeier, D. J. and Allan, J. (1996). Gender and crime: toward a gendered theory of female offending. *American Review of Sociology*, 22, 459ff.

Steffensmeier, D. J. and Brit, D. L. (2001). Judges' race and judicial decision making: do Black judges sentence differently? *Social Science Quarterly*, 82 (4), 749–764.

Steffensmeier D. J. and Demuth, S. (2006). Does gender modify the effects of race-ethnicity on criminal sanctioning? Sentences for male and female White, Black, and Hispanic defendants. *Journal of Quantitative Criminology*, 22, 241–261.

Steffensmeier, D. J. and Terry, R. M. (1973). Deviance and responsibility: an observational study of reactions to shoplifting. *Social Forces*, 51, 417–426.

Stevens, P. and Willis, C. F. (1979). *Race, Crime and Arrests*. London: Home Office, Study no. 58.

Stewart, J. E. (1980). Defendant's attractiveness as a factor in the outcome of criminal trials: an observational study. *Journal of Applied Social Psychology*, 10, 348–361.

Sutton, L. P. (1978). *Variations in Federal Criminal Sentences: A Statistical Assessment at the National Level*. US Department of Justice, LEAA, Utilization of Criminal Justice Statistics. Analytic Report 17.

Sweeney, L. T. and Haney, C. (1992). The influence of race on sentencing: a meta-analytic review of experimental studies. *Behavioral Sciences and the Law*, 10, 179–195.

Thomas, C. (2005). *Judicial Diversity in the United Kingdom and Other Jurisdictions: A Review of Research, Policy and Practices*. Her Majesty's Commissioners for Judicial Appointments.

Tillyer, R., Hartley, R. D. and Ward, J. T. (2015). Differential treatment of female defendants: does criminal history moderate the effects of gender on sentence length in federal narcotics cases? *Criminal Justice and Behavior*, published online 9 February.

Tonry, M. (1996). *Sentencing Matters*. New York: Oxford University Press.

Tyler, T. R. (1990). *Why People Obey the Law*. New Haven, CT: Yale University Press.

Ulmer, J., Light, M. T. and Kramer, J. (2011). The 'liberation' of federal judges' discretion in the wake of the Booker/Fanfan decision: is there increased disparity and divergence between courts? *Justice Quarterly*, 28 (4), 799–837.

van Koppen, P.J. (2002). The story of criminal proceedings: from fact-finding to police decision-making. In I. K. McKenzie and R. Bull (eds), *Criminal Justice Research: Inspiration and Ideation* (pp. 191–219). Dartmouth: Ashgate.

Vidmar, N. (2011). The psychology of trial judging. *Current Directions in Psychological Science*, 20, 58–62.

Walker, J. and McDonald, D. (1995). The over representation of indigenous people in custody in Australia. *Trends and Issues in Crime and Criminal Justice*, no. 47. Canberra: Australian Institute of Criminology.

Walker, T. G. (1972). A note concerning partisan influences on trial-judge decision-making. *Law and Society Review*, 6, 645–649.

Walsh, A. (1991). Race and discretionary sentencing: an analysis of 'obvious' and 'non-obvious' cases. *International Journal of Offender Therapy and Comparative Criminology*, 35, 7–19.

Warner, K. (2002). *Sentencing in Tasmania*. Sydney: The Federation Press.

Wasik, M. (2008). Sentencing guidelines in England and Wales – state of the art? *Criminal Law Review*, 251–263.

Welch, S., Combs, M. and Gruhl, J. (1988). Do black judges make a difference? *American Journal of Political Science*, 32 (1), 126–136.

Wheeler, L. and Kim, Y. (1997). What is beautiful is culturally good: the physical attractiveness stereotype has different content in collectivist cultures. *Personality and Social Psychology Bulletin*, 23, 795–800.

Wilczynski, A. and Morris, A. (1993). Parents who kill their children. *Criminal Law Review*, 31–36.

Williams, G., QC. (2013). *A Short Book of Bad Judges*. London: Wildy, Simmonds & Hill Publishing.

Wistrich, A. (2010). Defining good judging. In D. E. Klein and G. Mitchell (eds), *The Psychology of Judicial Decision-Making*. New York: Oxford University Press.

Wolfgang, M. E. and Reidel, M. (1975). Rape, race and the death penalty in Georgia. *American Journal of Orthopsychiatry*, 45, 658–668.

Zatz, M. (2000). The convergence of race, ethnicity, gender, and class on court decision making: looking towards the 21st century. In National Institute of Justice (ed.), *Criminal Justice*, 2000, 3, 503–552. Washington, DC: National Institute of Justice.

13 Reflections on sentencing in England and Wales

Nicola Padfield

Introduction

I sat as a part-time judge (in the Crown Court) for more than ten years (2002–2014), while working full-time as an academic in a Law Faculty and Institute of Criminology. Whilst sitting as a judge, imposing sentences, focused on both what might be called initial or 'front door' sentencing, my own research was on what has been called 'back door' sentencing, decisions to release and to recall offenders. The contrast between the two areas has ever become more readily apparent: the law has sought to constrain the discretion of 'front door' sentencers, whilst flexible powers of early release and recall expand. I, like others, originally looked at the two areas: 'sentencing' and 'parole/early release' as discrete subjects. But why should this be the case? Judges and magistrates, in their practice and their training, rarely look beyond the sentence they are imposing to consider its 'real' meaning. Indeed, it seems to be widely accepted amongst the judiciary that this is as it should be – post-sentence issues are explicitly not for the sentencing judge. This chapter questions this approach, reflecting on what seems to be a significant mismatch between 'judicial sentencing' and the experience of sentencing by offenders. It leads to the conclusion that it is time for a significant paradigm shift: if criminologists, judges, lawyers and policy makers shifted their gaze and saw 'sentencing' not as a one-off event but as an on-going process, the implications could be enormous for theory, law and practice.

Over the last 50 years or so, both lawyers and socio-legal scholars have turned their attention to the important subject of sentencing. In England and Wales, the subject was revolutionised for lawyers and judges by David Thomas QC: his book *Principles of Sentencing in the Court of Appeal*, first published in 1970, has since evolved into a four volume encyclopaedia. (For over 40 years, Thomas commented regularly on the case law flowing from the Court of Appeal, seeking to develop a principled analysis whilst offering trenchant criticisms of the often badly drafted legislation which floods out from Parliament, of poorly reasoned judgments and unnecessary (in his eyes) sentencing guidelines (see the Lord Chief Justice's tribute: Judge, 2009, p. 52)).[1] Other legal scholars have followed his lead, most notably Andrew Ashworth. Over the same period,

232   N. Padfield

sentencing has also been studied by a number of socio-legal scholars and criminologists, who have explored in particular the decision-making process in magistrates' courts, and less frequently the Crown Court. As a generalisation, lawyers (doctrinal analyses) have focused on Crown Court sentencing decisions, socio-legal scholars and criminologists (empirical research) on the magistrates' court, largely because there access has been easier (see Ashworth and Roberts, 2012; Dhami and Souza, 2009). Black-letter lawyers have, of course, focused on analysing the decision itself, not the wider surrounding socio-legal framework. But sentencing has now become a subject studied both in law schools and in criminology departments.

What remains striking about this scholarship is its emphasis on the initial or 'front door' sentencing decision: 'sentencing' is still seen as a one-off event, a public announcement in court. Academic lawyers have shown little interest in the enforcement of sentences, perhaps because as a subject it falls uncomfortably between 'criminal' law and 'administrative' law, areas which have traditionally been taken up by different groups of lawyers. Similarly, there was until recently a relative dearth of socio-legal or criminological research into the enforcement of sentences (despite the interest in the study of decision-making in other areas). This chapter seeks to explore the reasons for this, but also to consider the implications of this narrow focus.

'Back door sentencing' has been used to describe parole and recall decisions. Padfield and Maruna (2006) adopted the term when describing the dramatic increase in the use of recall to prison for breaches of release licences in England and Wales. As recalled offenders have continued to swell the prison population, there has been some increase in academic and policy interest in release and recall decisions, and indeed the term 'back door sentencing' was adopted by the Justice Committee of the House of Commons in their report on *Towards Effective Sentencing* (2008). Clearly anyone interested in understanding the changing shape of prison populations has to look not only at the law and practice of 'front door' sentencing, but also at the decisions taken later on which help influence who leaves prison and when, and indeed who is recalled to prison, when, why and for what reason (Ministry of Justice, 2013c). But what this chapter suggests is that even a focus on the 'front door' and the 'back door' suggests a paramount importance of certain decisions over others. A coherent sentencing structure requires a fuller understanding of key decisions taken over the 'life time' of a sentence.

The law and practice of sentencing has also changed immensely in the last 50 years, with more law and longer hearings (see Hutton, 2002). So we are looking at a fast-shifting world. What constitutes 'sentencing' is changing. Nor is this a purely English problem. The argument presented in this chapter could be equally relevant in many European or 'Western' countries. In France, for example, for many years academic analysis of 'sentencing' often started and stopped with the Penal Code: Delmas-Marty (2003) identified three different 'levels' of sentencing decisions: *la peine encourue* (which is found in the Code), *la peine prononcée* (the sentence announced in court) and finally *la peine appliquée* or *executée*

Sentencing in England and Wales 233

(the sentence actually served). To many of those involved in that project at that time, this felt like an advance: a recognition that academics were digging beneath the Code to find the 'real sentences'. But even in France, the execution of sentences remains a very different subject to the procedural law which covers the imposition of sentences (Herzog-Evans 2009, 2011; Padfield 2011a). The implications of the argument in this chapter are particularly important throughout the EU as attempts are made to facilitate the fair transfer of prisoners to their home jurisdictions.

What is a 'sentence'?

Beyond the scope of this chapter is a wider discussion of the line between penalties which are truly 'criminal' and those which are simply 'regulatory' or 'administrative', but the difficult boundaries must be recognised. This chapter, focusing exclusively on 'sentences' imposed in 'truly' criminal cases, also avoids another important area of debate: the current fashion for new civil 'offences'[2] and civil 'regulation' (see Cartwright, 2007 on consumer protection 'offences'[3]).

Nor can we avoid recognising the huge increase in out-of-court penalties: cautions, conditional cautions, fixed penalty notices, penalty notices for disorder and so on (Padfield *et al.*, 2012). The 'selection' of cases for court processing, what Ashworth and Roberts (2012) call the mechanics of sentencing, is shaped by a wide variety of players and processes. It is worth repeating the off-quoted statistic that only perhaps 3 per cent of offences committed in this country result in a sentence (Ashworth and Roberts, 2012, p. 872). Many crimes are of course not reported or 'solved'. There may be a deliberate decision not to prosecute. As well as the formal out-of-court penalties, more informal police diversionary sanctions, often of a 'restorative' nature, are being used. These may not involve 'sentences' as the term is usually used, but they feel like a penalty or sentence to the offender.

Another preliminary question is whether all sanctions imposed post-conviction are part of the 'sentence'. The most obvious sentences or penalties are fines, community orders and imprisonment. But the following orders are also often part and parcel of an English sentence, and worth listing to remind the reader of the complex components of the sentencing package:

- A confiscation order – which, under the Drug Trafficking Act 1994, the Proceeds of Crime Act 1995 and the Proceeds of Crime Act 2002 compel an offender to pay the amount of his benefit from crime, and, because of the way 'benefit' is calculated, the sums can be enormous.
- A compensation order – which, under the Powers of the Criminal Courts (Sentencing) Act 2000, section 130, is awarded to victims of crime for personal injury, loss or damage, arising from an offence. 'Personal injury' includes distress or anxiety. If there is personal injury/loss/damage and the judge or magistrates does not make a compensation order, they must give reasons for this in open court.

234   N. Padfield

- A deprivation order – these deprive offenders of property used to commit or to facilitate the commission of an offence, or property of which the offender was unlawfully in possession: Powers of the Criminal Courts (Sentencing) Act 2000, section 143.
- A disqualification – from driving, under the Powers of the Criminal Courts (Sentencing) Act 2000, section 146–147; from working with children or vulnerable adults, under s. 28 of the Criminal Justice and Court Services Act 2000; from directing a company, under the Company Directors Disqualification Act 1986.
- A restitution order – under the Powers of the Criminal Courts (Sentencing) Act 2000, section 148–149.
- An anti-social behaviour order – imposed on conviction under s. 1C of the Crime and Disorder Act 1998, added by the Police Reform Act 2002 and subsequently amended several times.
- A serious crime prevention order, a sexual offences prevention order, a foreign travel order – under sections 104–113 of the Sexual Offences Act 2003.
- A risk of sexual harm order – these broad orders may prevent an order doing anything which is necessary to protect children: sections 104–113 of the Sexual Offences Act 2003.
- A banning order – both drink banning orders, under sections 1–14 of the Violent Crime Reduction Act 2006, as amended, and bans from football grounds under the Football Spectators Act 1989.
- A binding over order – under the Justice of the Peace Act 1361.
- An exclusion order – Under the Licensed Premises (Exclusion of Certain Person) Act 1980, sections 1–4.
- A financial reporting order – under the Serious and Organised Crime and Police Act 2005, sections 76–81.
- A forfeiture order – an offender can be ordered to forfeit any personal property shown to the satisfaction of the court to relate to the offence, under the Misuse of Drugs Act 1971, the Knives Act 1997.
- A parenting order – under the Crime and Disorder Act 1998, sections 8–10.

There are others. Readers of this book may not be interested in the precise statutory provisions, but the list usefully reflects the chaotic nature of much sentencing law. Annual criminal justice and other legislation is passed which normally amends earlier legislation: the important changes to sentencing law enacted by the Legal Aid, Sentencing and Punishment of Offenders Act 2012, for example, are virtually all complex amendments to earlier statutes. Judges and lawyers spend significant amounts of personal and (costly) training time simply keeping up to date with these changes, both big and small.

All these orders should be seen as part of the 'sentence': it is no longer appropriate to think of them as ancillary to the main sentence. They may affect the offender's life, and how they are enforced is crucial – when the offender is brought back before a court and 'breached' for breaking the order, imprisonment

Sentencing in England and Wales 235

is often the consequence. Indeed, these 'ancillary' penalties are often the most burdensome components of the sentence, but they are often poorly understood by the offender as well as by lawyers (and ignored by criminologists?). Particularly important is confiscation law: many offenders fail to realise that if they fail to pay the often very large sums confiscated from them, they face significant lengths of time in prison, over and above the 'main' sentence they may already have served or be serving. The debt still hangs over them once the extra sentence has been served: imprisonment does not extinguish the debt. It is extraordinary how little empirical research has been carried out into the ways in which confiscation orders and other 'ancillary' orders operate. We can take the definition of sentencing yet further, to include other consequences of conviction, such as registration on the sex offenders register, which follows from conviction quite separately from the sentencing process. This first introductory section therefore serves to remind us that defining 'sentencing' is not easy, and definitions should not be taken for granted. But we now move to examine the 'classic' sentencing decision.

'Front door' sentencing

As has been pointed out, there has been significant academic interest in initial sentencing decisions, exploring in particular how the judge or magistrate is either affected or constrained by decisions taken by others in the process: the victim (Bottoms and Roberts, 2010), legal advice (Skinns, 2010; Souza and Kemp, 2009), police, prosecutors, probation officers, psychiatrists (Solomka, 1996) and other courts: see also Gelsthorpe and Padfield, 2003; Padfield, 2010. The advent of Guidelines in England and Wales has had a significant impact on sentencing law and practice: there is already a considerable legal literature on their use (see Ashworth, 2010; Ashworth and Roberts, 2013). As well, the decisions of the Court of Appeal in thousands of appeals against sentence every year continue to shape sentencing practice and to provoke academic comment.

As the discretion of the sentencer is increasingly constrained by law and Guidelines, so the 'power' or influence of the prosecutor grows. Plea bargains (encouraged in part by the statutory discount for guilty pleas) and deferred prosecution agreements (see s.45 and Schedule 17 of the Crime and Courts Act 2013) move the Crown Prosecution Service (CPS) ever more central stage (see the *Attorney General's Guidelines on the Acceptance of Pleas and the Prosecutor's Role in the Sentencing Exercise* at www.gov.uk/the-acceptance-of-pleas-and-the-prosecutors-role-in-the-sentencing-exercise). The Court of Appeal has made clear that both prosecutor and defence have a duty to alert a sentencing court to the many sentencing traps in the complex legal framework: *Qayum* [2010] EWCA Crim 2237, *Brzezinski* [2012] EWCA Crim 198. Yet there have been no recent studies of CPS decision-making in this area, of their role in sentencing.

It seems apt to cite Dworkin, the great legal philosopher, whose famous statement that "discretion, like the hole in a doughnut, does not exist except as an

236   *N. Padfield*

area left open by a surrounding belt of restriction. It is therefore a relative concept" (Dworkin, 1977, p. 39) paints a useful picture. That "surrounding belt of restriction", which includes many legal and other considerations, has been tightened around sentencers in recent years. Despite (or because of) this tightening belt of restriction, sentence lengths have increased dramatically in recent years: to 14.9 months in September 2012, compared to 2.5 months in the 12 months ending September 2002 (see Ministry of Justice, 2013b). This chapter does not suggest that we should ignore these developments: of course, lawyers and criminologists should continue to study front door sentencing.

There are many, many issues with which we should concern ourselves:

- the form and shape of Guidelines produced by the Sentencing Council (see its website at http://sentencingcouncil.judiciary.gov.uk);
- whether Guidelines may have unintended consequences, e.g. 'talking up' sentence levels (see Padfield, 2013b);
- the criteria for (and the fairness of) indeterminate (life) sentences;
- whether it should be possible to suspend a custodial sentence: in England and Wales, any sentence up to 24 months' imprisonment may now be suspended, but the judges have received little guidance on when this is appropriate;
- how, and in what degree of detail, judges should explain their sentences in court;
- measuring the effect of the offence on the victim, and how this should affect the sentence;
- measuring consistency, and indeed the value of consistency;
- whether and how much should be the discount for a guilty plea;
- the proper impact of previous convictions on an offender's sentence;
- the totality principle, and whether a defendant should be sentenced for every offence of which he is convicted, whether sentences should be consecutive or concurrent;
- the role of mercy.

But there is a paradox here: whilst there has been an increasing political and perhaps academic interest in constraining the discretion of the sentencer, the reality of the sentencing process is that discretion remains largely unconstrained further down the process. This appears to be accepted by the judiciary themselves: it is a 'principle' that the sentencing court has to decide the appropriate sentence for a crime without regard to the provisions for early release or parole: see for example *R.* v. *Round* [2009] EWCA Crim 2667, [2010] 2 Cr. App. R. (S.) 45, where the Court of Appeal held that it was wrong in principle for a judge to structure consecutive sentences either side of 12 months in a manner so as to make an offender eligible for release under the home detention curfew (HDC) scheme at the earliest possible opportunity. The Court said, "the general principle that early release, licence and their various ramifications should be left out of account upon sentencing is, as it seems to us, a matter of principle of some importance" (para 44). The main reason the Court gives for this was that since the release rules give broad discretionary powers to the executive there was no way of knowing in advance what future decision might be made about HDC release. But judges blind-fold themselves not only about the legal consequences of their decisions, but also about the social and criminological consequences. They are not trained to understand or to consider the implications of their sentences more broadly, for example by considering the literature on 'what works' to reduce re-offending to encourage desistance. Few visit a prison after the one-day visit included in their initial (very brief) training. Even those who serve on the Parole Board are unlikely to get beyond the area of the prison where an oral hearing takes place. We will return later to consider whether it should be the judge's role to consider the wider impact of their sentence. Now we turn to look a little more at the law and practice after the offender has been sentenced.

'Back door' sentencing

This expression developed out of a recognition that much of the current expansion in the prison population can be explained by decisions on release, in particular to revoke 'early release': prisoners were being 'recalled' to prison in ever greater numbers. Thus, Tonry (2003, p. 218) discussed 'back door strategies' for reducing prison populations. These include large-scale amnesties; broad-based parole release systems; absolute limits on prison capacity; petitioning for the resentencing of prisoners; giving the prison service the discretion to release inmates on a case-by-case basis; providing early release into community supervision programmes; and eliminating the extension of prison sentences as a sanction for violations of prison rules. These policies would not usually be thought of as 'sentencing'. Lawyers who work on these areas would be 'public lawyers' or 'prison lawyers', usually a separate breed from those 'criminal lawyers', whose job ends at the moment of sentence. We look here briefly at some important, if neglected, issues in back door sentencing.

Non-custodial sentences

The majority of sentenced offenders are fined: 816,600 fines were imposed in the year ending September 2012, 66.5 per cent of all sentences. (In fact, the numbers of fines has been decreasing in recent years, reflecting the decline in prosecutions and the growth in out-of-court sanctions: Ministry of Justice, 2013a). Many others receive a community order: 153,900 people (or 12.5 per cent of those sentenced) in the 12 months ending September 2012.

How are these sentences enforced? With fines it has long been a concern that so few seem to be paid promptly. They are enforced largely 'administratively', by court 'Fines Enforcement Officers' who can make deductions from benefits or attachment of earnings orders. They may also use private firms of bailiffs to collect the debt. In recent years there seems to have been a significant improvement in the payment of fines: according to the Green Paper *Breaking the Cycle:*

238   *N. Padfield*

Effective Punishment, Rehabilitation and Sentencing of Offenders (2010), 86 per cent of financial penalties were collected in 2009/2010 (Ministry of Justice, 2010, p. 61). Yet more than 1,000 people a year are imprisoned for non-payment of fines. And there has been increasing public concern about the methods employed by some bailiffs. The largest fines are often now imposed on companies, often under EU laws.[4] Here enforcement issues are often negotiated in secrecy, another area crying out for research. We get an insight from *R (Purnell)* v. *South Western Magistrates' Court* [2013] EWHC 64 (Admin) where the Administrative Court quashed an order requiring a fine defaulter to repay outstanding fines of over £2,500 at a rate of £5 a week. This was held to be disproportionate, as it would have taken him over ten years to repay. The court expressed strong misgivings about the current system used for the enforcement of outstanding fines in London.

As far as the implementation and enforcement of community sentences are concerned, one should start by noting the enormous pressure that has been placed on probation services in recent years to show that these sentences are serious, tough and credible. There was concern when the new 'generic' community order (one order, with a 'menu' of 11 possible requirements) was introduced in the Criminal Justice Act 2003 that sentencers would overload offenders with too many requirements, which would lead to more breach proceedings. This has not happened: many requirements are hardly used at all. Indeed, the scarcity of community alcohol services and the difficulties of accessing community mental health services have been something of scandal (Mair, 2011). There is a small literature on the enforcement of community orders: but it is only small: Hearnden and Millie (2004) rightly question whether vigorous enforcement is synonymous with compliance, i.e. effective enforcement; Cairns (2012) very usefully discusses some of the practical difficulties with enforcement. A breach of a community order is not itself a criminal offence, nor do enforcement proceedings form part of the 'criminal law' as such. This means that procedural statutes such as the Criminal Procedures and Investigations Act 1996 do not apply to breach proceedings. It is case law which has determined that a criminal standard of proof applies to enforcement cases. Yet there is no right of appeal against a finding of breach.

The 'new' version of the suspended sentence introduced in the Criminal Justice Act 2003 is a custodial sentence served entirely in the community (and therefore not properly classified as a non-custodial sentence: although the Ministry of Justice publishes the statistics alongside 'other' community sentences: in the 12 months ending September 2012, 44,400 people, or 3.6 per cent of those sentenced, were given a Suspended Sentence Order (SSO)). The SSO became increasingly popular with sentencers after the Criminal Justice Act 2003 removed the requirement that a sentence could only be suspended in exceptional circumstances, and we are likely to see another large increase now LASPOA 2012 has hugely expanded its potential use by allowing sentences of up to 24 months (and not just 12 months) to be suspended. The management and enforcement of requirements imposed under both community orders and SSOs lies

Sentencing in England and Wales   239

primarily in the hands of probation officers/offender managers. National Standards were introduced in the early 1990s in a drive to develop more consistency, and it would appear that National Standards 2005, to be found in Probation Circular 15/2005, still apply although this Circular technically expired in 2010; as Cairns (2012) shows, enforcement is clearly a challenge for practitioners as well as their clients. As we move to the enforcement and management of custodial sentences, it is interesting to note that the procedures are very different to the enforcement of non-custodial sentences.

Custodial sentences

There are currently more than 85,500 people in prison in England and Wales (monthly figure, December 2014: see www.gov.uk/government/statistics/prison-population-figures-2014). Many of them are serving only short sentences: in the 12 months up to September 2012, 97,500 persons were sentenced to immediate custody (a decrease of 4.7 per cent in the same period a year earlier and 12.6 per cent lower than the peak of 111,500 persons sentenced in the 12 months ending September 2002): Ministry of Justice, 2013b. But the size of the prison population is determined as much by release and recall decisions as by initial decisions to imprisonment.

Currently in English law there is a fundamental distinction between those processes which apply to those serving determinate sentences and those serving indeterminate sentences. Very different release processes apply to each category. In essence, those serving a fixed term are automatically released on licence conditions after half of the sentence, and may be eligible for up to 135 days earlier release before half-time on Home Detention Curfew (HDC), decisions on which are made administratively. Lifers on the other hand are only released after they have served a minimum term, and on the direction of the quasi-independent Parole Board. Release is very unlikely before the prisoner has spent time in an open prison, and decision to release will be taken after an oral hearing in the prison where the prisoner is currently held. Perhaps the most obvious unfairness here is that the law on 'front door' sentencing which labels the offender either a determinate or indeterminate sentence prisoner has changed significantly several times in recent history. There are many prisoners currently serving IPP for example, who because of the changes to the law enacted in 2008 and 2012 would no longer be sentenced to an indeterminate term. Instead, there is growing use of a hybrid, extended sentence.

This is a useful summary, but how much does this help the public, the journalist, the victim or indeed the offender understand the reality of the sentence? The offender is taken down to the court cells and the private security firm is told by the National Offender Management Service (NOMS) where the prisoner should be taken. That initial allocation is crucial: prisons vary enormously. Life in prison starts in what is usually a hectic reception and induction area. A bewildering number of forms are filled in (see Prison Service Order (PSO) 0550 on induction). Medical, suicide and cell sharing risk assessments have to be done.

240 *N. Padfield*

The sentence calculation has to be done within two working days of reception (see PSO 6650), and decisions are swiftly made about security categorisation and allocation, both crucial factors in the development of the prisoner's journey through the system.

Prison law is complex, not because of a surfeit of statutory change (as is the case with initial 'front door' sentencing decisions), but because of the curious mix of statute, statutory instruments, Prison Service Orders (PSOs) and Prison Service Instructions (PSIs). The main statute remains the Prison Act 1952, but this provides little guidance. Section 1 provides that "All powers and jurisdiction in relation to prisons and prisoners which before the commencement of the Prison Act 1877 were exercisable by any other authority shall, subject to the provisions of this Act, be exercisable by the Secretary of State". These powers include specifically, for example, the power, with the approval of the Treasury, to alter, enlarge or rebuild any prison and to build new prisons (section 33) and the power to "make rules for the regulation and management of prisons ... and for the classification, treatment, employment, discipline and control of persons to be detained".

Thus it is the prison authorities who are empowered to take crucial decisions which impact on the way the sentence will unfold: not only how and where it will be served but also, more subtly, affecting how and when it may end. Allocation depends not only on security assessments but also on the availability of places, and so the resettlement needs of a prisoner may well be outweighed by other more immediate considerations. Much has been made of the need for 'sentence planning' in recent years, but the reality appears to be often haphazard, particularly for those serving short sentences. There are also few positive activities, especially in local prisons (see the annual reports of Independent Monitoring Boards of individual prisons, available at www.justice.gov.uk/publications/corporate-reports/imb).

For most prisoners, of course, the central question is release. Calculating the release date has been a challenge for many years, especially when prisoners are serving more than one sentence simultaneously, confusing both prison staff and the courts (see *Olutu* v. *Home Office and another* [1997] 1 All ER 385; *R* v. *Governor of Brockhill, ex p Evans (No 2)* [2000] 3 WLR 843; *R (Noone)* v. *Governor of Drake Hall* [2010] UKSC 30 for some shocking examples). Prisoners will be informed of their Sentence Expiry Date (SED), their eligibility for Home Detention Curfew (HDC) Date and their Conditional Release Date (CRD). Even the SED is difficult to calculate, as it is frequently difficult to agree whether periods in prison pre-sentence should count towards the time served on the sentence. For example, it may well not be clear whether a period of imprisonment was 'remand' or 'recall' on a previous sentence. Between April 2005 and December 2012 the law required the sentencing judge to announce the precise numbers of remand days which were to count towards the sentence in open court (presumably to ensure greater clarity), but this has now become, once again, an administrative calculation (presumably to save time and money). Days spent on remand on nine hours a day electronic curfew also counts towards sentence: and this period must still be calculated and announced by the sentencing judge. The Conditional Release Date is the halfway point.

At this point, we should divert briefly to discuss the Parole Board. The evolving history of parole, and of the Parole Board of England and Wales, illustrates the shifting balance between 'front door' and 'back door' sentencing. The Parole Board was created in 1967 as an advisory body. The Criminal Justice Act 1967 allowed a prisoner to be released after serving one third of his sentence (or 12 months). This removed from the judge the power to decide how long a particular offender actually served. What Thomas (2002, p. 56) called the "effective authority of the judiciary, and therefore the importance of the decisions which they made" were reduced further when the minimum period for parole was reduced to six months in 1983. There was then no significant difference between sentences of anything from nine to 18 months' imprisonment, and the effective difference between nine months' and two years' custody could be as little as two months. This very flexible parole scheme was cut back in 1991, so that the only determinate sentence prisoners who were eligible for discretionary early release were those serving four years or more, and this only in a window between half and two thirds, decided by the Parole Board, with supervision continuing to three quarters. Then the Parole Board's role in relation to the release of all determinate sentences was removed completely by the Criminal Justice Act 2003, except for extended sentence prisoners. That too went in the Criminal Justice and Immigration Act 2008, leaving the Parole Board to decide only on the release of lifers and recalled offenders (see below).

The status of the Parole Board has also changed. It has moved slowly from being a purely advisory body to having increasingly independent and judicial powers. This has happened because the courts have recognised the 'rights' of life sentence prisoners, and of recalled offenders, to have a 'court or tribunal' review their detention. The Board now directs release, not merely advising it. Yet the Court of Appeal still (rightly in my view) held in *R (Brooke)* v. *Parole Board* [2008] EWCA Civ 29, [2008] 1 WLR 1950 that the arrangements for the Parole Board did not sufficiently demonstrate its objective independence of Government, as required by both English common law and Article 5(4) of European Convention on Human Rights, which provides:

> Everyone who is deprived of his liberty by arrest or detention shall be entitled to take proceedings by which the lawfulness of his detention shall be decided speedily by a court and his release ordered if the detention is not lawful.

It appeared in 2009 that the Government was about to act and make the Parole Board a 'real' court or tribunal (Ministry of Justice, 2009). But this did not happen: we return to this at the end of this chapter.

242   *N. Padfield*

Home Detention Curfew (HDC)

We turn now to consider HDC, which allows discretionary release up to 135 days, even before half-time. Then we will explore two other forms of discretionary release: that for extended sentence prisoners and for life sentence prisoners.

HDC was first introduced in the Crime and Disorder Act 1998, with the detailed policy/rules to be found in the frequently amended PSO 6700. Prisoners serving sentences for certain offences are presumed unsuitable for HDC, and will not be released unless the Governor agrees to their exceptional circumstances (eligibility rules have been varied several times). It is very clear that HDC is not an entitlement, it is only granted to prisoners who meet the eligibility criteria and pass a risk assessment, including a home circumstances check. Decisions are made by busy staff on the wing. Thomson (2008, 2010), writing of HDC in Scotland, calls it "one of the least popular sentencing innovations of recent years" in large measure because of the reality of poor assessment procedures (2010, pp. 814–815):

> Over worked and hard pressed prison staff rarely have time to spend carrying out in depth risk assessments of persons who may be in their establishment for a matter of weeks, and it would hardly be surprising to find that several assessments are superficial; indeed, when cases are given scrutiny after the HDC conditions are breached, it is not always easy to identify the process by which an offender was found to meet [the relevant] criteria.

Similarly speedy decision-making takes place in England and Wales. When HDC is refused, the prisoner is given brief reasons and may appeal internally to the Governor and through the Request and Complaints procedures of a prison (dealt with by the same prison). Whilst PSO 6700 talks throughout of the 'Governor', decisions in private prisons appear to be taken in practice by staff of the private company, and are simply signed off by the Controller (the public servant in the private prison: see s. 85 of the Criminal Justice Act 1991).

HDC prisoners are fitted with an electronic tag, and monitoring equipment is installed at their home address by a private contractor. If they are recalled for breaching the HDC curfew conditions, they will not be released again on HDC either for the rest of their sentence or on any future custodial sentences they may receive. Sometimes a prisoner is recalled for reasons beyond their control (for example if they are unable to stay at the curfew address any longer). There is then sometimes a possibility of re-release upon their return to custody subject to another suitable address being located, but most remain in custody until their automatic release date.

HDC is usually welcomed by prisoners as a way out of prison. It is also not ineffective: Marie *et al.* (2011) concluded that offenders who received HDC (under the then current rules) were no more likely to engage in criminal behaviour when released from prison when compared to offenders with similar characteristics who were not eligible for early release on HDC. This was the case, even when controlling for the additional time that offenders on HDC are in

Sentencing in England and Wales 243

the community, due to being released early. It also helps reduce the prison population. But important questions remain: about its purpose, and whether it is granted fairly. It grants a wide discretionary power to prison authorities. The Scottish Prisons Commission was damning (2008, para 3.43):

> Though we recognise that the current Home Detention Curfew Scheme (HDC) plays a useful role in reducing overcrowding, it is fundamentally inconsistent with the clarity and transparency in sentencing that the public need – and with the right of judges to determine sentence.

This argument, that judges should determine sentence lengths, is not currently shared by the English courts, which seem to have accepted without criticism that the current law provides for a distinction between a court's sentencing powers and the executive's administrative powers concerning the management of offenders. The House of Lords/Supreme Court has more than once recognised the executive's entitlement to take early release decisions (for example *R. (Smith)* v. *Parole Board* [2005] UKHL 1, [2005] 1 W.L.R. 350; *R. (Black)* v. *Secretary of State for the Home Department* [2009] UKHL 1, [2009] 1 A.C. 949; Padfield, 2009b). We return to this in the final part of this chapter.

Extended sentences

There have been many versions of 'longer than commensurate' sentences. In the past 20 years, we have seen three very different versions of the extended sentence, with different eligibility criteria and release criteria. The version introduced in the Criminal Justice Act (CJA) 2003 was a determinate sentence made up of an 'appropriate custodial term', plus an extended period of licence of up to five years for a specified violent offence and eight years for a specified sexual offence: section 227(4) CJA 2003. This sentence was, and is still, only applicable to offenders deemed 'dangerous', who pose a significant serious of harm. Under the provisions of the original CJA 2003, the precise date of release of 'extended sentence' prisoners was in the hands of the Parole Board, within a 'window' between the halfway and two thirds point in the custodial term. But amendments introduced by s. 25 of the CJIA 2008 meant that release from the custodial element became automatic at the halfway point of the custodial term. This was perhaps surprising given that the court at the time of sentencing must have decided that the offender was 'dangerous', but the reality was that it simply reflected a transfer of powers from the Parole Board to the administration, largely to save money.

After 2008, when the release of extended prisoners was no longer discretionary, recall became a more important and flexible tool. Crucial decision-making moved to the probation officer or offender manager who was responsible for supervising the offender and who initiate recalls to prison. Now political concern has recognised the cost of so many recalls – the Legal Aid Sentencing and Punishment of Offenders Act 2012 has introduced a new variation of what is now

244 *N. Padfield*

being called the Extended Determinate Sentence (EDS). For the new EDS prisoners, release will normally be at the two thirds points of the custodial term, unless the custodial term of the extended sentence is ten years or more, or the sentence is imposed for an offence listed in new schedule 15B of the CJA 2003, when the case must be referred at the two thirds point to the Parole Board, who will consider whether it is no longer necessary for the protection of the public for the defendant to be detained. This is an example of the current confusion between release decisions taken by the executive and those taken by the Parole Board. Most EDS prisoners will be released automatically at two thirds, some later. Do judges take notice of this at point of sentence? A prisoner who is sentenced to nine years' imprisonment will come out after four and a half years; whereas if it is an EDS of nine years with even a short period of extension, the custodial term will be six years. As we have seen, this six years may be a fixed release or an eligibility to be considered by the Parole Board. If a prisoner is recalled to prison, they may well not be re-released until the end of the custodial part AND the extension period: at the Sentence Expiry Date. The consequences of the initial sentencing decision are complex, and may be unclear to both judge and offender at the time of sentence.

Lifers

'Lifers' used to make up a much smaller proportion of the prison population than they do today. For many years, murderers have received a mandatory life sentence, and 'dangerous' offenders have been eligible for a discretionary life sentence. Until ten years ago, the vast majority of lifers were serving the mandatory life sentence: thus in 1999 there were 4,206 lifers in prison, made up of 3,308 mandatory lifers and only 898 discretionary lifers. The position changed dramatically with the introduction of Imprisonment for Public Protection (IPP) in the Criminal Justice Act 2003, which resulted in a huge increase in the number of 'dangerous' offenders serving an indeterminate sentence. At the same time, both the minimum term and the actual term served by those convicted of murder has increased very significantly. All murderers face very long minimum terms since Schedule 21 of the CJA 2003 introduced 15 year, 30 year and whole life starting points. And any released lifer is on supervision for the rest of his or her life. The consequences of the conviction continue forever. In 2011 there were 1,909 lifers under 'active supervision' (Parole Board, 2012, p. 38). There is no mechanism to remove the licence (unlike IPP, where ten years after release, the offender may apply to the Parole Board to have the licence conditions removed: see Sched 18 of the CJA 2003, and s. 31A of the Crime (Sentences) Act 1997, as amended).

In December 2012, the number of 'lifers' had risen to 13,577. Of these, 44 per cent were serving an IPP (5,920) while 56 per cent were serving life sentences (7,657). Most of the IPPs had a tariff length of six years or less (1,139 had a tariff length of less than two years, 2,706 had a tariff length of two to four years, 1,255 a tariff of four to six years). Particularly shockingly, 3,538 (60 per cent) IPP prisoners had passed their tariff expiry date (IPP is no longer an option since the provisions of LASPOA 2012 were brought into force, but thousands of prisoners continue to serve sentences of IPP). For those serving life sentences in 2012, 2,264 had a tariff of less than ten years and a further 4,106 had a tariff of 10–20 years and 1,039 had a tariff of more than 20 years. There were 43 offenders serving a whole life sentence at the end of 2012 (all statistics from Ministry of Justice, 2013b).

When imposing a life sentence, a judge explains at some length how he reached the 'minimum term' by reference to the statutory framework and the various aggravating and mitigating factors, but on the question of release he or she merely says (here I am quoting from the sentencing remarks of HH Judge Brian Barker QC, the Recorder of London on 4 March 2013 when sentencing Nicola Edgington (see www.judiciary.gov.uk/Resources/JCO/Documents/Judgments/sentencing-remarks-r-v-edgington.pdf):

> Taking all factors into account the minimum period of your life imprisonment term will be one of 37 years.... You will then be eligible for consideration for release by the Parole Board in their discretion. If and when released you will be on licence for the rest of your life.

There is no review of sentence length until shortly before the end of the minimum term. The growing number of lifers serving very long and unpredictable lengths of time in prison has had an unsettling effect on the 'management' of lifers and on the prison population more generally. This is obvious from the research evidence and from reports of, for example, the Chief Inspector of Prisons on individual prisons. In their study of HMP Whitemoor carried out 12 years after an earlier study, Liebling *et al.* describe "a new problem of relatively young prisoners serving indeterminate sentences facing 15–25 year tariffs coming to terms with and finding a way of doing this kind of sentence" (Liebling *et al.*, 2011, p. iii). The current rules for the management of indeterminate sentenced prisoners 'outside of the parole process' are to be found in PS0 4700, the Indeterminate Sentence Manual (formerly the Lifer Manual). The release process rules are contained in PSO 6010 on Generic Parole Process, which has been in force since April 2009. This division of the rules between management generally and the parole process highlights an important tension in the way that 'lifers' progress through their sentence. It is the Parole Board which decides when someone serving an indeterminate sentence should be released. But it cannot directly release unless "it is satisfied that it is no longer necessary for the protection of the public for the prisoner to be detained" (section 28 of the Crime (Sentences) Act 1997). Paradoxically, the Board has little control over the key factors which might lead to a decision to release: for example, whether the prisoner has been 'tested' in an open prison, whether he has completed recommended courses in prison, or whether a robust release plan is supported by a probation officer/offender manager.

246 *N. Padfield*

Other decisions which affect release

Crucial decisions are taken throughout the sentence by 'the administration', in reality by over-worked staff who are being increasingly asked to do more with fewer resources (see also Barry and McIvor, 2010). Thus there is not only a tension between the role of the courts and the role of the administration, but within the administration, there is still uncertainty about the relative role of prison and probation staff. Cambridgeshire and Peterborough Probation Trust (CPPT) told the Justice Committee of the House of Commons in 2010 that (Justice Committee, 2011, p. 17):

> There is currently a lack of clarity about what the term 'Offender Management' means, and CPPT believes that offender management should mean the effective engagement of probation staff with offenders to impact positively on their offending behaviour, achieving a reduction in offending behaviour. Within NOMS it seems that currently offender management is seen as primarily an administrative process, within which the offender manager is responsible for overseeing and sequencing interventions with the offender. This, in our opinion, ignores the capability and potential of offender managers to engage positively with the offender to reduce their offending behaviour. The professional base, training, skills, knowledge and experience of probation staff put them in the best position to supervise offenders effectively.

Currently, in most prisons, probation staff are not actively engaged with offenders. There is still an extraordinary gulf between what goes on in prison and what goes on outside.

After prison

On release prisoners are far from 'free'. Those released at half-time will often find that complex and often inconsistent terms are added to the six standard licence conditions, and those released even earlier on HDC will find they have an additional set of lengthy conditions. 'Going straight' is never easy, and the terms of the licence conditions can make it even more difficult. Inevitably, perhaps, conditions designed to protect the public may not enhance their chances of successful re-integration. Let us take a few examples: residence, drinking and computer access (examples taken from Padfield, 2013a). Prisoners will be released to a specific address, often told where to live, with little possibility of discussion or negotiation. A condition that they don't live with their family or friends is often made for good reason (perhaps these homes provide easy access to alcohol or illegal drugs), yet paradoxically these homes might have provided the best support network available. More serious offenders may be released subject to the condition that they live in Approved Premises. These are often difficult places in which to live, with tight rules, even compared to a prison,

Sentencing in England and Wales 247

particularly a Cat C, local or open prison, where 'doing time' may be relatively easy. Another negative condition (from the offender's perspective) is a pub ban – this excludes them from normal social environments, and has the effect of driving them to drink in less controlled environments. A third example is a condition which seemed to be added to many licences in 2011 (Padfield, 2013a, p. 17):

> not to use directly or indirectly any computer, data storage device or any other electronic device (including an internet enabled mobile phone) for the purpose of having access to the internet or having access to email, instant messaging or any other online message board/forum or community without the prior approval of your supervising officer. You must allow a responsible officer reasonable access, including technical checks, to establish usage.

The breadth of this condition makes reconnection with the modern world particularly challenging. How does one explore the job market or use a bank without direct or indirect use of a computer? Licence conditions imposed on prisoners for their own good, but without any real discussion or debate, are what Turnbull and Hannah-Moffat (2009) call 'unspoken expectations for reintegration'. These burdensome expectations are imposed by busy staff, with little time to consider conditions, and indeed to discuss potential licence conditions with an offender. Healy (2012, p. 392) gives a powerful message to policy makers:

> Government policy can exert a significant impact on the reintegration prospects of offenders but without genuine opportunities to strengthen social bonds, repair the harm caused by their behaviour and earn back the trust of their communities, their journey towards social inclusion will necessarily be curtailed ... policymakers should take account of these dangers when designing economic, social and criminal justice solutions to the current crisis.

Kemshall (2008, p. 31) puts it even more starkly, warning of policies which create "disillusioned and distanced non-citizens who are excluded from the neo-liberal social contract".

Once the conditions have been imposed, and the prisoner released, clearly probation services are hard-pressed to supervise offenders effectively. It is well known that living a life on licence is immensely difficult (see Appleton, 2010; Padfield, 2013a). Another small snap-shot of the difficulties of life on licence can be seen by the high death rates of those on licence (Gelsthorpe *et al.*, 2012). Emotional and financial problems multiply. It is not surprising that the number of offenders recalled to prison has been rising so steeply. When the offender manager is fearful that the offender may be 'going off the rails', they initiate recall.

248   *N. Padfield*

Recall and re-release

Over the period 1999 to September 2012, a total of 600,000 offenders were released from prison on licence supervision, and 147,000 of them were recalled to custody for breaching the conditions of their licence (Ministry of Justice, 2013a). Some are recalled for a fixed term of 28 days, but the vast majority are 'standard' recalls, who until s. 113 of the Legal Aid, Sentencing and Punishment of Offenders 2012 was brought into force on 3 December 2012, could only be re-released when the Parole Board directed it. Many serve the entirety of what remains of the second half of their sentence in prison. (Now the Secretary of State may cancel a revocation of a licence at any stage. The system may improve with these changes, which grant greater powers of re-release to the executive. But only time will tell whether this actually happens.)

So how does it work? Once back in prison, they are given a 'dossier' which explains the reasons for their recall (in a complex format, designed to ease decision-making within NOMS, not to facilitate communication with the offender), and they are asked in writing whether they want legal representation. This form does not tell the prisoner that it remains their responsibility to contact the solicitor. Although a copy of the form is sent to those responsible for administering the system in the Ministry of Justice, it is not clear what effect it is meant to have. The Parole Board also receives a copy of the parole dossier and within a short time, a one member 'panel' of the Parole Board then reviews the recall at a 'paper' hearing (i.e. it is a review of documents only). In *Understanding Recall 2011* (Padfield, 2013a), most prisoners had signed the form that they wished to make representations. Unsurprisingly, in no cases had representations been received by the Parole Board before the first review, which invariably upheld the decision to recall. The 'knock back' from the Parole Board invariably started:

> The Panel has received and taken into account the dossier referred by the Secretary of State on (date). The dossier does not contain an Annex H by the Offender Manager or any indication whether re-release is supported or not. The Panel has not received any written representations on your behalf...

The reasons were often glossed in expressions such as 'the dossier is silent as to any progress made since being returned to custody', or that 'the Risk Management Plan is somewhat underdeveloped'. This is hardly surprising since the prisoner has only just been recalled.

It is very difficult for anyone, prisoner, prison staff or academic researcher, to understand precisely what happens after this swift and invariably unsuccessful review by the Parole Board. The key to re-release is held by the offender's offender manager or probation officer, but they have no duty to maintain close contact with their 'client'. The Public Protection Unit (PPU) of NOMS may refer the case back to the Parole Board at any stage, but it is difficult to understand exactly when and if the PPU will do so. It would appear to be the usual practice to do so yearly, but the timetable is not strictly adhered to and it is not clear what might trigger an earlier review. It will be interesting to learn if the new rules which allow for executive revocation of recall (i.e. executive re-release) facilitate re-release.

Recalls happen both because of allegations of fresh offences, and because of breaches of conditions. For those recalled because of allegations of fresh offences, recall may be immediately on arrest or later in the process. It seems very unfair, given the consequences of recall, that it can be activated merely on the suspicion which leads to an arrest. At that point a prisoner should surely only be remanded in custody if the fresh allegations justify it, but this should be considered under the rules for remands in custody under the Bail Act 1976. In many other countries the 'rule of law' requires that only a fresh conviction justifies recall (see Cid and Tébar, 2012). This is much more appropriate: following arrest, charges are often not laid, or allegations are withdrawn, but by then in England it is too late – the offender has had his licence withdrawn.

The sense of disempowerment is enormous: many prisoners have little understanding of the process. There is little chance in prison to discuss the situation with anyone knowledgeable. Both probation officers and solicitors are difficult (and expensive) to get hold of:

> Nowadays you go into prison, and it's up to you to get on with it. Nobody answers you anything. It's up to you to get on with it. Everything you do in prison now is off your own bat. Nobody will come and see you for anything. You have to put in an app, an app for this, Oh can I see this person, can I see that person...

> It's an abuse of power. They've not given me a chance to put my end. It should go back to a court and a judge should decide it. The recall pack (the first time you get it is 10 days later) is ridiculous, but what can you do? It's one man against them, a lot of people.
>
> (both quotes from Padfield, 2013a, p. 28)

Lifers are both advantaged and disadvantaged by the current recall system. Advantages include an interview with a member of staff soon after they have been recalled, and the chance of an oral hearing with the Parole Board, which most prisoners believe to be a better and fairer review than those done on the papers only. The disadvantages for lifers include the extraordinary lengths of time they are likely to spend on recall, even when recalled for what appeared to be minor breaches of licence conditions. They are usually expected to follow the slow trajectory from recall to a local prison (with no specific facilities for lifers), where they wait for the Parole Board once more to recommend a transfer to open conditions, when they are 'tested' again in open conditions, often for at least a year before they have a realistic possibility of re-release.

When does a sentence end? Lifers are on licence forever, with no formal mechanism for bringing the licence to an end. This is in line with the tough

250   *N. Padfield*

English position on the 'rehabilitation of offenders' generally: unlike in many jurisdictions, there is no mechanism in English law that allows a conviction to be formally wiped clean from the offender's record. This was seen last year when otherwise worthy candidates for the elected post of Police and Crime Commissioner were barred because of minor youthful convictions. There is a strong argument for allowing some form of judicial rehabilitation, even for redemptive rituals (see Maruna and LeBel, 2003), but at this moment any likelihood of a formal form of judicial rehabilitation in the sense of record erasure seems inconceivable.

Conclusions

This chapter has identified various decisions and processes which affect the way a sentence evolves. What are the advantages of looking at sentencing as an ongoing process and not just as an event? My argument suggests that a coherent sentencing 'structure' includes not only the decisions made at the point of initial, front door, sentence – for example, whether a person is fined or given a community sentence or the length of a custodial sentence – but also what happens throughout that sentence, and at the end of that sentence. The implications are potentially significant.

First, perhaps, it would lead to fresh debate (and perhaps greater clarity) about the *aims and purposes of sentencing*. The current statutory aims, to be found in s. 142 of the Criminal Justice Act 2003, are in many ways contradictory: any court "must have regard to the following purposes of sentencing":

a   the punishment of offenders;
b   the reduction of crime (including its reduction by deterrence);
c   the reform and rehabilitation of offenders;
d   the protection of the public; and
e   the making of reparation by offenders to persons affected by their offences.

Whether or not it matters that the courts are offered a list of contradictory purposes is a challenging question (see Padfield, 2013b). But if one considers sentencing as a process, one can have greater clarity about the different aims (values?) which may take priority at different times in the process. In England and Wales at the moment it might be argued that, despite the wording of s. 142, the priority aim of 'front door' sentencing is consistent proportionate sentences, a desert-based, offence-based, system, where the judge calculates the 'right' sentence, adding an unspecified amount for those with relevant previous convictions and reducing a small amount for personal mitigation. During the implementation stage of the sentence the focus turns to more instrumental concerns: the risk posed by the offender in the community and to his or her rehabilitation. These two priorities clearly often 'clash' and prison and probation officers struggle to keep the balance between the competing interests of public protection and offender reintegration. Re-thinking the way that sentences are designed, or more accurately simply 'happen', might reinvigorate the debate on aims. For example, whilst the public denunciation of the crime at the initial point of sentence is clearly important, should there be more flexibility as the sentence progresses? Should we develop more ambitious aims? Hough *et al.* (2013) encourage us to identify the "positive goods" that court sentences exist to produce: might they be measured, they ask, by their capacity to support the development of constructive citizenship and to build community capacity and cohesion (Hough *et al.*, 2013, p. 17)?

This leads to a second advantage of thinking of sentencing as a process: it would lead to *greater understanding of the real meaning of the 'sentence'.* Currently sentencing is not only poorly understood by the public (Hough *et al.*, 2009), but judges, practitioners and offenders all struggle to understand the real meaning of the sentence imposed by the court. Although judges and magistrates when sentencing have a duty to explain the meaning of the sentence in open court, it is a challenge to do this without undue simplification. Let us take the hypothetical case of an offender sentenced to four years' imprisonment. When the sentence is imposed, the judge, having set out in some detail the reasons for the sentence, will say something like:

> The sentence will be one of four years' imprisonment. Unless you are released earlier under supervision you will serve one half of this sentence in custody. You will then be released on licence for the remainder of your sentence. While you are on licence, you must comply with all its conditions. At any time during your licence, the Secretary of State may withdraw it and order your return to custody.

For a lifer the judge will simply say something like:

> Taking all factors into account, the minimum period of your life imprisonment term will be one of 37 years. It is only after you have served the minimum period that you will then be eligible for consideration for release by the Parole Board in their discretion. If and when released you will be on licence for the rest of your life.

Despite these statements, the press frequently refer to a person who is sentenced to life as though they will come out of prison once the minimum term is finished. This causes particularly outrage with misleading headlines such as "man who rapes baby gets seven years". This as we have seen is very far from the reality: most 'lifers' spend many years in prison post-tariff. Another example: it is not well understood how many prisoners spend much of the period originally identified as 'supervision in the community' actually in prison. Some prisoners will serve longer on recall than they did on first conviction, especially with the growing use of extended sentences. An offender serving three years plus three or five years' extended supervision in the community, would until recently have been released after 18 months. Now they will not be released until the two thirds

252 N. Padfield

point at the earliest, but at whichever point they are released, there are many examples of such people being swiftly recalled. They may well serve the entirety of their 'extended sentence', including the 'extension', for which the offender might have been on licence, in prison.

The third advantage, again connected, is a *more credible, orderly and efficient system*. As sentence lengths are growing, and as prison resources are cut, an increasing number of prisoners are feeling that the system is 'unfair'. This has destabilizing effects (Liebling *et al.*, 2011). The criminological literature on compliance and legitimacy provides evidence that if the system is not perceived to be fair, there is less reason why people should obey the law (Tyler, 1990, 2010). This is in part why Sentencing Councils worry about public opinion (Hough *et al.*, 2009). Fair treatment is associated with compliance (Crawford and Hucklesby, 2012; Liebling, 2004).

But fair processes are not only necessary because they lead to more stable and orderly regimes. It is also morally right that *the penal system should be fair and just*. One obvious troubling sentence is a life sentence with a very long minimum term. Once the offender has exercised their initial right of appeal, this minimum term is absolutely fixed in English law. Should they not be able to ask a court to review this minimum term after a number of years? He or she may have been a model prisoner and be able to show that he is a 'reformed' offender? A French offender sentenced to any lengthy custodial term is able, after a period of time, to ask the *tribunal d'application des peines* to reduce his *periode de sûreté* (minimum term). The case of Nicola Edgington, sentenced in March 2013, involves a woman in her early 30s, with a history of serious mental illness, who was sentenced to a minimum term of 37 years for the murder of a stranger in the street, and the attempted murder of another. On the day of the murder she had sought help in hospital indicating that she thought she was dangerous and was having a breakdown, but had then left the hospital when she thought they were doing nothing. Is it right that there is absolutely no process in English law for reviewing this minimum term, even in 25 or 30 years' time?

There are many other examples of unfairness in the system. The failure to 'join up sentences' can as we have seen lead to an extraordinary hiatus as the prisoner comes out of prison and starts to serve the second community part of the sentence. This can be experienced as increasingly restrictive, with prisoners finding a move from a Cat C or D prison to Approved Premises difficult to achieve. Worse perhaps, many prisoners find the freedom of release impossible to cope with: note the numbers of deaths of those on licence (Gelsthorpe *et al.*, 2012).

The final, fifth, advantage is that a greater focus on the process of sentence might provoke *significant reform*. First, the law should be radically overhauled. The statutory law on sentencing and the enforcement of sentences is a mess and merits a fundamental review. Front door sentencing law is to be found in a number of frequently amended statutes; post-sentence law is found more in PSOs and PSIs than in statute. The Prison Act 1952 says very little, and is not fit for purpose. Since sentencing is in effect a whole series of inter-connected decisions, the processes which link them need review.

Sentencing in England and Wales 253

There have been important calls for a fairer and better system over the years, and many of the key official reviews repay re-reading today. Central to Lord Carlisle's *Review of Parole* (1988) was the argument that any release system should not undermine the proportionality of sentences passed by the courts, and that prisoners considered for discretionary release should have the benefit of appropriate procedural safeguards. Yet this influential report was constrained by its terms of reference: Lord Carlisle was asked to re-design proposals for parole but not the sentences within which parole operates. Lord Woolf's *Report into the Prison Disturbances* in April 1990 stressed the need for improved standards of justice within prisons (Woolf 1991); Halliday's *Making Punishments Work: Report of a Review of the Sentencing Framework for England and Wales* (July 2001) argued that courts should hold 'review hearings' to review progress of community sentences and the community part of custodial sentences, deal with breaches of conditions, etc., with power to order custody or return to custody for non-compliance. Further complaints about the failure of the penal 'system' to join up sentences led to Lord Carter's proposals to re-structure prison and probation "to provide the 'end-to-end' management of offenders, regardless of whether they are given a custodial or community sentence" (Carter, 2004, p. 34).

Judge Samuels argued (Samuels, 2004) for a system of review courts which would allow an offender to be more actively engaged in his sentence planning, and indeed to influence the time which he must serve in custody, as well as the time for which he will be on licence in the community, by complying in all respects with the requirements of his offender manager. Review courts, he suggested, as well as encouraging the individual offender to aim for early release through a structured rehabilitation programme, could have a significant impact on reducing the prison population. The idea is similar to the French system of *juge d'application des peines*, on which see Padfield (2011b).

Why is an offender not required to attend a formal judicial hearing at which conditions are agreed? The moment of release and the imposition of licence conditions at this crucial moment in a sentence, the moment when an offender moves from custody to life in the community, is crucial. There is no rite of passage: the offender simply signs some forms and leaves the prison. The assessment of the risks presented by the prisoner, but also of the likely success of the supervision plan developed by the hard-pressed probation services, merit careful judicial scrutiny.

But this, as we have seen, is not the only important stage in a sentence. Independent but interdependent agencies and decision-makers may be at cross-purposes with others. As Feeney pointed out as long ago as 1985, "in the criminal justice system interdependence occurs at many different levels – national and local; agency head and working officer; strategic, tactical and mechanical" (p. 8). Here we may be concerned both with strategy (a joined up approach to sentencing) but also tactics (particularly, the use of limited resources) and mechanics. To quote Feeney again, "process is rather like an assembly line in which each agency's workload is essentially controlled by the actions of the previous agency. In most instances the decision of the transmitting

254 *N. Padfield*

agency is largely discretionary, but the receiving agency generally has little or no say in the decisions made" (Feeney, 1985, p. 10). As Hutton argued, the responsibility for dealing with crime is shifting increasingly to non-state agencies (Hutton, 2002, p. 576). How much truer that is today. As the criminal justice system becomes more complex and fragmented by the 'contracting out' of services, the arguments for a supervisory body are strengthened.

This chapter has sought to show that the later stages of a sentence are currently too invisible, both in academic and political life. Because of the attention paid to the initial sentencing decision, and indeed because of its symbolic importance, too much attention has been focused on it. Sentencing in practice is a string of decisions taken by very many different players, often over a number of years. The effect has been that, at a time when there have been tighter guidelines imposed on constitutionally independent sentencing judges, the administration has been implementing more flexible early release and recall schemes. There are strong arguments for suggesting that the 'front door' sentence imposes only a provisional sentence, which can and should be regularly reviewed by a judicial authority. The extent to which a judicial body should coordinate a sentence, monitor progress and seek to ensure compliance should be the subject of further debate, with much more focus being given in that debate to sentencing as an on-going process.

Notes

1 I pay tribute here to two giants of academic sentencing: Dr David Thomas who died in 2013, and Professor Nigel Walker, who died in 2014. Both contributed immensely to our understanding of the theory, law and practice of sentencing. Professor Dworkin, cited on page **000**, another giant, also died in 2013.
2 See the consultations on the 'community remedy' and the Antisocial Behaviour Bill (at www.homeoffice.gov.uk/publications/about-us/consultations/community-remedy-consultation/?view=Standard&pubID=1143402).
3 What about cartel offences and the civil sanctions created in domestic, EU and international agreements? See the European Commission's Communication of September 2011, "Towards an EU Criminal Policy: Ensuring the Effective Implementation of EU Policies through Criminal Law" which promises to explore the relationship between criminal and non-criminal sanction systems in EU law (see http://ec.europa.eu/justice/criminal/files/act_en.pdf).
4 Thus for example, ExxonMobil was fined £2.8 million for failing to account for 33,000 tonnes of carbon dioxide emissions from its ethylene plant at Mossmorran in Scotland. See www.bbc.co.uk/news/uk-scotland-edinburgh-east-fife-17089378. This case illustrates another important and under-researched subject: the real difference between civil and criminal fines and enforcement procedures.

Bibliography

Appleton, C. (2010). *Life after Life Imprisonment*. Oxford: Oxford University Press.
Ashworth, A. (2010). Coroners and Justice Act 2009: Sentencing guidelines and the Sentencing Council. *Criminal Law Review*, 389–401.
Ashworth, A. and Roberts, J. (2012). Sentencing: Theory, principle and practice. In M. Maguire, M. Morgan and R. Reiner (eds), *The Oxford Handbook of Criminology* (5th edn). Oxford: Oxford University Press.

Sentencing in England and Wales 255

Ashworth, A. and Roberts, J. (eds) (2013). *Sentencing Guidelines: Exploring the English Model*. Oxford: Oxford University Press.

Barry, M. and McIvor, G. (2010). Professional decision making and women offenders: Containing the chaos? *Probation Journal*, 57, 27–42.

Bottoms, A. E. and Roberts, J. (eds) (2010). *Hearing the Victim: Adversarial Justice, Crime Victims and the State*. Cullompton: Willan.

Cairns, R. (2012). Legal status and positive practice in Community Order enforcement. *Probation Journal*, 59, 254–268.

Carlisle, Rt Hon Lord of Bucklow (1988). *The Parole System in England and Wales: Report of the Review Committee*. London: HMSO.

Carter, Lord (2004). *Managing Offenders, Reducing Crime: A New Approach*. London: Strategy Unit.

Cartwright, P. (2007). Crime, punishment and consumer protection. *Journal of Consumer Policy*, 30, 1–20.

Cid, J. and Tébar, B. (2012). Revoking early conditional release measures in Spain. *European Journal of Probation*, 4, 112–124.

Crawford, A. and Hucklesby, A. (eds) (2012). *Legitimacy and Compliance in Criminal Justice*. London: Routledge.

Delmas-Marty, M. (ed.) (2003). *L'Harmonisation des Sanctions Pénales en Europe*. Paris: Unité Mixte de Droit Comparé de Paris.

Dhami, M.K. and Souza, K.A. (2009). Breaking into court. In D. L. Streiner and S. Sidani (eds), *When Research Goes off the Rails* (pp. 81–87). New York: Guilford Press.

Digard, L. (2010). When legitimacy is denied: Offender perceptions of the prison recall system. *Probation Journal*, 57, 43–61.

Dworkin, R. (1977). *Taking Rights Seriously*. London: Duckworth.

Edwards, A. (2012). Legal Aid, Sentencing and Punishment of Offenders Act 2012 – the financial procedural and practical implications. *Criminal Law Review*, 584–591.

Feeney, F. (1985). Interdependence as a working concept. In D. Moxon (ed.), *Managing Criminal Justice*. London: HMSO.

Gelsthorpe, L. and Padfield, N. (2003). Introduction. In L. Gelsthorpe and N. Padfield (eds), *Exercising Discretion: Decision-making in the Criminal Justice System and Beyond* (pp. 1–28). Cullompton: Willan.

Gelsthorpe, L., Padfield, N. and Phillips, J. (2012). *Deaths on Probation: An Analysis of Data Regarding People Dying Under Probation Supervision*. London: Howard League for Penal Reform.

Hales, L. and Gelsthorpe, L. (2012). *The Criminalisation of Migrant Women*. Cambridge: Institute of Criminology. www.crim.cam.ac.uk/people/academic_research/loraine_gelsthorpe/criminalreport29july12.pdf.

Halliday, J. (2001). *Making Punishments Work: Report of a Review of the Sentencing Framework for England and Wales*. London: Home Office. http://webarchive.nationalarchives.gov.uk/+/www.homeoffice.gov.uk/documents/halliday-report-sppu/.

Hannah-Moffat, K. and Yule, C. (2011). Gaining insight, changing attitudes and managing 'risk': Parole release decisions for women convicted of violent crimes. *Punishment and Society*, 13, 149–175.

Healy, D. (2012). Advise, assist and befriend: Can probation supervision support desistance? *Social Policy and Administration*, 46, 377–394.

Hearnden, I. and Millie, A. (2004). Does tougher enforcement lead to lower reconviction? *Probation Journal*, 51(1), 48–58.

256   *N. Padfield*

Herzog-Evans, M. (2009). French post custody law (2000–2009): From equitable trial to the religion of control. *European Journal of Probation*, 2, 97–109.

Herzog-Evans, M. (2012). Non-compliance in France: A human approach and a hair splitting system. *European Journal of Probation*, 4, 46–62.

Hough, M., Roberts, J. V., Jacobson, J., Moon, N. and Steel, N. (2009). Public attitudes to the principles of sentencing. *Sentencing Advisory Panel* Report 6. London: Sentencing Council.

Hough, M., Farrall, S. and McNeill, F. (2013). *Intelligent Justice: Balancing the Effects of Community Sentences and Custody*. London: Howard League for Penal Reform.

Hutton, N. (2002). Sentencing, inequality and justice. In C. Tata and N. Hutton (eds), *Sentencing and Society: International Perspectives*. Aldershot: Ashgate.

Judge, Lord (2009). David Thomas. In C. Walston, *Challenging Crime: A Portrait of the Cambridge Institute of Criminology*. London: Third Millennium Publishing.

Justice Committee of the House of Commons (2008). *Towards Effective Sentencing*. London: House of Commons.

Justice Committee of the House of Commons (2011). *The Role of the Probation Service*, HC 519-I.

Kemshall, H. (2008). *Understanding the Community Management of High Risk Offenders*. Maidenhead: Open University Press.

Liebling, A., assisted by Arnold, H. (2004). *Prisons and their Moral Performance: A Study of Values, Quality and Prison Life*. Oxford: Clarendon Studies in Criminology, Oxford University Press.

Liebling, A., Arnold, H. and Straub, C. (2011). *An Exploration of Staff–Prisoner Relationships at HMP Whitemoor: 12 Years On*. London: Ministry of Justice.

Lynch, M. (1998). Waste managers? The new penology, crime fighting, and parole agent identity. *Law and Society Review*, 32, 839–870.

Mair, G. (2011). The community order in England and Wales: Policy and practice. *Probation Journal*, 38, 215–232.

Mair, G., Cross, N. and Taylor, S. (2008). *The Community Order and the Suspended Sentence Order: The Views and Attitudes of Sentencers*. London: Centre for Crime and Justice Studies.

Marie, O., Moreton, K. and Goncalves, M. (2011). *The effect of early release of prisoners on Home Detention Curfew (HDC) on recidivism*. Ministry of Justice Research Summary 1/11.

Maruna, S. (2001). *Making Good: How Ex-Convicts Reform and Rebuild Their Lives*. Washington: American Psychological Association Books.

Maruna, S. (2011). Reentry as a rite of passage. *Punishment & Society*, 13, 3–28.

Maruna, S. and LeBel, T. (2003). Welcome home? Examining the 're-entry court' concept from a strengths-based perspective. *Western Criminology Review*, 4, 91–107.

McNeill, F., Burns, N., Halliday, S., Hutton, N. and Tata, C. (2009). Risk, responsibility and reconfiguration. *Punishment and Society*, 11, 419–442.

Ministry of Justice (2009). *Consultation: The Future of the Parole Board*. London: Ministry of Justice.

Ministry of Justice (2010). *Breaking the Cycle: Effective Punishment, Rehabilitation and Sentencing of Offenders*. London: Ministry of Justice.

Ministry of Justice (2013a). *Offender Management Statistics (Quarterly) – July to September 2012*. London: Ministry of Justice.

Ministry of Justice (2013b). *Criminal Justice Statistics Quarterly Update to September 2012*. London: Ministry of Justice Statistics bulletin.

Sentencing in England and Wales 257

Ministry of Justice (2013c). *Story of the Prison Population 1993–2012 England and Wales*. London: Ministry of Justice (at www.justice.gov.uk/statistics/prisons-and-probation/prison-population-1993-2012).

Padfield, N. (ed.) (2007). *Who to Release? Parole, Fairness and Criminal Justice*. Cullompton: Willan.

Padfield, N. (2009a). Parole and early release: The Criminal Justice and Immigration Act 2008 changes in context. *Criminal Law Review*, 166.

Padfield, N. (2009b). The administrative implementation of sentences. *Cambridge Law Journal*, 68, 256.

Padfield, N. (2010). Discretion and decision-making in public protection. In M. Nash and A. Williams (eds), *The Handbook of Public Protection*. Cullompton: Willan.

Padfield, N. (2011a). An entente cordiale in sentencing?. *Criminal Law and Justice Weekly*, 175, 239–242, 256–259, 271–274 and 290–293.

Padfield, N. (2011b). *The Sentencing, Management and Treatment of 'Dangerous' Offenders: Final Report*. Strasbourg: European Committee on Crime Problems.

Padfield, N. (2011c). Time to bury the custody 'threshold'? *Criminal Law Review*, 593–612.

Padfield, N. (2012a). Editorial. *European Journal of Probation*, 1, 1–5.

Padfield, N. (2012b). Recalling conditionally released prisoners in England and Wales. *European Journal of Probation*, 1, 34–45.

Padfield, N. (2013a). *Understanding Recall 2011*. University of Cambridge, Faculty of Law Research Paper No. 2/2013. Available at SSRN: http://ssrn.com/abstract=2201039 or http://dx.doi.org/10.2139/ssrn.2201039.

Padfield, N. (2013b). Exploring the success of sentencing guidelines. In A. Ashworth and J. Roberts (eds), *Sentencing Guidelines: Exploring the English Model*. Oxford: Oxford University Press.

Padfield, N. and Maruna, S. (2006). The revolving door at the prison gate: Exploring the dramatic increase in recalls to prison. *Criminology and Criminal Justice*, 6, 329–352.

Padfield, N., van Zyl Smit, D. and Dunkel, F. (eds) (2010). *Release from Prison: European Policy and Practice*. Cullompton: Willan.

Padfield, N., Morgan, R. and Maguire, M. (2012). Out of court, out of sight? Criminal sanctions and non-judicial decision making. In M. Maguire, M. Morgan and R. Reiner (eds), *The Oxford Handbook of Criminology* (5th edn). Oxford: Oxford University Press.

Parole Board (2012). *Annual Report 2011/12*. London: The Stationery Office.

Samuels, HH Judge J. (2004). Judicial Sentence Review: A 'carrot and stick' approach to rehabilitation. *Criminal Justice Matters*, 57, 32–38.

Scottish Prisons Commission (2008). *Scotland's Choice*. Edinburgh: Scottish Prison Commission.

Sebba, L. (2001). When is a prisoner not a prisoner? 'Service work' in Israel – and in Britain? *Criminal Law Review*, 543–559.

Skinns, L. (2010). *Police Custody: Governance, Legitimacy and Reform in the Criminal Justice Process*. Cullompton: Willan.

Solomka, B. (1996). The role of psychiatric evidence in passing 'longer than normal' sentences. *The Journal of Forensic Psychiatry & Psychology*, 7(2), 239–255.

Souza, K. and Kemp, V. (2009). *Study of Defendants in Magistrates' Courts* (Ministry of Justice) available at www.justice.gov.uk/downloads/publications/research-and-analysis/lsrc/2009/DefendantsInMagistratesCt.pdf.

Tata, C. and Hutton, N. (eds) (2002). *Sentencing and Society: International Perspectives*. Aldershot: Ashgate.

258   N. Padfield

Thomas, D. (2002). *Exercising Discretion: Decision-Making in the Criminal Justice System and Beyond*. Cullompton: Willan.

Thomson, D. (2008). The use of home detention curfew as a means of prison management – its advantages and disadvantages. *Scottish Criminal Law*, 811–818.

Thomson, D. (2010). Home detention curfews; one of the least popular sentencing innovations of recent years? *Scottish Law Times*, 656–663.

Thompson, A. (2009). *Releasing Prisoners, Redeeming Communities: Reentry, Race, and Politics*. New York: New York University Press.

Tony, M. (2003). *Confronting Crime: Crime Control Policy Under New Labour*. Cullompton: Willan.

Tonry, M. (ed.) (2007). *Crime, Punishment, and Politics in Comparative Perspective*. Chicago: University of Chicago Press.

Tonry, M. and Frase, R. (eds) (2001). *Sentencing and Sanctions in Western Countries*. Oxford: Oxford University Press.

Turnbull, S. and Hannah-Moffat, K. (2009). Under these conditions: Gender, parole and the governance of reintegration. *British Journal of Criminology*, 49, 532–551.

Tyler, T. R. (1990). *Why People Obey the Law*. New Haven, CT: Yale University Press.

Tyler, T. R. (2010). Legitimacy in corrections: Policy implications. *Criminology and Public Policy*, 9, 127–134.

Weaver, B., Tata, C., Munro, M. and Barry, M. (2012). The failure of recall to prison: Early release, front-door and back-door sentencing and the revolving prison door in Scotland. *European Journal of Probation*, 4, 85–98.

Woolf, Lord (1991). *Report into Prison Disturbances* (Cm 1456, HO 370/1).

Index

abortion 36
age-crime curve 90
Antisocial Process Screening Device (APSD) 97
Area under the ROC curve (AUC) 84
arrest: case law 126; laws governing in the USA 126
attainment 9
attrition rate 48

Bavaria 35
Bavarian police 36
between-subjects design 87
birth cohort 7
British Academy 45
British origin 9
brothers 12
bullies 44
bullying 44; from bullying to violence 52; cognitive behavioural skills training 53; cyber 57, 58; cyber victimization 58; gender differences 65; preschool intellectual enrichment programmes 53; prevalence 58, 65; prevention programmes 52; school 38, 58; self-reported 48; willingness to report victimization 63
Burglary 26

callous-unemotional 99
Cambridge Study in Delinquent Development (CSDD) 7, 44, 100
child: rearing 38, 46, 49; sexual abuse 26; social skills training 52
children 13
clustering 13
Cohen's *d* 105
conditional release date 240; criminal justice system 176, 185, 193, 205, 206, 209–10, 254; interdependence 253

conduct disorder 99
control question technique (CQT) versus concealed information test (CIT) 158–66; contamination and confirmation bias 163; countermeasures 163–4; criterion validity 164–5; orienting response 160; preliminary process theory (PPT) 159; standardization 161–2; theoretical basis 158–9; underlying rationale 158–9
convictions 7; concentration of 15, 18; prevalence 14, 17; recorded 11
correlations corrected for attenuation 104
Cronbach's alpha 102
crime: drop 24, 39; rates 24, 26
criminal offence 48
Criminal Record Office 10
criterion validity 29
cyberbullying 57; and risk factors 68

dangerousness: prediction 78
daring 9, 48, 50
daughters 19
deception: concealed information test (CIT) 158; control question technique (CQT) 156–8; detection 155; National Research Council report 155; physiological measures/methods 155–8; pre-test interview 157; recommendations for psychophysiological detection 165–6; research paradigms 155
delinquency 99
demographics 37
design effect 13
dishonesty 9
disparity 203, 217
Dortmund 28
driving without licence 31
drunkenness 38

260 *Index*

ecological system theory 57
economic condition 36
ethical approval 9
extraversion 48

false accounts by children: boundaries
  between true and false accounts 138;
  criterion-based content analysis (CBCA)
  139–42; differentiating 138;
  distinguishing true and false 141–3;
  event-related potentials 138; features of
  138; functional magnetic resonance
  imaging (fMRI) 138; instruments for
  differentiating 138, 139–42; linguistic
  inquiry word count (LIWC) 142–3;
  neuroimaging techniques 138; reality
  monitoring (RM) 140–2; software for
  differentiating 138, 142–3; statement
  validity assessment (SVA) 139–42
false confessions: inadequate counsel
  180–1; perjury/false accusations 181;
  police interrogations 178–81; police
  misconduct 178–81; use of
  informants/"snitches" 180
false sexual abuse allegations by children
  136–8; conclusions 150; consequences
  of 137; divorce 137; judging children's
  testimonies in court 140–50; motive
  137; separation 137; stimuli for 137;
  uncommonness of 136
family income 49
father(s) 13
female partners 9

gender 57; differences 67
genetic influences 21
Germany 27: German Federal Police
  Office 35
grandfather(s) 19
grandmother(s) 19

head circumference 37
Home Office 11
hours spent online 68
hyperactivity 48

immigration 25, 37
imprisonment: public protection 244
improved security 25
impulsivity 99
incarceration 25
information: nomothetic 89; idiographic 89
intelligence 9, 48

interactive protective factors 50
Internet 57
interrogation 119: behavioural analysis
  interview 120; coercion 128; cruel and
  unusual punishment 128; custodial 126;
  deception indicators 120; eighth
  amendment 128; factors for evaluating
  juvenile interviews 130; false
  confessions 130–1; guilt-based
  indicators 121; high-value detainee
  interrogation group 131; information
  gathering approaches 131; innocence
  project 124, 175; juvenile suspect
  interviews 129; Kidd's police
  interrogation manual 120; legal
  framework 125; mandatory recording of
  suspect interviews 129; methods 119;
  'Miranda' rights 127; Miranda waiver
  130; Miranda warning 121, 127;
  miscarriages of justice 124; non-
  custodial 126; objective standard 126;
  per se rule 130; permissible tactics 29;
  permissible techniques 129;
  psychological domination 122;
  psychological interrogation 120; suspect
  interviews 129; third degree 119; in the
  usa 125–6; U.S. senate committee on
  intelligence 131; Wickerman report 119
intraclass correlation 13
Island of "Kos" 63
Italy 64

Journal of School Violence 47
judges: Canadian 204; female 213–4;
  verbal statements 207
judging: what is good 203
judicial: decision making models 217;
  defences against judicial prejudice 217;
  prejudice 217
judicial officers: age 214; characteristics of
  and sentence severity 214; crime victim
  214; gender 2015; legally trained 214;
  penal aim 215; politics 215; race 215;
  religion 2015; rural/urban towns 214;
  social class 214, 215
judiciary: concern within 212
jury: adverse inferences 192; challenges
  'for cause' 190; contempt of court 193;
  court architecture 197; disqualification
  190; effect of jury service 193; English
  jury 188–98; European court of human
  rights decision 197; excusal 190; expert
  help 195–6; fair 193–4; form of

summing up 196; guidance 190; judge summing up 191; judge to retire with 197; legislation in England 189–90; Lord Auld' review 194; majority verdict 192; miscarriage of justice 194; peremptory challenges 190; pretrial summary of issues 195; problematic acquittals 194; questions of fact 196; questions of law 196; role 188–9; royal commission 190, 194; sentimental attachment 189; stereotypical behaviour 195–6; summing up structure and content 191; trial in England and Wales 189–93; words used by judges 192
Justice Committee of House of Commons 232
juvenile delinquency: self-reported 24; shoplifting 26

latent growth curves 99
lead poisoning 37
low-income neighbourhoods 27

meta-analysis 38, 45
miscarriages of justice 175–85; *see also* wrongful convictions
mother(s) 13
Multidimensional Personality Questionnaire (MPQ) 98
Munich 34

narcissism 99
negative parenting 102
nervous-withdrawn 49
neuroticism 48
non-British origin 8
Nuremberg 28
nutrition 37

odds ratio 13
offence(s): aggressive 29; property 29; standard list 11; status 29; violent 29
offender(s): chronic 7; dangerous 243; management 246; rehabilitation 250
offending: frequent 32
Olweus questionnaire 64
oppositional defiant disorder orders 233–4

parent training 52
parental: mediation 63; monitoring 58; psychopathology 102; supervision online 57
parole: Board 241; decision making in

Israel 216; Lord Carlisle's review of 253; on licence 247–8; provisions in England 236; release 82
partial correlations 103
penal system: fair and just 252
penalties/sanctions: administrative 233; ancillary 235; community orders 238; fines 237–8; non-custodial 237–9; out of court 233; regulatory 233
personality 9
plea bargain 235
police interviews: achieving best evidence 145; allegedly abused children 144–5; approaches 144; appropriate techniques 144–5; echoes 144–5; facilitators 144–5; free recall 144; guidelines 147–8; inappropriate techniques 146–7; memory stages 144; P.E.A.C.E 145–6; sexually abused children 143
Police National Computer 10
poor housing 46
popularity 9
pornographic literature 88
prevalence rates 32
prevention programmes: school-based 38
prison: after 246–50; disturbances 253; law 240; population 25
prisoners: lifers 244–5; going straight 246; recall 248–50; release 248–50
probability theory 86
prosecutor: influence 235
prospective longitudinal study 7, 8
protective factor 39; interactive 46
psychology 24
psychometric quality 29
psychomotor impulsivity 9
psychopathic traits: absolute stability 97; adolescents 94; biological correlates 95; children 94; genetic correlates 95; longitudinal study 97; predictors of stability 94; stability 94; Youth Psychopathic Traits Inventory (YPI) 98
psychopathy 94; adolescents 109; children 109
Psychopathy Checklist-Revised (PCL-R) 97, 98
Psychopathy Checklist: Screening Version (PCL:SV) 100
Public Protection Unit 248–9

rational choice theory 25
Receiver Operator Characteristic (ROC) curve 84

262 *Index*

Reid interrogation model/technique 121, 124; assumptions of 123; civil lawsuit 123; evaluations 124; false conviction 123; innocent people 124; juveniles 124; naturalistic studies 124; nine-step framework 121; rapport 124; suspect's anxiety 122; techniques 122, 125
relationships: intergenerational 21; opposite-sex 21; same-sex 21
relative stability 95
release 248–50; home detention curfew 239, 242–3
resilience 45, 52
risk: relative 85; risk-based protective factor 46, 50
risk assessment: actuarial approach 75, 76; in California76; risk matrix 2000 76; static-99R 76; structured professional judgement 77; tool for sex offenders 76; violence 76, 86
risk factor(s) 46, 57, 77; recidivism 78
robbery 31
routine activity theory 25

Scotland 81
Scotland Yard 10
Scottish prisoners 81
security measures 37
sentence(s): attractiveness of defendant 211–2; community 238; concept 202; custodial 239; end 249–50; ethnicity of defendant 209–11; extended 239, 243–4; extended indeterminate 244; gender of defendant 206–8; impact of having a break 219; indeterminate sentence manual 245; judges' reasons for 207; length of sentence 207; life time of 232; mental illness and 207; non-custodial 237–9; part of 233–4; race of defendant 209–11; reviewing minimum term 252; sentencer characteristics impacting on 212–17; severity scale 206; suspended 238–9; what is 233–5
sentencing: aims and purposes 250; Australia 208; back door 202–3, 231–2, 237; balancing consistency 202; constraints on judicial excesses 202; decisions 201; discretion 236; disparities 203, 210–11; disparities in Israel 215; extra-legal factors impacting on 201–17; federal courts 210; France 232–3; front

door 202–3, 231–2, 254; guidelines in U.S. 202; Halliday Report 253; indigenous defendants 209; instinctive synthesis 204; intuitive process 204; issues 236; judicial discretion 201; judicial sentencing 231; law and practice of 232; legal formalism 204; legal realism 204; methods for studying variations in 205–6; nature of process 204; offenders' experience of 231; out-of-court sanctions 203; plea-bargaining 201; as a process 250–4; proportionality principle 202; racial discrimination at 209–11; reducing discrimination in 211; reform 252; sentencing council 212; studying variations in 204–6; Sweden 211; United States 207–8
sentencing decisions: levels of 232
sexual: arousal 87; conviction 81; recidivism 78; violent predator 76
sisters 12
social skills 38
socio-economic status 29, 49, 99
son(s) 19
South London 8
strain theories 25
Students' Needs Assessment Survey 64
Swedish National Council for Crime Prevention 45
systematic review 47

troublesomeness 9

within-individual analysis 87
wives 20
working-class 8
wrongful convictions: belief perseverance 183–4; confirmation bias 183–4; DNA profiling 175; dual threat of 184–5; eyewitness misidentification 177; factors contributing to 177–85; forensic error and incompetence 178; frequency of exonerations 176; investigation stage 177–81; jury 194; national registry of exonerations 175; police interrogations and misconduct 178–81; prosecutorial misconduct 181–3; tunnel vision 183–5

Youth Psychopathic Traits Inventory (YPI) 98